LOVED BACK TO LIFE SERIES

Out of the Darkness
An Autobiography of Love: Part One

By Pearl Sunshine

SCP - Shepherds Care Publishing

© SCPublishing / Shepherds Care Counseling Ministries
2473 S. Higley Road Suite 104 PMB 210
Gilbert, Arizona 85295

Loved Back to Life Series:

OUT OF THE DARKNESS

An Autobiography of Love: Part One

By Pearl Sunshine

Editorial Supervision: Michael E. Chalberg
Paperback Edition – ISBN 978-0-9746464-2-8
E-Book ISBN 978-1-7349703-0-2

© Shepherds Care Counseling Ministries is a nonprofit 501c3 org. All rights reserved. No part of this publication may be reproduced or Transmitted in any form or by any means without written permission Of the author.

Unless otherwise indicated, Bible quotations are taken from the New Open Bible, Study Edition, Copyright © 1990 by Thomas Nelson Inc.

Order:	scpublishing@shepherdscareministries.org
Email:	Pearl.Sunshine@scpublishing.org
Web:	www.shepherdscareministries.org
Editor:	scpublishing2020@gmail.com

TABLE OF CONTENTS

Forward - SCPlublishing V

Introduction of "Pearl by Jesus" VII

Preface – Pearl Sunshine VIII

<u>Chapters</u>

1. Out of the Darkness 1
2. Preparing the Way 4
3. The Bad Things 11
4. HELP?!! 17
5. Accepting the Truth 22
6. Help at Last 26
7. Company 29
8. Maisie 37
9. Susanna 48
10. Mum 56
11. Treasure in the Darkness 64
12. Plans and Purposes 74
13. AJ 83
14. Learning to Trust 93
15. The Enemy & The Big Lie 104
16. Letting Go of the Promise 117
17. Time Away 124
18. Being Seen 129
19. Losing My Old Life 144
20. Hello Holy Spirit 155
21. Out of the Well 168
22. Into Daddy's Arms 178
23. Never Alone 184
24. Blending 193
25. The Birthday 210
26. Season of Endings 219
27. A Home in My Heart 229
28. The Dollies 242
29. Together Again 263
    End Notes: 280

Forward by SCPublishing

Our new collections of autobiographies entitled: **_Loved Back to Life Series_**, are being presented to all who have lost hope in the power of God's unconditional love...to heal and redeem His purposes for our lives. We live in both the physical realm and the larger spiritual realm simultaneously, yet it is the physical experience which often defines our understanding of spiritual realities. So, we seek to find meaning to these realities, when we encounter suffering and pain, rejection and condemnation in our relationships with others...who are supposed to love, nurture, provide for our needs and teach us the truth about why our Heavenly Father created us to have an eternal relationship with Him.

When this relationship is broken by evil's influence, through control of those around and over us...we lose hope and trust in the power of God's love to overcome this evil and we cry out to the Lord, *"You would have been kinder to never have created me...just let me die."* This is often our primary mistake in seeking answers to why it seems that God isn't answering our prayers and we feel abandoned by Him as though our condition means we are unworthy of His love and presence in our lives. We are afraid to trust in and hope for, the fulfillment of God's promises and purpose for us in Christ Jesus. This is why this first autobiographical set by Pearl Sunshine is given in her own words, changing only names of those involved, without holding back any reality of abuses by evil controlling her life. The drawings given of the actual events from early childhood, depicting clearly the actions of others... family and Satanic cults can be triggering of painful memories for readers who are themselves survivors of such abuses. We ask that the readers have the strength and courage to continue reading when possible, to discover the joys as well of being drawn into God's heart. Her purpose here is not to convince anyone of the truth of evil in our lives, or her strength in continuing to follow the path that Jesus has set for her, to trust God's love again.

Her purpose, and ours, is to challenge our readers to understand more fully why Jesus is calling to us to trust in Him, and His love to heal and redeem us...to do for us what we can't do for ourselves...without Him. If we can believe in the promises that; **"I will never leave nor forsake you"**, **"I will come to you in the darkest depths and overcome the evil to set you free"**, **"I will love you back to life... eternal life with me"** and **"In this world you will have tribulations, but rejoice for I have overcome this world,"** then we can know the truth of who Jesus is in this life, and trust again in the plans and purposes of our Father God's unconditional love in action... right now... right here, where you are at. If these autobiographies, and the ones to follow in this series, help you to seek a renewed relationship of trust in Him...then the suffering you read about followed by their free will choices to continue on the journey, will have been worth it to each author. The introduction of Pearl by Jesus can challenge us all about what He means by saying, **"My grace is sufficient for you, for my power is made perfect in weakness."** This is the power of God's love freely given to us to survive this world with Him until we go home.

Ultimately these books and the others that will follow in this series, are about the personal commitment that God makes to each one of us to bring healing, as revealed in these private journals of one group of people with Dissociative Identity Disorder (DID) or Multiple Personality Disorder (MPD), who accepted God's call to receive His promise of healing for 'wholeness' in Him... living as one person with Him.

Our first series of books, **Shattered People: Journeys to Joy - Love**, focused on specific issues of people with DID and their struggle to receive healing later in life so they could be 'acceptable' to be loved by family and relationships in their closest circumstances. I offer commentary and counseling in this series as pastor, friend and counselor for them to promote treatment methods and dialogue about trauma and abuse survival, especially about our common questions to God on suffering, survival and how we all can know God through relationships within community and in our one on one time with Him. .

This series however, **Loved Back to Life**, looks at the individual searching for meaning and purpose directly from God in conversation with Him, expecting answers from no one else... not counseling or outside help for most of their lives. They seek meaning for a lifetime of feeling alone in darkness... evil that defined who they were, before discovering they were never alone. How they and Pearl come to trust in Jesus' love placed very deep in their soul long ago was as hard to believe for them, as the memories of suffering being revealed as true by those who had endured them... and the healing Jesus gives to both. These books allow you the reader to learn from their struggle to know God... to trust Jesus... to accept the Holy Spirit and their will for her life and how receiving God's love is the purpose of her life... a purpose she now wishes to share with all who suffer... to risk allowing Jesus in with His answers for healing.

Editor & Fellow Servant – Pastor Mike

- Dr. Joe Johnson, pastoral counselor. D.Min - Fuller Seminary 4/2020

"Pearl's miraculous story of redemption, healing, recovery and freedom from unspeakable suffering is a witness to what most people would say is impossible when they read these books. God brings Pastor Mike alongside of Pearl to share his love of Jesus to witness in confidence the power of Jesus to redeem and minister healing to Pearl, including each one of her dissociative parts (*alters*) more than I have ever known. Pearl opens her heart wide to the readers to the many ways she is healing and recovering from incredible abuses physically, emotionally and spiritually. I have learned that the biggest factor in healing trauma is to personally know that we are not alone... this is the cry of attachment pain, "Is anyone with me... am I alone?" Jesus never gives up on reaching her as Mike didn't, as He does with us, and I believe she'll never give up on them trusting they will be there for her."

Book One P1 – *Out of the Darkness: An Autobiography of Love: Part One*
Book One P2 – *Out of the Darkness: An Autobiography of Love: Part Two*
Book Two - *Becoming Pearl: An Autobiography of Love*
Book Three - *The City of Hope: An Autobiography of Love*
Book Four – A journey still being written.

Introduction of Pearl by Jesus

My little one you are my Pearl of great price. I have brought you out of the darkness and out of great suffering to be my jewel, my precious and beloved child. That is who you are and will always be. You will show others what it means to be a child of the king my little one. You will show them how loved and precious they are to me no matter what this world has taught them about who they are. You will show them the truth. I will take all of your pain my little one and all of your tears and I will use them to bring hope and joy to those who need it the most.

I will send you out my little one to those who are lost in the darkness, to my hidden children who do not know what it is to be loved or wanted. Your story will give them hope and through you they will see and understand that they too are loved and wanted. You will show the world who I am through the things that I have shown you my little one and through the person that you are. You will show them the truth about what it means to be a child, a true child of God. My little one you will know what it is to love and be loved. I will give you a heart that is open and free. Free to love those I give to you and free to be loved also.

You will teach others how to reach out to those who have been hurt like yourself my little one, not only in your words but also in your actions. You will be a light for me in places where few other lights shine. I will give you a joy that will shine out to those around you bringing hope and life to those who have not known either. My little one you will be my blessing and my gift to this world, a jewel in my crown. You know what it is to suffer my little one, but you will also know what it is to dance with joy. You will love me with all of your heart and follow wherever I will lead you and when all is said and done and I take you home to be where I am, you will be glad that you lived the life I had for you my little one. Though the cost is very high you will say that it was worth it. All this and more will be true of you my little one, because you are my Pearl... and this is who I have made you to be.

Preface by Pearl

I wrote these books because Jesus asked me to . He asked me to because he wants to show you who he is and how much he loves his children. It will be difficult to read sometimes, the things I talk about are real and painful. They are the truth of what happened to me, but it isn't the darkness he wants you to see so much as the light that shines in the darkness. I didn't hold back or hide what happened or my own pain and brokenness, because it's only when you see the darkness for what it is, it's impact and the difficulty of recovering from it that you can see the miracle of what Jesus has done in his healing of my heart. He wants you to see through my story what he is willing to do to bring his children out of the darkness into the light of his love. Whether you have been hurt like me or not, we all need Jesus to go into the broken places and bring his light and his healing. We all need to know that we are loved and safe, always.

I hope that you will continue to read even when it is difficult and painful, because it is in those places we meet Jesus and see him most clearly for who he is. Don't be afraid because he is right there with you as you are reading, ready to bring life and hope and healing to your heart just like he did for me. His love for you isn't any less, his truth is the same for you as it is for me. He is with you and loves you just as you are, and he knows who you can be, who he made you to be, which is more than you can imagine right now. He is faithful to walk alongside you and lead you forward as you say yes to him, even if your yes is very small to begin with, he will take it and work through it to draw you closer to him.

My story may seem extraordinary to you and parts of it are hard to believe or understand... but see it as the beginning of a journey to discovering more of who Jesus is. Allow yourself to question and to wonder. Give yourself time to ponder on his words which aren't just for me but are his gift to all of us. He is with us on our journey drawing us forward towards his heart of love for us. This is just another step, one that I hope you will be willing to take.

Chapter 1
Out of the Darkness

Walking out of the darkness and into the light is a difficult journey. It begins with the truth. It begins with the truth that you are in the darkness even though you don't know it. That is how it began for me. The truth of who I am was hidden from me for a long, long time. The truth of my life was hidden too, because they were hidden together. They were hidden from me so that I could survive.

Waking up to the truth and finding that you are so deep in the darkness, that you can't see how you can ever get out is a terrifying thing. It is so frightening that it seems easier to keep hiding in the darkness, pretending not to see the light, than it does to start walking towards it. Choosing to walk towards the light has needed a lot more courage than I have. I have had a lot of help on my journey so far.

My journey has been shared with many others. My life has been shared with them too. I needed them so that I could survive until the time when I could begin to choose for myself, until I was ready to begin the long walk to freedom…freedom from lies, from the pain and fear that was hidden away with the truth. Facing the truth meant facing the pain and the fear… a difficult thing to do. It has taken more courage than I have, so I needed a lot of help with facing the truth.

I am just a little girl, but my story began many years ago. I didn't get old with the body I was born in, because I was hidden away inside. Inside is difficult to understand maybe, because it's not a physical place… it is a spiritual one. You can't see it or touch it in the same way you can in the outside world, but it is just as real. I have an inside spiritual body, one that can see and hear and touch the things in the inside spiritual world, just like the outside physical body does in the outside physical world. I can be aware of the outside or the inside, and sometimes both at the same time. It can be difficult sometimes to see or hear or feel the inside world as clearly as the outside world. That is because like most people I learned to trust my physical senses… first. I learned to not believe in the spiritual reality that is all around me and even within me.

There are lots of different places on the inside just like there are on the outside. I spent most of my life hidden away in a dim corridor. At one end of the corridor there was a door to an inside world that I couldn't see or believe existed. The other end of the corridor was so close to the outside that it seemed like it was the outside. When I was there, I could see and hear and feel everything that was happening. It felt like it was me speaking and feeling and doing all of those things. But when I was at the other end, near the door, the outside seemed dim and far away like a dream. There I could hide away from the outside world and be safe, or safer from the things that were happening there. Maybe that seems strange to you. It did to me for a long time, but it is a part of the truth of my life and who I am that I have had to accept as I have walked forward on my journey into the light.

While I was hidden away inside there were many others who shared in the outside life. They lived the physical outside life, taking turns to be outside and then to go back inside to the places where they lived. There was a whole inside world behind that door where those that made up my shared life all lived. We all shared one physical body but there was a whole world for us to live in on the inside. It has taken me a long time to learn about these things and accept them as true, because for me it seemed like I lived on the outside. I didn't remember my corridor at all. I didn't know I was there. I didn't know that I was looking through the eyes of someone else on the outside. I didn't know it wasn't me. I didn't know that I was me, someone very different from the person I thought I was. I have had a lot of things to learn about and accept. It has been hard because I didn't want them to be true and they were so difficult to believe.

Before I knew any of these things about who I was or the inside or the others who shared the body, there was the truth about what happened to me. The truth was about what made me break apart into lots of different people, all sharing the same body and why I was hidden away all of that time. The truth was as difficult to accept as any of these other things. It was a dark and terrible truth that was held in the memories of many of those who had shared in the outside life… things I never knew or forgot that I knew, it is hard to be sure. Hidden away I was protected but not completely, I was broken but I was not destroyed.

I survived and was hidden away until I was ready to learn the truth of my life, but also to learn a greater truth. That truth would give me life in place of death and love in place of all the fear that I had known. This greater truth was waiting to be revealed to me on my journey. It is this truth that has given me the courage and strength I have needed to keep on walking into the light. This truth has given me the hope I needed when everything seemed lost, this truth that led me forward faithfully through all of the pain and confusion. It is this truth that makes my story one of hope and life, instead of one of despair and death. It is a wonderful truth, but I have found it as difficult to accept and believe, as the truth about my life.

The truth is that I was created in love to be loved… that everything I am is special and cherished by the one who created me. He made me with a purpose and even the things that happened, the brokenness of my heart or the lies I have believed, or the things I have done or have been done to me; none of these things can keep him from loving me with everything that he is and none of them can keep me from living out the purposes he created for me…not if I choose him…not if I trust and follow him.

He first started revealing this truth to me through the life of the one who was on the outside most of the time… and to me it seemed like I was Jennifer. Her thoughts were my thoughts, her decisions were my decisions, everything that she was and did and experienced, all of it seemed like it was me… so even though I know differently now, back then I believed I was Jennifer. She had been searching for the truth for a while, wanting to know if God existed or not. And if he did exist, what should she do about it. She said later that she was looking for the truth, but she never expected to find love. She found both.

Jennifer met Jesus in the hallway of the house where we lived. He had been calling to her for a while and finally she answered. I remember it like it was me, but it wasn't of course. I was still hidden away. I didn't know I existed, but Jesus knew. He never forgot about me and even when he was calling out to Jennifer, he called out to me too… I know that now.

This is the story of how Jesus revealed to me the truth, not just about my life and the things that happened or even about who I am as a person, but about how he has loved me and always been with me. He is still showing me the truth about who he is and who he created me to be. This is the story of how his truth is setting me free and how I am being loved back to life.

I have written my story as it happened to me, as I experienced it. I have included things that we wrote in journals and letters, conversations we had with Jesus and with each other. There are pictures we drew of the things we remembered and how we felt and of the things that Jesus has shown us along the way. It has been a long journey and there have been many changes, except for one thing… Jesus and his love for us.

My child why do you ponder so, where is your heart?
I don't know Lord.
It is in the darkness, come into the light.
It's safer in the darkness …no one can see me.
I see you.
Do you Lord? Where are you I can't see you?
Come into the light.
I'm afraid, I'm afraid of hope, I'm afraid of life. I'm not worthy of life.
I have given you my life, do not waste it.
I'm sorry I don't know how to live it.
I will show you; I am showing you. I breathe life into everything you do, if you allow me to.
I don't feel alive.
You are covered in death my child, but I have defeated death.
It feels like an old friend, safe and familiar. it keeps me from the life I fear.
Let my tears wash away your pain and your fear, I have paid the price.

I am not worth the price.
You are worth it to me. You are beyond price…
How can I live Jesus?
You can live in me. Come to me. Rest in me... let me live in you.
I'm so tired of hurting, when will it end?
Let me hold you in my arms and comfort you. Let me take your pain.
I'm so afraid Jesus. I don't know how to let go. I'm afraid it will consume and destroy me if I let go.
I am strong… let me protect you.
I don't trust anyone to protect me, not even you.
That is the truth my child. Why do you not trust me to protect you?
Because you didn't and you don't, and I can't. I am not safe. I will never be safe… Show me Lord...
My child let me show you that you are wrong.

Jennifers Journal Year 1

Chapter 2

Preparing the Way

It was a few years after I first met Jesus that he started to talk to me about needing healing. I didn't really understand for a long time, because I didn't remember about the bad things that happened. I knew there were things from the past that were still hurting me, but he seemed to be talking about more than that. He seemed to be making a big deal of it I thought. He wasn't of course, but I didn't know it. I was following Jesus with all of my heart. I longed to hear his voice. I prayed over and over for years. I want to hear you…I want to hear you. When I first met Jesus, I was part of a church that didn't really believe that God speaks to you except through the Bible, but that didn't stop me wanting to hear him or believing that he wanted to speak to me. It seemed obvious to me that if he was my daddy, he would want to speak to me, wouldn't he? If Jesus was everything…I believed he was, why couldn't I talk to him and hear him talk back?

I saw that God spoke to people clearly in the Bible, even before believers had the Holy Spirit living in them, so how could I be wrong? I read book after book and I prayed. I went to conferences and followed wherever I thought Jesus was leading me. My pastor didn't approve at all, but that didn't stop me. It did confuse me and make me feel afraid, because the pastor told me over and over that the Bible was truth, yet he didn't seem to believe what it said. Perhaps there was a lot of confusion in his heart, but he said and did some things that made me want to leave and find a new church. My pastor told me that I was wrong…but the Holy Spirit started talking to me and helping me see that I wasn't. After a very horrible time the church closed down and I was free to find a new one. That was difficult too. Even though a lot of what happened in that church wasn't right, it was a new beginning for me, and I had found friends and a different kind of family to the one I had known. Losing that was very painful, but Jesus helped me in so many ways.

While I was looking for a new church, I was also searching to know more about Jesus. The more I saw of other Christians the more puzzled…but more determined I got. I saw people who said they followed an amazing God who was full of love and awesome healing power, people who were supposed to be like him, but were not…not in any way. That was puzzling and frustrating. Then I found others who did seem to have something different. They believed in a God who speaks and who heals and who wants to be known. They had something I wanted. I knew that was what I had been looking for in my life.

I sat in the house one day and prayed for the Holy Spirit to come and baptize me like I was learning about. I remember being afraid that nothing would happen, that he wouldn't come. I felt silly. Maybe I thought I wasn't good enough…as I believed that for a very long time. But he did come, and I was crying and laughing and speaking in Holy Spirit language. It was amazing and everything changed for me then. I remember that it seemed like up until then, everything had been in 2D but now it was in 3D. I found a new church that helped me grow and discover new things about how to hear the Holy Spirit speaking and his gifts. It was a wonderful time when everything seemed new and so many things seemed possible.

I was learning a lot about how to hear God, but still it was the cry of my heart to hear him better, clearer, and Jesus answered. I went to a teaching conference all about how to hear God and nothing was ever the same again. I learned more about dreams and visions, but mostly I learned how to journal conversations with him. That was the beginning for me because I learned how to hear him clearly. I wrote down my very first conversation with Jesus during the conference. It was part of a vision and gave me a little hint of what he had planned.

I saw a city which I understood to be old Jerusalem. There were many ways, through narrow alleys. The Lord was speaking to me as we moved down the streets.

I am taking you down narrow streets- some dark, some light. You must follow me closely or you will get lost. Follow me to the heart of the city where I dwell. That is where we are going. I am holding your hand. You need me to lead. You can't find the way. We will go in unexpected directions. There you will find my heart and we will dwell together. It doesn't matter how far it is because we are journeying together. It will be a sudden revelation burst into revelation. Just hold on to me. We will get there.
I asked him can we run, and he laughed a little.
Yes we can run.
We went down many narrow streets which were empty, deserted, taking many twists and turns. At the heart I saw a place of such beauty that I thought it was heaven. I asked him will I be dead when I get there. And he laughed and said "**no**".

It was scary at first because I thought maybe I was making it up. I was afraid that he wouldn't talk to me, so it was always a scary moment to sit down with a pen and paper. I learned too that God isn't the only one who will talk this way. There is an enemy who wants to distract and deceive and confuse and they do it very well. I learned a lot about that yet, even so I did learn how to hear God the way I was wanting to. There is more of course...there is always more, but it was the beginning of so many things.

While all of this was happening, I was training to be a counsellor. I believed at that time that was what Jesus was calling me to do. I saw Jesus working through me to help a lot of hurting people and it opened my eyes to the things that happen to people and make them the way they are. I was clever and studied right up to master's degree level and then I went to work part time for a Christian charity. I loved the work but the more I learned about Jesus power to heal… the more frustrated I got. I could see things in the people I helped that I knew only he could heal but I was a counsellor and not a minister. Jesus worked though me, but it wasn't enough. I didn't think so...I cried for the people who were so broken and asked Jesus what I should do.

Jesus answered me but not at all in the way I was expecting. I went on a retreat day with the people at work. It was supposed to be a day to spend with God, but it turned out to be a lot of boring talk. At the lunch break I was overwhelmed by a desperate need to go to the little chapel I saw when I arrived. It was so strong I had to go even though the people I was with thought I was very rude I think. When I got there, I sat for a little while and I heard Jesus say so very clearly in my heart *'I have not called you to this'*. He said it three times so there was no mistake. I sat there not really knowing what to do. I saw a little alcove with some candles in it. It looked nice, hidden away and there was a little seat, so I went and sat and looked at the tiny tea light candles that were there and I heard him again. *'**I have not called you to this, this is tea-light ministry, a little light, a little power….**'* I looked up and saw a skylight in the ceiling and he said *'**the ministry I will give you will be as the sun compared to this. You will open up the windows of heaven and let the sunshine down on the people. Your ministry will be like the sun compared to the tea-light'**.* I was so shocked. I sat there with my mouth open for ages.

That wasn't all though. A few days later I went to a meeting where there was worship and a speaker. Most of it was very boring but then one of the speakers said that the Holy Spirit was calling people to go forward and make a fresh commitment. It was like there was fire in my heart and I practically ran to the front and fell on my knees. It was complete surrender to whatever Jesus was asking. It was a kind of scary no turning back moment, but I couldn't help it. I was crying and crying and shaking all over. I heard a click like something had clicked into place and I saw the word 'commissioned' written in little golden letters over me. Later on, while I was laying awake that night, Jesus showed me what the click was. He showed me a picture of railway points...they had shifted and clicked into place so that now my life was on a different track.

So now I knew that I was supposed to be doing something different than being a counsellor, or not just a counsellor. That was a bit scary because I had spent all that time training and working and now Jesus was saying he wanted me to do something different. I'd made my choice to follow him no matter what, even though it seemed very stupid to other people and some of the time to me too. Jesus led me to go and do some study at a ministry center. That seemed to make some sense at least, because it brought counselling and ministry together.

> *A vision…A dead tree stands alone on top of a hill. I climb up the hill, I wrap my arms around the tree and hold/hug it… signs of life begin to appear… leaves then fruit… bursting with life.*
>
> *This was such a difficult time for me. I felt I was taking ridiculous steps and couldn't see how any of it could possibly work out. I was full of self-doubt and doubt about what I'd heard from God…. This vision did encourage me. A promise that I will bear fruit.*

Jennifer's Journal. Beginning Year 1

So, I went to learn but it wasn't what I thought at all. It wasn't about me learning how to minister to people, it was about Jesus ministering to me... to start healing me.

I began my time at the ministry centre one weekend a month. They did a lot of teaching, all about healing. They also had times where students like me could be ministered to. Jesus used all of this to start showing me the truth. He began by showing me the truth of the things I already knew and remembered. I grew up never knowing my dad because he didn't marry my mum and lived abroad. I didn't think it mattered that much but Jesus showed me that it mattered a lot. A father's love is something that we all need. I was made with that need in me, but it was a need that my dad never met. Sometimes I would get letters or postcards, or a check for birthdays, but I never met him until I was about twenty. Then he wrote and said he would like to meet me and took me out to lunch, which I remember as being difficult and awkward but not terrible. He promised to see me again, but I didn't see him for another ten years or so. Jesus helped me to see my need and accept it rather than pushing it away and pretending it didn't matter. It was painful and at first, I got angry because I thought I was there to learn to help others not to have to face up to all these difficult things.

I discovered a book on my book shelves which talked about the fatherhood of God, which did help somewhat, but really it was the counselling of the Holy Spirit who showed me how I'd walled myself off and protected myself so effectively, from even recognising my need and the fear of abandonment which surrounded it. He gave me a really powerful picture of a newborn (me) lying in a dark and damp dungeon, no doors or windows. I was just lying there screaming in rage and pain because I was so alone and yet, I was the one who had constructed the cell. It was terrible, so much pain I never knew was there, or at least I'd never allowed myself to know. Just knowing that's how it was, however, didn't help at all, it just had me in pieces. One day I was praying and felt the presence of God, but it was God the father. I was so terrified I told him to go away and leave me alone. I was a bit of a mess. Anyway, I then realised that this was exactly what I had been doing all along. I didn't want to, but I was so terrified I couldn't help myself. At the same time, he was showing me that I was carrying a lot of stigma and shame about being illegitimate, the 'untouchable children in the sixties' and that the shame of both my parents had been put on to me. I knew that before but hadn't seen it quite in this way. I knew what I had to do was allow my father God to pick me up… but that was very much my choice. At this point I think the emotional pain was so great that it enabled me to overcome my fear, so that even though I was still very afraid, because I didn't want to risk abandonment, I did ask him to pick me up. I waited until the Sunday. The pastor prayed over us as a congregation and as he did so, the Father very quietly came and picked me up and held me close. It wasn't what I expected. I thought it would be really dramatic, emotional, painful but all I felt was peace and a real sense of safety and security… safe in my father's arms. That night I was awakened as I had a sudden revelation of who I am in Christ, a beloved child. That I was never unwanted or shameful… that was never who I was. I have always been and will always be a beloved child of the king. Amazing.

By the time Jesus started to heal me before this, I was meeting with my dad for a few years and had gone to visit him and meet his side of the family. It was always difficult I think, maybe because of the pain I was holding and because of the kind of man he was. But I got to know him a little bit and some of the time it was nice, and I think it was a good thing to spend time with him. Now he was ill and dying of cancer and so all of the past stuff was getting mixed up with grief. I was hurting a lot.

Jesus was showing me other things too. I learned how important it is to be comforted. That seems obvious now, but I never knew it for myself. I gave comfort to my children, my friends and the people I was helping, but I never expected it or even wanted it for myself. I found it hard to accept even when it was offered, because I didn't know what to do with it. I realised that comfort was something I never had. Growing up there were no hugs and crying was usually ignored or seen as bad. Seeing the 'need I never knew I needed' and never met, was like finding big holes in my heart and it hurt, it hurt a lot.

Jesus sat on a throne at the top of some steps. There were a lot of children coming and going up and down the steps. They were dressed in lovely clothes and they were happy and not afraid or shy. They went to talk with Jesus, they sat on his knee and cuddled him and kissed him and he cuddled them back. He gave them gifts that they happily took. I sat huddled up on the bottom stair. I was a young girl with a shaved head, all dirty and dressed in rags. I sat and watched the other children with Jesus. I loved Jesus but I didn't feel like I belonged with those children. Jesus looked at me every so often and I could see the love and compassion, but I couldn't look him in the eye. I wanted to go to him, but I was afraid that if I even moved, he would send me away. I was only allowed to stay because I was still and quiet. I didn't believe I could ever be like one of those children.

Jennifer's journal. Early year 1

I held on to Jesus and didn't change my mind about following him, even though what was happening wasn't what I expected or wanted. Jesus told me what to expect of course in conversations and visions many times.

I see an owl (spirit of wisdom?). It has a golden 'look' about it. It turns its head this way and that with huge black eyes that see everything. I look down, I think through its eyes and I see two people on horses riding slowly along the road below. One is a woman, she has really long hair. So long it hangs down the back of the horse and trails in the dirt collecting twigs and leaves. They stop by the side of a lake. The other who I can't see clearly (the Lord?) builds a fire. I see that there is danger to the woman because of her hair, she can't go near the fire. The water looks inviting but how can she swim with all that hair? I just knew that she spent a lot of time tending to all her hair, taking all her time and energy. I noticed before that the top part of her hair was blonde, the bottom part dark. I see the Lord? Take some old-fashioned scissors almost like shears and cut off the dark part of her hair. The woman weeps and tries to gather it up so she can keep it. But I know she has to let it go. Now she will ride faster, she won't be in danger from the fire or the water and she can move her head, not be weighed down anymore.

Is the dark hair from the past, before I was saved? The blonde hair represents righteousness in Christ. The lord wants to cut off the past, finally and completely. He wants to burn it in his holy fire so that it no longer hinders in any way.

Jennifer's journal early year 1

Somehow, I didn't pay attention to that very much... I was thinking about his promises for the future. He had given me lots of promises in words and visions and dreams, like the one about the tea lights.

A dream
I saw a dragon, huge, really huge, green and scaly. Myself (and another) killed the dragon (cut it's head off?). The dragon had eaten many people and I felt we needed to cut them out of its belly and try to save them. Some others thought this was a waste of time, but I insisted. We cut open the dragon, got the people out and began to resuscitate them. For some it was too late, they were dead, but many were brought back to life.

A vision.

I saw a kingfisher and a river, a fast-flowing crystal-clear river. At the bottom of the beautiful river were many gems and precious stones of all kinds. I looked upstream and saw a very large and strong 'monster' coming towards me. He had the head of a falcon and the body of a muscular man with talons. He was a reddish, brown colour. As he walked through the water, he crushed the gems underfoot. He passed by me and disappeared. Suddenly I knew that it was my task to put the stones back together. The river is the church and the gems its people. The monster is the destroyer Satan. I started to question 'how will I do this'. First, get in the river. As I did so, the monster looked around and came straight for me to stop me, but he couldn't touch me.

From Jennifer's journal. Year -1

Now I understand why he had given me all those promises. It was like before he began healing me, he gave me a treasure box. He filled it up with his plans and promises, reasons to keep following and keep hoping even when it got really difficult and I couldn't see where I was going. This was only the beginning for me, but my treasure box has helped me through my journey so far. Jesus has added to it along the way, but he has never taken anything out.

I finally did realise that Jesus' main purpose for this time was to heal me. I still didn't know about all the hidden things. I thought there was quite enough already, but all Jesus had really done was to prepare me for the real healing that was to come. He had started to open up my eyes so that I could see my need. I didn't understand of course, I didn't know what I was asking for when I asked him to heal me.

I am coming to stir things up. I am coming to change things. There will be a great shaking and things will never be the same. Things cannot remain the same, they must be torn down so that I can begin to build. Things cannot remain the same. Structures that are there cannot remain in place if I am to build. They cannot co-exist. The old must give way to the new. I am about to shake your very foundations. I am about to tear down the old so that I can build the new. I cannot build on what is there it must be torn down. The old must go completely. Then I can begin to build in your life what I want to be there. I have hold of you... do not be afraid. Everything may look uncertain; you may lose sight of who you are, but do not lose sight of who I am. Trust me completely. The foundations you have built your life on must be removed. You cannot build the life I have for you on those foundations. They will not support anything. My work in you must go deep, so deep that you will not be able to follow it or fathom it. It will require you to trust me my child with all that you are. You must stay with it... you must allow me complete freedom and access. Do not fight me... do not hinder me... do not run away. Do not be afraid for I am about to do a mighty work in you. I will not tolerate the presence of the work of the enemy in my precious child any longer. Now it begins. I have laid the foundations for this work and I am going to begin. You know that I am with you, you know that you can trust me, you know that I will give you all you need every step of the way.

Jennifer's journal year 1

About three months after beginning my course at the ministry centre, I went away to a weekend conference with my good friend Ruth. I knew that Jesus was going to do something, because he gave me a dream which told me the barriers in my mind would be removed, so that I could leave the place I was and go to a new one, where something new would be built. I had no idea what this meant but I knew it was important. We arrived in time for the evening meeting. Ruth wanted to sit right at the front. She knew the woman who was speaking so maybe that is why, but I wanted to hide at the back. I was feeling very scared. I was scared that Jesus was going to do something, and I was scared that he wasn't. I'm not sure how much I managed to worship or pay attention to the message, but I did pay attention when the lady speaker stopped in the middle of her sermon and pointed straight at me. I was right in front of her of course. She said to me *"you are called to be an evangelist, you don't know it, but you are"*. Maybe I looked as shocked as I felt I don't know. I just sat there. I think I felt sick and very, very confused. This was not what I had been expecting at all. Why was he doing this? How was it meant to help? I didn't want to be an evangelist. I thought it was stupid, but I couldn't argue with it. That lady was very, very certain about what she was saying.

The lady continued with her message, but I wasn't listening. I was having a little rant at Jesus. Meanwhile, the lady stopped preaching because the presence of the Holy Spirit was so strong, she couldn't even stand. She called people to come forward for prayer and even though I was confused about what happened, I knew I had to go. I was overwhelmed by a terrible fear… a despair that said to go forward was a waste of time, that nothing was going to happen. Jesus wasn't going to do anything. I struggled and wrestled for a while. I knew I had to go even if I thought it was a waste of time. At least that way I was letting Jesus decided what to do and not getting in the way of that. Even so it was like I was glued to the seat. A lady came and sat next to me. She said she could see I was afraid, but felt I really needed to go forward. I started to cry and said yes, but I couldn't. I prayed and I prayed, and I suppose Jesus helped me, because I found myself on my feet walking to the front. I know now that it was the enemy trying to keep me from what Jesus was about to do but right then all I felt was fear and confusion.

I joined the end of the row of people who were waiting for the lady to pray for them. She got back on her feet by now, but she never prayed for me. The Holy Spirit came instead, and I fell to my knees crying and crying. There was so much pain that came from somewhere deep, deep inside. I didn't know what it was or what was happening, but I knew it was the Holy Spirit at work. I knew this was why I had come. I cried and cried and cried. I made a lot of noise. I am glad it was a noisy room full of people, but even so I made a lot of horrible wailing noises. I couldn't stop it. It just kept coming and coming. People came and gave me words, like I would do great things for God, because I had surrendered, and he was giving me a testimony. That was nice but what I really wanted was someone to give me a lot of tissues because I was very much needing them!

When I asked Jesus later about being an evangelist, he said *'you have no idea who you are. You are who I say that you are'*. That is something he has said often to me as I have been learning about who I am. Learning that he sees the truth about who I am and accepting it has been so important.

You are not who you think you are, not in any sense but I will give you a new identity, a new name. This is what I will do. I make all things new. Do not be afraid for I am holding you. I will give you the strength to see the truth, trust me to do that. There is nothing to know that you cannot bear. You are strong in me my little one, so strong. Nothing can stop this now. I will completely heal and cleanse you. It will not be long now. Just hold on to me and know that I am all you need. I will show you the truth and I will bring you out of that into a future full of life and freedom. Take it one step at a time, just follow me. Don't worry about the path and where it leads.

Jennifer's journal year 1

I still didn't want to be an evangelist though. Jesus kept talking to me and showing me things for the rest of my time away, but he didn't do any more healing which was good because I was exhausted. I came home knowing that Jesus had done something very big but not really understanding what it was.

I saw a great rugged rock. Waves were crashing against it. I saw myself standing on top of the rock facing out to sea, arms outstretched.
What am I doing Lord?
You are trying to catch the wind. Now look out to sea. What do you see?
I saw a giant tsunami wave out to sea, but not far out, headed towards me.
But Lord that will kill me. I'll be washed away.
No. I've got you, I'm holding you.
And Jesus was there beside me on the rock, arms holding me tight. He told me that in the

same way an earthquake triggers a tsunami in the natural, my allowing him into the deep places, like saltwater in the deep places of the earth, had triggered this spiritual tsunami. I told him I didn't understand how that can be but once again I gave him complete access, renouncing all my walls and defenses. Jesus told me the wave will sweep them all away and will cleanse completely. I can run or I can stay. I said I wanted every hindrance to be gone, that I would pay any price if only I can have him.

Jennifer's journal entry two weeks <u>before</u> the conference.

A few days later dad died. I knew that it was going to happen, so it wasn't a shock but still somehow it was. Jesus was very kind to me with the timing, I think. My children were going to stay with their dad for a few days, so I had time and space to be with Jesus and to grieve. I spent three days crying and sleeping and not much else, like all the grieving was crammed into those days. I think maybe that is because of what was to come, and Jesus knew I needed to have this done. He always knows what I need.

Don't be afraid little one, don't be afraid to come to me. See I'm holding you, my little girl. I'm holding you close. I'm not afraid of your pain. The greater your need the closer I will hold you. I will never push you away. Bring all your pain to me, don't hold any of it back. I will never tell you it doesn't matter. Your pain matters to me. It matters. You will never wear me out, you will never hear me say not now. I will always be here to hold you, to wipe away your tears. You matter to me. I will always be here. Don't ever be afraid to come.

Jennifer's journal year 1

Chapter 3
The Bad Things

The dream Jesus gave me before the conference told me the barriers in my mind would be removed. I think He began as gently as he could. Being with Jesus is the safest place to be and it was in that place that I began to remember. It was just a picture at first, of a place I knew when I was little. I was in the local park in the sunshine, sitting on a bench eating an ice lolly. I think I was about three years old. There was someone with me, a man, but I didn't see his face at first. The man was sitting with his arm around me, but his hand was inside my clothes, touching me. I was confused and afraid, but I needed to know if it was true, so I kept asking Jesus to show me who it was. When I saw him I didn't believe it. I didn't believe Granddad could have done that. Jesus just kept telling me to trust him. In the next few days I remembered other things that were kind of the same. Things that happened at home or in the woods... all of them were with granddad.

I saw myself, maybe a little older 5… going down into the woods at the back of our house with him. He sat me on his lap and put his hand there again. I was aware of feeling fear, confusion and completely alone. I wept. Jesus came again and picked me up in his arms and carried me away.

I have come to fix your broken heart...I will fix it. You know you can trust me utterly, do not falter now, lean on me. This may be the most difficult time of all when you lose the sense of who you are, but your security is in me, in who I am. I do not change. I am the everlasting unchanging one. I am holding you so close, so close. I will give you all you need. Comfort, security, love and identity.

When I was small, I lived in a house with mum, with grandma and grandad. I lived there until I was five, so I spent a lot of time with grandma and grandad while mum was out at work. I didn't remember very much from that time but what I did remember was grandad playing with me, listening to records together, being tickled and playing games. Nothing bad, nothing that ever made me think he wasn't anything but kind to me. I remembered him as the only person who ever showed me any affection.

I didn't want to believe he did those things, but it seemed like that was what Jesus was telling me was true. I prayed and prayed and asked Jesus to show me the truth. I hoped it was all some mistake, but all that happened was more memories came. Jesus did help me. I went to a meeting hoping and praying that he would help me in some way.

The Lord began pouring out a revelation of his love for me. I had a revelation that I have the spirit of the overcomer in me, and that he has overcome. As the music played over us, I heard him talk about my grandad. He said 'I am your grandad and your dad. I loved you. I will always love you. Even if no one else loved that little girl I did. I am all the love you will ever need. Let it go'. And I did. What I had been struggling with and made it so hard to accept, was that my grandad had been the one person who had shown me love and affection… who would spend time with me and made me things. It was so hard for me to let go of that and believe no one had shown me love.

Finally, I accepted that it was true… it must be true. Then I started to remember other things. This time grandma was there, and she knew what he was doing. She was helping him. This was even worse

and more unbelievable to me. Grandad died when I was eight, but grandma had been there all the time I was growing up. I thought I knew her, who she was, but all the time I didn't. All the time she had known what was happening and even helped. It took me a long time to accept that this could be true. Believing these things changed who I knew them to be. It changed how I saw myself and my past. I didn't want to believe it, but I knew that it was Jesus who was showing me these things, most of the time I did anyway. There was so much pain and grief that came with the things I remembered. I knew that I wasn't making it up, there was no reason for me to do that. I had never even for one moment thought that this could have happened to me.

My times at the ministry center helped a lot because I had people to talk to and who prayed with me. I had space to cry too. It was hard at home because I had to care for two children. I couldn't let them see or know what was going on. I had to be very good at keeping things hidden and contained. I suppose that was one way I had of keeping safe. I kept everything hidden except from Ruth and another good friend Cheryl. It was difficult for me to talk about the things I was remembering even to them, because I wasn't sure if it was true and because I felt like I was betraying people who loved me and cared for me as a child. I felt that way for a long time. There was a battle going on, though I didn't really understand that at the time. The enemy didn't want me to know the truth, be healed or set free. Most of the time they attacked in whispers that told me it wasn't true, that I was sick or just wanting attention. Some of their attacks were more direct.

Last night I had an experience… I don't think it was a dream. I was only half asleep and I was suddenly aware that the enemy was right there. I said No and started to tell it to get off… I'm not sure if this was out loud or not but it must have been because I was suddenly unable to speak or move and I could hear a snarling. I prayed in my head **"Father help me"**. *And whatever it was left.*

Jennifer's journal year 1

Jesus was showing me other things too, not just memories. He was showing me things I believed about myself. I began to notice things and remember them as things I had always known but never really accepted. I had thoughts about wanting to die. I always had them, but somehow, I never saw them or admitted to myself that they were there. I remembered things I thought about my body and how it was somehow separate from me, just a thing I had to have but didn't like... I hated it. The more things I noticed the more I knew that the things I remembered were true. I was shocked that I never saw them before, especially because I was counselling people who had the same kinds of thoughts and feelings, but I didn't see them in myself. Now I understood why Jesus asked me to stop working as a counsellor a few months before that. I was glad I listened and did what he asked. I could never have continued to help people that way when I was in so much pain and turmoil. I never expected this, I thought I was going to help others. Now I was the one needing help.

I look but don't see
I listen but don't hear
I touch but don't feel
Laughing on the outside
It only goes skin deep
I'm breathing
But not living
Knowing but not experiencing
Giving little
Receiving less
Protected and detached
I try to keep safe
Isolation
Is all I've achieved

Jesus talked to me a lot about my need to be in control and keep safe. He asked me over and over to surrender control to him. That wasn't easy because it meant trusting Jesus completely. The more uncertain things were, the more I wanted to try and be in control… things were very uncertain. One way I had of trying to be in control was by needing to understand everything. I tried very hard to try and work out everything that had happened, what was happening, what would happen, what Jesus was doing, how I could get healed, and how I could move forward. But it was hopeless of course because I understood

Isolation

practically nothing of any of those things. Trusting Jesus meant not needing to understand everything but trusting that he does and that he is in control and what he is doing is good. It meant trusting him to give me everything I needed, including understanding when I needed it. I got better at this, but it took a long time. I think the reason I learned as fast as I did was because I had no choice. I had nowhere else to turn.

I started to notice other ways that I kept myself safe too. I didn't see it before. Safe meant keeping away from people, keeping them out, not letting them see, not letting them close. People were a threat…all people, some more than others but no one was safe. It was kind of a shock to see that and to see how it kept me away from others… kept me alone.

I noticed too that when I got afraid or very distressed I could kind of switch off so that nothing was real, and everything faded away. I didn't mean to do it, it just happened. Sometimes I would stare at something, just gaze and gaze at it, so all of my attention was on that and nothing else. Sometimes I would stop breathing, not like holding your breath but I just stopped breathing. I had lots of things like that I did when the feelings were too much. Those things had helped me survive but Jesus wanted me to learn to run to him and let go of my own ways to survive and keep safe. He wanted to teach me that he was my safe place. That has taken a long time to really learn. Feeling safe has taken a long time to come.

It was the start of a new year. There was a lovely little place in the countryside that I had been to before, a log cabin surrounded by pretty woodland, quiet and safe and away from the world outside. Me and Ruth wanted to spend some time away with Jesus and it was the perfect place to spend a few days together. We knew that he had plans for our weekend, but we weren't expecting what happened. We spent a lot of time together and all of it was centered around Jesus. We knew that our friendship was his idea. We longed to know more of him and to follow wherever he was leading us, so the weekend wasn't just about spending time with each other but most of all it was about spending time with Jesus and allowing him to do whatever he wanted.

He didn't waste any time and began working straight away through our conversations together. I didn't know what he wanted to do about me, but he began with Ruth helping her to see some things he wanted to heal. It was difficult but we both knew it was good and encouraging to know that Jesus was with us. The next day was the same until the evening when his focus suddenly seemed to change onto me. Ruth knew about the things I had been remembering and we were talking about it a little bit and I started to remember something else. I remembered standing at the bottom of the stairs in the house where grandma and grandad lived. I think we had moved out by now, but I still spent a lot of time there because of mum being at work. I was standing looking up the stairs, feeling afraid. I had just got in from school and needed the toilet, but I was afraid to go upstairs in case grandad was there. So, I stood there listening to see if it was safe.

Then I remembered when I first started school and I went to the doctors to have an injection. It wasn't a new memory, but I started to wonder about it. I had never remembered being in the doctor's room I only remembered what happened afterwards. I remembered how angry mum was because she said I screamed and cried and made a fuss. Now I wondered why because I had never seemed very afraid of injections since then. The Holy Spirit started to show Ruth something. He showed her the doctor's room and she described it to me perfectly. I went to the same doctor for years, so I knew the room well. Ruth had never been there. She said she could see something on the desk, something that explained why I screamed. I started to say I had no idea what that could be and then I saw it. As clear as if someone had given me a photograph to look at. It was a metal kidney shaped dish and in it was a speculum. That is why I screamed, because I saw that. It had nothing to do with the injection. I went cold because I knew that I shouldn't have even known what that was at age four. There was no reason I knew of that it should have meant anything to me so why was I so afraid and why did it make me scream in terror that day in the doctor's?

I felt afraid. So afraid and kind of numb. I went home still not knowing the answer to the question, not really wanting to know, but it seemed like there was no turning back now. Like the door wasn't just opened but was flung wide and the memories started to come. What I saw and remembered was like nothing I ever imagined could be true. Not for anyone and definitely not for me. It made the stuff I remembered before seem easy. I don't remember now what came first because there were so many that came one after another.

Even though I was scared and horrified I wanted more than anything to know if what I was remembering was true. It didn't seem like it could be. How could those things have happened and I didn't know anything. Then the things I was remembering weren't like anything I thought I could make up, not like anything I had ever really heard of or thought about. I didn't see how I could have made them up.

I knew now why I screamed when I saw the speculum. It was something I knew a lot about. It was put inside me to stretch me and make me ready. Not just for grandad but for his friends too. And there was more, so much more. It was so hard to spend time with Jesus. There was so much fear and confusion. Everything and everyone seemed threatening. But I did still hear him somehow.

I will reclaim you and restore you my child. There is none that can stop me. I will have my way. You must find all of your strength in me, all of it. Do not rely on your own strength for anything. Lean on me in all things. I am sufficient. I will supply every need you have. I will make you whole again my beloved child. Only I know the way, the way I have chosen for you. Do not lean on your understanding but only on mine. I will not let you falter or fall. I am with you. I am with you. Remember these words. I am with you. I never leave you. I never forsake you. I am working for you. I am fighting for you. I am your protector and your healer. I will save and deliver you from all the works of the devil. Place yourself completely in my hands. You cannot do this. You cannot do this. I am completely trustworthy. I will not let you down. I will not hurt you. I will not give you more than you can bear.
I saw a picture of me climbing up an almost sheer cliff face- reminded me of Frodo and Sam on the winding stair.
Yes the way is difficult, dangerous, painful and arduous. It is dark and treacherous but see you are not alone, you are surrounded.
I saw the same picture but now I see I am completely surrounded by angels- there's no way I can fall. Some support me from below and supply the strength I need to climb. Some are guiding my hands and feet to the right place. Some go ahead of me. All are protecting me. **You will not falter or fall. You will have all the strength you need. Do not be afraid. Allow me to carry you. Allow me to be your all sufficient one.**
Jennifer's journal year 1

That helped me to keep holding on and trusting but I had no idea what to do with all of this stuff though it seemed to me that I was going to the ministry center for just this reason, so that they could help me. It was about two weeks between the weekend away and the next weekend at the center and in that time I had remembered a lot of things. So many things seemed to trigger them. Things that I saw or heard, like the call of geese flying overhead or the sound of rain on the window. I knew that I needed to tell someone, but I had no idea how to do it. I was very afraid I wouldn't be believed, or they would think

I was sick in the head. But I prayed and trusted that Jesus was going to make a way since he kept telling me he was.

Every weekend at the center they taught and ministered on a different topic. This weekend just happened to be sexual abuse. I knew that wasn't an accident and I knew it was going to be very difficult. I sat in on the first session. As far as I remember they were talking about all the different types of abuse and there wasn't one I didn't remember having happened to me. It got more and more difficult to keep sitting there listening, so I decided to leave quietly and pretend I was going to the toilet. It almost worked. I made it to the big, heavy wooden door and pulled it open but then lost control and even though it was such a big heavy door managed to slam it shut behind me as I ran out in terror. Everyone must have looked; everyone must have known but I didn't seem to care. I ran into the toilet and locked the door and huddled in the furthest corner crying. It was a strange feeling, like I was far away and not really connected to what was going on. I could hear voices in my head telling me, I thought, to open the door to the lady who was knocking on it now, asking if I was alright. But I just kept on crying. I was so afraid. The inside voice kept talking telling me it was ok, and I needed to get up and open the door. Eventually I did…but it was very hard not to start running again. The lady took me into a different room and sat with me, trying to get me to talk. But I couldn't. I didn't. I just sat there, not looking at her, not moving or talking, just breathing and staring at the sofa I was sitting on. It seemed to take a long time but eventually I felt more in control and able to talk.

I asked to speak with one of the other ladies there. A lady called Beryl who had been very kind to me and prayed with me about the other things I remembered before. I told Beryl as best I could the things I was remembering. I told her the worst memory I had at that time...I'm not sure why...maybe because I wanted to know if it could be true and if Beryl would believe me. She did. That was bad and good all at the same time because I wanted to be believed but I didn't want it to be true, even though that would mean there was something very, very wrong with me. The memories came in different ways. Sometimes they were just pictures, sometimes clear, sometimes not. Sometimes they were like silent movies. Sometimes they were like little movies with sound and color, sharp and clear. This was one of those.

I told Beryl about the Goatman. He seems to have been the leader of one of the groups I remember being at. He is in a lot of the memories I have. I think this is probably one of my first memories of this group but there were many, many more after this one. I must have been five or six because I was wearing a white dress that I recognized as the one grandma made me for the school nativity when I played the part of an angel. It was dark and I was in woodland. There were trees around, but I was in a clear space where there was a fire. I was laid on a big flat stone that I know now was an altar. I was laid on my back on this cold stone and I was looking up at the Goatman.

He was wearing a red robe that was open at the front. He wasn't wearing anything underneath. His face was covered by a mask that I think was dark red though it was hard to tell because it was dark and in his hand, he had a knife or maybe you would call it a dagger. It wasn't like any knife I ever saw because it had four blades. He held up the knife over his head. I was surrounded by people all dressed in the same kind of robes. He said something but I don't know what and then he put the knife inside me between my legs, so it cut. He collected the blood in a cup and drank it and then he did the sex thing with me. He leaned down and spoke right into my face and said you will always belong to me; you will always be mine.

And then he stood me on my feet and said behold the bride. Then he gave me to the crowd so they could do the sex thing with me, but I didn't remember that.

Then I was sitting high up in a tree looking down at my body. I think there were angels in the tree with me. I could see dark shapes all around my body like they were trying to get it but somehow, they couldn't like it was protected. I think maybe I was almost dead. And then I heard shouts and there was running and darkness and suddenly I was over grandad's shoulder and he was running. I didn't remember any more.

That is the thing that I told Beryl and she believed me even though it was so very unbelievable to me. She prayed with me and said that she would speak to the person who was in charge of the ministry at the center. She said they would be able to help me. That was such a big relief to me, to have been believed and to know that there was help.

A vision...I saw the Lord coming towards me across a floor of what looked like thousands of gemstones. His feet were at my eye-level and I couldn't see where I was. I couldn't see myself. Jesus squatted down and held out His hand towards me and pulled me out of a pit. I didn't see it then, but I was covered in black goo. As we walked back across the gems, I could see I was leaving a trail of black goo across them. We then came to a perfectly white environment, and then I saw myself. I was filthy, ragged with matted black long hair which trailed on the floor behind me. I was disgusting. The Lord continued to almost pull me along, as I grew more and more distressed at my state and the mess I was leaving in my wake. I tried to stop, I tried to let go of Him, but He kept a firm hold and urged me onwards.

We came to a door which Jesus opened. Inside was a storm. Crashing waves, gale force wind, driving rain and in amongst it all... fire. Jesus motioned for me to go in. I knew this was where I would be cleansed, but I was afraid, it was terrifying in there. As I stepped into the room Jesus came with me. As I was engulfed by the storm, I was aware of Him holding me and that is what I focused on. Finally, Jesus led me out by a different door on the other side of the room. Outside everything was still and completely white again. I stood before Him, bedraggled and battered in my rags. I looked at Jesus. He was in the same condition. He had experienced every blow and every pain that I had. He had truly been with me.

As I looked at Him a great blinding light shone on us. It was warm and gentle. We were warmed, dried and healed. Jesus exchanged my rags for a white gown which sparkled. My hair was now shoulder length, golden in color. Jesus put a netting of golden gems onto my head, he took my hand and we walked across the floor again. This time I left a trail of crystal-clear footprints. Jesus led me to the floor of gems. This time as I walked across them... what had been dull jewels now sparkled and gleamed.

Jennifer's journal Year 1

Chapter 4
HELP!???

I waited to see what the lady in charge of the ministry at the centre would say to me. I waited and I waited. After about two weeks I spoke to her on the telephone and answered a lot of difficult questions about the things I remembered and the past and my relationship with God. It was very, very difficult for me because of all the fear inside.

Then I got an email with a questionnaire with lots more difficult questions, many of them asking if the memories were real. The ministry lady had told me she didn't think they would be able to help but she asked me all these questions anyway. The next time I was at the centre for the weekend I spoke to her again. I had written down all the bad things I remembered so I didn't have to say them. That made it a lot easier, but it was still very difficult. While I was talking, I heard a little voice inside saying 'I deserved it'. I think the ministry lady knew that there were others inside. I think she knew if what I was telling her was true there almost had to be others inside.

I was still hoping that they could help me at the centre...why did they ask me all these things otherwise? The lady didn't say no just that she didn't think they had the people. And so I kept waiting and hoping because I couldn't understand why I was there if they weren't going to help me. I went to talk to my pastor about the things that were happening. He listened and was kind but didn't seem to have any help to offer. He didn't seem to know what to do. I decided I would have to help myself as best I could. I started to keep a journal that I called the book of death. I drew the memories that came. It seemed to help somehow, and I wrote the thoughts that were in my head, some of them weren't my thoughts but the thoughts of those inside. And I drew the way I felt, or what others felt. It helped because mostly I had nobody to talk to.

Beryl, the lady at the ministry centre was very kind and gave us her email address and said I could email any time. When I was at the centre she would spend time with me, but I didn't want to be a nuisance. I never wanted to be a bother to anyone but because she came to me, I did spend time with her and talk to her...about lots of things. And she told me things about herself and it was like I had found a kind new friend and that was such a good thing in the middle of it all. I struggled because I got very attached to her and wanted to be close to her but I was afraid I would make her go away. I was very afraid that she would leave me. I had fights with myself all the time about whether to write or not because I didn't want to make her go away, and I didn't want to depend on her and I suppose I didn't really trust her either. So, in the end I didn't write very much. I did check and check and check to see if she had emailed me,

Can't speak.
There's so much to say but I can't speak
A mind full of pictures that I can't describe
A heart full of pain that I can't express
A life full of fear that I can't live
There's a silence inside me that I cannot break
It stops up my mouth and clogs up my brain
I see it but can't say it
The words won't come
my body trembles
my mind freezes
my heart goes numb
I can't speak
How can I speak
help me to speak.

I'm alone
I'm all alone
nobody sees
nobody hears
I'm right in front of them
but still they don't see
they don't see me
Only the outside
not the inside
they not looking
they don't care
what's on the inside

I want to die
please let me die
I'm lost inside and it's so dark

no more

especially if I was waiting for a reply. I got so anxious and so disappointed day after day after day when she didn't write. It was very horrible and added to my fear and distress.

The memory flashbacks kept coming, more and new terrible things. And I started to hear the voices of those inside more clearly. I wanted to know if I really was a multiple, but there was nobody who would help me find out what was going on or what was true and what wasn't. Jesus kept reassuring me that he was in control and that he was showing me the truth. He said that there was a particular man who would understand and who would help me. I just needed to hold on, wait and trust him.

. I read all the books I could find on multiple personality disorder trying to work out if I had it. It was so difficult to know because there seemed so many different ways it could show itself. I wasn't sure I fit... except that now I was hearing all of these different voices inside and feeling the things that they were... and sometimes not feeling like I was in control of what was said or done outside. It felt like pressure all of the time to stay normal and not let anyone see. Like all these other voices and feelings and thoughts and memories were all going to burst out at any moment.

When I believed that there were others there it did help me to understand some of the things that were happening. It helped me to understand what had happened at the ministry center that time. I understood now that it was an alter who had switched out and had run and hidden in the toilet. And the voice I heard talking to me was another alter talking to her trying to get her back inside. They weren't talking to me at all. I don't know who they were, not even now but it made sense to me once I understood that there were others inside

I found a website that had been set up to help people who had been hurt like me and had DID. I emailed the person who ran it and asked lots of questions and I got replies...that was amazing to me. And it did help, and I thought maybe I wasn't so alone, but they didn't have any answers about where I could find help.

Eventually the lady at the ministry center told me a final no. They couldn't help me. They didn't have the people who were willing to make that kind of commitment. They didn't have the time or the resources that someone like me would need. The lady said that people like me needed to have a lot of support because they rang up a lot wanting help and needed ministry for years. They couldn't help me because I needed too much. That made me feel like I should crawl away and die somewhere because I wasn't worth the effort. I was too much trouble. It was easy for me to believe that. I knew it already.

Beryl seemed to change her mind about me after the centre said no. She started to avoid me and didn't reply to the few emails I sent. I was very confused because she had said she wanted to be my friend and spend time with me and then suddenly she didn't want to have anything to do with me. And just when I felt like

If you shut your eyes
Do I still exist?
When I'm gone from your sight
Do I leave your mind
Can you remember my name
When I'm no longer here
Do you give me a thought
Or do I disappear
Am I even real
When you're not around
Do I cease to exist
Can I even be found?

I'm broken and dirty
Nothing worth saving
Don't look at me please
I'm trying to hide it
I long to be loved
But how can that be
There's nothing worth loving
On the inside of me
I want to be held
Given comfort and warmth
I can't let you touch me
I won't spread my filth
I want to be noticed
And valued it's true
But I keep on hiding
I won't let you see
I can't even look
At the thing that is me

I'd accepted she wasn't my friend I would get an email asking how I was… like we were good friends again. I got so upset time after time and it was making things more difficult and not helping at all. I was feeling abandoned and rejected time after time and then given hope that she would be my friend and then rejected again. Eventually I emailed her and said thankyou for all her help and support and that I wished her well for the future...goodbye in other words. Beryl replied straight away and said something like yes, ok goodbye. I was so hurt, but in the end, it was a relief. It was too hard.

I didn't give up though...how could I? If I gave up, I knew I would die and even though a lot of the time that was what I wanted, I couldn't die because I had two children who needed me. I couldn't do that to them. And Jesus kept encouraging me to hold on and trust him. That he was in control and he had a plan. And I kept choosing to trust him.

I guess it's true
I'm angry with God
Why did he lead me here?
Only to desert me?
Why show me the truth
Just to bring me more pain
And do nothing
To relieve the suffering
Why surround me with people
Who do nothing to help
And take me to places
Where they are able
But not willing
Why rub my face in the dirt
And cover me with shit
And then leave me
To enjoy the smell
Why?
Why show me a future
I can never have
Why give me a taste
But withhold the meal
Why give me a hunger
Never to be filled?
Why make me love you
And then abandon me
Why make me trust you
Only to betray me
Why make me follow you
To this dreadful place?
Why don't you help me
Why don't you answer
Why?

Jesus why must I always be waiting?
My timing is perfect for you.
Why is it always about waiting?
I am teaching you to trust me
Why does that mean I have to wait?
It is in the waiting you discover who you are relying on, hoping in.
So am I not truly hoping in you?
What do you think?
I think only when I have to, I'd like to transfer my hope to someone more tangible. Oh dear, easier to control. Is that it, I still want to be in control?
Your lack of trust drives your need to be in control. As you learn to trust you will give up that need, you will allow me to be fully in control.
So all this waiting has purpose, a good purpose.
I use everything to good purpose.
So it comes down to the same old issue...trust, and who I am trusting?
Yes.
Then help me Lord to trust you, I'm so tired of waiting! The waiting doesn't matter because you are with me, you are in control and I can trust you.

Jennifer's journal year 2

I cannot face those words again
I cannot hear them said
And be polite and gracious
When I wish that I were dead
I'll just go away then
And quietly waste away
And you can live your life
Knowing you did your best
If you will not help me
Then tell me just who will
Who will put the effort in
To help me live again
I cannot ask this from you
For desperate as I am
I know that I'm not really

I went back to my pastor and told him the ministry centre couldn't help. He didn't seem to have any suggestions but did an online search while I was there and suggested I try a ministry he found. I wasn't very sure, but I went away and prayed. I asked Jesus to make it very clear because I didn't want to go to the wrong person...and I didn't know anything about this man except what the website said. So, I sent an email and the man rang me back. It is hard to know exactly what it was, but I don't think I liked him from the start. He asked some strange questions and he didn't ask about things I thought were important like about the support I had or how I was or my relationship with Jesus. Nothing like that. He did tell me how much it would cost for each and every ministry session...and it was a lot and they were a long way away from me. I trusted Jesus to provide if this was what he wanted but it didn't seem right to me. But on the other hand, he was actually offering help.

I spoke to my pastor about it... he didn't seem to have much of an opinion. So, after much prayer and anxiety I decided to say no to the man. I didn't like him or trust him…and there was no way I could afford it. So, I had to say no to the one person who offered help. I got angry and upset with Jesus. I didn't understand what he was doing. Why wasn't he helping me?

After a while my pastor said he had a colleague who might be able to help. He had worked with people like me before. I wondered if this could be the person Jesus had told me about, so I emailed him and told him the things I remembered. He emailed back and said he had ministered to people who had similar pasts. He said he was very busy…but he would get back to me. I waited. I waited over two months feeling anxious and wondering if the promised help had come. Eventually I decided I couldn't just keep hanging on so I emailed him again and asked if he could help…and he wrote straight back and said no, he was too busy.

shut your eyes
don't stare
don't look
don't see
I'm not here
its not me
there is not me
I don't see
I don't know
won't tell
can't tell
didn't see
wasn't here
wasn't me
don't tell no no don't tell
can't tell wasn't me
didn't see didn't see
telling lies telling lies
I not see no I not see
I not here
don't tell

There were a lot of things I wrote and drew in my journal about how it all felt. I lost hope so many times. I didn't even know what was real and true and nobody wanted to help me even find that out never mind recover from it. How would I ever get out of this nightmare I didn't know. I hung on and kept going. I don't know how really because I was having to pretend to everyone that everything was ok, that nothing was going on. I was caring for two teenage children and looking after a house. I was having flashbacks and nightmares and inside people were talking and crying and wanting to hide away or hurt themselves and die. Every time I asked for help it was a big fight because I was so afraid, they were going to say no. I didn't think I deserved it or that anyone would care enough to help. And every time they said no, I was right, and I thought I should die. And every time I told about the bad things, there were those inside that were terrified. They were afraid of what would happen because I told. They were afraid they would be punished or killed.

I don't know how I did it except that Jesus was helping me giving me the strength I needed just like he promised he would. I wasn't very keen to go to a counsellor. I knew it was going to take a lot more than counselling to recover and find healing, but I thought at least it would be a start. At least it would be someone to talk to about things, someone who could maybe help me to know what was true and what wasn't. It was a bit tricky because of course I knew a lot of the counsellors where I lived. I didn't want to go to anyone I knew. There weren't very many who worked with DID but I needed someone who knew something about it because I wanted help and advice. I knew that Jesus needed to be at the centre of my healing so I looked first of all for a Christian counsellor but there just wasn't anyone where I lived. So, I tried to find anyone, anyone at all. There were a few but not many near me. Most were too expensive but eventually I found one...the lady didn't have much experience but by now I was willing to try anything. The counsellor lady was very nice and kind. She helped me to accept more that the memories were true and that the alters were real.

I know I'm bad
I'm bad right through
and I deserved everything
they did to me
I'm bad on the inside
and that's why
they did what they did to me
the devil chose me 'cos I'm bad
thats how bad I am
No-one is badder than me
so I should be shown how bad I am
thats why they hurt me
thats why they hate me
they know how bad I am
know one else can know
but they know
I deserve to be hurt

Dirty

I didn't go for very long, only about six weeks but it did help a little bit. Some of the inside people wrote to her. It was very strange for me to see that and some of them weren't very polite, but the lady didn't seem to mind. She was happy to work with me long term, but she didn't know Jesus and I believed that I needed to work with someone who did. But I was struggling a lot to keep on trusting Jesus and didn't see why he had bothered to do all the things he'd done if he wasn't going to help me get better. I kept on with my journaling and my reading. I found a book that I found interesting and helpful and I read that the author had a ministry working with people like me. So, I thought I would try because I didn't have any other ideas. I emailed the American pastor and told him a bit about what was happening. I didn't see that he could help much because he was so far away, but I decided to try. When I didn't get a reply, I wrote a letter, helped by some of the inside people and sent it in the post. But he didn't answer.

Chapter 5
Accepting the Truth

I didn't seem to be getting any closer to finding the help I needed but Jesus was helping me. I was still going to the ministry centre once a month and he was working through that but not in the bad things. He used it to start healing me from the things that happened when I was married and from a miscarriage I had and things like that. That was good and helpful, but it still left all of the bad things and all of the inside people.

I was desperate to know if the things I was remembering were true. Sometimes it seemed obvious that they must be. There were lots and lots of reasons to believe that they were true, but it seemed hard to hold on to any kind of certainty somehow. I went back and forth. It's true it's not true, it's true it's not true. It must be true it can't be true and on and on. I got sick of it. I found out through the things I read that what I remembered did happen to people. I found out that the Goatman was real and it seemed like he was someone a lot of people had in the bad things they remembered. The things I found so very unbelievable, the really sick things, other people remembered them too. That was terrible but it did help.

I woke up from the lie
And found myself in a nightmare
Truth not what I expected it to be
If this is freedom
Then what was the lie
My whole life
Lost in deception
What then is real
And just who am I?

There were other things in the memories that were more about just me that told me that these things had to be true. I couldn't have made them up. I made a list of them when I was having one of my arguments about whether any of it was true or not.

I remembered that when I was little, I always seemed to have a scab down my nose. I had thought it was from falling over but when I thought about it that didn't make much sense. Who falls on their nose all the time? I didn't ever remember doing it. But one of the things I remembered made it make sense. It was horrible but it made sense. I had a lot of things I remembered from being in the garage. It was a meeting place for grandad and some of his friends. They did very bad things there. One of the things I remembered was kneeling down with my hands tied behind my back. The floor was cold concrete. I was made to bend forward so they could do the sex thing with me from behind. That was why my nose had a scab on it so often.

One of the other things I remembered from the garage convinced me I couldn't be making it up. It was one of the memories that was like a movie with pictures and sound and everything with vivid details. I could see and hear but there weren't any feelings. I am glad about that. I think I was about three or maybe four years old it is hard to be sure. I was laid on what I realized was a hospital trolley. Like the ones they take you to operating theatre on. The bit you laid on was black and the poles were silver. I don't know how they got it. I was being held there by Barbara, the lady who lived next door to us. I didn't have any clothes on.

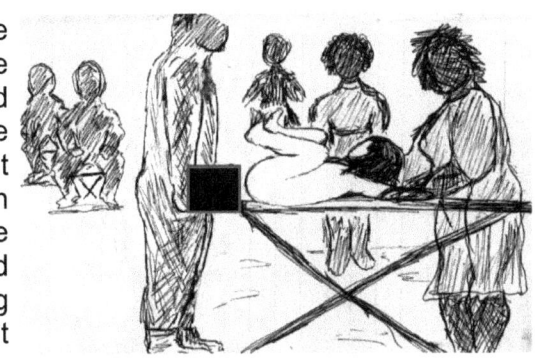

There were maybe four men there. I am not sure who they were except for grandad and a man called uncle John. He is in a lot of memories and now I am sure that he was grandad's brother in law. I had a speculum in me. I think it was to stretch me and get me ready. I expect Barbara put it in, but I didn't remember that part. Grandad was wearing a string vest but nothing else I don't think. He said to me are you ready for grandad? He did the sex thing to me. I didn't remember much about that except that it happened. The other men cheered him on...go on Ed give it to her. That kind of thing. I had forgotten people called him Ed because he was always grandad to me. So, when I heard people calling him Ed in the memory, I knew it must be real because I had forgotten that. Then it was uncle John's turn and he was excited, but he looked at me and said Christ Ed you've made a mess.

So, then grandad told grandma to come and clean me up. I didn't know she was there until then. That's when I saw the bottle. It was a small plastic bottle with a tube on the end so you could squirt water out of it. She used it to squirt water in me and clean me up, but I recognized it. I remembered that she used to do home perms. Those you get in a packet and do yourself. This bottle was part of the kit. She used to get me to put the stuff on the hair rollers using this bottle. It was the same. Seeing that bottle and recognizing what it was, even though I had forgotten all about the home perms, helped me believe the bad memory. I couldn't make that up. So, grandma cleaned me up and the other men took turns. Then Barbara stood me up and told me to say thank you to them. They laughed at me.

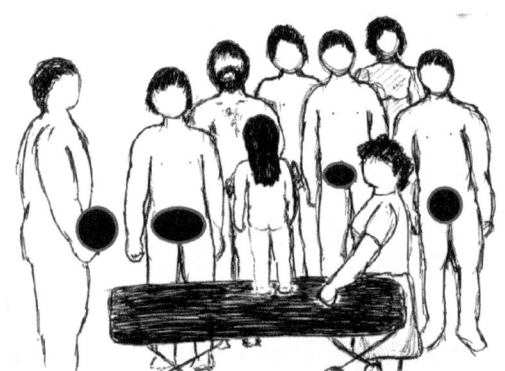

There were other things I remembered too that helped me to know I wasn't making it up. I tried to hold on tight to those things. Sometimes it was the smallest detail I remembered that was so convincing to me. Some of the things I remembered happened in caves. There are a lot of caves near where I lived. In one memory I remembered walking down narrow tunnels to get to a big cave where the meeting was. It was the Goatman group, so they were all wearing the red robes but the Goatman wasn't there this time. There was a table that they put the children on. When I saw it in the memory I was surprised because it looked like one of those folding tables people use to paste wallpaper on. I wondered why they would use something like that but then later I realized that they would have needed a folding table to get it through the tunnels. It was things like that that told me this is really true. It really did happen.

Those moments were terrible for me. To know that those things really did happen and that most likely all the other things I was remembering happened too. It was a terrible kind of freezing fear that would hold me. But I had to know the truth. Even though there were so many reasons to know it was true the battle to hold on to believing that went on for a long time. It went on for years. Sometimes I would think I had accepted it and then something new would be revealed and I would start to doubt all over again.

How to accept
The unacceptable
How to think
The unthinkable
How to speak
The unspeakable
How to forgive
The unforgivable
How to heal
What's been broken
How to recover
What's been lost
How to answer
Such questions

Much later on I decided one day to do an internet search. I typed in the name of the place I grew up with the word witchcraft. I don't know what I expected to find…nothing probably but what I did find was some online chat between some people who had grown up in the same place around the same time as me. They were talking about things they remembered. Things like weird happenings in the streets around where I lived, a stone altar with the remains of a dead cat in the very place I had memories of, rumors of strange noises and people meeting in the woods near there and of a dead child…It seemed like while I had forgotten all of those things others had been aware of them.

But it was still difficult for me to believe that such terrible things could have happened, to anyone. It was difficult to believe that people who were supposed to love me treated me so very cruelly and did such terrible things. That was part of the reason I struggled to hold on to the truth.

There were other things that made it difficult though. There were inside people who didn't want the truth to be known or told. Some were terrified about what would happen if it was. And the enemy didn't want me to know the truth. The enemy wanted me confused and afraid. The enemy wanted to drive me to despair thinking I had gone mad or was a sick pervert to come up with this stuff. It was a long hard battle to believe that Jesus was showing me the truth...and that there was hope for me.

Jesus helped me in other ways to accept the truth. One unexpected and nice surprise was a trip to Florida. I went with Ruth who had inherited some money and paid for me to go, but I wasn't really going to Florida, I was going to the revival that was happening there. I went knowing that Jesus had a plan. I didn't know what, but I was praying mostly that I would come back knowing whether it was true about the memories and the inside people, so I could stop arguing to and fro.

> I don't want to share your memories,
> Your thoughts. They hurt me
> They drive me to despair
> And still I wonder
> Are you real or only a delusion
> I can't tell, I don't know
> I guessing time will tell
> I don't want you to be real
> But if you're not what then?
> What does it mean if you're not there?
> Either way its bad
> There's no way out that I can see
> No good end to this
> So I guess real or not
> This is it.

I found out almost straight away that the church where the revival started had a special ministry to people with DID. I knew that couldn't be an accident. I went to a meeting there and when it finished, they prayed with people. I stood in the line waiting, it went all the way around the walls of the room. There were hundreds of people there. I saw a lady, one of the ones who prayed for people look at me from the other side of the room. She came straight over to me even though I was nowhere near the start of the queue. She seemed to know about the bad things. She asked me about them. It was scary but I knew it was God. I told her a bit about it and the lady prayed for me and then offered me a ministry appointment during the week. I knew it was Jesus' idea so I said yes even though I didn't really know what good it would do because I was only there for a week.

I went a couple of days later and I was very, very afraid. I talked to the lady and told her about things that I remembered. The lady prayed and then some of the inside children came out and started talking to her...just a little bit because they were all afraid. I kept my eyes closed the whole time. I think there were four of them that talked to her all young girls. I don't remember now what they said but the lady asked them about Jesus and if they knew him. I think maybe some of them met him there, but I couldn't tell what was happening on the inside. It was a very strange thing and it answered my prayer because I knew now that it was real and that I had DID.

> We are not safe
> We are not safe
> they will find us
> and hurt us
> they will take us away
> and kill us
> where can we hide
> I want to hide
> don't tell anymore
> please don't tell anymore
> they will find us

There were a lot of things that happened while I was there. Some of it was lovely. The sea there was like a warm bath and there were pelicans diving and I went on a boat and saw dolphins. I loved all of that. Some of it was very difficult. In the meetings the Holy Spirit did a lot, I suppose I don't even know what he was doing a lot of the time. There was one time though when being there seemed a very bad idea. The Holy Spirit came like a wave that swept over the whole crowd. I never experienced anything like that before or since, but he comes in different ways at different times and this time he came delivering people of evil spirits.

That was very bad for me. I was doubled up in pain and fear. I suppose that it was the enemy who was feeling that, but I felt it with them. I was crying and crying and begging God to stop because it was so very horrible. To me it felt like I was full of snakes all squirming and screaming in pain. That is what it felt like and it is one of the worst things that I remember ever feeling apart from the bad things. I don't ever want to feel like that again. Maybe you might think that would make me afraid to be with Jesus again, but it didn't. I needed him and I understood it had been the reaction of the enemy to what he was doing. He wasn't hurting me.

So, I came back from Florida knowing much better what was true, and that Jesus hadn't forgotten me. I felt more hopeful, but I still couldn't find anyone to help me. The lady at the Florida church gave me a number to ring of some people she knew who she thought might be able to help. I tried to ring but I never got an answer.

My child this is a long journey which I will carry you through you do not need to know how to do anything. I will show you the way. Do not look at your life and the way you think it should be. Your life is in my hands and I am making it what I want it to be. I am making you who I want you to be. Do not be distressed my little one for all things are working for good. You do not see as I do. I know where I am taking you. You have not yet seen all that I have planned for you. There is no reason to despair but every reason to hope for I am at work my dearest one. All is not lost. There is great hope to be found in me and in who I am. I will redeem everything my child. What you consider to be lost or damaged beyond repair will be recovered restored and brought back to life. I know my little one that it is hard for you to accept your life the way it has been revealed to you but it is not the end my dearest one it is the beginning. It is the beginning of the new life I have for you. Do not be tempted to give up but trust in me and in all that I have said. I know you do not see. You cannot see for I have not yet enabled you to see. Trust me then because I am the one who sees everything. Trust me because I am your beloved. I will not leave you and I will never let you down. Trust me with all that you have. I will not disappoint you. Your life will be turned into something beautiful my dearest one. Where you see desolation, I will bring life where you see despair and pain I will bring hope and joy. Do not give up my little one. I am here.

Chapter 6
Help at Last?

It was hard for me to understand why Jesus had done all the things he had if he wasn't going to help me get better. It seemed very cruel. It didn't make any sense. By now I knew that everyone I had asked for help had said no. Everyone except the American pastor who hadn't said anything at all.

But the day came at last, the one that I had been waiting for. It was almost a year since the first memories had come. A year of searching and hoping, despair and anger and confusion and anxiety. The day before at church someone gave a word from God in the service. It could have been for anyone, but I knew it was for me. I could feel the presence of the Holy Spirit so strongly and the words went straight into my heart. The message was that it had been night for a long time but now there was a new day dawning, new light, a new beginning. Even though it was a message of hope it made me afraid. I was afraid to hope after so many disappointments.

*This ray of hope terrifies me
to move forward
to stay where I am
to see possibilities
to see nothing at all
hope terrifies me
It awakens more pain
that I'd dulled myself to
more disappointment coming my way
I've had my fill
I don't want any more
hope ~~~~ awakens pain
I don't want any more
I need hope to live
but it terrifies me*

The next day I got an email from Mike, the American pastor that I had written to months before. He said that he would help me. That was wonderful and terrible all at the same time. I didn't know what to expect and I was afraid it wouldn't work out.

I think I must have thought that if Mike was going to decide I was too much trouble he should do it straight away so I would know and not keep hoping for something that wasn't coming. I hadn't forgotten that Jesus had promised me that there would be a man who would understand and who would help me but I didn't always trust what I heard and I didn't always trust Jesus. So I wrote a very long email telling him all about the things I had remembered. I didn't try to make it sound better than it was I wanted him to know the worst so he could say straight away if I was too much for him.

*When you don't respond
It feels like I don't exist
And fear takes hold
Will I be here forever
Alone, not noticed
Is anything real
Or will I sink
Into oblivion
Lost without trace
I need you to hold my hand
Keep me from falling
Into the black hole
That awaits me
I see it waiting expectantly
Don't let go*

I didn't hear back for a week and I thought that was it. I thought he was horrified and didn't want to help me after all. I had a very bad time because it wasn't just me of course it was inside people too. But he did write back saying he would help. He encouraged all those inside to write to him, not just me. There were so many inside people who wrote to Mike and all of them wanted him to write to them and help them. I thought he would run away but he didn't. He didn't do what I wanted either. I suppose he did what Jesus wanted but that wasn't the same at all and made a lot of us angry and upset with him and with Jesus.

I was angry and upset with Mike for a long, long time. The inside people would get together and have meetings to decide if we should give up on him. A lot of them thought it was a waste of time and it was making it more difficult for me because of my anger at him.

*Quiet, be very quiet
Stay alone where it's safe
Say nothing, stay hidden
Never let them see the pain
Never let them know your need
Never ask for help
Do not utter a cry
Make no sound
Not a whimper or a sigh
Be ashamed of your need
Be ashamed of your pain
Feel the shame of woundedness
Never let them see
They do not want to know
They push you away
Your pain is not real
Your needs are unimportant
Be quiet.*

Even though Mike had agreed to work with us I didn't see how that would be enough, not for all the inside people that there were. He was so far away and for whatever reason didn't seem to want to write very often. Definitely not as often as I, or anyone else wanted him to. It was kind of like Beryl all over again. I was checking lots of times every day to see if he wrote to us but mostly, he didn't. It was hard for us to bear the anxiety of that. Everyone found it difficult.

But Jesus told me over and over to trust Mike. He told me over and over to keep writing. He told me over and over that Mike was safe. I had a lot of arguments with Jesus about this. He said that I was to write down my thoughts and feelings and send those too. I didn't want to do that at all. I didn't trust Mike. I thought he didn't care, and I didn't see why I should tell him anything if he wasn't going to help, but Jesus said that is what he wanted so I did. I argued about it a lot, but I did it.

Lord why must it be this way…isn't there enough going on for me?
My child I ask you to trust me. Things are not always what they seem.
I don't understand how a man who does not have time and does not care can help me in any way at all.
You must trust me to work through all this. I know mike's heart and you do not...it is all in the palm of my hand. Do not doubt me.
I don't like it. How can I stop it from hurting?
By holding on to me. I will help you bear the pain.
But why must I bear this extra pain. Don't I have enough already?
Remember that I am working all things for your good. All things, even this.
Yes I remember but I'm not sure that I can keep going Lord…how can I write so personally to this man?
Think of it as writing to me...know that I am listening and I am responding, whether you see it or not. Know that whether you are aware of it or not Mike is listening. He is paying attention. He is bringing all of you before me. He does care.

I didn't understand, none of us did. I thought he should be doing something like praying with us or ministering like I knew other people did. But he didn't. He would reply to our desperate emails sometimes and answer questions to help us understand but he didn't do any of the things I wanted or expected him to do.

So I found help but I was angry and confused about it a lot of the time. My pastor said he would be willing to work with Mike to help me and he'd send an email to him. But that never seemed to happen and after a while I stopped asking my pastor for help or even telling him what was going on. He never asked. Not long after I started to write to Mike, I started to see a counsellor again because I still didn't believe Mike was going to be the help I needed.

This time it was someone I knew, a lady I worked with when I was counselling. That made it feel a bit safer for me I think but maybe more difficult for Julie, the counsellor lady. I went to see her for about a year, but it never really seemed to help that much. It was only me who talked to her. None of the inside people wanted to come out and talk. They got upset because they thought that Julie didn't think they were real people. They didn't want to talk to her, and they didn't see the point of going.

> I'm alone
> I'm all alone
> nobody sees
> nobody hears
> I'm right in front of them
> but still they don't see
> they don't see me
> Only the outside
> not the inside
> they not looking
> they don't care
> what's on the inside
>
> I want to die
> please let me die
> I'm lost inside and it's so dark
>
> no more

Dear Julie. You don't know me, but my name is Maisie and I'm one of the alters in this system. I heard you talking last week and man I was pissed, because you keep saying that we are all part of her. The one you call Jennifer. I was pissed, because you think I am part of her. Well man I ain't part of no-one, I'm me and that's that. Same goes for everyone here. I am who I am and I ain't no-one else. I mean, what's so special about her? Why do I have to be part of her? She could be part of me you know just the same. But anyway, she's not and I'm not. I am who I am like anyone else, and I would appreciate it if you would get that and stop treating us like spare parts. Thankyou Maisie

I stuck with it as long as I could, almost a year, and tried my hardest, but the things I told Julie seemed to scare her or confuse her or both. Eventually I decided that it wasn't helping so I told Julie I was thinking about taking a break. I am not sure really how it happened but within a few minutes it was agreed that I wasn't going any more ever and that was it goodbye. I think Julie was very relieved. We had been too much for her. I don't blame her because we were too much for us, but it didn't help. I gave up looking for people to help me after that. There didn't seem to be anyone who would or could and it was too hard to keep looking and keep hoping.

Who is this man?
And does he care?
Can I let him in?
And allow him to touch the pain?
Will he understand
Who I am?
Will he be with me
When I need him the most?
Dare I reach out
And let him see
What no one has ever seen?
Will I be able to be present?
Not one step back
Keeping safe.
Is he safe, really safe?
What does that mean?
Am I just another job,
Another case on file.
Will I be a burden?
A heavy load to bear
Would I let him carry me?
Or even lend a hand
Will he let me fall?
If I lean on him too hard
Can I lean on him at all?
Who is this man?
Who's standing here at my side
A thousand miles between us
Seems so small somehow
Will I run and hide from him
Will I grow to need him?
He doesn't know me,
Not at all
Why would he want to know?
I'm more afraid that he will stay
Then that he will go
Can I do this, let him in
Will he want to stay?
Who is this man?

Will my life change?
I'm afraid to hope
Will I be different?
I'm afraid to hope
Do I have a future?
I'm afraid to hope
Will the pain go?
I'm afraid to hope
Will I be loved?
I'm afraid to hope
Will I matter?
I'm afraid to hope
Will someone notice?
I'm afraid to hope
Will someone help me?
I'm afraid to hope
Is there any hope?

A vision…Jesus lead me by the hand down a dark and rainy street. There were lamps giving off a little light, but the cobbled street was deserted. I went into a house and into a small sparse room lit only by a fire in the hearth. Jesus introduced me to a man who was maybe in his 40's with a beard and a checked shirt. The man and I laid hands on a group of children and prayed for them. They were happy and Jesus pressed my hand into that of the man...partners?

Jennifer's journal year -1

Chapter 7

Company

I spent a lot of time talking with the inside people who came to the surface. I tried to help them and talk to them about Jesus if I could. I would write down all of the conversations I had and send them to Mike because that is what Jesus said to do. I wrote down all the things I heard and remembered and some of the inside people wrote to Mike and I sent those letters too. It was so confusing with all of those inside people around. The thoughts and feelings would get very mixed up, so I didn't know what belonged to who. It was very hard to know who I was.

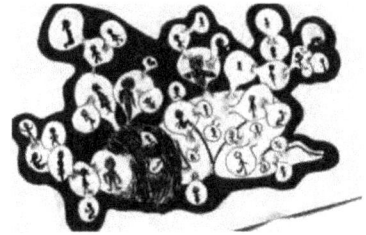

By now I had more or less accepted the DID. Sometimes I still thought maybe I was just crazy but mostly I accepted it. It made a kind of sense to me when I looked back over my life. It helped me understand why there was so much even of normal life that I didn't remember. It was a shock to realize I had no memory of my wedding day. What did that mean? Was it someone else who got married? Did that mean I wasn't ever married at all? I didn't know. Sometimes it was overwhelming. I remembered another time, there were lots of times like these I was remembering, of 'waking up' in my classroom at school. Some of the other children were looking at me and laughing. I looked down and saw I was wearing a summery pink and white cotton skirt...with thick woolen orange brown socks. I wanted to disappear. I couldn't understand why I had worn them but now I understood. Someone else had got dressed that day...someone with no idea about what to wear!!

Why

Why did He let me live
when so many others died
why do I hate Him so ?
the one that I love
Why did I suffer
only to forget
why have I remembered ?
only to suffer
why am I alive
not able to live ?
why is it so dark
if I'm full of light ?
Why is there no escape
if I am so free
why I am I so lost ? ?
if I have been found
Why am I so broken
if He's made me whole
why am I here
and what's it all for
why am I crying
tears nobody sees
why does He love me
when He sees what I am

The more I accepted it the more I saw and the more I saw the more I knew it had to be true. I didn't want it to be true though. In some ways it was worse than the bad things. At least the bad things were in the past but the alters weren't. They were here, now and I couldn't get rid of them. I felt ashamed and like I was some kind of freak who should hide away and never be seen. I didn't understand why I had to survive all of that, why I had to live like this. I didn't understand why I had survived when so many others hadn't, and I felt bad that I had given my pain to others.

When I looked back at my journals, I could see that Jesus had been telling me in different ways about the alters but I hadn't understood then of course. How could I, this was before I knew any of the really bad things or suspected about the DID.

I'm falling
I'm falling down and down and down
it never stops I never stop
I just keep falling
in the darkness
falling into darkness
no end no bottom
endless falling
endless darkness
Save me Someone save me

I saw a flower, a bit like a chrysanthemum. At first it was white, then yellow, then pink. Then there was a bunch of them. The lord picked one out and gave it to me. It was white with a red centre. Then he gave me a yellow one, then pink. All with red centers. He said you are not one thing but many. I saw a diamond and it was full of many colors. Again, I felt the lord was saying not one but many.

Sadness

Sadness covers me, like a shroud
Grey and tattered, hanging down.
It moves a little in the breeze
But never blows away.
Sadness always over me

Writing things down did help though and gave each person a chance to talk for themselves. Even though most of them never really came out to the outside, a lot of them would be close enough to see and experience the outside world. They all wanted to be heard and understood. Some of them were very sad and wanted to die, some were angry and thought Mike should get lost and so should Jesus. Some were more friendly, some were desperate for help, some didn't want any help at all. Most were in pain.

There were adults and children, girls, boys, men and women and they came and went not really knowing or caring about the outside life. I was in the firing line for everything. I had to do all the normal life stuff and keep pretending everything was fine and I had to talk to inside people and help them. Then there were flashbacks and all of the pain and fear. I was writing it all down and sending it to a man I didn't trust, and everything was confusing and seemed hopeless.

A lot of the time I coped somehow but sometimes it all got too much for me. Even though I didn't really trust him I did share some of my thoughts and feelings with Mike just like Jesus asked me to, I couldn't tell if it was all me. Mostly, it seemed like it was, but I got tired of trying to work it out.

Hi...I thought I'd write a quick response to your e-mail. It's not always easy for me to organize my thoughts but I'll just give them to you as they occur. You ask why I would doubt that I was hearing God...why would I not? What is there that I can count as certain in my life whether it's my inner or my outer life? I've never been the kind of person who felt they could be certain about anything. I always believe there's every possibility that I could be wrong. In the past year my whole life has turned out to be one big lie...my family, my past and even who I am. I have no real idea about the truth of any of these things. Why would I trust any of my thoughts, perceptions, feelings? How can I be certain of anything? I'm so afraid of believing lies that its hard for me to believe anything, and I certainly don't trust my own judgment. Then add to that the knowledge that I have so many different voices in my own head, who turn out to be other people and not me at all. HOW THE HELL AM I SUPPOSED TO BE SURE OF ANYTHING? You might think I'm sure the alters are real, but I'm not. I sent you what 'they' said, because I just don't know what else to do. I am so confused and distressed about all of that.

When I got your reply to them, I just sat and sobbed for a very long time, because it really hit home that this is real and yet it seems so unreal. I don't want to be the responsible one. I can't do it anymore. If there are other alters there, I'm happy to hand it over. My only concern is for my children, as long as they are ok that's all that matters. Frankly I think that one of the others could do a better job than me. I don't see I have anything to offer anyone, probably all my good qualities belong to someone else. This life has NOTHING that I want to hold on to. The idea of living in any kind of community...inner or outer terrifies me. I feel completely trapped and unable to see any bearable options. What kind of future is there, because I can't see anything? What is it I'm supposed to see? I'm so tired I don't even care anymore, and all that there seems to be is a promise of years of more of the same. I don't think I can do that. I don't want to do that. All I can seem to do at the moment is sit and cry, or just be completely numb. I can't pray...apart from God please help me... that's the extent

of my dialogue with him at the moment. I feel so lost….and so trapped, all at the same time. Sorry this is a pathetic ramble but that's how it is. I'm good at pretending most of the time, conceal and contain that's what I do in public. In private I unravel. There you are, the real me, whatever and whoever that is. I don't think anyone actually really knows me...they think they do, but they don't really.

Bye. Jennifer

Some of the alters only surfaced and spoke when they were triggered by things that happened. Like the little one who was triggered when I did some digging in the garden.

I not want to go in hole not put me in hole with worms. No more worms no more worms. No more hole. Not like worms not like cold not like it. I frightened and they leave me in hole with worms. I not know my name it is gone. Worms ate it. Will eat me if they touch me. No more worms. I am six but I not too big to be eat by worms they can do it they have teeth and eat me slow. They get my toes they like toes best.

I found out I couldn't go digging in the garden without little one's being triggered because of the things that happened to me, to us. There was a lot of that going on and it was hard to avoid all the triggers because they could be anything. When I heard about someone who had tried to kill herself by cutting her wrists, a little one called Hilda was triggered. She had a job collecting blood from the Goatman who would cut his arms

He cuts and he cuts and blood it comes out and he is shouting and laughing and they is shouting. I am hiding. I not looking not want to look but I can not run. My name is Hilda and I am 8. I am holding the knives. I give the knives. They are special for this cutting they are small and sharp like tiny daggers. The Goatman cuts his arms and they collect the blood in little cups. I hold the cup. It is my job to hold the knife and the cup. They drink the blood it makes them strong like magic. It is for the big people who are strong not for little people like me. I hold the cup. I must not drop it. That is my job. It is very important and special for me.

It could be very difficult when memories and inside people were triggered. I could be anywhere, with anyone. My bedroom became my safe place. If I could hang on long enough to run there, I could let the little one, or sometimes an older one, talk or write or draw which seemed to help them and then they would go back inside. Then I could recover and face the world again.

Sometimes when someone was triggered, I could bring them to Jesus and listen to him talk to them in their fear and their pain and their anger. Some of those were the most difficult but also the most wonderful conversations.

Angry child please come out and talk to my father. He won't hurt you...he just wants to hear what you have to say.
I HATE YOU I HATE YOU SO MUCH. YOU NEVER LOVED US YOU NEVER CARED. YOU STOOD BY AND WATCHED. I SAW YOU. I SAW YOU. I SAW YOU THERE AND YOU DID NOTHING. YOU JUST LET THEM HURT ME AND HURT ME AND HURT ME AND YOU DID NOTHING. NOBODY DID ANYTHING. THEY JUST WATCHED. NOBODY CARED.
I cared.
NO HOW COULD YOU CARE. YOU DIDN'T HELP ME.

I kept you alive.
WELL THANKS FOR THAT. YOU KEPT ME ALIVE SO THAT THEY COULD HURT ME SOME MORE. AS MUCH AS THEY WANTED. THAT'S HOW MUCH YOU CARED.
It hurt me too.
SO? WHAT YOU WANT ME TO SAY I'M SORRY. I SUPPOSE THAT WAS MY FAULT. WELL I DIDN'T MAKE YOU COME AND WATCH I DIDN'T WANT YOU THERE. YOU DIDN'T HELP ME.
I did help you.
HOW? DID YOU STOP THEM RAPING ME...NO. DID YOU STOP THE KNIVES...NO. DID YOU STOP THEM LAUGHING...NO YOU DID NOT.
I gave you the strength and the means to survive.
I DIDN'T WANT TO SURVIVE. I WANTED TO DIE.
But I did not want you to die. I wanted you to live so that you could be with me. I wanted you to stay alive so that you could come to know me. I did not want to lose you.
THAT MAKES NO SENSE TO ME. WHAT WOULD YOU WANT ME FOR. YOU DIDN'T WANT ME THEN... YOU DON'T WANT ME NOW. THE ONLY REASON ANYBODY EVER WANTED ME WAS TO HURT ME. IS THAT WHAT YOU WANT?
I will never hurt you.
NO... YOU JUST LET OTHERS DO IT FOR YOU.
Do you believe that?
I DON'T KNOW. I'M CONFUSED HOW AM I SUPPOSED TO UNDERSTAND.
I have never hurt you. I will never hurt you. You have always been so precious to me. But you have been so hurt and you are right to be angry. I am angry about the things they did to you. I was angry then. I am angry now. Think about the time you saw me. What did you see?
YOU WERE STANDING LOOKING AT ME. YOU LOOKED INTO MY EYES. YOU WERE CRYING. I WASN'T CRYING. I DIDN'T FEEL ANYTHING BUT YOU WERE CRYING. I DON'T UNDERSTAND.
I felt your pain. I felt what you could not. That was how I helped you. I kept you alive, all these years I have kept you alive because I have a special purpose for you... to use all the suffering you endured.
BUT YOU NEVER STOPPED IT AND YOU COULD HAVE.
Yes, I could have, but sometimes I have to take the long hard path to do what needs to be done. The cross was the long hard path I chose for myself.
AND YOU CHOSE A LONG HARD PATH FOR ME.
Yes, I chose that for you. You did not choose it, but I did.
WHY WOULD YOU DO THAT TO ME?
Because I see what you cannot. I see what lies ahead. I see what you will become and what will be accomplished because of this choice. You could not choose but as your father I chose for you. I chose a long hard path for you because that is the best path for you. The very best. That is hard for you to understand now but I am your father, even then I was your father and I chose for you.
SO... YOU ARE SAYING IT WAS A GOOD THING.
I work all things together for those that love me.
I DON'T LOVE YOU. I HATE YOU FOR WHAT YOU LET THEM DO. THANKS FOR CHOOSING ME!
Do you really hate me? Is it me you hate or those that hurt you?
I HATE YOU ALL.
Think. Really think.
I HATE THEM...I'M CONFUSED ABOUT YOU.
I am for you
SO YOU SAY, BUT YOU HAVE A FUNNY WAY OF SHOWING IT.

It seems so to you but that is because you cannot see what I see.
WHAT DO YOU SEE?
I see all things. I see your past, your present and your future... into eternity. I see all you have done and all you will do. I see every impact you make on others; I see everything you set in motion. I see what a difference you will make and the life you will live and the glory you will bring to me. I see the joy and the peace and the life you will enjoy, and it is because of the choice I made for you. I could have chosen less for you, I could have chosen a little of those things, but I chose to give you much, an abundance, beyond your wildest dreams. That was my choice for you my child.

Both sides of that conversation were difficult for me. It was difficult for me to listen to that child/teen who was so angry and hurting, but it was also difficult to hear what my father said, that in some way he chose this for me... for us. But I know the path chosen for Jesus ...so that I could live. That made me more willing to accept it even though I didn't understand it and most of the time I wished it wasn't so...that there was a good reason why he had allowed this to happen.

A different kind of conversation made me wonder too.

> *Gnawing pain deep and biting it penetrates my soul*
> *There is no end... no end to torment and suffering*
> *What hope is there for one so twisted and broken*
> *Where is the light that was extinguished so long ago?*
> *I sit in the darkness*
> *Covered in filth*
> *Held in the chains they bound me in*
> *I cannot get free*
> *I am so weak and the chains so heavy*
> *What use is there in life*
> *What is it for?*
> *When will it end?*
> *Tell me when it will end*

Hello.... I feel the echo of your pain, it is in me too. I feel the echoes of your despair. But there is a light. There is One who can set you free from the heavy chains that bind you. Will you let Him do that?
I do not know of whom you speak. How is it possible that the darkness should end? I have been alone in the darkness so long. Who are you?
My name is Jennifer, I am part of your system. I know the light bringer and the chain breaker. He is mighty and can overcome any darkness. He can be with you and set you free.
How can this be? Who is strong enough to break these chains? Who has enough light to pierce the darkness? How can this be. I have been alone so long. Who would come to me?
There is One who is light and love. He is strong enough for you and will come to you if you ask Him
I do not know Him. What should I call him?
He has many names. He is called the Lord of Hosts, the Light of the world, Yahweh and Jeshua. He made me and He made you. He wants to rescue you from the darkness. Will you let Him come and save you?
I want to be set free from my chains and to see the light of the one called Jeshua. Will he come if I call?
Yes He will come. Call Him now.
Jeshua, light of the world will you come and set me free?
Yes my little one I am with you even now. I will set you free from the chains that hold

you and the darkness that surrounds you.
Yes I see you.
Come to me my dearest child. Will you come?
Yes. Here I am. Are you strong? Can you break the chains and make the darkness go away?
My light is here for you. I am strong and mighty to save. See your chains are broken.
Yes I am free. Thankyou Jeshua. I see your light, but I am so dirty and now I must hide because you are so clean.
I can make you clean if you are willing
You can? How can you do that?
By the power of the cross and my blood which I shed for you. I paid the price so that I could make you clean
I don't understand but I want to be clean like you. Please if you can I would like to be clean.
Will you accept me as your savior? The one who saves you?
You have saved me from my chains and the darkness. You are my savior.
And will you have me as your lord. Will you love me and obey me?
What will that mean?
It will mean that I will always be with you and I will give you my love to surround you forever. It will mean you will suffer for my sake, but these things will remain true.
I have suffered a long time alone. To suffer with you surrounded by love would be a good thing. I will accept you as my lord and I will obey you. Will you make me clean?
You are clean my child.
… and then it just went quiet.

I know when I was writing my part it felt like I was being guided, like I was given the words to say and I am sure that is true. That Jesus was speaking through me. I don't know who it was that was saved, and I don't know who the angry child was, but Jesus came to them both and offered his love. One rejected him, at least for the moment and one gladly accepted.

Some of the inside people were very afraid that we were telling about the bad things. I could hear them crying. I tried to help them not be afraid, but I don't think it worked. Some were afraid because they thought they were bad and some of them were very afraid of Jesus or someone they knew as Jesus. They had been told a lot of lies about him. Then there were the dark ones. I am not sure who they were. They spoke together which made them sound very creepy. They wanted Mike to go away.

> I am nothing I am noone
> do not touch me I will hurt you
> I will hurt you bad.
> Thats what I do I hurt
> I kill do not come near me
> my evil will hurt you
> I can't stop it
> the evil in me

Go away go away tell him to go away
Tell who to go away?
The man the pastor make him go away and leave us alone. We don't need him we don't want him, make him go away.
Who is this?
Don't want to tell you make him go away
Why do you want him to go away?
He will hurt us he will break us. We don't want him, make him go away
Please tell me your name. I won't hurt you.
You are like him we don't trust you make him go away
I can't make him go away he doesn't listen to me
You write to him and tell him to go. He must go or we will hurt you.
Why would you hurt me? Who are you?
We are the dark ones. He must go away. They will find us he is telling about us make him go away.

I've told you he won't go away. I can't make him go away.
You are writing. You tell him...we will hurt you.
It won't make a difference he won't go away
He will he must he is hurting us with the light make him go away
Who is hurting you with the light?
The man he is bringing light we are the dark ones we are in the dark…the light hurts us and he must go away.
The light is good.
We will hurt you make the light go away

Other inside people were afraid that Mike would leave us. That he would go away and not come back because they were bad. When we didn't hear from him for a while, they would get more and more anxious and afraid.

We were bad and they left us

We didn't do what they wanted

Please don't leave us please don't leave us we are sorry we should not be bad we will not be bad any more please don't leave us we are very sorry we were bad we won't be bad any more we'll be very good please don't be angry we are sorry we will not do it again we will be very good please don't hate us we cannot be here any more please help us we don't know how to get out

My mammy left me she left me because I am bad. I don't want to be bad please don't leave me I am sorry I will be very good

My grandad he is angry he says I am a bad girl they shut me in the dark and left me please don't leave me I am sorry I am bad

We won't be bad anymore please come back don't leave us here we will be good and quiet please come back we tried very hard to be good please come back

The inside people that came to the surface and told their stories were hard to believe at first. They told me about an inside world where they lived together. It sounded a bit like the outside world I knew with a forest and a lake and mountains and caves. I wanted to see it so much. I think I wanted to go hide there and let someone else be on the outside. If I couldn't die because of the children, then I could go inside and let someone else do the life I didn't want. That way everyone would be happy. That's what I thought. I tried to come up with so many ways of escaping. I thought about all the ways I could die. I thought about all the ways I could do it. One time I even stocked up on pills and alcohol because I didn't want to keep on living. I think now I understand that at least some of that didn't come from me or those inside, but from the enemy. Sometimes alters would turn out to be the enemy. That made everything even more confusing for me, because I didn't know whether to believe the things I was told or not.

You think you had it rough you should try being me. Well like I said I've had it. You're the one with the power here. You're the one who can end it all why don't you go on and do it. What are you waiting for? It only takes one quick slash with a big knife. I've seen it done a hundred times. It's not hard, it's quick. Its so easy and then it would be over. You could rest and not keep struggling. No more making yourself do anything. No more struggle you'd just be at peace. Imagine that just to be at peace… no more pain no more fear no more nothing. You can do it. You can do it today. You've got nothing to live for… what kind of future do you think you have. People like you don't have a future. They only exist. There's no hope for you. All there'll ever be is pain and suffering. You know that. Why not just end it now. No one will miss you, not really, don't think they will. People say they care but it's not true.

That wasn't very subtle, but often it was, and I just didn't know what to believe. Sometimes the enemy didn't even bother to pretend...they didn't want me talking to Mike and would tell me all the things we feared the most were true. Mostly that went on in whispers...all the time it seemed but sometimes they just said it out loud.

He doesn't believe you he thinks you are a liar that's why he doesn't reply. Why would he waste his time with a liar like you? He knows you are just making all this up. Don't think he doesn't know. Don't you think he laughs when he sees what you have written. He just thinks you are sick, he just thinks you are a liar. No wonder he doesn't pay attention no wonder he doesn't care. Why would he care about you? You are a disgrace you don't deserve anything and that is what you are going to get. Nothing. No-one is going to help you. You might as well give up now. There's no point going on you know. No one will listen. No one really believes all that stuff. Who would believe it? It's too sick to be true. You know that but you just want their attention don't you. Poor little me I'm in so much trouble please help me. So pathetic. No one is taken in, nobody cares you are just going to be left alone to lick your wounds. Forget writing to Mike, forget your counselling, forget it all. Just get on with your sorry pathetic little life because that's all you've got. It's never going to change. It's that or nothing. If I were you, I'd take the nothing. After all what have you got to live for. Those children of yours don't appreciate you, anyone would do as well. Your friends don't need you, your whole existence is pointless. You might as well give up. You can't shut me up... no I'm not gotten rid of so easily. I'll always be here reminding you of what you are. A disgusting slut who got everything she deserved... there is no help for people like you. You deserve nothing. Hoar, bastard child of the devil;

But there were other voices I heard. One time when I was feeling very desperate and the enemy was not leaving me alone, I heard another voice that brought with it peace.

The presence of the Lord is with you. Do not fear. You are in the midst of a mighty battle, but the Lord is fighting for you. Stay strong in him. Trust him and you will see a new day. It will be a day of victory for the Lord is doing a mighty thing. Stand strong then and wait on the Lord who is your defender. He will not leave you abandoned but will rescue you with his mighty arm of victory. Do not be afraid.

I didn't see him, but I think it was an angel.

**Plunged into darkness, unable to see anything but terror and pain and death
I clung to the robe of Him who took me there. Though He held me tightly I feared
the precipice which beckoned enticingly, tempting me to fall into black despair
I cried out to Him 'Help me!', time and time again but He only held me firmly, not
moving, steady as I trembled and fell, pulling me to my feet, enabling me to stand
confusion and doubt pulling me down again as I looked into the darkness. Pain
and fear and sorrow crushing me in my weariness gentle arms drew me close
and gave me strength, His words bringing comfort and hope I looked into
His loving eyes and clung on even more He led me slowly by the hand
towards a chink of light. The journey it was long and hard and I
faltered many times but always He would pick me up and help
me on my way He led me oh so slowly through the darkness
and the pain pointing out His servant He put my hand in his.
A companion for this journey, one who knows the way. The road
before me is so long, it's dark and dangerous so many are my
enemies, so close that precipice but I'm still clinging to the robe
of the One who brought me here, I know He'll never let me fall,
I know He's always near.
Alter unknown?**

Chapter 8

Maisie

and a window to the inside...

Maisie was one of the first inside people I met. She was about twenty and she told me she had been on the outside a lot when we were in our teens, but not really much since then and she had only just found out about the bad things like I had (though later I found out that wasn't true). She didn't mix much with the others inside and lived on a different level closer to the surface than most of them. When I first met her Maisie was angry. She was angry with Mike and she was angry with God.

Hi there Mike, this is Maisie. We haven't met but I heard about you. I heard you are a pastor and you're into all this God and Jesus stuff, right? Well God makes me sick what does he think he's doing sitting up there on his cloud in the sky while little kids suffer. You can't feel the pain of that little girl, but I can and if God cared he would do something instead of just sitting there watching. That's if he's paying attention at all. I don't know how you manage to justify bothering with God at all. He doesn't give a shit about anyone else but himself and why should he. He can do what he likes. I don't get it though. What are you doing? Why do you bother? We are no one to you, what do you want to bother with us for? There isn't much in this world that makes any sense it's all pretty futile if you ask me. I was talking to Jennifer the other day. I know she believes all this crap about Jesus and how he loves us, well I don't have any time for that if he loves us so much let's see it. I've only got to look at someone like Anna and I know he doesn't care, and you can't convince me otherwise. The proof in the pudding...I've seen enough pain to last me a lifetime and nothing ever suggested to me that if there is a God, that he gives a shit about if he likes of me. Why would he when he doesn't even care about little kids. Like I said he makes me sick. So, stick that in your pipe and smoke it Mr. pastor man.

She came and talked with me for a few months and I learned a lot about the inside world through the things she told me. She learned a lot too. Even though she didn't trust him and didn't see the point of him Maisie did write to Mike asking for help when something happened on the inside.

Hi there pastor Mike. This is Maisie here. We've got a bit of a situation and we really could do with your help. I hate asking for help it makes me bad tempered but there you are I don't know what else to do. There's someone on the inside and they are causing a lot of trouble. I don't know who they are... I don't recognize them, but they are a nasty piece of work I can tell you. He's going around all the little ones whispering about how bad they are and about how they deserved everything they got. Some of the bigger ones are hiding too. I don't now what he's been saying to them, but they are scared. This whole place is full of voices telling us how we are beyond hope and how the whole thing is hopeless. They talk endlessly about all the terrible things that have happened and nothing seems to shut them up. Who this person is I don't know but he won't go away he just laughs in our faces and he's scary too? I don't think he would stop at anything he just wants to hurt everyone. We don't know what to do. Can you help us? This voice goes on and on about you too, about how there's no point talking to you and how you don't care, and you won't help us, it never shuts up. Maybe its right I don't know but we have nowhere else to turn. Everyone is desperate, what should we do, do you know? We've never come across this before. I don't know what else to say. Hope to hear from you soon. Maisie

Mike did reply but Maisie didn't like what he said and decided to ignore it. But Maisie wasn't the only one worried, Mary was another inside person I would talk with sometimes. She said she had talked to Jesus about the men...there was more than one, and this is what he said to her.

Mary my child I know your heart and I am glad, but this is not your battle. There is one who must come to me, another who must gain victory in this fight, but it is not you. I would have you wait and pray for that person so that they may see my power and know that I am God and Lord.
So I asked Him who that person was but He only said that was for Him to know.
Maisie overheard this conversation...
What the hell was all that about?
Maisie? You heard all that?
Yes, I did what a lot of crap. If Jesus is waiting on me to sort this lot out, then we are all in deep shit why doesn't he just get on and sort it out himself if he's so hot.
I suppose He's got a different agenda. He usually does.
Well he can go hang cos there's no way I'm going down there
Aren't you even a little bit curious?
Nope not me… I'm not stupid you know, and I won't be manipulated into doing anything I don't want to do. Not by you and not by him either.
Ok. Sorry. Maybe its not you He's waiting for anyway.
Maybe. Let's hope not for everyone's sake! Do you think this is how he gets his kicks making people squirm and feel guilty?
No. but He is very persistent.
What for. I mean what does he want anyway… why me?
Well I suppose He wants you to know Him, or at least to take a first step.
But what for?
Because He is the answer. He's the one who will bring healing and life and freedom, and He wants you to have it as much as anyone else...and He's the only one who can give it to you.
Shit I don't need all that. I'm alright as I am. it's the others who are in a mess.
We are all in a mess Maisie and we all need Him. I need Him.
Well you can have him. I just want him to stay away from me. He's trouble with a capital T as far as I can see.
Ok well it's your choice Maisie, He won't force you.
Let him try.
He won't. He'll just wait patiently until you are ready.
Well he'll be waiting a long time then. Right I'm off. You not crying today?
I think you missed it
Well give it a rest will you. Waste of time. Right I'm off. See ya
Bye

Jesus did have a plan, but Maisie wasn't quite ready yet, I don't think.

Yes, it is me
So how's it going?
I'm pissed off. Why do you keep bothering with that man? He really is a waste of space. He's never going to help us. He doesn't give a shit
Maybe you are right Maisie I don't know. I don't know anything really.
Oh God quit your crying we are not going to let any man beat us why don't you write and tell him to just piss off.
Well for starters what would be the point? It wouldn't make a lot of difference now would it.
No but it would be satisfying, and we'd feel more in control. Not hanging around waiting for him to help us and pray. It just makes me sick. What the hell are we going to do?
Keep going like we always do.
Well there has to be something better than that. You keep saying your Jesus is going to come up with the goods I'm not seeing it. If this Mike is supposed to be his help I'm not impressed.

I have to believe that Jesus will come through for us one way or another.
It is the only thing that keeps me going… no, He keeps me going.
Well bully for you. What about the rest of us… and quit crying?
How am I supposed to know Maisie I'm just doing the best I can? You shouting at me isn't helping.
Yeah well, I can't help it I'm pissed off like I said…. man it stinks.
Yes it does.
Stop crying.
What have you got against crying? Don't you ever cry?
No I do not… stupid waste of time.
I suppose you get angry instead.
Well it's a whole lot better than all those pathetic waterworks.
What good does that do?
What good does the anger do?
Well at least I can stand up for myself.
I don't see you standing up to Mike, you've just run away
Yeah well, I don't believe in wasting my time either. When does he ever listen to what any of us say or even bother to reply?
He did reply to you to be fair
Yeah with a whole load of useless baloney. Doesn't seem to care much what happened either does he.
No… he doesn't. But don't ask me. I don't understand any of this.
Me either kiddo. I'm off now. You have a good day and stop with the crying.

Sometimes Maisie would see things on the inside when she came to talk with me. I couldn't see what was happening most of the time and the things she told me were surprising and interesting.

Hi. What is it Maisie?
I saw it again. I saw it. I mean you were covered in it...everywhere
Slow down. What did you see?
Well you were just covered in golden light… like before... only more, much more and I saw, I don't know, I saw ... I saw men, well not men, but like men around you and they were pouring something on you. I don't know what... What's going on? come on I want to know.
Well you are seeing something I don't Maisie. So, I don't know exactly what you saw. But Jesus was with me, healing me…. I guess the light was the Holy Spirit again and the men were angels but what they were doing I don't know.
Man, this is weird. I don't get it. Its freaking me out. What's it like?
Well… its kind of wonderful and painful all at the same time…I don't know if I can say more than that really… its painful because I'm feeling the pain that I'm giving him and the wounds that he's healing and its wonderful because I'm being held and loved.
Mmm… I don't know... You were doing a lot of crying…
Well ... Yes... Like I said it was painful.
But don't you get fed up of it all? I mean you are always crying, and he just seems to make you cry more. I couldn't cope with that.
Certainly, I get fed up with crying… give me a good laugh any day... But this is where I'm at, I can't really do anything about it.
Well it doesn't make a lot of sense to me... I can't see the point.
To be better... that's the point
Well I don't see how crying is going to make you better…
I'm so tired Maisie…maybe we can talk later.
Whatever... Just you were freaking me out that's all.
Why don't you just go talk to him Maisie?
Me... What would I say?

Anything you like... Ask him about the golden light, the angels, whatever. I'd be interested to know what he says.
Yeah well don't hold your breath. I told you I'm not going down there.
Is he still there? I mean has anything changed?
I haven't been out to see.
You're hanging round with me, instead right?
Well why not? It's kind of interesting.
I think it would be more interesting talking to Jesus.
Man, you don't let up do you. I'm not going down there. I'm not going to talk to him ok.
Ok... But I thought you didn't do scared.
I don't... I mean, hey I don't have to explain myself to you.
No, you don't... you do whatever you want Maisie.
I will don't you worry. right well I'm off. Might catch you later.

I think that Jesus was showing Maisie things and helping her to learn about him. One day I, and maybe someone else? had been talking to Jesus. I got really upset and angry and shouted at him.

Hi there Maisie... I'm ok now if you want to talk.
Man, that was something... Don't think I've ever seen you that upset and angry.
Haven't you? well it happens you know. I wasn't entirely sure that was all me mind you... What do you think?
I couldn't say but whoever it was took a bit of a risk...
Whoever it was should really say it to Him themselves... because He knows who it was anyway.
He does?
He is God... He knows everything.
Oh... Yeah, I forgot that.
But of course, everything He said was also for that person... Not just for me.
You think... I mean why would he talk to them if they were so pissed off with him?
Because He understands... And because He loves them.
But he's God, right? I mean you can't just start raging at God and expect him to put up with it.
Well, He puts up with me raging at Him. That's not the first time you know.
But you don't get angry... that's what I do!
Of course, I get angry I'm just not that good at expressing it... I'm afraid of it, I'm afraid of conflict.
Oh ... Right... that's mad... I like a good fight but man to tell God that your pissed that's something else.
Well He knows how I'm feeling anyway. A lot better than I do...He prefers it if we are honest because then He can respond and help.
Well I don't know about that... All he ever says is trust me... Why the hell should we trust him?!
Because He doesn't lie. Because He loves us and because He is who He says He is.
Yeah but.... I mean we only have his word for that don't we... So, its kind of trust me because I say you can.
Yes... But you will find if you trust Him that He will do what He says. Not in the way you think He will most likely, but He will do it.
Well I don't know what I think about that. I mean how are you supposed to trust someone who lets all that bad stuff happen. I mean look what happened to us... the kids... If he's God, he could have stopped it right?
Yes He could.
But he didn't did he so how do you trust someone like that and believe that he cares... I don't get that at all.
I don't always get it either, but I think it's all down to free will…He allows every person to

make their own choices... even if that means they hurt someone else.
Why would he do that if he knows what they will do? And he's God, he knows, that right?
He knows everything... He gave us free will so that we could choose to love Him.
Huh?
When He created mankind, He created us to have relationship with Him, He loves us, and we love Him.
Ok... weird but ok.
But we decided I think basically that we wanted other things more. To have our own way, for life to be about us and not about Him or our relationship with Him. So we turned our back and did our own thing... our choice.
Alright but why does that mean that he has to allow such terrible things to happen?
In order for us to get back into a relationship with Him we have to choose it. He can't make us want Him. He can mmm... What I'm trying to say is He wants us to freely choose to love Him so that He can restore the original purpose He had for creating us in the first place. You can't force someone to love you. That free choice means that we can choose to go against Him and do all manner of terrible things. He allows that because He must... I suppose. It gets a bit deep and I don't pretend to be able to completely get my head around it. This is where Mike would be a help... but hey all you've got is me I'm afraid.
Ok... So free will means bad stuff can happen and he lets it so that we can choose to love him?
Basically...
Well that sucks... I mean that's just plain selfish isn't it. Letting people suffer so that he can have his big love fest. Man, that stinks he's worse that I thought.
Calm down... You're missing something.
Go on then what am I missing?
We were created to love Him and without that we are stuffed basically... He's giving us a chance to get back what we lost... which is Him
Well what's so great about him that we should go through all this shit to get him?
That is a very big question Maisie... and probably one that you need to discover the answer to yourself. But the more you get to know Him and the more you see how much He loves you the more you will realize that He is worth it.
Must be good.
Yes... He is.
So why were you shouting at him then if he's so good?
Because sometimes I forget and sometimes it all gets too much and I have to shout at somebody. And since He's the one I know loves me and won't push me away because I'm not perfect He's the one I shout at. And besides He's the only one who can do anything about this anyway.
It's all confusing you know.... And I don't get it.
Well just mull it over cos there will always be stuff you don't get... there's a whole load of stuff I don't get...but I trust Him anyway
Bonkers.

I was still going to the ministry centre every month and learning things and Jesus was healing me or maybe more than me at times. Maisie thought our trips were a stupid waste of time but she still paid attention...

Ok then Maisie what is it you want to say?
I want to say this is a right load of bollocks...I mean do you actually believe this stuff?
Well.... I think there's a basis in truth yes, but I will have to think about it. I'm sure it's not as black and white as they are making out.
What about all these agreements and ritual stuff. I mean where does that leave us? Does that mean we are in league with the devil... whoever he is... or is it just the kids or what?
Honestly, I just don't know how it applies to us or even if it does. There's too much I don't

know about it and there's too much I don't know about what actually happened to the children. But I admit it looks a bit bad for us...
So tell me about the devil and demons and stuff... I mean are they real?
Yes they are definitely real... and they are definitely a problem for us.
Go on then how do you know they are real?
Well two ways I suppose. First, the bible is very clear on the subject that Satan, the devil, is the enemy of God and demons are bad angels who rebelled against God. Satan is a bad angel too... but more powerful.
Right so these bad angels... they are out to do bad stuff, right? I mean...like what happened to us?
Yes... they do it I believe by influencing people... and they provide the spiritual power behind the supernatural stuff that goes on... Like all the stuff he was talking about like astral projection and that sort of thing.
Ok so there's Satan and bad angels and there's God and good angels...
Yes but Satan isn't like God. He's just an angel gone wrong... Nothing like as powerful as God
Mmm...but how can you tell the difference? I mean he was talking about that angel who went around killing people right, well.... I mean how can that be good?
The people he killed were the enemies of God.
So that makes it ok?
I guess....
Well I don't know I'm just confused. I mean how is anyone supposed to figure this stuff out... I mean who made it so complicated anyway... ha ha I made you laugh!
Yes that was very naughty of you.
Couldn't help it. He's stood there thumping his bible... What am I going to say!
You made me smile its true....
So do you think we've got demons ... bad angels cus if we have that's not good is it...I mean man if the good angels are that powerful what about the bad ones and what about this Satan where's he?
So many questions in one sentence! I think the answer is yes there will be demons who are hanging around us and yes, they are powerful...though no more so than good ones I'm sure. But Jesus can deal with them. You remember what Mike said to do? that's what he was talking about.... getting Jesus to get rid of a demon, or possibly a demon because that's what it sounded like. Either the man you described was a demon or a part who was acting under the influence of a demon.
Shit I get it now... so the bad angel things have got it in for us yeah and the only one who can protect us is Jesus?
Exactly yes that's exactly it.
Oh... so that's what Mike was saying... right it makes more sense now... kind of... I mean its completely weird but then I've seen a lot of weird stuff this week... this morning when you were singing... sorry, worshipping it was weird... I could have sworn I saw fire... I mean like flames all around you but that can't be right can it... cos here you are not singed or anything!
Well that would be the fire of the Holy Spirit... do you remember Mike said something about the demon being consumed by the fire of the Holy Spirit? I think that's what he said... well the Holy Spirit can come as a fire... Not always in such a violent way of course but still...
Oh man... So Holy Spirit... What's that?
The Holy Spirit is God. He's a He not an it.
Confused! I thought Jesus was God according to you.
He is...dear me... some of this stuff is hard to explain and makes my brain want to explode cos this is God we are talking about. There is only one true God, yeah...but He has three alters...I suppose you could say... There's Jesus, the Holy Spirit and there's the Father and they are all God, all equal with each other, but also quite distinct from each other.

…… Mmm so a bit like us… we are in one body, but we are different…
In a way but...Oh dear... This is a bit beyond me Maisie…can we come back to that one... It feels like a very long conversation.
Sure... I think I've got enough to think about…so Jesus can get rid of these demons right... What about Satan? Where does he come in?
Well he's the boss…. How demons relate to each other and to Satan I really don't know Maisie…but I shouldn't worry too much about Satan himself if I were you…. we've got plenty on with the demons…but you are right, Jesus can get rid of them…because he's God and they are nothing to him... even though for us they are very powerful supernatural beings.
Scary stuff……
Yes…but Jesus is always there if you call on him...always… I've had some encounters with demons and Jesus has dealt with them.
You have?
I do wonder what you've been doing these past few years Maisie...not paying attention obviously.
Well I can't be watching everything you know... most of your life bores the pants off me... I only bother with the interesting bits.
You seem to have missed all the interesting bits if you ask me…
Yeah well… I have to admit its more interesting than I thought.
Is there anything else Maisie cos I've got to go soon?
No... you've given me plenty to think about thanks.
So, I guess Maisie did just that. It was all part of the plan of course because Jesus definitely hadn't forgotten her.
You said you had things to tell me. I haven't forgotten.
Yeah. Yeah, I do. But its not easy you know.
Well… I'm listening…
Ok well I thought you know after the stuff we talked about and all that other stuff that happened last week, that I would just go down again, and maybe see if Jesus was about. I mean I don't know what I thought I was gonna say, but I was curious you know.
So what happened?
Well I only got halfway there, and he was just in front of me. Standing there like he's been waiting. in fact, he said he had been waiting.
Ok...go on.
Well I said something lame like, hi I'm Maisie... and he just came out with all this stuff about how he'd been waiting for me, and how he was longing to show me just who he was because I didn't get it. You know that I didn't understand who he was. You know all that stuff about how God thinks.
Uhhum.
So he took me down to the place. You know where all the angels are, and he led me into this valley type place. Well I was a bit nervous about this you know because there I am with this strange man, God... whatever, surrounded by all these massive angel things and he takes me into this valley, right?
Yeah…
Well right at the end of this valley which is a kind of a dead end are these 5 men…things… I don't know and they are kind of being held prisoner I suppose... guarded by a few angels. So I'm thinking man what am I doing here and I wanted to run away you know, but Jesus he just says to me don't be afraid... like he knew or something and then he went up to these men who started howling and crawling about on the floor...I've never seen anyone act like that... Not even Susanna has that effect!... Ha! So he turns to me and says your enemies, Maisie, will bow before me because they know who I am. Do you know who I am? And he looked me right in the eye. It made me shake all over... So, then I said I don't know who you are, but I heard you were God, which ought to have sounded daft... telling someone you

heard they were God but somehow it didn't. So then he turned back to these men and he said something like reveal your true form and man you should have seen 'em squirm but then... I can't even describe it... suddenly they weren't men any more they were these things I mean they were disgusting with teeth and everything and man they were scary, and I was glad to have all them angels and Jesus too, cos I could see they weren't scared. So then he turns back to me and says these are your enemies Maisie, sent by Satan to destroy you and the others in this system. Should we let them stay? And I said no way! Please get rid of 'em. You can do that right? And he smiled and just told them to go and they like disappeared before my eyes. That was it ... gone, I mean weird... And a whole load of angels left too so there were only three or four left with Jesus and me.
Wow... So what happened next?
Well he, Jesus just looks at me and says Maisie I know your name, I know who you are. Do you know who I am? And I have to tell you it had been pretty freaky up till then but in that moment, I was scared. I mean really scared and I couldn't even look at him. Because well I knew who he was didn't I. I mean I just knew, and I was scared because you know this is God and he's talking to me and I can't run and hide I mean... yeah well, I was scared.
So what did you say?
I said I think you might be God...like they said. And he smiled and that was weird too and he said don't be afraid Maisie. Well I mean I was afraid wasn't I, and then he said we will meet again soon...look out for me... and then he was gone I mean poof... just like that.
I don't know what to say Maisie. Wow…that's quite an encounter.
Yeah... It's got me freaked out. I keep expecting him to pop up with a posse of angels you know, but I haven't seen him.
Well you will. You can be sure of that.
Yeah well anyway that's me. I don't know what else to say about all that I mean ...were those things demons then?
Yes I'm quite sure they were.
Man they were nasty...I mean you wouldn't want to tangle with one of them... so how come they looked like men?
They can take on different forms. The bible says they can even appear as angels of light. They deceive people into thinking they are something other than demons, sometimes they even seem to be good. The test is whether they can be in the presence of Jesus. You saw what happened to them when he approached them.
Yeah man they were sweating' I can tell you. They looked pitiful...which is quite something when you consider how evil they look.
So you've seen Jesus' power over evil and you've spoken to Him. So what do you think now? Does God stink?
Er… maybe not, but I still got a load of questions. There's still a mountain of stuff that makes no sense to me.
Well, maybe you can ask Jesus Himself when you see Him.
Maybe I don't know…. well I'm gonna go now cos I can see you are tired.
I am Maisie but I'm really glad you told me that…I mean I know that… well I've never seen anything like that. I think you are fortunate to be able to see the spiritual world…I get glimpses sometimes but mostly it's a mystery.
Yeah, I guess… its freaky though! Anyway, see ya later.

It wasn't very long before she met Jesus again and this time, I was there to hear it even if I didn't see it.

Hi Maisie.
Hi.
How are you today?
I'm ok what about you?
Yes I'm doing ok today…no crying you'll be pleased to hear.

That's a relief. Can't be doing all that crying… what are you doing?
Talking to Jesus.
Is he here?
He's here with me.
Oh... I can't see him
Well…. Maybe you have to ask him to be with you as well…
That's ok…
Tell Maisie I am always with her.
Did you get that?
Er yeah... Er...
Don't be afraid Maisie.
Er…
The things you fear are not from me….I will never hurt you.
Man…. Help me...
What do you want me to do!
I don't know... why is he talking to me?
Why don't you ask him?
Er ok… Jesus. Why are you talking to me?
Because I want to.
Ok…. Er….
You wish to ask me many things.
Well…. Maybe...
Lord three-way conversations are a bit of a challenge…do you want me to go and leave you to it?
No my child I wish you to stay and listen.
Ok.
You wish to ask me many things do you not Maisie?
Well I guess I mean there's a lot of this stuff I don't get…for starters, why you have suddenly appeared...I mean where have you been all this time - I never saw you.
I have been right with you Maisie, never more than a heartbeat away.
Well I never saw you.
You did not wish to see me. You were angry with me.
Well yeah, I mean... why not? You're God right you could have stopped all that rubbish that happened to us… and that was before I knew about the kids... Man where do you get off saying you love us when you let stuff like that happen?
You think I am responsible.
You're God. You're responsible for everything.
Am I? Am I responsible when you choose to hurt people?
What do you mean?
Your actions and your words Maisie are often designed to hurt are they not? You have no answer…am I responsible for that?
No... I guess that's me.
And when others hurt you...is that my doing?
No...
So is what happened to you...to the children, my doing?
No, but you could have stopped it.
If I stopped every wrong and hurtful thing that people do Maisie, the world would have ceased to be long ago.
And what would be so bad about that...I mean it's a shitty place... Sorry.
The world is full of pain and darkness that much is true... It is not the way I would have it ... But I am working to restore all things to their original state... As I intended them to be.
Why are you taking so long about it? I mean, you could do it straight away couldn't you?

Perhaps... But my ways are not your ways Maisie.
Yeah, I kind of figured that.
You wish they were perhaps?
Probably not...like you said I can be mean... and what do I know anyway...
You see Maisie all people long for life, true life. They spend their whole lives searching for it. Many of them never find it although the answer is always with them. What do you think that answer is?
You?
So what about it Maisie...will you accept the answer?
Er... what do you mean?
Will you accept me as your answer... the answer to all your questions...and there are many I know?
Yeah I got loads of questions. I don't know... I mean …
You have seen what darkness is Maisie…will you choose the light? Will you choose me?
What would that mean...I don't know what that would mean.
It would mean that you choose my side, that you choose life over death, that you recognize who I am in all of your life...you know who I am?
Sure... You're God right... Shit... God's asking me to be on his team…. Help
Sorry... Your choice here Maisie!
Man…. Well I don't want to be on the other team that's for sure…. I mean I know what they are… there's only two teams right?
You must choose.
Man…well ok, I guess...I choose you Jesus… oh man what am I doing?
You are choosing life Maisie…
Well ok then so …. Man… Ok then Jesus, I do choose you cos I ain't gonna be on that team... But …well…. I'm scared…I hate to admit it, but I am.
Don't be afraid Maisie you have chosen well.
Shit... There you are... Sorry... Does that mean I've got to be all good now, if I'm on God's team? Man, I ain't never gonna be good...why would you want me anyway?' Like you said before, I'm mean and rude and man I ain't no good.
You cannot run away…you will be all that you can be in me Maisie... Do not worry that you are not good enough, for I will make you into a mighty warrior for me and the enemy will fear your coming.
I kind of like the sound of that but it sounds a bit unlikely I mean... I've seen them demon things and man I wouldn't want to mess with them.
Nevertheless, Maisie now you are on my team they will fear you, because I am in you and you are in me. They will not see you...they will see me... And they fear me.
Yeah, I saw that…
I will teach you Maisie…do nothing but what I tell you…you must rely on me for everything. You will find this hard to begin with but fear not I will show you the way.
Mmm… well... Man what have I got myself into? I blame you for this.
Me...what has it got to do with me?
Well if you hadn't gone on about him, I wouldn't have been curious...what have I done?
Nothing to do with me Maisie… it's all Jesus… Lord are you still there?
I am watching... My two daughters whom I love...you delight me.
I don't understand.
Nevertheless, I tell you that it is so.
I would spend the day with you as I said… and with you Maisie...if you will have me?!
Er...man... Ok ...I don't know how this works…
I'll see you Maisie... Have a good time.
Right... See ya
Thankyou lord for letting me share that…

I wish for you to share many things…many things lie ahead my child that you cannot yet see. I want you to know that I am in control and that I have every single person in this system in the palm of my hand... Do not be afraid for them there is nothing... and no-one who is too difficult for me to reach.
That's good Lord… I know I often doubt that... I can't see how you are going to work all this out, but I will try and trust you day by day.
That is all I ask my child.

Maisie visited me at the surface for a little while after this and told me what was going on inside. She was learning how to live with others and finding it a bit difficult sometimes. Jesus gave her the job of protecting some of the children inside and I think she found that kind of hard too, but she loved the things that Jesus showed her and taught her and always said that he was cool. After a while she stopped coming to the surface and I didn't see her again until I wrote this chapter. She came back to the surface with Jesus to visit one last time, but that part of her story is for another time.

Chapter 9

Susanna.

and the darkness

Jesus had promised that no one was too difficult to reach. That was good to know. Susanna seemed to me too difficult. If Maisie was angry Susanna was full of rage… everyone inside was afraid of her and she seemed to take pleasure in coming to the surface to threaten and torment me. The same day Maisie joined team Jesus, Susanna turned up.

RIGHT I WANT TO KNOW WHAT THE FUCK IS GOING ON IN THIS PLACE. I CAN'T HEAR MYSELF THINK FOR STUPID FUCKING ANGELS SINGING. WHAT THE HELL IS GOING ON? WHERE DID THEY COME FROM? THEY CAN GET THE FUCK OUT OF HERE BECAUSE I'M NOT LISTENING TO THAT FUCKING ROW.

Is this Susanna by any chance?

OF COURSE, IT'S ME WHO ELSE WOULD IT BE. IS THIS YOUR FAULT? YOU'RE INTO ALL THIS GOD SHIT. DID YOU SEND THESE ANGELS DOWN HERE TO MAKE ALL THIS FUCKING ROW?

I don't order angels about Susanna. I think Jesus is the one you need to talk to.

JESUS! WHO THE FUCK IS HE AND WHAT'S HE GOT TO DO WITH ANGELS?

Well he's their boss, he's the one who sends them wherever he wants, to do whatever he wants.

WELL, YOU TELL HIM I WANT THEM TO GET THE FUCK OUT OF HERE NOW.

Well I can certainly talk to him about it, but I don't think he takes orders from anyone Susanna… not even you.

WHY- WHO THE FUCK DOES HE THINK HE IS ANYWAY?

Well. God, I suppose… since that's who He is.

WHAT? WHAT CRAP IS THIS? WHY WOULD GOD HAVE ANYTHING TO DO WITH THIS? I THOUGHT YOU SAID HE WAS CALLED JESUS.

Well he is but He's still God.

YOU ARE A COMPLETE SHIT-HEAD. YOU BELIEVE THAT?

Well I don't know where else you think angels would come from.

WHAT THE FUCK DO I KNOW ABOUT ANGELS EXCEPT THEY MAKE A FUCKING ROW.

Look I'm sorry but there isn't anything I can do...you need to find Jesus and tell Him about it.

I'M NOT TALKING TO ANYONE WHO THINKS HE'S GOD. WHAT THE FUCK DO YOU TAKE ME FOR?

Then you'll have to put up with the noise.

I talked to Jesus about her…

Lord… Er... this conversation?
My child I know all things.
Yes…I know. She seemed a bit confused to me.
Rage opens a person up to much deceit and much confusion.
She's impossible to reason with.
I can reach anyone remember.
Yes… so what should I do?
Simply be calm and patient and speak the truth as you have done. I know the plans I have for Susanna.

Ok Lord. Please give me the wisdom and the compassion and the patience!
I will be with you my child.

Susanna confused me... and scared me at times. She wrote to Mike. It was hard to know why except she liked to cause trouble... and she wasn't impressed with his reply.

Right now, let's get something straight. I don't take no shit from no-one right, so you keep your mouth shut because I'm not interested in anything you've got to say this is for the pastor right. Nothing to do with you so I don't even want to talk to you right because you've got nothing to say that I want to hear you got that. And don't be thinking you can ignore me because I can get your attention, you only make it worse for yourself you know. Don't think you can stand up to me because I know what a pathetic wimp you are. You couldn't stand up to piece of wet lettuce. Yeah so anyway for the pastor…

So pastor I read that letter you sent me. You think a lot of yourself don't you. Who are you to tell me how to behave and how to be? What the fuck do you know anyway? Have you lived my life? No so don't take that fucking attitude with me right. As for this one here I'll treat her anyway I choose. What are you going to do about it? You gonna come and sort me out, are you? Ha. There ain't nothing you can do you can't touch me. I don't have to take your insults either. I don't have to take being called a fucking demon. Who are you anyway? What the fuck do you know about anything. As for Jesus fucking Christ well up his and yours too.

That's it you send that off like the good little secretary you are. Stupid fucking idiot. I'll be back don't you worry. This is just the beginning. Now I see how it is. I don't have to take no fucking crap from you or the fucking pastor… See you got nothing to say have you.
Why are you doing this?
Because I fucking hate you get it and I like to cause you pain and that's what I'm going to do. So, watch out. It'll be fun. More fun than I've had in years. See you.

Susanna kept on visiting, but she didn't have it all her own way though because Jesus was helping me, I'm sure.

Oy you stupid fucking idiot answer me.
What do you want Susanna?
What do I want? I want your attention. I'm not going to wait around until you decide you want to answer me.
What do you want?
I want to know what you are doing here. I mean what is it that you and that pastor think you are doing anyway. I've been watching and all you ever do is talk about stupid fucking Jesus. I mean don't you have anything better to do.
No I don't. The whole point of me being here at all is to serve Jesus and what He wants is for me to point others to Him so that He can show them the truth and help and heal them.
Fuck that.
Why do you care anyway?
Care! I don't fucking care I just thought I'd come and tell you that I'm not going to be allowing that anymore. I'm going to stay right here with you and no-one else will be able to talk to you and you won't be able to talk to them. You'll just have me for company.
Who are you serving Susanna?
I don't serve anyone except myself. I do what I like and what I like is to make your life a misery.
Everyone serves someone, either you are serving Jesus, or you are serving Satan.
Well I'm not serving fucking Jesus.

So you are serving Satan?
What if I am?
As long as you are aware that you are making that choice... is that what you want?
What do you fucking care what I want or who I serve?
Because if you serve Satan it will end in your destruction. There is no other end for the enemies of God. Is that what you want?
I just want to do my own thing with no-one fucking telling me what to do.
Well Susanna you are being told what to do. You are being controlled and manipulated by evil to do their work for them.
Fuck that. I'm doing my own thing
Satan doesn't believe in free choice or free will. He's all about slavery and captivity and right now he's got you right where he wants you, doing exactly what he wants.
What the fuck do you know about it?
I can see Susanna.
Fuck off.

Jesus told me that no matter how it seemed the true victim was Susanna because she was being controlled by evil. That made it a bit easier for me I think... to see her that way.

So what is it you want?
I told you I want to make your life a misery.
So how are you going to do that?
Hey, I can just hang around here and tell you what I think about you. That will make your day.
I don't know why you think that would make me miserable. It might annoy me I suppose.
Yeah right, I've seen you doing all that sniveling...all that poor me it hurts so much. I want to die. Well go on then why don't you. No-one wants you around anyway. Just get on with it and put an end to your sorry pathetic life.
Supposing I did that? What would happen to you?
Fuck I don't know. I don't care as long as you aren't here.
Well I hate to tell you this but if I die, you're dying too. Can't really avoid that.
Shit like I care. What's the fucking point of life anyway?
Without Jesus... nothing at all.
Not fucking Jesus again.
Well He is the point of living. He's the only one who can make it worthwhile. The enemy of course just wants us to die. What about you? What do you want?
It doesn't matter what I fucking want this is what I've got isn't it. Just me in this miserable fucking life with no way out except one.
It doesn't have to be like that. There is someone who can change your life. Make it worth living.
Fucking Jesus right.
Jesus can turn your life around and give you hope.
Why the fuck would he want to do that?
He loves you Susanna. He sees the mess you are in and He wants to rescue you and give you a new life.
Shit there is no life for me, this is it so don't give me no fucking speeches about life and hope. Jesus can go fuck himself. I don't need him or you.

Susanna kept on with her visits, always threatening to make my life a misery or worse but I didn't back down because I trusted Jesus was with me and I'm sure he was helping me.

Fuck what are you doing?
I was talking to Jesus He gave me a message for you.
What too chicken to come and face me Himself is He?

This is the message Susanna.

Susanna, I know the forces that are holding you captive. You have given yourself into their hands. Do not believe the lie that you cannot escape. I will deliver you from their hands if you turn to me. I can save you Susanna, but you must turn away from the evil that you are currently involved in and you must turn to me. There is nothing that you have done that I cannot forgive. Your life is not lost. It can be restored. Turn to me and I will show you the true meaning of life. But do not delay the time is short.

What the fuck? He's got to be kidding right? I don't need his fucking forgiveness and I'm not interested in his fucking life either so you can tell him that. Shit I never heard so much crap. I can't stand it here, but don't you worry I'll be back.

I didn't back down, but I wasn't finding it easy either.

Can I ask again about Susanna?
My child you may ask me anything, share all your concerns and worries with me. Do not carry anything alone.
Well...I don't know what I'm doing when I'm talking to her and it seems so futile. I don't know... I suppose I'm just getting shot at without... not without a reason but... well you know.
My child do not give up. Love is patient and endures. I would have you show Susanna my love towards her. She will not see it anywhere else.
I don't think I know how to do that. I'm not that good at loving people I love let alone people I don't.
I did not ask you to show her your love, but mine.
Well yes... that is a better idea... but...
Do not fear. I will enable you my child. My love dwells within you and will flow through you.
Really? Well ok... are you sure I can do that?
You are my child.
Yes but... I'm a very flawed one.
Are you willing?
Yes... I am.
Then I am able. Be patient and persevere. Be my servant and be obedient to my Spirit as He leads you.
Yes... Alright. I don't feel up to this you know.
I know.

So I kept on going even when Susanna was at her worst. I stayed calm and didn't crumble or back down. I knew it was Jesus who was giving me the words to say. I don't think I could have done it otherwise...

You stupid fucking bitch why don't you pay attention to me. Now I'm just going to have to make you pay...
Susanna... did you want me? You know I'm happy to help but if you just want to call me names...
What the fuck do you think I need your help for? I keep telling you I'm just here to make your life miserable not to get your help. You stupid pathetic cow like you could help anyone. Do you think I don't see all that fucking pathetic wailing you do? How the fuck are you going to help anyone?
Well you are probably right Susanna. I don't think I can help you except to remind you of the one who can.
Fuck give it a rest I don't need any fucking help ok.
Do you remember what He said to you? Its not too late but you do have to admit you need help.

Fuck off you stupid bitch how many times? I don't need your fucking help or his.
You can call me Jennifer you know. I don't mind.
Ha why would I call you that… we all know you don't have a fucking name that's because you're nobody…just a piece of shit.
I might not know my name but I'm a child of God, not a piece of shit.
Same difference.
You think? Well … did you know you can be a child of God too. That's what He wants. He wants you to be part of His family.
Shit I don't want to be part of any family. Do you know what family does to you? Fuck families.
I do know, yes. Family isn't my favorite word either but I'm glad to be God's child. It's not like being the child of a human parent who will let you down and hurt you… even the best one's do that, but God never will.
You really believe all that shit?
Yes… I'm betting my life on it.
You're fucked then.
And what about you? What are you betting on?
Shit I know who I belong to. There's no escaping that. All this talk of love and shit that's not for me. Never was never will be.
Love is for everyone. God's love is for everyone. You only have to choose to accept it, no matter who you think you are or who you belong to.
You think you're so fucking clever with your answers to everything well shit on you. What do you know? I've seen things and done things that you could never even dream of shit head. God doesn't love people like me.
It doesn't matter whether I know about you or not. God knows everything about you and yet He still offers to save you and love you. You heard Him yourself. You heard what Jesus said to you.
SHUT UP. FUCKING SHUT YOUR MOUTH OK. I'M NOT LISTENING TO YOU AND YOUR FUCKING LIES.
I'm speaking the truth. I think you know that.

Susanna did seem to be running out of steam a bit I thought. It was a small glimmer of hope.

Susanna... She seems to be softening a little.
She is becoming more aware of the pain and turmoil within my child as she begins to hear the voice of my Spirit within her… she will resist for a little while longer for deep down she is afraid of what it will mean and what she will have to face if she surrenders to me. She is also afraid of the consequences of not surrendering to me for she begins to see the truth. The battle is fierce, and it is not yet won. Persevere my child I will be with you.

Jesus knows what is happening in everyone's heart. He knew Susanna's heart with all of its fear and anger, and he knew how to reach her, just like he said. So much to my surprise…

All you have to do is to turn to Jesus and say yes Lord.
That fucking easy is it.
Yes. He doesn't make it complicated… He's done everything. All we have to do, each one of us… is choose. He's making that offer to you…all you have to do is say yes.
So… he is God... I mean... he's still a man but he's God.
Yeah.
Fucking hell shit, shit, shit.
Don't be afraid… He loves you so much.
Shit what have I done I mean shit, shit, I can't I mean... Shit… hell's real right?

Yes... It is.
Shit... And I'm on my way.
You don't have to be.
Fuck what do I do?
You get on your knees before Jesus and ask him to forgive you, knowing with absolute certainty that He will.
Shit... I can't do that.
Yes you can... You must.
Shit.
Maybe this is the moment Susanna where you make your choice. Maybe this is it for you. Don't lose your opportunity. It may not come again.
Shit... help me.
Only Jesus can help you Susanna... Ask him. You can do it right now.
Shit I don't know.
Ask him to come and confirm what I've said. What you've begun to see... You can do it.
What do I do... shit what do I do?
Take a breath... and pray... Lord Jesus please come.
Shit ok... Lord Jesus please come... Fuck this is stupid. Shit here he is.
Stay calm Susanna. You are ok. Just breathe.
Shit... shit...shit.
You may go now my child; your work here is done for now. Come Susanna I have much to say to you.

That was a big surprise to me. I think the Holy Spirit was helping me a lot with my answers! I wasn't usually so bold. I really wanted to know what was happening, but I had to wait until Susanna herself came to see me a couple of days later.

Hello Jennifer, this is Susanna.
Hello. How are you? I've been thinking about you.
Erm... I've been with Jesus. I can't tell you what that's been like. I wanted to say I'm sorry for everything I said and the way I hated you and everything. So I'm here.
You are completely forgiven. I'm just so glad you met with Jesus. What's happened, you sound so different.
He took all the anger and hatred Jennifer. I never knew really that it was there it seemed like it was me but really it wasn't... it was them and now they are gone and I can be just me. I don't know who that is, but I don't feel the same. I hate the way I was. I feel ashamed. I'm sorry.
Well Jesus is a God of new starts so why don't you and I start over Susanna? I'm so glad to see what he's done... really, I am.
I need to write to the pastor too. I was... well you know
Yes I know. Do you want to do it now?
Yes... I don't even know how to start. This is so hard...
Just start by saying hello. Tell... well whatever it is you need to say.
Ok. Hello pastor Mike. This is Susanna. I don't suppose you recognize me... I don't recognize myself. I met Jesus. The one you told me about...and well he showed me the truth about myself and all the lies I believed. He told me he knew everything I'd done. So many terrible things, so very many but that he loved me. How could anyone love me? No-one ever loved me. Anyway so... after that when I knew I had to do something because I didn't want to be that way anymore, so I asked him to help me and he said he would. He forgave me for it all. He put his arms around me. No-one ever did that. Anyway, so I said I knew he was right, and I was wrong, but I didn't know what to do. So he said he could help me change if I would choose him and turn my back on Satan and all that stuff. But I was afraid because I know what they can do. So I said no at first, but he knew and said he could protect me... so then I said yes... and he told the anger and the rage and the murder to go

and they did... Just like that. I never saw anyone who could tell them what to do like that. And now here I am and ... I'm not the same. I wanted to say sorry for the way I was. Jesus says I have to say sorry to the people I hurt and try and help them now. I don't think I can do it. They all hate me. I hate myself for what I did. I don't see it can ever be put right and I'm still afraid that they will get me. They will be angry... they will know. I think they will want to kill me and I'm afraid... I don't like being afraid. So that's it so I'm asking if you will forgive me for the way that I was. Thankyou

Susanna came to see me again after that. She was having a bad time I think because nobody inside trusted her or wanted to be friends. Maisie was horrified and didn't want anything to do with Susanna... and she started to avoid Jesus so he wouldn't ask her to. My advice to both of them was the same, talk to Jesus, spend time with him. Susanna told us a little bit about the things she had believed that had helped to keep her in the enemy's power for so long.

Ok... well right from the beginning I was always told that God hated me because I belonged to Satan and that Satan and his followers were the only ones who could protect me from the wrath of God. I was told that there was no way I could ever escape from that, because of what I'd done and because I belonged to Satan. Erm... so Jesus... who I was told was the one who would come looking for me. He was the one to be really afraid of because if he found me, then he would not only kill me but he would torture me forever because I am evil and so... and they said that because I gave my soul to the devil that Jesus wanted to punish me and that he had ways of doing that. I have always been afraid of Jesus and always believed that Satan was my only hope, we were told we could avoid being found and tortured by Jesus, if we remained faithful and under Satan's protection. That he could keep us alive even after we die and we could go to another place then, where Jesus can't get us, and we can do whatever we want forever. There was a lot of other stuff too, about how in this place we would be the torturers, but I don't really want to talk about that. I suppose now that I've met Jesus and I don't think... I mean he says he loves me, and he hasn't hurt me and ... but I suppose I'm still afraid of him because I think... Well I don't know because of who I am... maybe... I suppose I think he might change his mind and then there's Satan because I've betrayed him, he will get me and then I will die, and I don't know what will happen. I'm confused and I'm afraid. Can you help me because...? I'm not sure anymore. I can't talk about this anymore. Thanks.

I think Susanna had a long journey ahead of her to get free from the enemy and their lies but now she belonged to Jesus and that was the important thing. I didn't hear from her again and I don't know yet what happened to her in the months and years after. Hearing Susanna talk about her life made it more real for me about the things I was remembering. Not just things that had been done to me or us, but things that we had been trained to do and how we had been in the power of the enemy for so long. Now Jesus was setting us free one by one.

My child the days ahead of you will be dark and difficult but I will be your light. I will guide you every step of the way. You will not falter, and you will not fall, only hold on to me. This dark tunnel does not go on forever and at the end there is new life and hope awaiting you. Do not ever give up hope. Keep your eyes fixed on me and know that I am always with you. I will never leave you. No matter what you learn about your past, no matter how dark and difficult the path becomes I am with you and will give you everything that you need. All that I ask is that you trust me. Trust me with everything that you have. I will not let you down and disappoint you. I will keep all my promises to

you. The future is not as you suppose. You do not see what lies ahead. You have no concept of what I have planned for you. So do not give up my dearest one. Allow me to carry you through this knowing that the victory is already ours. You are mine my beloved child nothing can separate us in this world or the next. I am wholly on your side. I am a strong and mighty warrior fighting on your behalf. You do not need to be strong you only need to trust me. I am all you will ever need. I am your beloved Jesus and I love you with an everlasting love.

Chapter 10

Mum

and the struggle to forgive

My struggle to accept the things that I remembered continued for a long time. I especially had trouble with the things I remembered about mum. It had been very difficult to accept that Grandad and Grandma did what they did, but it was even harder with mum because I still saw her all the time. It was so hard to believe she could have done the things I remembered and allowed all those terrible things to happen to me. When I saw her it was worse. Sometimes inside people would be triggered and I could hear them and feel their pain. Sometimes it was all just so normal that I couldn't believe all those bad things.

The mum I remembered when I was growing up wasn't always very kind. I often felt like I was bad and not good enough. When I did jobs for her, she would do them again because I did a bad job, but she never said how I could do it better. She never said anything she was just angry. Sometimes she would stop talking to me for days, but I didn't know why. I never knew what I did to make her angry. I would cry and beg her to forgive me but that just made it worse. There were no cuddles or comfort that I remember. I learned not to cry because it got ignored and it felt like I was bad to cry, and I felt ashamed because I did.

I went into the kitchen and mum was there...doing something but with her back to me, ignoring me. I went into the little room under the stairs. The only thing I remember about this room was that was where we kept the record player. One of the old one with the lids... I loved the record player; it was a treat to be allowed to put the records on. But anyway, this had nothing to do with that. I put myself right in the darkest corner under the stairs, there was no natural light in this room so it was dark...and tried to make myself so small that I would disappear. I didn't want to exist. I didn't so much cry as howl with the pain of this memory. Jesus was there reassuring me, comforting me. And then I saw Him in the memory, holding me in His arms. I wasn't alone. He was there with me.

Mum took care of me, I had clothes and food and toys to play with but there wasn't much affection that I remember. I always knew these things; I didn't forget them, and I suppose it makes more sense why she was the way she was now I know about the bad things. But I still had a very hard time believing the things I was remembering now because I didn't want them to be true. I didn't understand how she could let those things happen to me.

I was in the small room between the kitchen and the hall in the house where we lived with my grandparents, I think it was mostly used for storage. I was maybe three years old. Grandad was there, it was dark, the light was off and he was... it doesn't really matter because that's not the point of this memory. The door to the kitchen opened and the light was switched on. It was mum. She saw us there, switched off the light again and left closing the door behind her.

I remember the shock of this memory. I had been wondering how she didn't know. How could she have not known that all of those things were happening? But now I knew...she did know. At least she knew some of it. I spent a lot of time talking to Jesus about her. I didn't see how it could be true, how she could have pretended not to see. He said he would help me to understand in time.

My child do not be afraid for I am at work in her life. I know you are confused and uncertain, but the past is past my dearest one. Accept your mum as she now is

without needing to understand or to judge. Leave those things in my hands. Simply accept her and love her as she is. Do not be burdened by the past but allow me to work.

I suppose I am still trying to figure it all out because I still worry, I've got it wrong and that its all a terrible lie.

And yet you know the truth.

I'm trying to trust that you have revealed the truth.

I am the truth my dearest one. I will not lead you wrong.

Then I will try Jesus…

I love you my child. When you do not understand, and you cannot see trust in my love for you.

Yes, I suppose I tend to think I'm looking for answers, but really I'm looking for you. Help me.

My desire is that you should find me all the days of your life and into eternity. I am always working towards this my little one. I am here to be found.

But the more I remembered the more upset and distressed I got because it wasn't just that she was pretending not to know but like grandma she was helping.

I saw grandad coming towards me looking angry. I don't know why. I was very frightened. He pinned me down on my back on a table with one hand on my chest. I didn't have any clothes on, and I must have been three. He called over his shoulder, Eve get me some rag. Eve is mums name. He took the rag she gave him and pushed it up between my legs inside me. I suppose it was to do stretching. Mum walked away. I cried mammy don't go... mammy don't go, but she left me. Maybe it was because I was crying, I don't know but grandad picked me up by one arm and dragged me into the punishment room. He put me in the luggage trunk, shut and locked the lid. I cried and cried mammy... mammy. In the trunk I could see Jesus curled up in there holding me close. He didn't leave me.

And it wasn't just grandad that she let hurt me. There was a priest who would visit. He came to grandma and grandad's house with his big black book. It looked like a bible on the outside, but it wasn't. It was Satan's book. He came to the house where I lived with mum when I was a bit older as well. The Holy Spirit was coming in waves… and then I was in the inside of my Wendy house. It was yellow and when the sun shone it was a bright golden color on the inside which I loved. There was a pink blanket on the grass inside for me to sit on. I was playing with my doll. I called her Goldilocks because she had long golden hair which you could change the length of by turning a knob on her back. Mum called me out and led me into the kitchen. Father T was there. He held out his hand and took me into the little room under the stairs. I think I must have been about 6 or 7. He was wearing a long black cassock with a narrow belt. He took off the belt and started to undo the buttons down the front. He got me to come and help. There was a gap here so I'm not sure what came next, but then I saw that he was sitting in the pink bucket chair we had. He was still wearing his cassock, but it was open, and he was naked underneath. I was sat straddled across him so that I was sat on his lap facing him. I was naked. I had my arms around him and my head on his chest. He was stroking my hair. His penis was inside me. The very distressing thing for me was the knowledge that I was in some way enjoying this because he was holding me, stroking my hair and showing me physical affection. He had a hairy chest, but it was warm and comforting….

I remembered too that mum would take me to the park and hand me over to men. I didn't know who they were at this point, but they took me into the woods.

What are we going to do?
We will continue with the relationship with your mum my dearest one for there is much to do.
Ok.
Rest a little then my dearest one and we will begin. My little one do not be anxious. Rest in my love for you my little one.
I'm sorry I don't want to do this.
I know my little one I know, but are you willing?
Yes Jesus I am.
Then let us begin. I want you to think back my little one to when you were five.
Mmm.. I don't remember anything good about being five.
Yes my little one I know but I have more to show you.
Ok.
My little one I am with you do not be afraid. Close your eyes.

I saw the park. The park where so much happened. It was hot day. I was with mum. I was surprised because I don't have many memories of being with mum at the park... but then I don't remember much. Right away I felt I knew what was coming. I know I was resisting but trying not to. I saw her handing me over to a man, I don't know who. But then because I was resisting probably it became unclear again… and then I saw the boating lake with the boats. I never got to go on them. But there was a suggestion here that mum handed me over to a man who took me on one of the boats but again I pulled away. Then I saw that we were in the little café. It wasn't really a café, they sold ice lollies, maybe sweets and drinks and there was a room with chairs and tables. Mum bought me a lolly and we sat at one of the tables. It was cool after the hot sun... again she was handing me over to a man. But I didn't want to see... And I was pretending, hoping I was just making it up…

Jesus
Yes my little one.
What am I supposed to be seeing?
My little one be patient. Do not be afraid. Close your eyes.
So I did but I was still fighting it. I was back in the café again…
My little one I am here. Do not be anxious but trust what I am showing you.
Well I saw the park. I was there with mum. We went for a lolly and sat in the café a bit which was cool… did I see that right?
Yes my little one that is what I showed you but there is more. Are you willing to see?
Help me to be willing. I don't feel willing.
My little one you know who I am.
Yes... I know you love me and want to heal me. I'm sorry. Have your way Jesus.
Come then my little one and allow me to show you the truth.
I'm afraid.
Yes my little one I know you are but I am here. I will not leave you.
Ok then. Show me.

It was such a struggle for me to allow myself to see. But it was just the same. She handed me over to a man who led me away into the woods… I didn't see anymore. I was overwhelmed by grief….

My little one I understand your grief. I am here with you.
I don't want to see any more of this stuff... why must I see?
I want you to know the truth my little one. Do not fear it for it leads to healing and

freedom.

Jesus, I don't understand. I know you keep saying I will eventually but how do I understand that. How?

My little one your mum was caught in a trap she did not know how to escape. Like you she had many ways of protecting herself from the truth. This enabled her to do and to be many things that are difficult for you to understand. This did not mean that she didn't love you in her own way for she did, but there were so many conflicts for her and so much fear my little one that she failed you and betrayed you as should not have been done.

I don't want to accept any of this.

I know my little one, but this is the truth.

Crying... I just want to hide I don't want any of this to be true. Please .

My little one I know you are in great pain. Let me come and comfort you my little one. Rest in my arms a while. I will enable you to continue. To take the next step my dearest one. That is all you must do.

The overwhelming feeling that came with this memory apart from the grief was one of despair. It made me want to give up, to lie down and die... like I am and always will be utterly alone and defenseless.

Jesus

Yes my little one I am here.

Help me. I don't want to do this, be here anymore.

I know my little one, but you are not alone. I am with you. I am bringing you life my little one.

I'd rather come and be with you. This whole thing looks so hopeless to me. Its hard to care about anything except escape.

Hold on to me my little one. Keep your eyes fixed upon all that I am. We have many things to do together my dearest one. We have all of eternity to enjoy each other but I have much for you to do here my dearest one. Do not despair I am well able to do all that I have said. My dearest one I understand your despair, but it does not come from me it does not tell of my hope and my love. Do not listen to it my dearest one. Though you have been hurt and betrayed by those who should have loved you the most I will restore everything to you my little one. All of this and more. Hold on to me and I will bring you through this.

I spent some time just staring blankly...

My little one.

I'm sorry it's so much easier not to feel anything. I don't want to feel anything anymore... I don't want to be alive. I'm sorry. Help me.

I am here my dearest one I am here. Do not give up before you see all that I will do my dearest one. It will be worth everything you are going through. I have so much planned for you. So much for you to see and do and experience. So much work for you to do for my kingdom. Do not let the enemy rob you of all of that my dearest one for that is his intent. He wishes to rob you of every good thing it is my desire to give to you. Do not let him have his way.

Just more sitting...

I'm sorry... I don't have anything to say really.

My little one trust in my promises, allow yourself to hope. For life and hope go together my little one.

I can't seem to do that... hope is painful.

My little one I am your hope.

I wish you would just let me come... but I want to stay for you. I feel pulled in so many different directions.

Then listen to me my dearest one. I want you to stay and let me heal and restore you and all those in your system. I want to use your life to bring glory to my name and to draw many of my children back to me. I want to bring you life and hope and joy and peace. To give you a life worth living my dearest one. Listen to my voice and mine alone.

Yes. But...

I will help you my dearest one. I am always with you…. My little one do not be afraid to ask for anything.

I need more of you... I want to know you more, hear you more clearly... Love you more. I'm not going to make it otherwise.

I will give you everything you need my dearest one. I will give you more that you seek and so much more besides. Hold on to me my little one and trust me with all that you have.

Some of the other alters would tell me the things that mum did. Matilda was especially full of anger and hatred towards her. She was very hurt by the things that mum did and didn't do.

… shit that woman left us, she left you. She walked away, time after time she walked away. I saw it, I saw it all. I can't believe you can even look at the bitch, she left us for god's sake. She didn't care, none of them cared!

Matilda told me about how mum had let the men into the house when I was much older, a teenager. The men would do the sex thing to me. I didn't know what that meant until later but maybe Matilda understood. She was full of anger towards mum and towards me because I didn't feel the same. Some of the little ones would be triggered when I talked with mum. That was very difficult to manage and made me feel very unsafe to meet with her or talk to her on the phone.

She'll never love me. No she'll never love me. No matter what I do. No matter what I say I'll always get it wrong. She'll never be pleased no matter how I try. It will never do. She will never love me she never wanted me, and she'll never love me. I'm too bad to be loved I wish I could go away far away. Make it [the pain] go away let me go away please let me go away.

I was finding it very difficult to spend time with her because of all this turmoil and because of the triggering that was going on. I was out with mum for a coffee. There was no apparent problem and we spent an hour or so together but by the time we parted I knew there was a problem… I did my few errands and then went home even though I'd planned to look around the shops. There was too much pain and distress and I could hear a little voice saying 'the mammy she hurt me'… it made me want to weep because I didn't want to hear anything else especially not about mum. So, I got home as fast as possible and into what I suppose is my safe place... my bedroom. And started to sob….

The mammy... make the mammy go away she hurt me. She hurt me in there I don't like it. Make the mammy go away…

Jesus I can't do this

I am with you my little one, she has nothing to say that you cannot bear in my strength.

My mammy… that mammy, she hurts me she puts the thing in me to make it big, so grandad is happy. It hurt me. Make her go away I don't want the thing in me.

Jesus please….

My child I am here. do not be afraid.

You help her then I can't do it.

I will help her my little one. I will help you both. My love is here for both of you... it is not wrong to grieve my little one. Do not be afraid...
You've got to help me understand... please.
In time my little one this is enough for now.

I knew that Jesus wanted me to forgive her, but I was so confused and unsure about the truth that I couldn't seem to move forward at all.

You cannot forgive her my child until you have admitted the truth, until you see it for what it was.
I know that's true Jesus... perhaps I'm using the fact that I don't know the whole truth as an excuse for not facing this.
My child the truth will be revealed in time. Do not wait for the full revelation before you begin to deal with what you already know.
But if I... deal with what I already know and then I find out there's worse I will find myself back at square one.
No my child you will have laid the foundation for what is to come. You are working towards an end. This will not be an end in itself.

Even though I understood that Jesus was right, I got more and more confused and distressed and the enemy was tormenting me. I think because I was refusing to accept the truth. No matter how difficult it was I did know deep down that it must be true. There was a big battle going on and I needed to choose to trust Jesus. So, I got in the bath but was again just overwhelmed by the most intense pain and grief, and a feeling that it could not possibly be true. How could she have done that... but then I thought really it all comes down to whether I trust Jesus. Do I really believe He would allow this if it wasn't true... hasn't He promised time and time again to reveal truth?

Who do I trust- my God or my mum? So I was on my knees in the water bent almost double with the pain crying out, I trust my God, I trust my God... and then it hit me afresh... that meant it was true and this time I couldn't control it and I just screamed and screamed. But I didn't make a sound, why I don't know but once again they were silent screams... It was a good thing of course because Sophie and Richard were downstairs, and I was not in control at all. Once again, I heard Jesus whisper that He was holding me, and I gradually became calm again. It did feel like He was holding me, preventing me from physically hurting myself, holding me mentally because I did feel on the edge of losing it and emotionally, He brought calm. I would not have made it through that without Him.

Jesus did help me though. He helped me to let go of my need to know and to understand. He helped me to let go of my need to judge whether she was 'bad' or not.

I was reading the passage where David goes into Saul's camp... but chooses not to kill him because its up to God to judge him... David still treats Saul with respect as the king.... It's really not up to me to judge my mum. I don't know the truth, perhaps I never will but even if I did its for the Lord to judge not me.... and having let go of that need to judge whether she's innocent or guilty, good or evil, I am free to honor, respect and love her... no matter what. There's so much freedom in that and so much peace. Where there was intense grief and turmoil there is now peace... sadness yes and no doubt still many tears to be shed... but a sense of peace, nonetheless. Whatever the truth, whatever she did and didn't do I can trust Jesus to bring justice, I can trust Him to reveal whatever truth is needed in order for all of us to find peace and healing. I can trust Him... and whatever the truth is, whether she loved me or hated me, whether she's multiple or not... I still belong to Him... and He loves me and is my security and that's really all that matters. So... I feel like a huge weight has been lifted from me... like I can see again, from darkness to light I suppose.

It took a long time I think before I was ready to hear more of the truth, but Jesus did slowly help me to understand. I wondered for a while if mum had alters too. That would make it easier for me to understand how the person I knew now could have done those things. Maybe she had alters like I did who did bad things and others didn't know about it.

> **My dearest one I understand your confusion, but her behavior now does not mean that the things that you remember, the things that I have revealed to you, are not true my little one.**
> But... I have never understood how the person I see most of the time now could be the same one...the one who hurt me.
> **My little one the human heart is complex and not easily understood, but the person that you see now and the one that you remember, the one who hurt you, are one and the same my little one. They are not different.**
> Not alters?
> **No my little one not alters.**
> That makes it harder to understand Jesus. Not easier.
> **I know my little one but there is no need to be afraid of the truth. My dearest one the things that she did then, the person that you remember, is locked up deep inside and has been forgotten by the person that you see now. I am not speaking of alters my little one, but of a protective mechanism which enables a person to forget the unbearable and to become someone else. It is not the same my little one. The person you remember is still there, she is just not expressed outwardly.**
> It sounds a lot like alters Jesus.
> **But it is not my little one. It is not the same.**

Jesus helped us to see and understand that mum was a victim of her father just like I was. I don't know what happened to her when she was growing up but, in the things, I remembered it seemed to me that she was afraid of him just like grandma was. I had a lot of memories of grandma too of course.

In all of them she seemed afraid. I don't know really how it was between them, how could I, I was just a small child, but I know what I remember and the things he made her do. It never seemed to me that it was what she wanted, only that she was afraid and like her, even though mum was helping that doesn't mean it was what she wanted, or she had a choice about it. In time it helped me a lot to see that. I chose to let go of her, to trust Jesus with her and to forgive. A few years later I talked to Jesus about mum and the things we had learned about forgiveness.

> I remember the thing about mum. We were tormenting ourselves, or maybe it was the enemy who was tormenting us. I don't know with why she did what she did and how could she do it...and struggling to believe it but knowing that at least some of it was true and feeling so much pain about it. I don't think I even realized it was something that forgiveness could help but you took us to that bit in the bible where David has a chance to kill Saul but he doesn't because it is up to you to judge him and he is going to honor the king because he was the king. And we knew you were speaking to us and telling us that we had to surrender mum to you and leave you to judge and know what she did and why she did it. And that we needed to love and respect her because she is our mum no matter what she did. And that should have been really hard to do Jesus but somehow it wasn't because we saw and understood that you are God and we are not and that we could trust you with that. And that was when we forgave her and trusted you with knowing and judging and the pain went, and it was so much better. No more tormenting and we have been able to spend time with her and love her and though it has been a bit scary sometimes because I get hurt easy it has been ok and we never felt that same way again. I just want you to save her and love her Jesus. That's forgiveness isn't it?
> **Yes my little one it is.**
> And I think forgiveness is...you are helping me to forgive... that was a gift to me Jesus.

Maybe to her I don't know but mostly to me because it set me free and... I think brought healing.

Yes my little one it did. My dearest one holding on to the need to judge and to bring some form of punishment to those who have hurt you is to put yourself in my place. That is never a good thing my little one. It twists your soul and brings pain and torment as you have seen.

But what about...like seeing someone convicted of a crime...that's not wrong is it?

No my little one that is not wrong. The criminal justice system allows for punishment to fit the crime my little one and to bring protection from that person committing the same crime again, but it does not mean that you cannot forgive that person my little one.

No... I see...kind of...but no one will ever be put in jail for what they did to me Jesus.

No my little one perhaps not, but that does not mean that there is no justice for you my little one.

No. But I am not very sure what that is. Do I need to know there is justice before I can forgive...I suppose, I trust you to bring justice so...maybe yes?

Yes my little one trusting me will always help you to forgive those who hurt you.

I expect…there will be a lot more forgiving for me to do.

Yes my little one there will. As we journey together you will discover many more people from the past who will need to be forgiven and there will be those in the present who will hurt you my little one and you will need to forgive them also.

You will help me though Jesus.

Yes my little one I will.

I think... You forgive me for all the things I do wrong Jesus and that is a big gift and I am not sure I know how big it is but I think you helping me to forgive those who hurt me, that gift is big too...and maybe I see that a bit better.

My little one I will help you to see and understand the true power of forgiveness both in your life and in the life of others. You are right my little one in saying that it is my gift to you. One of many that must be taken hold of time and time again my little one as you journey with me.

Some people, they don't seem to want your gift Jesus...not either part of it. They don't want forgiveness for themselves and they don't want to forgive either. Why is that?

Sometimes it is because they do not fully trust me my little one, sometimes it is because they are unwilling to face the pain of what was done to them and sometimes my little one it is because they have allowed the enemy to enter their heart and cause it to turn bitter. Bitterness is a terrible thing my little one. It destroys those who have it and has only one cure my little one.

What is that Jesus?

Forgiveness my little one. That is the cure. Forgiveness for their own wrongdoing and forgiveness towards those who have wronged them.

But...they have to see that they need help...they need truth first Jesus. Like with everything I suppose.

Yes my little one they do and as with everything it begins with choice my little one, a willingness to see the truth of the condition of their own hearts.

You helped us to do it Jesus…all of those things. They are all hard and painful.

Yes my little one they are but they are possible, for everyone they are possible.

That is good news.

Yes my little one it is very good news.

I don't remember forgiving grandad Jesus…maybe...it just seemed to happen.

My little one you made a choice in your heart to forgive everyone who hurt you. It is your heart that matters my little one and the choices that you make, the rest follows.

Chapter 11
Treasure in the Darkness

Jesus kept on healing me. I would spend time with him most every day. I did a lot of crying. There was so much pain and grief even when there didn't seem to be any other alters about. Jesus would hold me and love me and comfort me. Sometimes I would hear a song that would touch my heart and I would know it was the truth and I would cry and cry.

> A refuge for the poor, a shelter from the storm.
>
> This is our God
>
> He will wipe away your tears and return your wasted years.
>
> This is our God…
>
> A father to the orphan, a healer to the broken.
>
> This is our God
>
> He brings peace to our madness and comfort in our sadness.
>
> This is our God…
>
> A fountain for the thirsty, a lover for the lonely.
>
> This is our God
>
> He brings glory to the humble and crowns for the faithful.
>
> This is our God…
>
> This is Our God   Chris Tomlin.

It hurt a lot to be loved and comforted. I never had that before. Jesus said that as his love went in the pain came out and that is why it hurt so much. I had to trust him a lot because sometimes it would hurt so very much, and I wanted to run away and not feel it anymore. Jesus gave me the courage I needed. It all came from him, but I had to choose to let him. He never forced me or gave me more than I could bear.

Tell me what you believe about yourself.
Lord…
I will enable you, are you willing?
crying…I want to be willing.
That is enough.
crying… I don't know if I can do it Lord… Everything gets stuck you know, and I definitely don't want to know.
You wish to keep running from the truth.
Yes.
I am truth... If you run from the truth you run from me.
Oh dear…You will have to help me Jesus… crying, there's nothing there right now... crying. I mean nothing.
I know what is there... do not worry... I can do all things... can I not?
Yes… crying.
Then begin...
Well you said yesterday that I believe I am nothing and I can see that's true… crying… that I don't matter, that the fact of my existence makes no difference to anyone...
You think they don't care whether you live or die?
Yes… and no. In my head I see that isn't true because obviously my children love me and

need me and my friends... well I suppose they would miss me… but
Go on...
If I had died before...you know...if you had let me die rather than helping me to survive...
Would that make any difference?
crying… Yes... I suppose.
That is because you do not understand anything of the impact you have had or the impact you will have... that will make a difference for all eternity.
Lord... I can't believe anything that I do is that significant.
I told you, you don't understand... continue.
Then help me Lord because there's nothing there, except fear...
My child the doors are unlocked and open already you have only to go in
Show me how.
Take my hand.
I saw myself taking his hand and he led me through a door into a dark room. The only thing I could see clearly was a baby, naked and lying on the floor, crying. There were lots of other things in the room which I couldn't see with my eyes but... crying... I am unloved and unlovable, I am alone, no-one cares for me, ...crying... I am vulnerable and unprotected... I am not worth protecting...crying... I have no rights, no worth... I exist for the pleasure and gratification of others... crying… I belong to no-one …crying... and no-one wants me, except Satan who wants to use me and cause me pain and I must allow him to do that, because that is my purpose, to serve Satan by allowing him to do whatever he wants. That is my worth and my purpose…crying... Lord that can't be right surely? I mean how can I live for you, with a purpose like that?
Keep looking...
I am an object, not a person, my feelings and opinions do not matter, they do not even exist... crying … I am dirty… shameful… bad… completely corrupt with nothing good in me... crying… Utterly worthless … My life has no good purpose and I can achieve nothing of value... crying… I am waiting to die, that is what I deserve … I am nothing but a pile of shit.
You see my child what you have hidden away, closed the door on and yet what you believe about yourself affects everything
Can we come out now Lord and shut the door?
We can come out, but the door must remain open, these lies will be removed one by one. Only then will the door be shut and sealed so that nothing can ever be put in there again.
crying…
Remember what I told you... What is in that room is not you, only the lies that you have believed about yourself... That is not who you are.
Then why is it so painful?
Because you still believe it.
How do I manage to even keep living believing all that?
By shutting it away my child and not allowing yourself to acknowledge it. Which is where we began.
Yes... Ok
Now you have faced this fear and you have seen the lies we can begin to remove them. Are you willing my child?
Yes…. What will that mean?
It will mean dealing with the source of those lies, with the memories and experiences that you have buried and shut away. There are many rooms my dearest child that we must enter together.
I will do it Lord... with you… please… I need your help. How can I even bear to look?
I will give you the strength and the courage do not be afraid.

I think that a lot of the healing he was doing was to take out the lies and put in the truth. This took a long time because the lies were so deep in my heart and there was so much pain and fear that got in the way. He always told me that pain wasn't the enemy fear was. I don't think I really understood that to begin with, but I understand it a lot better now. It is fear that keeps us from healing. Fear of pain, fear of having to face difficult truths, of seeing ourselves as we really are, fear of change. So many things that we get afraid of. So, we have to choose over and over to face the pain and the fear trusting that it isn't endless, and that healing is happening even if it seems very slow.

Set me free from this life I'm in
From the pain and confusion within
Let me go where it's peaceful
Surrounded by love
Set me free
Wipe up the tears that spill from my eyes
Hold me in your strong arms
Tell of your love
and faithfulness given to me
wipe all my tears away
take all the memories that terrify me
soothe all the anger and fear
pour in the oil of healing and grace
and mend my broken heart
please mend my broken heart

I was determined to push on because it was the only way out that I could see. Jesus once told me he wouldn't take me out of the valley of the shadow of death but that he would walk through it with me. That is what he has done. Of course, I wanted him to take me out. I wanted him to make it stop. I wanted to be healed and free NOW. Either that or to die. Often, I didn't care which it was. But he has been teaching me to be patient and trust that the path he has for me is the best path and if I will follow it there is life and hope and joy and meaning and purpose to be found along it. Sometimes it has been a battle every day to choose the way Jesus has for me.

My little one come.
I don't know... There isn't anything to say I can't talk to you. I don't even want to hear what you are going to say.
My little one my words are life and they are truth do not turn away.
But they seem more like death and lies to me so why would I listen.
Because they are not. my little one I am your hope, there is no hope outside of me.
I know. I think that just means there is no hope. I might as well accept that. I keep... believing there might be, but it doesn't bring anything but pain. There's no point.
There is every point my little one for hope founded in me is not in vain, it is never in vain. Everything I have said to you is the truth my little one. I do not ever lie.
I don't want to cry any more. I don't want to hope any more. I don't want to try and believe that I might ever have any kind of life. It's not true.
It is true my little one I have not lied to you.
I don't know what to say. You know I've wanted to believe that, and I have tried, and I have tried so hard to do everything you asked and believe what you said but I can't not anymore because……. I don't think it is.
My little one do not let the pain you feel rob you of your future.
Why not. You could help me, but you choose not to. Mike could help me, but he chooses not to. Why should it matter to me if it doesn't matter to you? All I want is to be free of all of this. That's all.
My little one do not choose the way of despair and of death. There is hope before you my little one. All that I have promised is before you. I will not let you down but I will fulfil every promise I have made.
I don't know when this time will be Jesus because I don't see... anything... I'm not even sure you care... or are that interested. You seem content to let me drown in all this... stuff.
My little one I am always here for you.
So you say. What is it you want from me?

I want you to trust me my little one, to trust in my love for you and in every word, I have spoken to you.

I've been trying.

Yes my little one you have. Do not give up now.

Why not? Jesus there is no point to this conversation. I feel like you've already let me down. Like you've turned your back on me. I can't do what you are asking me. I can't. I asked you to help me. I asked Mike to help me. The answer was the same as always. No, you're on your own. Alright then. I know how to do that. I know how to survive on my own. It's all this, promise of all the things I can't ever have that I can't handle. It stirs up too much pain for no reason. I don't know why you would want that if you love me. I don't know why you tell me all that stuff about Mike when it makes no difference. There has to be a point where I say that's enough. I've given it my best shot and I can't do any more. So that's where I am.

My little one I know exactly where you are. I see everything my little one and I know you have not given up. I know that you are still hoping in me I know that you are still holding my promises close to your heart and that you long to believe that they are all true. My little one I have not lied or misled you. Everything I have said is true. Hold on to me and don't give up.

I can't. Crying...... It hurts too much. I can't keep believing for all these things I can't see when even the things that are here and now don't seem to be true. You say so much about Mike, but I've never been able to see it. Every time I cry out for help no help comes, no response comes. It's been a long time since I let myself do that, because I know the pain that comes when he doesn't answer. I don't know why I thought it would be different this time, but it's not and I've no reason to believe it ever will be. He won't ever help me or be there for me. I can accept that. I've accepted it about a lot of other people just don't keep telling me to believe all those things because I can't survive the pain of that.

My little one everything I have told you about my servant is true. He does not answer you because I have not asked him to. My little one he is obedient to my voice and will do all that I ask of him because he trusts me. My little one I do not do this because I am unkind or because I wish to confuse you I do it so that you will continue to turn to me. My little one your trust and dependence must be upon me and me alone.

So why is he there then. There's no point to him Jesus, not for me. I'm just wasting his time and he's just causing me pain. Why tell me he's there for me when that is a big fat lie. Why ask me to believe that, it serves no purpose except to cause me pain when it's shown to be untrue as it is time after time. I can't do it anymore. Why should I believe anything you say when that isn't true? Why should I think that any of it is real if the things I should be able to see prove to be the opposite of what you say? If you want me to trust you Jesus I don't think its working.

My little one we have been here many times and each time I have asked you to trust me because I know his heart and I see all that there is to see. My little one I know that you do not understand this still. I know that it brings you pain when he does not answer you but my word to you is true. He is there for you my little one and will always help you when I ask him to.

Well since that doesn't seem to be any time at all my argument still stands. There's no point to him...

My little one will you follow me?

You want me to choose now in this moment when I don't trust you at all and I've had enough.

Yes my little one I do.

Crying.... Please don't do this to me please.

My little one I will not let you go. I understand your pain my little one but do not turn away from me. Keep hoping, keep trusting. I will not let you down.

I can't I can't you are asking something I can't do I can't... Crying... Jesus you are all I have... Crying... I can't live without you but I can't do this...

My little one will you follow me?
I can't.
I will help you my little one. will you follow me?
Please don't ask me that please don't.
My little one my word to you is true. I know you cannot see it and you are afraid. I know you are hurting my little one but will you follow me?
Crying… Why won't you help me?
My little one I am helping you for I know what it is you need. My little one I am holding you so close. I will not let you go. My love will never let you go. This path is not too hard for you my little one for I will carry you through. All you must do is choose.
But what if it's not true… I can't do it… Crying…
Yes my little one you can. I am here. Hold my hand and let me lead you down the path of life that I have chosen for you. My little one I am leading you towards all that I have promised. Do not give up now but choose life. Choose me.
Please just leave me alone leave me alone so I can just die please… Crying…
No my little one I will not leave you. I will never leave you.
I can't do it…. Crying…
Yes my little one you can. Take my hand.
Crying… I know if I do then the pain will just go on and on and I'll have to keep on hoping. I can't do it I can't do it…
My little one look at me. Remember who I am.
Crying… I don't want to, if I do that, I'll say yes… I can't keep doing this. I can't.
My little one my promises are true. Take my hand and follow me. I will lead you to life my little one. Do not take the path of death. Follow me.
Crying… Your way is too hard.
I am with you my little one. I will not ever leave you.
But why won't you help me.
I am helping you my little one. I am helping you in the way that you need the most.
Crying… I don't think I can keep hoping, I don't think I can do it.
My little one I am here with you. I am your hope. Take my hand and walk with me. I will lead you faithfully even through the darkest place where there seems to be no hope. I will not leave you. I will not abandon you. I will fulfil every promise I have made to you. All you must do is take my hand and follow me.
Crying…

Despair makes me quiet
It turns out the light
It closes my eyes
And shuts my ears
Till it's all that there is
Filling me up
Whispers of death
Surrounding me

I couldn't resist any longer and I fell into His arms

My little one I will not let you down. Do not be afraid but rest in me and in my word to you. My little one my promises are true and will all be fulfilled. My servant is all that I have said my little one. Hold on to these truths. Hold on to me. The future is before you as I have said. I will not fail you my little one. I will not ever fail you.
I don't understand you.
I know my little one but my love is true whether you understand it or not. Hold on to me my dearest child. It will not be very long now.
I can't find anything to say Jesus. I wanted you to let me go so I could give up and not do this anymore.
I know my little one but I will never let you go. You cannot push me away my little one. It will not work…
I still don't think I can do it.
I know my little one but you have me and I am all that you need. Rest now my little one and know that I am here with you. I will not leave you but will lead you through everything. Trust in my word to you my little one and do not be afraid to hope for

your hope will not be disappointed.

That was one kind of battle but the battle to accept the truth of the past lasted a long time too. Sometimes I would think I had accepted it and then I would find I was back doubting again. Maybe that happened when more pain and memories started coming to the surface I don't know. I suppose I was always wanting to find a way to escape from it all but there didn't seem to be a way. Not a good one anyway. The only way I could escape from it was to die. I called that Plan B for a long time. Jesus' plan was Plan A but then when I thought that was too hard...impossible or I was just too hurting or confused I would think about Plan B. So I would struggle and pull away from Jesus but always he would draw me back and help me to choose the truth. To choose him and his way for me.

My child I am always speaking to you. I reveal truth to you constantly.
I can't face it, I'm sorry I just can't.
I do not ask you to face it alone my child.
But I am alone... it's the truth about me...crying
It is the truth about all of you, the community that is your system.
I don't seem to be part of that... I'm just here on my own. They each have a burden to bear, terrible some of them... but do they see the whole thing... I don't know... I just know it's too much and I don't know how to see it and still keep… living. So that's why I'm hiding but if I hide from you then I won't make it and I don't want to hide from you…
I am still here my child.
crying… then help me please.
I will strengthen you, keep your attention on me. The enemy is seeking to devour you. He is using the truth as a weapon against you. Do not listen to him the truth will bring you freedom and life. It will not destroy you as you fear. That is what he is telling you. Listen to me my dearest child. I will give you the strength you need. The truth is just that, it cannot be changed but it can and will be redeemed. Cling to that for that is the truth. Do not listen to his lies my child. He seeks to drive you to despair and to separate you from my love and my power in your life. He is afraid my little one. Be encouraged. We will overcome. The truth is your friend and not your enemy.
crying... It's very difficult for me to see that... It's difficult for me to see anything except the horror… and I don't feel anything but grief and despair. How do I survive and not run away? I don't know how to do that.
We do it together my child. Do not turn away from me but trust me to carry you through, giving you all that you need so that you don't need to run. My child you are right I could have brought you, all of you home long ago. I could have let you die; you could be in heaven with me right now, at peace with all suffering ended. But I did not. I have purposely kept you alive. I have planned the road ahead of you. All of your life I have watched over you. I have walked with you, weeping for you my child. I weep for you still. Your time here is not ended. I am with you in your suffering my dearest child. I understand your pain. But I see what you do not. I have prepared wonderful things for you. To bring you home now would mean forfeiting those plans. That is not my desire my dearest child. Travel this road with me though the cost is great. You will not regret it my dear child. Do not give up.
I know it's all your plan, that this is your will for me… crying… help me understand or at least to bear the … I don't know… crying...
My child I have charted your course carefully. Your feet are upon the road I have marked out. This is my will for you. To you it seems illogical but to me it makes perfect sense.
I don't know because I don't always see clearly... I just want to be cared for, not left to fend for myself... crying... I don't know how I will ever be…
My child I see what you do not. I have promised to meet your every need and I will... but in my way.

When I wasn't fighting against the truth, I would rest in Jesus arms and just cry. I didn't know why really a lot of the time there was just so much pain. It never seemed to end. I thought I would never stop crying.

Sometimes it felt like I was drowning in it, that it would swallow me up and I would never come out of it. But I found out that no matter how it felt to me sometimes that I was always held. I was always safe, and Jesus was always in control. I learned slowly that I could trust him with the pain. I learned that I could let him do whatever it was he was wanting to and no matter how much it hurt, I was safe, and I did come out of it. He told me that I would be able to help others because of what I was learning about how I could trust him.

I am tired, but I'd like to try and understand what you're doing... if that's ok.
I want you to understand as much as you can my child and not merely for your sake but for others who will come after you.
What do you mean?
There are many others my child who also require my healing.
Yes... I know.
I do not want them to be afraid. I want you to help them not to be afraid of the pain that comes with healing.
Who are these people, and how can I help them?
You can help them because you have experienced the power of my healing love for yourself my child. There will be many people that I bring to you, many people who are afraid to surrender themselves and trust me with their pain as you have done. You will help them to trust me my dearest child because you will know and understand that no matter how terrible the pain, that I am there with you in it enabling you to bear it and loving you through it.

Even though I was learning to trust him, I didn't want to see or know those terrible things that had happened. I didn't want to face up to the pain of it, but Jesus knew that sometimes it was the only way for me to find freedom from the lies and things that were holding me.

The first thing I saw was that Barbara was rubbing the skin on my knees away with wire wool... so they would appear grazed. This made me tense up and Jesus comforted me and  *reminded me that I was safe and that I needed to relax and let Him in. Then she had the speculum, she was inserting things... I don't know what. Then I saw she was holding something. When I saw what it was, I gasped with horror. I don't know what you call it, but I think they are called a rasp, a metal tool a bit like a long thin cheese grater used for filing down wood or metal. She inserted it so that it cut me, and I bled on the sheet. Then she washed me out with the saltwater. I suppose to stop the bleeding, maybe infection too. And then Jesus said that was enough for today and I cried and cried for a long time.*

Remembering these things and feeling the pain and horror of them often seemed like more than I could bear. There was so much of it day after day and week after week. Somehow Jesus gave me the strength I needed to not run away and to let him heal me.

My little one I am here. Do not be afraid but come to me with everything. My dearest one. I am here with you. I will strengthen you and sustain you through everything my dearest one.

I'm sorry I just don't want to do this anymore. I don't want to face it. I don't want it to be real...crying.

My little one I am here with you. There is nothing you cannot do with me helping you. My dearest one I understand your pain and your fear but all you must do is hold on to me and follow me step by step. Do not worry about what lies ahead but concentrate on what I am giving you today. My little one that is enough. I am here with you. Hold on to me and all that I am. My little one the healing I have for you will come slowly that is true, for it is all that you can bear. But it will come my little one. Do not be afraid of what lies ahead but follow me. I know the perfect way for you. I will not lead you anywhere you cannot go.

Crying... I know... but help me because I don't want to do it anymore. I don't I'm sorry. Please don't make me talk about it please... Crying...

My little one I will only go at the pace you can manage. I am not asking anything of you that you cannot do in my strength. My little one I know you are afraid but do not let that fear keep you from stepping into all that I have for you. My little one there is life before you, even in the midst of all the pain. My little one I would not ask it of you if it were not so. Do not be afraid of anything I will ask of you for it is all working for you my little one. My way is perfect for you. Keep walking then and do not be afraid.

Sometimes he helped me to remember so that he could heal the pain and loss that I had.

Then suddenly I was in a memory and I knew that's what it was. I was standing at the entrance to the graveyard, where some of the abuse happened and it was dark. I knew I was older, in my teens, not a child like in the other memories. I didn't want to see; I didn't know what it was going to be. I was afraid and I said to Jesus please don't make me go in, please don't make me go in...even though I knew I would have to...and that He was with me. And I saw it, the baby, the one I saw in the dream. I'd forgotten about the dream, convinced myself that's all it was. They were burying it...It wasn't very clear, but it was enough...and I understood, I knew that what I'd dreamed or seen before wasn't a birth it was an abortion. And that this was where they did it. In the graveyard... and then I saw Him, standing cradling the baby in His arms. He was smiling and surrounded by light. There were no words, but it seemed to me He was saying that the darkness was gone and that everything had been made right… and then I really cried. The pain hasn't gone but its less anguished... I can still see that scene, but not without seeing Jesus standing there smiling, holding the baby. He is so amazing…. only he could bring light and hope into that.

Usually Jesus chose to heal me when I was alone with him. Maybe that is because he was teaching me to trust him and depend on him for everything. Maybe it is because I didn't have anyone to do that stuff with, not really. But sometimes he would heal me when I went to meetings. I went to quite a lot of events with my friend Ruth. Sometimes the Holy Spirit would just come, and I would be crying and crying. Sometimes I would be prayed for and then he would start to work. Jesus never wasted any opportunity and I tried to give him as many opportunities as I could. I went away with Ruth to the little cabin in the woods quite a few times, even though it was scary because it could be very painful. Sometimes though Jesus chose to heal me in a different and much more enjoyable way, even though it still meant a lot of crying!

When we were outside, we were talking about what we would ask the Lord for… my answer is always the same. I just want Him. I want Him to be real. I want to see reality. While Ruth was getting dressed, I read my daily readings. The one which caught my attention was John 9 & 10... Jesus restored the man's sight, but he was then persecuted for being able to see… I said I don't care Jesus... I want to see...I have to see… and I just started to weep with a kind of desperate longing. Ruth appeared at this point... saying that she just needed His presence… the Holy Spirit had arrived. Within seconds we were both on our faces crying out in complete desperation for Jesus... for His presence... uncontrollable sobbing, complete desperation…. very much like I experienced the week before at the meeting. This went on for some time, until it eventually subsided by which time we were completely wrecked. Ruth heard Jesus say... for both of us, you were worth my life... which is a bit hard to accept... But we were then just surrounded by this profound sense of being loved and accepted... which made us cry again but in a different way. He told us we had touched His heart, that we were His beautiful daughters... makes me cry just remembering it. And for both of us ... it's difficult to describe but we just knew that nothing else matters, only Jesus. He's the only thing worth living for, the only thing worth having... everything else is rubbish (like Paul says) ... and then came a knowing which I expressed as... oh my God, He has put His hand upon us, picked us out and set us apart for His very own... I knew it as surely as I know anything... and it was a fearful and humbling moment... We sat for a long time barely able to move because His presence was so strong... It seemed a little foggy in the room, though outside it was still bright sunshine. We had barely recovered from all of that when we were overtaken by uncontrollable laughter... rolling about on the sofa for no apparent reason... except that to me anyway it felt like I was being tickled on the inside... when this subsided the atmosphere changed again, very perceptibly and I found myself getting very still... I 'saw' angels, two of them with large pitchers from which they were pouring out golden dust... The atmosphere was what I would describe as reverent. Ruth said it was like holy awe. She saw the golden dust, with her eyes, falling between us... spreading out over on us... Gradually the presence lifted. We were so exhausted we actually had to sleep for an hour to recover. This description doesn't do it justice of course...how could it?

There was still the really difficult things he had to show me while I was there. I suppose sometimes I needed time and space to recover from the things he did. Time and space, I didn't have at home.

...then we sat chatting. I could feel His presence quite strongly, but I was feeling terrible, like I just wanted to cry and cry. Except I didn't want to cry at all, so I was trying to ignore it. It just got stronger, and I was getting extremely edgy. We decided to put on some worship music and listen/wait. The feelings got stronger and I began to weep, though I didn't know why except that I suspected a memory was trying to surface. The Holy Spirit was coming in waves and with each wave, it was as if pain was being pushed to the surface. I began to 'see' a memory. I was in my bedroom in the house where I lived with mum and with her sister for a time. I seemed to be hiding in the dark under my bed. I was wearing a blue coat and red shoes which I remember vaguely and have photos of me wearing it. I must have been about six or seven. I say 'I' but it probably wasn't me... though that's how it felt. The memory and the emotions came and went for a time. I was talking to Jesus, He reassured me constantly that He was with me and I could see Him under the bed with her. I asked Him to 'get on with it' but He told me to be patient and wait. He was taking it slowly. Gradually it became more and more vivid... it was clear that I was dressed and ready to go somewhere, somewhere I didn't want to go.

Three men had arrived. I don't know who they were, I didn't see them, they were like dark shadows. She was crying with fear and trying desperately to be quiet, so they wouldn't hear her. I was also crying in fear and pain and trying desperately hard not to make a noise, because I didn't want to disturb/ distress Ruth. They were pulling her out from under the bed and she was crying don't make me go, I don't want to go, please don't make me go... I couldn't tell if she was saying that out loud to them or just crying to herself. At the same time, I was weeping with fear and echoing her, please don't make me go, I don't want to go... because I knew that Jesus was going to take me into a memory, something I didn't want to see. It faded again and I was fully back in the room with Ruth, but I knew I had to go, that Jesus wanted me to go. So I closed my eyes again and asked Him if He was there, He was. It seemed to me He was holding my hand, so close. I said I would go, that He could take me where He wanted me to go. That was the difference I suppose... she had no choice, but Jesus gave me the choice. They walked her/me down the stairs. I was both her and me at the same time, seeing through her eyes but observing as though watching, all at the same time. Jesus was with her, but He was with me too. They took me down the street in the darkness to a car, a kind of boxy, old looking, tan colored car. They put me in the back seat, and I sat at one end with two of the men. I recognized the car from another memory, it may have belonged to 'uncle' John, I don't know. I'm not sure how long the journey was.

We arrived at a large flat open space ringed by trees, there was a kind of stone alter in the middle, which I assume was put there specifically by them. There were lots of other people there, I think. Jesus kept reassuring me that He was with me. By this time Ruth was next to me, holding my hand but I was barely aware of her... unable to respond... I saw/felt them take off all my clothes and put a white robe on me. It hung lose, open down the front. Then they took me to the stone alter and stood me on it. There was something said, that I barely caught, about me being the priestess. Then they put a knife in my hand with a long thin blade.... and the rest was a blur, but I knew suddenly and with certainty what had happened, what I'd done... it was a little girl, just like me.... her blood was on the white robe... and they made me drink. With this knowledge came so much pain and distress it just burst out and I sobbed and sobbed. Jesus held me. Ruth held me. I knew that Jesus was with me, that He loved me, was with me... and I cried. I found myself saying take me home, that's enough please take me home. I didn't want to be alive, didn't think I should be alive, but He just held me....

When I think of it, all that I experienced in seeing that memory, I am glad I chose to go. In spite of the pain and the horror and the shame I didn't feel alone. I wasn't alone and I knew it. Perhaps more than I ever have. I said to Ruth 'I wasn't alone.' I think with a kind of amazement or wonder. She thought I meant her, but I meant Jesus. I'm glad she was there but if she hadn't been, I wouldn't have been alone. He didn't leave me, even though I felt as if He should, He just held me and comforted me. I could feel His strength flowing into me as I cried out to Him... He didn't leave me. He didn't turn away in disgust or horror He just kept on loving me. That really is treasure in the darkness. I'm glad I chose to go.

I was learning that no matter how deep the darkness was Jesus was always there in it with me. He never left me. He showed me so much love in those places. He showed me that He is my treasure.

I will go before you and will level the mountains. I will break down the gates of bronze and cut through bars of iron. I will give you the treasures of darkness, riches stored in secret places, so that you may know that I am the Lord, the God of Israel, who summons you by name.

Isaiah 43:2-3

Chapter 12
Plans and Purposes

Jesus was right when he said it was a long journey. To me it seemed endless and a lot of the time it seemed hopeless too. Sometimes it seemed like I couldn't take one more step.

Jesus
Well you already know everything I'm thinking and feeling and all the reasons for it which are many. The point is I'm done. I can't do this anymore. If you want this to happen so much, then it can't depend on me so now you do something ok. You've made a lot of promises you tell me you are everything that I need. Ok let's see it because right now all I have is me in my little pieces with nowhere to run. I cannot do this on my own which is what you seem to think. None of the alters are interested either in healing... that is Mike or Julie, nor are they interested in helping in any way that's constructive with outside life. I don't know what they are doing but its not that. So what am I doing? Mike as usual isn't around. I don't know what his definition of abandonment is but its not the same as mine. He doesn't reply to me... he doesn't reply to the alters. I've just been left to deal with them, help them by myself. I can't keep going like this. How many times do I have to say this and beg for help? You stand me back on my feet but nothing changes and so I end up on my face again. What's the point what are you trying to prove? I'm not getting it whatever it is. There is no point going any further like this because I can't do it. How many times do I have to prove it to you... and anyone else who's paying attention I need some help I need some reality. Nothing is real. Everything is still just voices in my head...memories of alters...you...Mike even. Nothing real about any of them. What am I doing with my life... day after day I sit here writing... talking to voices... You, demons, alters... and the illusive man. What a waste of time. What is it for? Is this supposed to be helping? Are we supposed to be healing…it's not happening…and the truth? What's that? How can I ever know the truth? Even if somehow it was revealed through memories or alters it would still be unreal...like the rest of it. I can't live like that. I know I should have more faith, be more courageous and all the rest of it but I'm just one little messed up person. You're the God here, you sort it out. I'm not doing another thing until you show me that this is real and that you are going to help me through whatever that means because I have had enough. No more.

I had had enough. I wrote to Mike to say goodbye because I didn't think I could do it anymore. I don't remember if I was surprised that he wrote back, but I was surprised by what he said.

Hello Jennifer

I do not say goodbye because I think that there is much yet to do together for the Lord...much to learn and share...not only for you, but for your alters as well. I receive letters like this often from my clients when the journey gets tough and seems endless, with no improvement in sight. But the Lord is with you as you know and will bring you through this today and probably many times ahead. Do not give up on Him as He will not give up on you. His love and purpose for your life is very real and true and you can depend on the truth that is in Him alone.

I will catch up on questions from your alters this week and next, as I have time available, while you rest from sending me anything for a week or two. Contrary to some who have attacked you with lies...I do believe your stories of abuse... your conversations with the true

Jesus Christ, as well as evil pretending to be Him so as to cause confusion and disbelief. He is stronger than them and will continue to offer His strength for you to grow and continue. The enemy will not give up their fight, until you are with Him eternally or He returns. I will continue to be your friend and offer counsel as He leads me. I believe He has me waiting to write often instead of immediately, because He wants your full dependence upon Him and not on me. He has plans for you to affect many for His glory and He must have first position for all support to accomplish that.

One day we will meet as partners in ministry more than pastor/counselor and client. I mentor several clergy couples and individuals around the world, and I foresee that you will be in that group of relationships soon. Be ready at a moment's notice to return to His side, as the enemy is already preparing to move against you, the further away from Him you move. You may want to quit, but they won't let you as they increase their attacks at deception...for they already have heard some of the plans He has for you. He will give you rest in Him. Trusting in Him to sustain and empower you.

Pastor Mike

What he said gave me some hope, that there was something ahead for me after all. I didn't know what he meant by 'partners in ministry' but it helped me enough to decide to keep trying to follow Jesus. Over the next few months Jesus started to talk to me more and more about the future he had planned for me. He had told me lots of things before of course and I hadn't forgotten them, but they didn't seem very real in the middle of everything I was going through. Jesus told me that I would write a book about my story and that the things I was writing to Mike would be a part of that.

When you say all this stuff, I'm writing I suppose you mean my letters to Mike?
Yes, my little one. That is part of their purpose.
And you want to… publish those?
In time my little one… Come my dearest one I know your thoughts already
Well I suppose... I mean I'd suspected., you dropped enough hints.
Yes my little one I have been speaking to you about this in many ways.
I can see why... because it does show... you, but... it shows me too.
Yes my little one it does, it is necessary that you should be seen in order that I can be seen.
I... don't know how well I'll cope with that.
I will be all that you need my dearest one.
What about... my mistakes… I know I don't always hear you perfectly and probably some of your words are really my words.
My dearest one I am big enough to cover your mistakes. Do not worry about that.
And Mike?
He is part of this too my little one as I have said.
Well yes... because they are letters written to him… there's a lot of stuff in there... well I've spent a lot of time talking to you about him.
He is willing my dearest one.
And... you want me to keep writing... How long?
Until my work in you is complete my dearest one for the full story must be told.
But... that could be years.
Yes my little one.
That's a lot of writing... a big book.
It is a story worth telling my little one. I know how it will be.
And the speaking… I'm terrible at public speaking. I hate it. Is that what you are talking about?
I want you to share your story with my church. I want you to tell them in your own

words all that I have done my little one. I want you to share who I am in your life. I will be with you my little one. I will help you. I will give you the words and the boldness you need.

But... the abuse.

My little one you will not always carry the pain and the shame that you do now. I will enable you to share all that is necessary.

No-one will believe it…Crying…

My little one many will not believe the truth of the abuse or of your testimony of my work in your life for they are blind and cannot see the truth. My little one do not be afraid. I will be with you. I will strengthen you and enable you to withstand everything that comes against you. I will not leave you alone. My dearest one your trust in me will enable you to withstand all the attacks that come your way. I will give you all you need.

I don't know... if they don't believe it... what's the point?

Some will believe my dearest one, some will see. Each one is precious to me. Each one is worth the price.

It's hard not to feel afraid of what you are asking.

I know my little one, but I will give you the courage you need.

Why are you telling me this now?

My little one there is much still for you to face, much for you to overcome. You are on a long and difficult path. It will help you to see some of the reasons I am asking you to do this. It will help to give you purpose and direction.

I have a lot of questions.

Yes my little one. Ask them all.

How does Mike fit into this?

He will be with you my dearest one, helping you, guiding you. Sharing his wisdom and his love with you. You will not be alone. I do not ask you to stand alone my little one for I will always be with you and I have also given you my servant to stand by your side…

I'm sorry... I'm afraid.

My dearest one there is nothing to fear. I am asking much but I will give you more than enough, I will enable you in everything.

Help me not to run away.

I am with you my dearest child. I have told you this because I know that it will help you though it is hard for you to hear. I am preparing you for many things my little one for I have much for you to do. This is only the beginning.

What do you mean?

That there is more my little one but that it is not yet time to reveal this to you. Accept what I have said for now. Know that I will use your life and your testimony for my glory. That I am doing many things and preparing many things…

I don't know what to say.

My little one I am here for you. Rest a little now.

It did frighten me to think about what Jesus said but really it wasn't so new. When he was filling up the treasure box before he started to reveal the truth, he had told me.

> *A vision... I'm standing on a very small raft facing Jesus, holding on to him. We are in the middle of a river... the water is cold and laps over the side of the raft which seems in danger of sinking. The water gets rougher and rougher and the sky darker. I wrap my arms around him, and he holds me tight. He tells me to open my eyes and look around. I let go a little trusting him to hold me and I look around. There is a storm raging. The water is very rough, the sky is full of black clouds and lightening is flashing. Jesus shows me all this- he's not perturbed and, in the distance...there is a*

small patch of blue sky and sunshine. The raft runs aground on a very small beach. We climb a grassy bank and look down into a valley where I can see thousands of lights...a vast city. We make our way down to it. The buildings are tall and dark, the streets are dark. We make our way into the city until we come to a church, an old church with the feel of a castle with a drawbridge. It is lit up and seems to be on a small hill. We go inside. It smells like an old church and looks like an old church. I fall to the floor as the power of the spirit hits me. I look up at Jesus. He and the spirit are embracing, communing, perfect unity, perfect joy. The spirit intertwines and envelopes Jesus in golden light (this is the most beautiful thing I have ever seen). Jesus reaches down and pulls me in. The golden light fades but now we are moving as one. I am in Jesus and he is in me and there is no distinction. People start to stream into the church through many doors. They are covered in grey blankets. They are coming to Jesus/me. As we touch them the grey blankets fall away and there is light, light in their faces. I see light spreading from the church, throughout the whole city which is now light and full of life and joy.

While I was trying to accept these things the lady preacher who had stopped in the middle of her message to tell me that I was called to be an evangelist came to visit my church. I was scared. I was very scared that she would give me some kind of public prophesy in front of people who knew me. That she would give me away and they would know. Of course, that didn't make much sense because any prophesy would come from the Holy Spirit who didn't want to hurt me but help me...but I was still scared. I wrote to tell Mike what happened.

I had prayed repeatedly and very specifically... Lord PLEASE no prophetic word, at least not publicly. PLEASE. Not hard to guess what's coming is it. She stands up to give the message and immediately points to me and says she's been getting a word for me all day (so much for my hiding) ... so she gives me this word in front of the whole congregation... and it was quite long... And I was getting redder and redder and tenser and tenser and wishing for some kind of trap door to open up in the floor... and then she gets everyone to pray for me. I should just add that this was the only prophetic word she gave in the service...Not really what I had in mind... so much so that it's almost funny. Almost. So anyway, this is what she said, as far as I remember it ...

She said she'd got the word 'healing' repeatedly and that she felt it referred both to the healing the Lord was doing in me and the healing the Lord would do through me. She said she'd then seen a stone... a precious stone which was a kind of amber color, but it wasn't amber it was topaz. She said the Lord was chiseling and working on this stone so that it could reveal the light within... She emphasized that the light was coming from deep inside and had nothing to do with the outside... And that the light was the glory of the Lord. She wasn't sure what the significance of the topaz was though she felt it was significant, she mentioned that in Revelation topaz is one of the foundation stones of the holy city and also on the breastplate of the priest. As I said she then prayed over me, but don't ask me what because I'd lost the plot by then.

I think I realized something today... maybe, I don't know, about that word I was given on Saturday... and the reason it was given publicly which I hated but Jesus clearly had a purpose for... It was something I half thought at the time and dismissed but it came back to me today... it sounds a bit wrong, but it was almost as if Jesus was bragging about me... because He's proud of me and all that I will become. Does that sound wrong? I don't know... but that's kind of how it felt and was probably part of the reason I wanted to crawl under my chair and hide... I don't know it doesn't seem possible but that is how it felt.

I found out that the amber colored topaz is considered to be the most valuable, that the name topaz means fire and that the stones become electric when heated... electricity suggests power to me. I don't know if that means anything in the context of what I'm talking about, but Jesus chose that stone for a reason.

I spent a lot of time asking about the future. I didn't see how it could work. Jesus said that eventually all the alters would be blended into one and that I would hold the full truth of everything that had happened. I didn't see how that could be. How could anyone hold all of that and survive...that surely was the whole point of being multiple, that it wasn't possible. He said I would live openly and that the people around me would know the truth...but I didn't see how that could work at all. If I was going to tell my story and live openly, I was worried that the children, Sophie and Richard and mum and the rest of the family would find out. That made me very afraid because more than anything I wanted to protect them from the terrible truth. Jesus just kept telling me to trust him. I asked about how I would live and whether I would have to get some kind of job, even though I didn't feel like I could do anything...but he said no. He said my whole life would be given over to the ministry he had for me. I wouldn't have time for anything else. I didn't see how that could work either. He told me that he was going to send me away from all the things and people I had known but I didn't understand that either. Where would he send me and what about Sophie and Richard? I couldn't just leave them. His plans made no sense.

These things were hard enough to understand but it was the things he said about Mike that worried me more. I was so afraid I was making it up. I didn't want to hear it because then I would have to write and tell Mike and I felt afraid and ashamed of what he would think of me.

What do you want to talk to me about?
I wish to talk with you about my servant Mike.
I really don't want to talk about him again. I don't. Please...
My little one this is important. Listen to what I have to say…
Alright.
My little one your path and Mike's path will increasingly come together until they are running side by side. Your destinies are joined, connected in many ways my little one.
Must we?
Yes my little one for I know that you are still full of doubt and fear about this.
Yes. I am. For lots of reasons. Jesus how am I meant to believe this? You won't even let him write to me... I don't get it.
My little one I have many reasons for the things I have him do but that does not mean that he overlooks you or that you are not important.
Why are we talking about this? You know it makes me afraid. I don't want to talk about this please.
My little one the time is near when things will begin to change. I do not want you to resist this when it comes.
I will do my best to be obedient to everything you ask of me.
I do not want you to be obedient in your actions only, but willing in your heart also my little one. And I do not want you to be afraid.
I don't understand you. I don't understand why you are doing this now. Why now?
Because he is part of your future. The future you are struggling to see and are so fearful about. I do not want you to be full of fear I want you to know that you can trust me.
Jesus... It would help me more if you told him and let him tell me. Then I wouldn't panic about making it up... or feel ashamed for all the reasons I've said already. Why don't you just do that. Please. If you want me to know.
My child I want you to trust that you hear me, that you know my voice. I will be speaking to Mike also for this concerns him closely but my child I want to speak with you personally about your future and the things I have for you.
You said you were going to reveal things in a way that wouldn't shame or embarrass me...
And so I will my child. Do you feel ashamed or embarrassed?
No... I think I'm past caring. If I'm getting it wrong or making it up, then so what. He knows what I am anyway.
Yes my child he sees you for who you are but he does not see what you see.

It doesn't matter what he sees or doesn't see.
My little one do not give in to your despair. I know my little one that you are struggling, and you do not feel able to really believe anything I am telling you, but I am the truth and you do hear me.
I'm not sure what I believe any more. I feel very lost and confused. I'm holding on to you but I'm not sure who you are.
I am all you have believed me to be my little one. Do not be afraid.

I had a lot of trouble with Jesus plans for me even though I didn't know really what he meant. Like always Jesus asked me to share my thoughts and feelings with Mike. Of course, it wasn't just my thoughts and feelings...but it was hard to tell, who was who, back then.

Hello Mike
I don't think I'm afraid that you will embarrass or shame me, I'm not even sure how you would do that, but I am afraid that I will be embarrassed or shamed in front of you, even more than I am already. I suppose that's how I feel most of the time. I am so ashamed of the things that happened, of what was done. Logically I know that isn't my shame, but logic doesn't have much to do with that. I feel dirty and disgusting and naked... all the time. I'm ashamed of how I am now... of what it's made me, and I know that every time I write you see that, you see me, and it makes me want to crawl under a rock, but I can't. I think believing that I will never have to talk to you or look you in the eye helps me to cope with that. But then Jesus talks about the future and it's like I can't get away from you, which isn't anything to do with you it's all to do with how I feel about myself - sometimes I can see that. I don't know what He means when He says you are part of my future, but I get afraid that you will think I'm making it up because of some weird, needy, fantasy thing I've got going on in my head.... I'm afraid to imagine anything because I'm afraid that's what I'm doing, that I'm making things up... because I've spent my whole life making up 'futures' in my head so that I could survive the present. I'm so afraid to want anything, because I know I can't have it. So when He says He's going to say things about the future I'm afraid He'll say things that involve you and then I have to send that to you and I'll feel ashamed and embarrassed because I think I must be making it up. I'm sorry I hope that makes sense. I'm not worried you will shame me... I'm worried I will shame myself.

Mike didn't seem very worried by what Jesus was saying, but it was hard for me to really know what he was thinking and I always feared the worst...that he didn't want me or thought I was making it up so that he would finally pay attention to me. But Jesus kept on talking to me. It was like he was dropping hints or leading me one step at a time towards the thing that he wanted to tell me but that I was so afraid of hearing.

Jesus.
Yes my little one I am here.
There's an obvious question I want to ask but I am afraid to ask... I'm afraid to be seen asking it and I'm afraid of the answer.
My little one I know your fear and I know all your questions. Ask me my little one and do not be afraid.
I am afraid.
Nevertheless, my little one.
Well... you are telling me that I will leave everything... but you haven't said where I will go.
No my little one I have not.
Are you willing to tell me Jesus... where you are sending me?
I am willing my little one, if you will ask.
Why must I ask?
My little one do you remember what I said to you about taking risks, learning to trust

in the place of vulnerability.
Yes... I do.
Come then my little one. Trust me and ask your question.
Well... It's hard not to come to the conclusion that you are sending me to America, to be where Mike is. Is that where you are sending me?
My little one I have been speaking to you about this for a long time and you have resisted me and all that I have been saying, for you have been afraid have you not.
I'm still afraid.
Yes my little one I understand your fear but you do not need to be afraid. My dearest one I have told you many times that you will be with my servant. That you will be where he is. I will send you to him my little one. That is where I am sending you.
To America?
Yes my little one. To America. Do not be afraid for I am there also.
Mmm... I know... Sorry.
My little one I know you are afraid of what I am asking of you both now and in the future but there is nothing to fear my dearest one. My servant will welcome you as I have said.
But... I can't even speak to him without feeling sick.
My little one I am at work. You will come to love him and trust him as your friend and your brother. Fear will have no place in your relationship my little one for though the enemy will try to cause you to be afraid and mistrust him yet as you both cling on to me I will enable you both. It will be all that I have said my dearest one.
It's such a long way away... Crying...
Yes my little one I know and yet I will be with you. I will bring such good things into your life my little one. Do not be afraid... My dearest one come and hold on to me. I know what I am asking of you. It will not be too much for you my dearest one for I will give you the strength and the courage you need. I will bring such blessing to you through the life that you will lead there.
Crying... Jesus I love you.
Yes my little one I know you do. Hold on to me and trust me. I know what I am doing.
Crying... Why must I go?
So that you can fulfil my plans for you my little one. So that my purposes in your life can be accomplished for it is in partnership with Mike that you will do and be all that I have purposed for you.
I don't understand that. I'm afraid of that.
Yes my little one I know. I know it would be easier for you if I told you I had things for you to do alone for that would be familiar to you but that is not what I have for you my dearest one. It is not my desire for your life. Accept my will for you my dearest one for it is better than anything you could think of.
And why are you telling me now Jesus... because it must be... some way in the future.
It is not so far away my little one and I am preparing many things for much change is coming my little one as I have said, and I am preparing many things. You must trust me and hold on to me my dearest one. I am showing you these things so that you are not troubled by them and can begin to accept them even as I begin to lead you towards them. Do not be afraid my little one.
What about... the children... mum?
I have not forgotten my little one. Trust me with them. Trust me to work out my purposes in their lives as I work in yours.
It's just... how can I go... and leave them. I mean I can leave mum but what would I tell her?
My little one I know all things. I know how it will be, how it must be. I will show you the way. Do not be anxious about Sophie and Richard for I will be with them... My little one do not fear the things I will ask of you for many things must change as I have said. You cannot yet see how it will be possible for you to accomplish all that I

have said but I know the way. I know all things. I am making a way my little one.
Ok...
Come my little one.
I'm afraid of what Mike will think, say.
Yes my little one I know but do not be afraid for I am speaking to him also. He hears me my little one.
I think I will need to come back to this.
My little one I will be here. I want you to be at peace with this for you have much to do and much to overcome before it can come about.

I was very afraid of what Mike would say. For what seemed a long time he didn't say anything and when he did, he didn't really seem like he believed it... to me anyway maybe because I was so afraid, he would think I was making it up or even that I was hearing the enemy. Jesus didn't help much because he didn't seem to want to say anything to Mike about it. That was confusing and scary and I didn't know what to believe. But Jesus never changed his mind or said it had been a mistake. His plan was to send me to America to be with Mike and work with him to tell my story and show people who Jesus is. Sometimes his plan gave me hope. It gave me hope that all the things I had been through would be used for good. That it would somehow be worth it, the past and even the present because often the pain of healing was so great. It gave me hope that there was a plan and that maybe there was something better ahead for me. But there was a lot of fear too. I didn't see how any of it was possible. I didn't understand how any of it could ever happen. I was very afraid that Mike wouldn't want me and that I would just be a nuisance. I was afraid of what it would mean if I had to depend on him for the things I needed. I still had a lot of trouble trusting him even at such a big distance and the thought of being with him and talking to him was terrifying a lot of the time. I was afraid to go to a different country where everything was different and strange. I was afraid I wouldn't be able to do all those things Jesus said and be all those things he said. It all seemed too big and impossible. Most of all I was afraid about leaving Sophie and Richard and even friends. I thought they would hate me for going and wouldn't understand at all. I thought I was going to lose everything and everyone. I wanted to know when and how it was going to happen. I wanted to know it definitely was going to happen. Jesus had told me his plan but a lot of the time I didn't like it and I was very afraid.

I have told you many times my dearest one that I will use your life to bring me glory. I will do this through the power of your testimony my little one for I am giving you such a powerful testimony to my love and power and grace. This will require you to trust me with everything you have for the world will not be willing to receive such a testimony. The world has never been willing my little one. But I will hide you in my love and give you all that you need as you follow me. There are those who will come against you and try to pull you down, but I will enable you to stand my little one. Do not be afraid of anything that comes against you for I have overcome the world and I am with you and for you. Your testimony will be both written and spoken my dearest one. The words you are writing, all that you have written and will write are to be shared my little one as I direct, when the time is right. I want them to see who I am through your eyes and through all that I have said and done in your life my little one. I know that you are afraid, but I will be with you my little one. This is your work for me, this is your offering of love for me, to let the world see my little one. To let them see all that I have done. My little

one I will never leave you. There is nothing that can come against you but that I allow it and everything I allow I use for good my little one. There is nothing to fear.

Your testimony will not only be written, it will be spoken also for the power of the spoken word is not yet understood by you. I will use you greatly, to speak to my church of the things you have learned, of who I am and all that I have done my dearest one. I will make you able do not be afraid. The church needs to see who I am and the nature of the enemy they face. They need to understand what is at stake my dearest one and be shaken out of their apathy. I will use your life to do this my dearest one. Do not fear what they will say and do *[at this point I had a picture in my mind... what I saw were many snakes coming straight for me as they were disturbed out of their hiding places]* I know my little one that you see what I am showing you but you will trample on the snakes in my name. No weapon formed against you will prosper as you stand in who I am. My dearest one I tell you these things so that you can choose to follow me. This knowledge is not too much for you to bear my dearest one. It will help you when you cannot see where you are going. Know that I am in everything. I am working through everything. I will never leave you my dearest one. I never will. Do not fear anything I will ask of you for I will give you my strength and my grace. My arms of love will be around you supporting and strengthening you in everything.

Chapter 13

AJ

The healing continued but Jesus changed what he was working on to the more recent stuff. He started to heal the things that happened when I was married. He had me write the whole story down and helped me to understand and see it better. He helped me to forgive my husband and myself too. My marriage wasn't very good. My husband didn't seem to love or care about me very much, only really about himself. We had two children, but he wasn't very interested in them after a while. It was difficult as well because Richard was diagnosed with special needs when he was two. He couldn't communicate like children normally do so he got upset and frustrated a lot of the time. That meant a he did lot of screaming and was very difficult to manage. His future didn't look very good and there was a lot of grief for me in that too. My husband just seemed to get angry and didn't do anything to help Richard or me. I was afraid of what he would do if I left him alone with the children, because he got so angry with them. There were lots of other problems too of course and eventually I left, and we got divorced but it was very difficult along with trying to care for two little children and Richard needed a lot of extra care and attention with therapy groups and hospital visits etc. Jesus took me through it all and did a lot of healing.

I didn't really notice it for a while, but Jesus was doing something else too. I had thought for a while that maybe Jennifer wasn't my name at all and I was confused about the way I was sometimes. I felt more like a child than an adult some of the time and more and more I didn't recognize who I was. Mike started to call me AJ because those were my initials and that seemed better somehow. For a while I didn't really understand that Jennifer and Aj were different people, but Jesus was beginning to show us Aj as different to Jennifer. For now, Jennifer thought she was AJ...AJ thought she was Jennifer. I think to both of us felt like we were both Jennifer and AJ. We were very confused for a long time.

I didn't sleep very well... still feeling poorly and too much going on in my head. Around 5am I was awake and found myself thinking about this person that I seem to be... that I don't recognize. This person... who you call AJ isn't the person I thought I was, that person (Jennifer), the one who everyone but you know would not be crying and getting anxious... she would just get on with it. That's the person I think of as being me, but now it seems that's not me at all, it's just the me I've been pretending to be... so I spent some time thinking about that and how I don't want to be AJ because she's... the way she is. I don't particularly want to be Jennifer either... She's more together and copes a lot better but she spends a lot of time keeping safe... AJ isn't that good at protecting herself....

Jesus was showing us in lots of ways that Jennifer and AJ weren't the same.

I know that this will sound strange and I don't understand it, but I think I saw AJ in my mind as it were. I was making lunch and thinking about how protective I feel towards AJ, then suddenly I saw her. She was sitting on a stone step, kind of in the shadows. She was hugging her knees and looking at the ground so I couldn't see her face, because she had longish straight brown hair that was hanging down. She looked young, I am guessing mid teens and she looked very forlorn and kind of... thin I suppose. Understand that this body has never been thin (more's the pity). She looked neglected and shabby. I thought maybe I was imagining her but then I realized the clothes she was wearing were like something people wore in the late seventies- long wool socks and a plaid kind of skirt and a jumper, very plain and dull colors. I suppose that would be about right. I don't think I was imagining it. It's strange to see her because in a way I am her, even though I am Jennifer. I don't understand it. So I think that is who AJ is.

Jennifer had started to chat online with Mike once a week. Just typing not seeing or speaking. That was very scary. I expect Jennifer would have been ok with it, if it had just been her but AJ was very afraid. She would sit and shake and cry a lot of the time. I was very glad he couldn't see me, but it was hard not being able to see him. I struggled to trust that he wanted to talk with me or bother with me at all. I thought he wanted me to go away. I don't think he did, but that is what I thought. We were still very mixed up... Jennifer and AJ when we talked to Jesus about it... it was Jennifer and AJ talking about themselves.

I think I got afraid yesterday...because I started to see how things would be different without her, how I would have to stop pushing everyone away and all of that.
Yes my little one that will come in time. For now I want you to let AJ be seen and accepted by yourself and by my servant Mike. I will keep you safe my little one. Jennifer will still be there to help you in your life for she has many skills that you need. But my little one I want you to try and keep Jennifer away from your relationship with my servant for he has not come to help her but to help you.
What you are saying is that I mustn't try to protect myself when I'm with him?
Yes my little one. Let him see the real you. Trust him and do not listen to Jennifer for she will be full of reasons to hold him at a distance. But he is safe my little one.
Jesus I am going to find that difficult.
Yes my little one but I will help you. Choose to be yourself my little one and trust me to keep you safe ... Come my little one share your thoughts with me.
You know them already.
Yes my little one but sharing them with me will help you.
I'm thinking, wondering about these chats... I've no idea what to expect, what we are going to talk about... he knows everything already.
My little one you are not chatting to give him information you are building a relationship.
Why?
Because that is part of your healing my little one, to learn to be in a relationship.... AJ does not yet have any friends.
Crying…. that's because nobody would love her.
My little one that is why you need this. You are loved my little one but you need to receive it. Being loved will bring healing my little one. You need this.
But I'm afraid.
Yes my little one I know. To be seen for who you are is frightening for you. You have been protected for so long my little one. But my servant will not hurt you.
Crying…
Speak my little one.
I'm thinking about how AJ, me…. how I feel more like a child. Crying…. I can't …. Crying….
My little one I am with you. I will keep you safe. Come my little one tell me.
I feel like a child... Crying… who needs to be held... Crying… And loved.... And it makes me afraid and ashamed because I'm not a child... Crying…
My little one you never received any of the things you needed as a child. You need to have those needs met in order to grow and to blossom into who you are meant to be. Do not be ashamed my little one. For I will love you and meet every need that you have. Do not be ashamed to be a child for I love my children. My little one your child-like qualities will be an asset to you in my kingdom. The world may view them with disdain, but I do not. I will enable you to live both as a child and an adult my little one, wise in the ways of the kingdom and yet with the trust and dependence of a child. Do not fear this my little one for it is in this way that I will work through you to do so many things.
Crying… I don't know who I am. Who I will be? Crying...
You are my child. My beloved one. That is who you are my dearest one. You are not

any of the things that you have believed yourself to be but you are all that I create you to be. Hold on to me my little one…… My little one do not try to hide the pain or the fear that you feel for I see it all. I know my little one that you feel vulnerable and afraid but you will not be hurt. My servant will not hurt you but will love you with the love that I give him. Do not hide from him my little one … My little one.

I'm afraid he won't like me. I'm afraid he will leave me. I'm afraid I won't be good enough or something and that he'll get impatient. I'm afraid I won't know what to say... or that I won't be able to say anything.

My little one he understands all of this. He will not leave you. He does not come expecting anything of you...he comes to help you and to share my love with you. You do not have to be anything but yourself.

But...

My little one he will not leave you…

I'm worried about all the times I go blank… that I won't be able to think.

Then tell him my little one.

But...

My little one you do not have to be anything with him. Just be who you are. That is all.

I don't know how to do that.

Yes my little one I know. I will be helping you. It will come.

I was thinking about Julie.

Yes my little one I know but he will not run away, he will not leave you… He will be AJ's friend and companion.

Crying…. She doesn't deserve to have any friends.

My little one you have believed that for so long but it is not true. AJ is my child, my beloved child. Allow me to show her how loved she is, how special she is…

I think I'd like to stop this conversation ... I'm sorry.

My little one we will go at a pace that you can manage. Do not be afraid for I will take you down the path to healing. You are my beloved child and I will bring you through.

I'm finding it hard to accept AJ.

Yes my little one I know but it will come. Do not be anxious but allow me to work.

How can I be so damaged?

My dearest one you have survived great evil, evil which was designed to destroy your very self. You have survived and now I am healing and restoring you. Do not be surprised at what the enemy has achieved but focus upon me and all that I can do. I will bring you through to newness of life my little one. You will be all that I desire you to be.

It's just the further we go, the more you reveal, the worse I can see it is.

Yes my little one for we must uncover the damage in order for it to be healed but do not be discouraged for I am well able. Look to me my little one. I am your healer and you savior. I am doing great things.

Now when I look at our conversations with Jesus, I can see that they had changed, and it wasn't all Jennifer any more talking to him. Jesus talked to us all at once because we were so mixed up together. At first the person who answered him was Jennifer, but now that was changing to AJ. Jesus was always in control and knew exactly who was who, but we didn't. Not for a long time.

So now there was Jennifer and there was AJ. Now I was learning that I wasn't Jennifer at all, that I was AJ, even though I didn't really understand what that meant for a long time. The other alters seemed to have gone back inside and Jesus told us that he had closed the door for now. When Jennifer saw me sitting on the step... she saw me sitting on the doorstep of the door that led to the inside. Jesus said it was me, Aj, that needed to be writing and chatting with Mike. That was very scary for me, to be seen and to do anything without Jennifer was strange and frightening. It was frightening to see myself as different to her. When I wrote to Mike for the first time, that was very strange because it was like I could hear my own voice for the first time... I was talking for myself and saying what I thought in my own way with my own words.

Hello Mike
This is difficult and frightening and I have no idea what I'm going to say or even if I'm any different. I know there's things I want to say sometimes but I haven't been allowed. I don't know if I want to say them now. I know that Jesus is my best friend and that He says you are my friend too. I want you to be my friend, but I don't want to be a nuisance and I don't know if you would like me. I'm not sure anyone would like me. Except Jesus. I think He likes me. I hope all of this makes sense to you. I'm not sure I understand it. I'm not sure I understand anything very much. It's all very confusing but maybe you understand how I can be two people at the same time. It's hard for me not to hide behind her, but Jesus says He wants me to talk to you myself because this is the real me. Not the one that everyone else sees. Jennifer tells them about me sometimes, that's ok sometimes, but nobody gets to see me or talk to me. Just Jesus and now you.
I'm worried because I need you to be kind and patient. I still don't really know who I am or how to be with people. I might get upset a lot. I don't know. Jesus says you are kind and patient, sometimes I think you are angry with me. Please don't get angry with me and please don't send me away. Not even to Jesus. If I need to run away, I will always run to Him... and He's always there waiting for me when I am running away. I don't think you need to worry about me. It's nice that you are but I don't think you need to. I'm feeling better about our chats. I don't feel sick anymore. Please be patient with me because I might be afraid... and I don't know how it will be without Jennifer because this feels very strange. I already want her to come back, I want her to come back and be 'normal' again. But Jesus says that's not really me, this is. I think that's what He said anyway. Maybe when I'm better I will be like her again but maybe not. I can't tell what I will be like I'm not even sure what I am like. I feel like I'm going on too long now so I'm going to stop. Maybe I will come back again later on and write some more. Please be nice to me.

I started to chat online with Mike too. That was kind of hard at first because it seemed difficult to get past Jennifer and be AJ and I got scared very easy and then Jennifer would be in control again, because I ran away even though I didn't mean to. It was strange and frightening to be seen and to be AJ after all those years of being Jennifer.

Jesus
Yes my little one.
This feels very strange. It doesn't seem like me. It seems like someone else.
I know my little one but that is because you have been hidden away for so long. You do not even really know who you are. Don't be afraid my little one. You are wonderful in every way. I will show you.
Will you? I don't feel wonderful. I feel weird. I want to get back to being Jennifer... she wants to explain...
You can explain my little one. You don't need her for that.
Don't I?
No my little one you are much better at explaining yourself when you are being yourself.
I suppose. It just feels strange. Not with you. I'm used to being me with you now.
Yes my little one I do not want you to be anyone but who you are.
But you are safe, you don't ever hurt me, you always understand and say the right things.
Yes my little one but my servant wants to be those things too. He will try to be as safe and as understanding as he can. I will help him my little one.
Good. Maybe it will be easier for him to understand if it's just me.

Yes my little one it is always easier when people are who they really are and not trying to hide away or pretend.
Yes. I see that. I've been afraid for so long of wanting and needing anyone… of being me. Please help me. It doesn't even seem like me.
But it is my little one. It is the you I have been longing to reveal.
Was that what the tapestry was? What you were talking about?
Yes my little one. I want you to be seen for who you really are. You are not the way you see yourself my little one. Let me show you who you really are and how I see you.
Yes. This is strange. It feels better.
Yes my little one it is better. Do not be tempted to go back.
What about with other people?
My little one be yourself with me and with Mike. That is enough for now.
Yes, it is. But help me to put her aside when I need to.
Yes my little one you have made the first step. It will be easier.
Ok. Thankyou.
I am always with you my little one and I will always help you to be who you truly are.
Thankyou Jesus. I love you.
And I love you my little one.

Jesus said he wanted me to let go of Jennifer. He told me that eventually I would be the one on the outside and Jennifer would be gone…that he would give her back to me because she came from me in the first place. This was terrifying to me because I didn't see how I could ever live the outside life.

My little one I want you to be prepared to let go of Jennifer for you do not need her anymore.
I think you might need to say a bit more about that. I'm still a little unclear on all that. And, I'm not entirely sure who Jennifer is.
She is the one who protects you my little one, she is the one who has found so many different ways of protecting herself. She protects herself from the truth of her life and her past, she protects herself from being hurt in relationships, she disappears when things get hard or confusing.
Mmm... Yes but she's more than that surely.
Yes my little one she is much more than that for you have put much of yourself into her but those things belong to you and not to her. I want you to take them back and to let her go.
But… that makes me very afraid... I don't know. I can't be AJ all the time. I can only be her with you, maybe Mike eventually.
My dearest one I am not asking you to do this instantly. It will be a process my little one and is part of the healing that I have for you. AJ is who you are, you can't hide behind Jennifer forever.
But I don't even know who AJ is.
No my little one but I do. I am beginning to heal her and as I do so you will begin to see who she is, who I made her to be. Who I made you to be. She cannot be that person if Jennifer remains.
Ok… I think I understand. Do I understand?
Yes my little one you understand perfectly. Are you willing to let her go?
I don't know... She's me. I don't know who this other person is except I know she can't keep safe. Jennifer can keep safe. She can do that. That's what you want me to let go of isn't it.
Yes my little one. I will keep you safe in my way. Jennifer keeps you safe but the cost is very high my little one. It costs you the love that you so desperately need. That I want you to have.
Crying…

My little one you are already safe and you are already loved. You do not need her anymore. She only keeps you from receiving all that I have for you. She has done her job... she has done it so very well but now it is time to let her go.
Crying....
My little one...
I need you to help me... Because I'm afraid.
My little one I know you are very afraid, but I am here with you. I will keep you so much safer than Jennifer ever could. I will give you more than safety my little one, I will give you love and security and enable you to live without fear. Jennifer cannot do that my little one. She keeps you safe, but the fear never leaves you, the fear controls you my dearest one. I would not have it so.
But who would I be without her?
You would be yourself my dearest one, the beautiful child that I created, whom I am loving and restoring, who will be so much more than Jennifer could ever be, who will live a life that Jennifer could never live.
I want that... I do.
My little one you do not need her. I am here with you.
I don't know how.
I will show you my little one. I will lead you. Will you allow me to work? Will you allow me to make AJ into all that she can be.... Will you let Jennifer go?
Wrestling and crying.... Yes.
My little one....
Crying....
My little one I will be with you in everything. I understand your fear my little one and I know how hard this is for you, but I will not let you down. Depend on me for everything and trust me with all that you are. I am all you need my little one. AJ is hurt and vulnerable, but she is so many other things also... You will see my little one as the defenses fall away and you become free to be who you truly are. Do not be afraid my little one for you have chosen life over death. I will not fail you.
Jesus... I just need to spend some time with you.
Yes my little one come I will strengthen and comfort you.

Letting go of Jennifer meant trusting Jesus to keep me safe. It was very hard for me to feel safe when there was so much fear inside. There were always thoughts about how Jesus had let the bad things happen to me. He didn't stop them even though he could have so how could I trust him to keep me safe now? I didn't understand.

Jesus
Yes my little one I am here. My dearest one I am always here for you. Do not fear that I will ever leave you my little one for I never will.
Sometimes... sometimes it's still like you are not real.
I know my little one but that is not so. I am more real than anything my little one. I am reality just as I am truth. Just because you are unaware of my presence does not mean I am not there my little one.
No. I suppose not but I want to be aware of you Jesus. I want to live my life knowing you are here and that I am safe. I don't think... I don't know if I am safe.
You are safe my little one. Do not listen to the enemy who is seeking to fill your mind with fear and mistrust. I will not ever leave you my little one. I will keep you safe.
I think maybe... I still don't understand that.
I know my little one but understanding will come as you move further into the truth of who I am and the nature of all things. My little one I understand that it is difficult for you to feel safe when so many terrible things have happened to you but I never left you my little one. Not for one moment.

But that didn't mean I was safe Jesus. They still hurt me.

Yes my little one they did. That was not my will for you my little one. That was never what I wanted for you. But I allowed it to happen my little one for I knew what good would come from it. Even though it hurt you so very much my little one I knew that I would save you and heal you and that all that was done to you would be redeemed my little one.

How can you do that Jesus?

Because my little one I understand what you do not. I see what you do not. My dearest one I allow many terrible things to happen in this life. It is not my will that it should be so my little one. That was not my desire for my children or for this world, but I know that there is more at stake than just the temporary things of this world. Even the pain of this world will not last my little one, but the pain of the next world will last for all eternity. My dearest one though it was never my desire for you to be hurt in this life, I will use all that you have endured to save my people from the pain that is to come. My little one such pain is without measure and without end and I do not wish for any of my children to be lost to it.

I see that Jesus. But it doesn't mean I am safe. I think it just means I am eternally safe but not safe in this life Jesus. Because I'm not.

Your safety is indeed found in me my little one and whatever befalls you in this life you will never lose that my little one. I am holding you safe in my hands. But my dearest one you have not yet understood the safety that I bring. I am your protection my little one, your shield and your defender. That is for this life my little one for you will not need any of these things in the life that is to come.

No. I don't understand it Jesus. I suppose maybe a lot of the time you are protecting me from things, and I don't even know it.

Yes my little one that is so. If I were not protecting you, you would have died long ago my little one for the enemy has wanted to destroy your life from the beginning, but I have kept you safe my little one.

Safe?

Yes my little one for though he has wanted to destroy you and to take you from me I have kept you safe. I have kept you for my own and I will heal you and save you from everything he has done my little one.

I suppose I want you to promise me that I won't ever be hurt again but I know that's not what you mean.

No my little one that is not what my safety is. My safety is such that even when you are hurt still you are safe for there is much pain in this world my little one. You know this.

You didn't spare yourself pain Jesus. I understand that.

No my little one I did not. I endured everything that was necessary to save mankind my little one. And yet I was always safe in the hands of the father. My little one I never doubted that.

I don't understand Jesus... but you chose that. I don't understand it but you did. I didn't choose what happened to me.

No my little one you did not but that does not mean that you were not safe in my hands. My dearest one I knew from the very beginning, before you were even created, all that you would suffer. I knew what they would do my little one. I knew what the enemy would do but I also knew what I would do and all the good that would result from all that you suffered as you surrendered yourself to me. My little one I know these things are hard for you to fathom for you do not see as I do but you know that I love you.

Crying… Yes.

Trust in my love my little one. Trust in who I am even when you cannot see and understand. My dearest one I will keep you safe from all the schemes of the enemy

as you cling to me. I will not leave you my little one. You are never alone. I will never abandon you. I know you do not understand my little one but trust in who I am.

Crying.... How will I ever be able to feel safe Jesus?

My little one I will help you. Hold on to me and keep trusting me. Do not listen to the enemy my little one. He is trying to distract you and to cause fear and mistrust. Do not listen to him my little one. Even if you do not understand remember who I am. I will not leave you my little one.

I don't want those things to be true.

I know my little one... My little one hold on to me and do not let go. I will bring you through everything my dearest one. I know you are afraid, but I am holding you and I will not let you go.

I think... how will I ever be able to come through all of that Jesus?

In my strength my little one. I am all that you need. Even for this. Do not be afraid my little one. I know the way. It will be painful little one, but it will not be too much for you. I will work through it all to draw so many to myself. My dearest one I will redeem everything that enemy has done. Your life will be worth living my little one. Keep holding on to me.

Is it worth it Jesus?

Yes my little one it is worth it. I would not ask it of you otherwise.

Everything I will give up... my children, my friends... everything. Is it worth it?

Yes my little one. It will be more than worth it. My little one you will never regret following me for though I am asking so much of you I will give you so much more in return my little one. Everything you give to me will be given back with an abundance of blessings. Do not be afraid my little one. It will be worth it.

This life that you have for me Jesus... can I really live it?

Yes my little one you can for you have me. I will help you with everything. My dearest one the life that I am giving you will be good in every way. Even if it is hard and painful at times it will be worth living my little one.

I love you Jesus.

Yes my little one I know that you do. Do not give up your hope in me my little one. Remember that all that I am is truth my dearest one. I will keep you safe. Even if you do not understand what that means or how it can be true that is my promise to you, to protect you and keep you safe.

I don't know if... I don't know what it means Jesus. But I will hold on to you.

My little one I will lead you forward, and I will show you what it means to be safe in me. I will not ever leave you my little one. I will hold you and love you all the days of your life. My dearest one everything that I have promised is coming soon. It will not be long now my little one. Keep holding on and you will see all that I have promised.

Ok.

My little one I will never leave you. I am holding you close to my heart.

I'm glad Jesus. That's where I want to be. Help me to see you and not listen to the enemy.

Yes my little one I will help you in every way that you need.

I talked to Jesus about these things a lot because I knew he said he was my safe place and he was all I had... but I would get sucked back into the past and it was hard to feel safe there. I found it hard to feel safe in the present too. When I got hurt, I wanted to protect myself and keep from feeling that kind of pain ever again. I got hurt a lot because of all the pain inside. I suppose it is like if you have a wound on your leg say... and it gets bumped. That hurts a lot more than if there was no wound there... and you are especially careful to keep it from being bumped because it hurts so much when it does. Jennifer was really good at that... she had lots of ways to keep us safe but following Jesus meant that I had to trust him and not her... it meant giving up all those ways of keeping safe. Because I let Mike see me and know me, that meant I got hurt more by him than anyone else... so that was where the battle for me was most of the time.

I didn't sleep very well. I was still hurting a lot and trying to find ways of keeping myself from feeling that way ever again. I thought about not talking to you, not writing to you, except maybe occasionally but I couldn't come up with anything that wouldn't mean being disobedient. Eventually I saw something that I suppose is obvious, but I saw it more clearly than I ever did before. I saw that it is impossible to follow Jesus and be obedient to him and to protect myself, in all the ways I have always done, from the pain that comes. Either I have to not follow him, or I have to trust him to protect my heart. And I thought about all the things he has been showing me about my heart, and the house that he is building and how he is making it new and beautiful and he wants to fill it with who he is. And he can only do that if I follow him. So I made my choice to follow him and to trust him to help me with the pain that comes and not try to keep myself safe because I can't do both and it doesn't work anyway. And I felt much better and at peace even though I was still hurting.

Jesus was teaching me about what true safety is and helping me to trust him to protect me and help me when I got hurt. A new part of our journey with Jesus was beginning. I was discovering who I am in so many ways. He was promising a future that seemed impossible to me and that I would be a person I didn't even know. I needed to hold on tight to him.

My little one I am here with you. Your chats with Mike will continue my dearest one for that is my will for you and for him. Do not be afraid of what I have promised. Though you do not understand yet all that I have said... will be my little one. I am at work. My little one I know it is frightening for you to be seen in this way. I know that you feel ashamed of all that you are but my dearest one I am not ashamed of you. You are a delight to me. My dearest one do not listen to the enemy's lies. There is life and hope before you. My promises are true. Take hold of them my dearest one and do not be afraid to believe. Do not be afraid to hope. Do not feel that you are unworthy of my notice or of the things that you are called to. Do not feel ashamed because I have promised you good things. I made you to have needs and desires.

I will meet them all my little one as you follow me. I have placed many desires in your heart my little one, but you are still afraid to see them or acknowledge them. You believe you are not good enough for any of these things but my child it is my desire that you should have them. I have called you to a hard path my little one which will require much courage and endurance for my sake but I have also called you to live a good life my dearest one, where you know how to love and be loved and you are able to receive all that I have for you. I know how to bring this about my little one. Do not be afraid of what I am doing. Remember that I am in control of everything and I know how it will be. I know what you need my little one so much more than you do. Do not be afraid but keep following me.

I am your guide and I am your healer. It will all come in time my little one just as I have said. Do not fear what you see in yourself and do not be ashamed but know that I am with you, that I love you, that I am healing and changing you little by little. My little one the road to healing is long and painful and will take many years as I have said but along the way I have so many good things planned for you my little one. Along the way you will find your new life and start to live it. It is in your new life that you will find the most healing my little one. This is only preparation for all of that. Do not be afraid but be willing to follow me. My plans are perfect in every way. I will not

fail you my little one. Your life may not be the way you expect for you have not yet seen my plan for your life my little one, I have revealed only a part. But it will be a good life, a full life and I will be with you, in ways that you have not yet imagined. Keep following my little one. Do not falter but fix your gaze upon me. I am all that you need.

Chapter 14

Learning to Trust

Even though I had a lot of trouble trusting anyone and everyone, Jesus only ever asked me to trust him and Mike. To me everyone was a threat. People weren't safe, not one of them so to trust anyone was something that seemed impossible.

People are too difficult for me. If you don't give them what they want, you get punished but sometimes you can't and sometimes you don't even know what they want. It is hard to work it out. I try hard to work it out Mr. mike but sometimes I get it wrong. Sometimes I try out saying no or doing what I want but it isn't any good Mr. Mike. I wish I wasn't me.

Mike was the one Jesus trusted to help me learn that some people are safe. He told me it was the safest relationship I will ever have, outside of my relationship with him because he is there right at the center, with both of us. Our relationship is centered and grounded in him. I am still learning that but knowing that Jesus trusts Mike was always the biggest and best reason I had to trust him.

Jesus told me he wanted me and not Jennifer to write and chat online with Mike. That seemed to be a hard thing to do and I would realize over and over again that it was Jennifer and not me that was writing and chatting. It was hard for me to be seen. I was very afraid that Mike wouldn't like me or want me. So, I would hide away but not on purpose and then Jennifer would be the one on the outside. Then I got upset that Mike didn't see me and treated me like Jennifer and that made me think he didn't want me and I would hide away even more.

It is still very hard to let you see me. I don't even want to see me because I feel wrong all the way through. I don't want to see me. I don't want you to see me. I think you might say you don't want to have anything to do with me if you see me because ... you won't want to. So, I keep hiding and you get to see Jennifer instead. I think you might see me a bit because sometimes I try but mostly it is still Jennifer. I am sorry because I said I would try and I did but somehow I hid again. I think if you don't see me and say that its ok that its her and not me, I will hide again. Maybe because I think you want me to go away. I think maybe it is hard for me to keep writing and letting you see because its like you don't because you don't ever write back. That makes me afraid it's not ok to be me and I hide again. I know its not your fault and you can't write for lots of reasons, but I think that it is hard for me to keep writing. It was hard for Jennifer too for a long time, but she is better than me at doing without things that she wants or needs. She is very good at that I think but I am not so good because I get scared. I don't know if you understand anything I say, and I think you must be tired of reading these letters. I would like to stop and just hide away and not come out again, but I am trying to trust Jesus. It is hard to do I try very hard and it makes me afraid still. I try very hard not to be a nuisance and that makes me hide too because I don't want to ask for things I can't have or shouldn't want. I know Jennifer will never do that, so it is safe to hide behind her. Then I don't say bad things. I don't know why Jesus wants me to be me. I think it would be better to get rid of me and keep Jennifer. It would be much better. I am trying to listen to what Jesus says but it hurts a lot and I don't think it can be true but then I get worried because it must be. I don't know anything. That makes me want to hide too. I don't know what I will do when Jennifer is gone. That makes me very afraid it makes me more afraid than anything. I don't know if I can do that and be... anything good. It seems more impossible to me than all of the other things He is asking me to give up. I think if I can ask for one thing when I come it would be a safe place where I can hide away and not be seen. I don't know if that is ok to want that or to ask for anything, but I would like that please.

It was hard too to face Mike because I felt very ashamed about the plan Jesus had to send me to America to be with him. I thought he must be feeling horrified by it and not want me to go, or worse that I was trying to force myself on him so even though Jesus was talking to me about his plans I didn't want to talk to Mike about them.

I'm sorry I got afraid to talk to Mike again. I just got afraid. I am afraid to ask him things. Why am I afraid Jesus?
Because my little one you still feel like you do not deserve to be here asking questions or even talking to him my little one. You do not really want him to see you. Asking questions makes you feel vulnerable and exposed. It exposes your need of which you are so afraid.
Oh. That's a lot of reasons.
Yes my little one and that is why it is hard for you to ask him anything but it is especially hard for you to ask about the future for you still believe you should not have it.
It does feel a bit like...a giant present that I'm being given by mistake.
But it is not my little one. There is no mistake. This is my gift for you. Not for anyone else my little one but for you, my child. And it is a gift my little one. It is a wonderful gift that I am giving to you.
Yes. It is.
It is not a mistake my little one... My little one cling on to me and do not fear what I am doing or anything that I am giving to you. My little one it is my desire to give you many things. I will help you to receive them all my little one for I know and understand that it is difficult for you to accept these things.
I wish I was different Jesus and that I didn't get afraid. I don't want to be afraid and I don't want to have to keep on pretending that I'm not.
I know my little one. Freedom from fear will come my little one. I will help you not to pretend but to just be all that you are in the moment without shame.
That sounds... I can't imagine that.
I know my little one.
I'm glad Jesus that I have you.
My little one you will always have me. My dearest one I am with you, watching over you and caring for you. I never leave you my little one. I will help you to take hold of all that I am and become all that I desire for you to be. My love is unfailing my little one and will see you through it all.

There were things from the past that made it difficult for me to be seen. Jesus showed me those things so that he could help me break free of the fear that was holding me. This was Jennifer talking but I don't think the fear was hers.

The day went on but I got increasingly distressed... and fearful... about writing to you, letting you see.
My child I am here.
Lord... I can't do it... I just want to weep, and I know it's silly and I want to be obedient but...
My child be still. I have not asked you to do this because I am unkind. I understand how difficult it is for you and yet I still ask you to do this in the strength I give you.
(I began to cry and then I saw an image... Me as a small child in my bed hiding under the bedspread...grandad was trying to pull the covers off me... when I was able to stop crying enough to continue...)
What was that? A memory?
Yes my child. A fragment of a memory which you have hidden so very deeply.
I don't want to see please...
It will help you to see this my child. It will help you to understand.

I don't want to understand... Please.

Will you allow me to show you? Trust me. I am here my child do not be afraid.

I am afraid... crying... but I will trust you. (I saw only enough to know what happened. The covers were ripped off me. There were several people in the room, but I didn't see who. They laughed at me as grandad raped me...) crying... I don't understand the connection... why does that memory have anything to do with this?

You do not want him to see. You connect being uncovered, unwillingly, with humiliation and shame and pain of the worst kind. You try to cling on to your covering believing it will protect you. Not wanting it to be removed at any price.

But its not the same surely?

It is the same feeling and the same fear my dearest child. To you it seems the same.

crying... It is the same feeling. The same fear of being exposed and humiliated... but... it's not the same. I don't know... what are you trying to show me?

I am uncovering the lie that you have believed for so long, a lie rooted in that and other memories that you have buried so deep. The lie is that if you let anyone see you, that you will be mocked and humiliated and violated. You need your covering, your hiddenness to stay safe.

Is it a lie? It seems true to me, now that you say it. I do believe that yes... and you are asking me to put aside my covering as it were... and I can't do it because...

You believe he will do what your grandfather did.

That doesn't make sense... because he can't and logically, I know he wouldn't, but it doesn't feel safe... and I suppose I do think, believe that...

Say it my child.

That he will laugh at me, think I'm stupid... Lord why are you showing me this?

I need you to understand where the fear comes from my child so that you are no longer at its mercy. If you understand the source of the lie you are more able to stand against it.

It doesn't make me want to give up my blanket.

I know my child, but it helps you to believe me when I say it is now safe to come out... and it is now safe.

crying... It doesn't feel any safer.

He is safe my child. If you let him see you he will not mock you or hurt you.

I still don't think I can do it... I don't even know how... What that would mean... and I am afraid...

I will be here with you my child.

Jesus kept on telling me that Mike was safe and that he was my friend and to share my heart with him. I didn't understand about him being my friend. I didn't know what it meant. Jennifer thought he should be like a professional person and help us but not pretend to be our friend. She didn't understand why that was a good thing or even why we needed it.

I understand that you have reasons for wanting me to write, some of which I can guess at maybe, some which I don't know about.

Yes my child I have many purposes in this as I have said.

Well... that's kind of ok. I think there are two main things that are troubling me... that's the friend thing and the future thing... I don't know.

My child you can tell me anything for I know it already. Do not be ashamed and do not be afraid.

You said that he's my friend and companion, he says he's my friend. Why?

Because it is so my little one. He is your friend though you are reluctant to see him as such. You wish for the friendship to be more do you not?

I don't know... I wish it were one thing or another. How can I see him as a friend? Friend suggests a relationship, sharing, affection, caring... that kind of thing. I don't even know him.

My little one he can be your friend, even in the way that you are experiencing right now. It is not how you expect to experience a friendship and yet that does not mean it is not one.
That's the point... the word friend automatically brings with it expectations. How can it not?
You fear disappointment my dearest one. You fear that you will expect too much and that he will not be your friend in the way that you want him to be. That you need him to be.
Yes… and I'd rather not expect anything. I don't need him to be my friend. I never asked for that. I don't want to have that fear. I always get it wrong. Why do I always get it wrong? I don't know what to do with this friendship. I don't know what it means. It doesn't make sense. It doesn't feel safe and I don't want it.
My little one he is your friend in the truest sense of the word. You may not know him but still he cares for you as a friend would. He is there to answer your need as I direct him. He is there to share this journey with you my dearest one just as I have said.
I don't think I understand. I can't imagine that he would care anything about me. I'm nothing to him. Why would he want to? It doesn't matter. I don't need him to care or be my friend. All I wanted is for him to help me.
My child this friendship of yours is in my hands I am making it what I want it to be. Whether you accept it or understand it or not he is your friend and he does care. You care for him do you not?
A little I suppose.
My child it is not wrong to care for him. Do not be ashamed for this is my doing. It is right that you should care for each other as friends do, for that is what you are.
It's still not making any sense to me. I don't know how to be or what to expect. I'm confused by the whole thing. How can he be my friend? I still don't like it.
You fear it my dearest one because it is not of your doing, you did not seek it or ask for it. You can give very little to this man who knows so much of you but who you know so little. You are afraid my dearest one, that is all it is.
All?
Yes my little one but I have told you so many times that he is safe and that he will not hurt you.
But if I expect him to be my friend and all the things that means to me, I will get hurt because it doesn't mean any of those things. How can it... It can't possibly.
Why not?
I don't like this conversation.
I know my little one but do not run away. That will not resolve anything for you.
A friend, to me anyway, is someone who is involved in your life, someone you share experiences with... good and bad. You share a common affection... I don't know. He isn't my friend. I suppose…
Say it my dearest one.
As far as I'm concerned, he's just a kind of overseer who keeps an eye on things and only gets involved when things are going wrong, when I'm losing the plot like I am now. That's a good thing. It's helpful, a bit like a safety net… but it's not friendship. So why call it that? Why not just call it what it is?
My child I am calling it what it is. I know you do not see this as friendship in the way you understand. I know you are afraid of it being less than you want or expect. My child listen to me you do not have to know or understand something in order to make sure that it is safe. That is what you are trying to do. You are trying to fit this relationship into your limited understanding of friendship so that it feels safe. It does not feel safe to you because you don't understand it. That is why you are trying to push it away. To push him away.
It would be better. I don't want him to be my friend.

My little one you know this is not so. You desire his friendship, but you are afraid of it. You want to know him but are afraid you never will. You still fear rejection and abandonment my little one but that is not what I have planned for you. He will be your friend in the best way possible. He will be a friend to you in the darkest places for he is not afraid of the darkness. He will not abandon you when everything looks dark and hopeless, for he knows and understands that I am with you, and with him in all of this. My little one he will be the friend that you need him to be. Do not be afraid of this. Do not try to run away my little one for this is a gift from me to you. You may not understand it. It may look strange and unfamiliar to you but do not be afraid. This friendship will not bring you pain. Embrace it my little one. I will be with you in it all as I am in everything. Do not be afraid.

I'm still afraid of wanting what I can't have… I'm not sure I know what I want to say… should I expect it to ever be more than it is now? I just don't want to be thinking it's something that it's not... you know.

Yes my child I know. Do not be afraid. I will lead you through this just as I will through everything. There is much more to any of this than you have guessed my little one. Do not be afraid of disappointment. I know all your thoughts...all your hopes and dreams and I will meet them all in my way and in my time. My dearest child there is so much yet to be revealed. It is not yet time. Simply accept my word to you which is the truth. Mike will be your friend in the best way possible through everything that lies ahead for you. He will be the friend you need him to be. I will be in the midst, leading and guiding you both down the path that I have for you. There is so much my dearest one. Wait upon my timing. It will be revealed in time.

You are smiling?

Yes my little one I am smiling for I know what lies ahead. You will look back on our conversations together and you too will smile and wonder why you ever doubted. Do not be afraid my little one. All will be well.

I.... AJ… wanted him to be my friend even though I wasn't very sure what it meant but I didn't believe he would be, because I was bad and didn't deserve to have a friend. Jesus helped me a lot because I was very afraid and didn't think I deserved any kind of a friend, especially not Mike.

Jesus
My little one I will heal you and enable you in this as in everything.
Crying......
My little one it would not be better for him if you went away.
Crying......But I don't see that.
I know my little one. Hold on to me and keep following where I lead. I will help you my little one. I will help you and I will heal you and I will give to you good friendships, not only with my servant my little one but with many others. My little one you are worth his time and attention.
Why are we talking about this?
Because I am longing for you to see the truth my little one.
But I am not believing any of these things Jesus. I am sorry.
My little one just because you don't believe it does not mean it is not the truth. My dearest one my servant will not stop reaching out to you. Take hold of his hand my little one. I will help you to do this.
I don't know what that means.
It means my little one that I will enable you to accept his friendship and to trust him, if you will allow me to...
But does he want me to?
Yes my little one he does.... It is not wrong for you to have a friend my little one. It is not wrong for you to have Mike as a friend.
It feels wrong.

But it is not my little one. It is my desire for you...
Are you sure?
Yes my little one I am very sure.
Well... it is up to you Jesus. I don't know about it.
Will you follow me my little one?
Yes.
Even into friendship with my servant?
Crying.... Crying.... I can't do it Jesus.... Crying....
Yes my little one you can. I will help you.
Crying.... But he won't want me.
He wants you to be his friend my little one and to accept the friendship that he is giving to you.
Crying... But why?
Because he cares for you my little one. Because he longs to see you healed and restored, because he is your friend.
Crying...
Hold on to me my little one and let me lead you forward. I will not leave you. I will help you.
Jesus I want to follow you.
Yes my little one I know that you do.
Help me.
I will help you my little one. Take my hand and let me lead you forward. This is a good thing my little one, it is not something to be afraid of.
But...
My little one take my hand.
Yes Jesus... Crying...
My little one I will be with you and I will not leave you. My dearest one in allowing me to lead you forward you are overcoming the work of the enemy in your life. It is another step towards freedom my little one. Do not be afraid then but trust me and follow me wherever I will lead you.
Yes. Ok. You are sure?
Yes my little one I am sure. My dearest one you have a great future together, you will accomplish many things for my kingdom and for my glory but most of all you will be a great blessing, each to the other my little one. Do not be afraid.
I think ... I need you Jesus.
Yes my little one you do but you always have me my little one. I will not ever leave you. My dearest one your friendship with my servant is a good thing. Do not fear it.
I will try. Please... will you look after him and help him to get some rest and feel better?
Yes my little one I will. Rest is coming to him my little one. I will sustain him until it comes.
Thankyou.
My little one I will care for you both for you are both my beloved children...
Thankyou.

Jesus told me that receiving help and allowing myself to be seen was part of learning to trust. For me that was a very hard part. I didn't believe that anyone wanted to help me... not really. I remembered that when I was little, some of the people in the cults would pretend to be my friend and tell me they were going to help me and save me. But it was a lie and they would hurt me instead. They did it so I would believe there was no help and I wouldn't tell anyone about the bad things. That made it hard for me to believe that Mike wanted to help me or that I could trust him not to hurt me when he said he did. And I felt like every time I cried out for help, he didn't answer so we made a rule never to ask for his help, at least not openly because it was so very painful when that help didn't come. Sometimes we broke this rule but almost always wished that we didn't.

I did learn though that Jesus would always answer my cries for help. He never left me and always, always saved me when I was sinking into a big black hole. That was the point of course. Jesus wanted me to trust him first…and then Mike, but I found it very confusing and didn't understand a lot of the time why he said Mike was there to help when it seemed to me that Jesus didn't want him to. Even though it was difficult for me I was thankful in the end. It is much better to trust Jesus over and above any person. Jesus is always there and never makes mistakes.

It was difficult for me to recover from mistakes that Mike made sometimes, or the things that just happened that seemed to tell me all the things I believed were true and all the things Jesus said were lies. I don't think I would have kept on writing and talking to Mike, if I hadn't trusted Jesus first, more than what I saw or felt or believed about Mike. Sometimes it would happen that Mike would miss his chat appointment with me. Jennifer would get very angry with him and have arguments with Jesus about how she was supposed to keep on trusting 'that man' as she called him. I just wanted to die.

I don't know what I want to say. I don't want to say anything except I think I'm sorry for being here. I know you have lots to do and I don't want to be a bother. I don't want to bother you with any of this, because I know I shouldn't make a fuss. It should be ok for you to do whatever you want, and I shouldn't make a fuss. I'm sorry that I do, and I still get afraid and don't trust you. I think it would be better if I just went away and didn't do this anymore because I can't seem to do any of it. I try very hard to trust Jesus when He says you are my friend and you won't leave me and sometimes, I think I'm doing better and then something happens and I know that I don't at all. I don't think I'm getting anywhere just running on the spot and falling down a lot. I'm tired and I don't want to get up again. That's all. I don't think I can keep on wanting to do this, because every time I think I'm doing better I fall down again. I don't want to keep doing that. I don't want to keep feeling like this. I don't want to keep writing these letters that just say the same thing over and over. I don't really think there is any hope for me. I know I should, and it should all be ok, because I've got Jesus but somehow it still isn't. I think maybe I'm just one of those people who don't make it no matter what Jesus does. I don't think I want to say anything else.

It was especially hard for me when I thought he forgot about me. That is because I had been alone and forgotten in the dark for all of those years. I was terrified of getting lost again and being left alone. I thought I was unimportant and didn't matter at all. I was so afraid that Mike would leave me. When he didn't come to our chats... I thought it was because he hated me and because I didn't matter. The enemy had a lot of fun I think, and I listened to a lot of lies over and over again. It was only Jesus who helped me to keep on going. He held me and comforted me and told me the truth that Mike was my friend even if I couldn't understand what that meant yet. He told me that Mike cared for me and wanted to help me and that he was safe. I didn't believe any of those things for a very long time, but I held on to Jesus and I kept on trusting him, even when I didn't trust Mike.

Very early this morning…
My little one I am here with you and I will never leave you. My dearest one I understand your pain and your fear but I have not lied to you I will never lie to you. Everything I have said to you about my servant is true my little one.
That's very hard for me to see. You tell me he won't hurt me, but he's hurt me more than anyone has for a very long time and I'm not expecting that to stop. He will just keep on hurting me because that's what he does. I don't think that can matter much to you or you wouldn't keep asking me to go back for more.
My little one it does matter to me. It is not my intention that you should be hurt. It is my intention that this relationship should be healing and life giving. My little one I know you are hurting so much and you do not feel that you will ever be able to trust him but my little one I ask you to forgive him and continue as before. I do not ask this of you because I want to see you hurt but because it is my desire that this relationship should grow and flourish into something beautiful, something strong

and powerful not only for yourself but for others also. My little one the enemy will oppose this whenever and however he can, and he will use every circumstance and every mistake that my servant makes to try and destroy both this relationship and ultimately you my little one. My dearest one I know you do not understand how he can care for you and yet forget you but my dearest one I have not lied to you. He is your friend and he does care. He will not leave you my little one.**

How can I argue with you? You are God and you know and understand all things. I don't know or understand anything. I don't know how you can keep forgetting someone you've made a commitment to help even if you don't care about them, it would be better to say go away I don't want to help you.

My little one he does want to help you. He wants to do all the things he has said to you. Give him a chance to do so my little one. Do not give up on him… My little one this is a hard and difficult journey you are on and many obstacles will be put in your way. Do not allow them to drive you off course but rely on me to help you overcome these things. My dearest one I am always here.

But mike isn't supposed to be an obstacle he's supposed to be helping me.

No my little one he is not and he will help you in many ways. My little one do not allow the enemy to have his way. Keep trusting in me.

I don't see that the enemy has to do anything here. Why does he even need to try?

My little one you do not see or understand the true nature of what is happening here. The enemy is seeking to destroy you as I have said. If he cannot destroy you he will try to destroy my purpose for your life which is wrapped up in your relationship with mike. Do not underestimate his subtlety or his determination my little one. Keep standing in my truth despite what you see and believe about my servant. My dearest one keep on trusting him. He is all that I have said.

I don't see it at all Jesus.

No my little one I know that you do not that is also the enemy's intent. He does not want you to see the truth.

Well I don't know... it seems to me easy to blame the enemy for everything. How hard can it be to remember your appointments? Its not a hard thing, it's basic. I can't find anything in me that is believing you. I'm sorry. I understand I just don't believe. I don't even want to believe because that means going back for more. Why must I do that?

Because I am asking you to my little one. Because this is my way for you difficult and painful as that is.

How can I see that as anything other than you asking me to get hurt again? That's all this is Jesus.

But my little one that is not all as I have said. My dearest one everything on this journey of yours will come down to trust and obedience. There will be many times when I will ask you to do things that will cause you pain. That is not my will my little one, that you should be hurt, but it is the nature of this world. It is a world which desperately needs me my dearest one. Do not allow the enemy to keep you from all that I have for you. From the life that I have promised you my dearest one. Keep trusting and keep following in spite of the pain and the fear. I am greater than those things.

Why would I even want the life you've promised Jesus when it's so wrapped up with a relationship with a man who continually hurts me and breaks his promises. Why would I want that?

Because my little one that is not how it is and that is not how it will be. The life I have for you is good. The relationship I have for you with mike is good but you must persevere to take hold of these things my little one for there is a great deal of opposition as I have said.

I have nowhere else to go Jesus. No other plan, no other life. But I don't even know if I can do it. I don't know if I can even find anything to say to him or find the courage to talk to him

again. That seems beyond me at the moment.
My little one I am here for you and I will help you but first you must forgive him my little one.
I don't really feel anything Jesus. I don't know if I can do it from my heart.
I will help you my little one I know what is needed.
Then I do forgive him. Help me to do it.
I will help you my little one. You will come through this.
Will I? I don't know. I don't even know if I want to. But I do want to sleep. Please help me to forgive him and be at peace even if it still hurts.
Yes my little one. I will help you. Give it all to me my little one. I do not want you to carry this burden. It is my job to protect and lead you. It is yours to follow my little one.
Yes. I know that it is. I will follow Jesus. Even in this. Please take the pain I'm holding on to and please help me to forgive him. Please because I don't think I can do it.
Come then my little one. Do not be afraid.

It was a very big battle for a long, long time. The enemy didn't want me to trust Mike and they played on all my fears and the lies I believed about myself, to make it seem too hard for me. Jesus always helped me somehow even when I thought there was no way out of the hole I was in, he made a way. Time after time after time. Sometimes though it did seem like too much and I didn't always do what I knew Jesus wanted me to do. Jennifer felt protective of me I think maybe like a mummy is or should be of her children. She thought she needed to protect me from Mike when I would get upset.

*The reason I/we can't talk with you any more is to help us survive. AJ would continue to throw herself at the brick wall no matter how much it hurts in the hope of finding what she needs. She isn't going to find what she needs, she is just getting hurt and so it is better that we stop. AJ needs to know that she matters, that you see her and that she's not alone. She needs reassurance that if the promise is true that you will be her friend and help her and not want her to go away. I don't know if the promise is true or not, everything is very confusing, but I do know that talking with you isn't making it easier for us to keep going or even to want the promise to be true, mostly it makes it harder. So we need to stop and that is why we aren't coming to chat anymore. There doesn't seem any reason to write unless there is something to say. There isn't anything to say at the moment so I don't know if we will write. I know that this isn't what Jesus has told us to do but that is just more confusing to me. I don't know what is true and what isn't so I just need to survive the best way I can.
Jennifer*

I would get upset and scared about the things that she said to Mike sometimes, because I thought he would think I was bad and would tell me off or leave me, but he never did.

*Hello Mike
It is me AJ. I am not knowing what to say because everything is jumbled and confused in my head. Jennifer wrote you that letter and I wished that she didn't. I didn't go away, but she just pushed past me and took control and I was confused so I let her, because I don't know what to do about anything. But she doesn't know either and I don't think she was right. She wants us to stay away from Jesus and you and everyone to keep safe and figure that out. That is how she keeps safe, but I don't think that is right. I don't know and it is hard to write because I am crying too much, but we have been talking about me saying I am in trouble so that you will know, and you can help. I don't know if you will help or what will happen but that is what you said so that is what I am going to do. If I don't learn new ways of doing things, then I will always be living her life. I don't want to live her life I want to live mine. She doesn't get to choose if I talk to you or not, I get to choose. I always let her choose those things before but now I am choosing. I am very confused because I don't know if I am me. When it was Jennifer it felt like it was me, but it wasn't. It was me looking out through her. I think. I don't know. I am sorry I thought you forgot me. I am sorry about*

those things she said. I don't think that. I don't think I do. I get confused but I think Jesus wanted me to come to you and it isn't her choice it is mine because it is me talking to you not her. I don't want you to go away. Please don't go away. I am in trouble I think because I am confused, and it doesn't seem safe to go to Jesus. I don't know what else to do. I don't know what to do.

Jesus wanted me to trust Mike. He wanted me to know that he was my friend. I needed his help because I didn't know how to get past all the fear.

So in the vision I walked forward to where you were standing next to Jesus and I reached out to take your hand. But you took me in your arms and held me and I cried and cried...
My little one you are safe and you are loved. Not only by me my little one but by my servant my little one. Stay in his arms my little one for it is where you belong. You are safe there my little one. There is nothing to fear.
Crying... But... in real life Jesus...
My little one my servant accepted you into his arms long ago but you were not willing my little one. Now that you have gone to him, now that you are standing in the light, I can begin to truly build your friendship my little one. There is nothing to fear from this. I am holding you both in my arms of love my little one...
Your ways are strange Jesus.
Yes I know it seems so my little one but that is only because you do not yet understand. My little one what I bring together in the spiritual world cannot be torn apart in the natural world.
Yes... I just get surprised that you would put us together Jesus.
I know my little one but you will see that I have chosen perfectly for both of you. Do not be afraid to love him my little one and do not be afraid to accept the love that he gives to you. It is my love my little one, given to him for you. There is nothing to fear from my love my little one.
No.
My little one I will make all things possible for you. You will come to love and trust him my little one, both as your friend and as your partner.
I still think he wouldn't want me.
My dearest one he has accepted you into his arms. That was real my little one.
Yes. I have to let go of that lie.
Yes my little one you do. He has already accepted you my little one.
Yes. He has.
My little one I am making a way for you. Keep following my little one and do not be afraid.
I will try Jesus. It is a lot of things to get used to.
I know my little one but you are able.
Yes.

I got stronger over time and made my own choices to trust Mike and eventually to love him... no matter what Jennifer thought about it.

It is finished Jesus.
Tell me about it my little one.
It is me and Mike and we are joined together by you, so I put you in the middle holding our hands. I drew two Holy Spirits because he can be everywhere and he is with us both all the time. I know you are too Jesus but I didn't need two of you.
What else little one?
I got worried about what color the Holy Spirit should be, but I made him pink because I was thinking about how we are joined together by love and that is why we are all surrounded by pink. I think that is all Jesus.
My little one your picture describes perfectly how it is. I am joining you and my

servant together in love my little one. I know it still makes you afraid but your picture is a good one. It is good to have my spirit with you both little one for he helps you to love each other with my love.

It is a bit scary to have him there Jesus.

I know my little one but it will not stay scary. It will seem normal and natural to you my little one and you will want him to be in more of your pictures.

I hope he will like it Jesus.

He will like it my little one. Do not be afraid.

I am glad you are in the middle.

Yes little one I will always be at the centre of your relationship. You will always have me with you my little one.

My little one this time ahead of you will be filled with many challenges. Do not fear this but know that I am greater than anything that will come against you. The enemy is not happy my dearest one for he has seen your trust in me. He will try to cause you to doubt in every way he can. Do not listen to him my little one but hold fast to my word to you. I will not leave you. My servant will not leave you. My little one it is important that in the next few weeks and months that you allow yourself to truly trust my servant, for in the times ahead you will need to know that he is there for you, that he will help you and guide you and not leave you.

My little one he is everything I have said. He will be your friend through everything that comes my little one, through your healing and beyond. Do not be afraid of this for he is safe, and he is faithful to me. My dearest one I will hold you and I will keep you through the coming storm. Do not be afraid but know that I am in control. Know that there is nothing the enemy can bring against you that I do not allow for my purposes my little one. My dearest one I want to accomplish a great deal in this next little while, for the time is short. I am longing to bring you to a place of total trust and dependence upon me, for it is in that place that I can truly begin to do all that I desire.

It is in that place that I can begin to reveal who I am my little one and who you are also. Do not fear this but know that it will bring you great blessing my little one, for there is much that I wish to do that you have not guessed at. My little one I will do things in your life that have not been seen before. I will do this because it is my pleasure to do so and because it will bring great glory to my name. My little one I know you do not understand my words to you, but you will see in time that they are true. I do not ever lie my little one. For now, hold on to all that you know me to be. Trust in my great love for you. I will never fail you.

Chapter 15

The Enemy and the Big Lie

Being able to trust Mike was made a lot more difficult by the enemy. It was a big target for them because they knew how important it was. It was important because he was there to help me get better and to follow Jesus and it was important because of Jesus plans for us to work together in the future. So they put a lot of effort into trying to convince me that he wasn't safe, that he didn't want to help me and that I couldn't trust him. Jesus had to help me a lot.

My little one the enemy takes your fears and he uses them against you. He takes your fears which are based on true events and he turns them into lies. My little one he will not stop trying to undermine and destroy this relationship. He will try everything he can to cause you to fear and mistrust my servant. He will oppose your move to America in every way that he can my little one. Opposition will come at every point, but I can overcome all things my little one. All you must do is hold onto the truth. My servant is safe, and he will never hurt you. He will not harm you in any way my little one. I have entrusted you into his care because I know his heart. The love that he will give to you comes from me my little one. Do not fear it and do not listen to enemy lies who would tell you that he is going to hurt and abuse you. That is not true my little one.

When I was chatting online the enemy would take what Mike said to me and twist it, so I thought he was angry with me or wanted me to go away. Every time he missed his chat time with me or didn't reply to my letters when I so wanted him to, it was the same battle I had to fight. To trust Jesus over what I saw or felt. They didn't want me to write to Mike either. Jesus had told us how important it was that we kept on writing for a lot of reasons, but it was a big fight for us to keep doing it. The enemy would tell us all the reasons why it was a waste of time and we shouldn't do it. The other alters never seemed to want us to write either...maybe that was the enemy too I don't know. Jennifer was always under pressure to stop writing.

The enemy has been persistent...giving me reason after reason why I shouldn't write, saying that you will abandon me, that you don't care anyway and won't even talk to me, that all this future stuff is rubbish and I should just concentrate on getting by on my own. At least I assume it's the enemy... I've been doing my best not to listen. It doesn't make any difference anyway because even if all of that were true, I will still keep writing, because that's what Jesus has asked me to do. It's not my decision to make whether I write or not. It does seem to bother them a lot and I often wonder why...well I suppose I still wonder why they bother at all...but then I assume there's a lot going on here that I don't understand or even know about.

The past things and my feelings of despair and abandonment were places they attacked too. They wanted me to give up, lie down and die. I would have if it wasn't for Jesus. I am very sure of that. We didn't know how to fight against those things. It was too much for us. We had to hold on to Jesus and trust him to save us. He always did.

Last night I'm afraid things went downhill fast. I don't even really know what was going on, but I just found myself completely distraught and just asking Jesus to please let me die. He spoke to me in the midst and I managed to write it down.

My child, my dearest child I will never leave you, I will never leave you. Trust me, trust me to show you the way. The enemy has you in his sights my child, but I am your shield and your protector cling to me.... stay my child and listen to what I would

say. Do not listen to the enemy he is seeking to confuse and overwhelm you, but nothing has changed my child. I am who I have always been. I am your savior and I will save you. Wait then and see what I will do. Do not be tempted to give in to despair or desperation. Wait my child for I am at work in ways that you cannot see. Wait. I am worthy of your trust my child I will not let you down. Trust me then and know that I am the overcomer and that I will overcome everything of the enemy in your life. I will break every hold he has over you and I will make you completely mine my child. Nothing else will satisfy me. Wait on me then and know that I will not fail you. You will see the truth my child, you will see it for I am the truth and I will reveal my truth to you. Wait then and trust me. Remember all that I am and all that I have said. Wait.**

Somehow Jesus gave us the strength we needed and caught us every time we fell, which was a lot. Sometimes we thought we would never make it through. They used things that other people did and said to trigger things from the past, to bring alters and memories to the surface in places and through people that took us by surprise. That could be little things they said or did and we would have to hold on until we could get somewhere safe to be with Jesus or to let the little one that was triggered cry and tell their story. We were always having to run away into our room. Sometimes though it was much worse. Sometimes the enemy made a whole situation that we couldn't escape from. That way they attacked the inside alters, they attacked us at the surface, and they attacked Jennifer's relationships. Those times were very bad.

Before I tell you what happened on Thursday, I need to give you some background. At the church youth group which Sophie and Richard go to they often have little competitions where they make something. It's just a bit of fun and the prize is usually a few sweets or something. They always ask me to judge these things when I come to pick up the children and I hate it. I really hate it but every time they put me on the spot, and I have to do it. On Sunday two of the leaders, one of which was Cheryl, were talking about decorating biscuits as part of the bonfire night party. I said quite clearly that I didn't want to judge it, because I hate doing it… when I went to pick up Richard (Sophie has been unwell all week) I found them waiting for me. They had arranged themselves in a semicircle facing me as I walked in and started chanting judge, judge, judge, judge. There was a moment where I really thought I was going to turn and run, probably screaming and crying but somehow, I kept control and managed to pretend to be ok. I picked out a winner, but I couldn't even see the biscuits... not in any way that made sense. I just picked one at random... not the best by any means. Delighted winner gives me a hug, everyone else complains. Cheryl approached and started talking about something, no idea what because I was just aware that she was too close. I tried to take a step backwards, but she stepped forward to hug me. I still kept control. Then she started to talk about Monday which we are spending together… wanting to know what I wanted to do where I wanted to go … and getting 'arsy' when I said I didn't know. I was torn between crying and telling her where to stick her day, but I didn't do either, I just did what I always do. I smiled and pretended I hadn't noticed her attitude and made my exit with Richard. Richard was in an awful mood.

I made it home said I was going for a bath. I locked the bathroom door and leaned against it and finally let go. I couldn't stop crying. I was completely out of control. Curled up in a ball trying to hide under my own arms. I kept curling up my hands. I seemed to be trying to hide my index fingers and it wasn't clear and I didn't want to know but I did anyway. That they made 'me' choose who was next… and I wish I could say I was over it... that the distress has gone now but it hasn't. I'm not out of control anymore but I still can't stop crying when I'm on my own like now. I keep having flashbacks of when I opened the door.

I heard Jesus in the midst of it all... except I wasn't sure it was Him. Even when He was talking to me, I wasn't sure. I got out of the bath, still crying... and tried to listen.

My child do not be afraid for I am with you. The enemy cannot hurt you my little one for I am protecting you do not be afraid… My little one I am holding you. The distress and anguish you feel will go my little one. It will not overcome you. I am with you.
Please don't leave me. Help me.
I will not leave you not ever. I am always watching over you my little one do not be afraid. I will not leave your side. I am your protector. The enemy wishes to hurt and destroy you, but I am with you and he will not have his way as you remain in me. Do not be afraid…I will stay with you. I will not leave you my little one. I am watching over you constantly. I do not ever take my eyes from you. My dearest one you are safe. I will not let you go, trust in all that I am for I will never let you go. Do not be surprised at this my little one for the enemy has many plans and many ways he wishes to attack you, but I will always be there with you. He will never take me by surprise. I will always be everything you need my little one in everything. I will never let you go. I will sustain and protect you through everything. Stay close then my little one and know that I am your protector. The enemy cannot overcome me.

I just sat with Him and gradually calmed down…. and stopped crying. Sophie knocked at my bedroom door and it must have been obvious I'd been crying because I had no way to disguise it… but I pretended to be fine. And then I went to see to Richard and his skin… he was still in a bad mood... I couldn't take it. I just left him to it. He knew I was upset.

We had a lot of bad dreams too. Sometimes that was memories coming to the surface but often it was the enemy…telling us in lots of ways that we were bad and worthless, that there was no hope for us, and the future Jesus promised us was a lie.

I had a dream this morning. I was dreaming I was with a group of people and they promised me lots of things. Things that would make me feel beautiful and special and wanted. At first, I was afraid and said no but then I changed my mind and said yes. Everything was ok when suddenly they said I was too ugly and too bad to have these things and they were very mean. They said they would take me to a certain place I wanted to go, because I thought it would be safe there and there might be people who would help me. They put me on a minibus and drove me but didn't stop at the place even though I asked them to a lot of times. They just ignored me and kept driving. They came to a big factory place in the middle of nowhere and made me get out and told me to go away. They didn't care.

So I walked all the way to the place where I wanted to be. I wasn't sure of the way and it took me a very long time. On the way I was thinking maybe Jesus will help me, maybe He will send someone but then I thought no He won't help me. I came to the place and it was dark and deserted. I had nowhere else to go so I just laid down on a bench and I wanted to die. And then I woke up. I checked the time it was 6am and I saw I had an email from you. I couldn't help it. I tried very hard not to, but I cried, and I cried, and I heard Jesus but I didn't want to talk to Him. But then the thoughts in my head were getting worse and I was feeling more and more out of control and I knew I needed His help, so I came to talk with Him, but I knew almost straight away it was the enemy. I got even more distressed and asked Jesus to come but the next voice I heard was the enemy too. I knew it wasn't Jesus because of the things it said. So I got really desperate and I was calling out for Jesus to come and save me but all I got was the enemy again. I don't know what was happening, but I stated to shake and shudder, but I don't think it was me it was like it was something else. It was frightening and I kept calling out to Jesus. It stopped and I thought that this must be Jesus, but it wasn't. I felt completely abandoned and very afraid. I couldn't seem to stop crying. I don't know how but I got back some control and told myself that Jesus hadn't left me and that He was there with me. I was still very distressed but then I heard Him…

Jesus

My little one I am here with you. I did not leave you and I will not ever leave you. My dearest one things are not always the way they appear to you. So many things lie hidden from your sight my little one that is why you must trust me and my words to you. My little one I know you do not always understand my ways or my plans, but I will never leave you and all my words to you are truth. My little one nothing that I have said to you can ever be changed or taken away. All that can change is whether you choose to believe them. My dearest one keep choosing to believe the truth. The enemy will continue to feed lies to you my little one. He will not stop. It is not his desire that you should take one more step on this journey for my plans for you are dangerous to the kingdom of darkness. My little one you know the truth. Hold on to it and do not let go. Hold on to who you know me to be my little one. I will not fail you in any way. I will always be there to help you my little one. Do not listen to the enemy.

Jesus you know all the thoughts in my head. They make me ashamed. They do.

My little one the way that you feel and the thoughts that you have all come from a wounding that goes to the very core of who you are. My little one I will hold you and love you and enable you to stand in the truth even in the midst of an attack such as this. My dearest one everything is just the same as it was. Do not be afraid.

It doesn't seem to matter what you say I can't seem to stop feeling like this.

I know my little one but choose the truth. Choose me.

I don't want to be like this Jesus. It was better before when I didn't even want to be helped or loved or anything. It hurts.

My little one it was not better before. I know that you are hurting my little one, but you are not abandoned. Not in any way. Do not fear it my little one. It will not come.

I still think it will. I know that's not what you say, and I try to believe it but I'm still just waiting.

My little one I know all your thoughts I know everything about you. I will meet every need that you have my little one. I will hold you and give you my strength in times like this. I will give you the truth when the enemy is filling you with lies. I will not leave you my little one. My servant will not leave you. Circumstances cannot change the truth my little one. What you see with your eyes does not change the truth of my word. My dearest one do not listen to the enemy. He has no truth or life to give to you. His desire is to bring destruction and death. Hold on to me my little one and I will help you stand.

It takes so little Jesus and here I am again. Will I ever make it?

You will make it my little one for I am with you. I will not leave you. I will meet every need that you have, and I will love you and strengthen you my little one. You will make it if you do not give up.

Sometimes I think that's true but...I want the pain to stop.

My little one I am with you in all the pain that you feel. It will not destroy you my little one for I bear it with you. I will not leave you to carry it alone my little one. I will not ever leave you.

I expect this will pass Jesus because it always does. Please keep me safe and help me to believe you. Help me not to give up.

I will help you my little one. Do not be discouraged. Every time you come through an attack you grow stronger and more able to stand. It is not for nothing that I allow these things my little one. I always knew how it would be my dearest one, but I know you have the strength to make it through and to become all that I have said. Do not give up then but hold on to the truth. Hold on to me my little one. I will not let you go.

It doesn't really feel like that Jesus. Not right now. My reaction is always the same.

But you recover faster my little one. You still fall but you rise again so much faster than you did before. My little one be encouraged. The enemy will not have his way. I will enable you to overcome everything he brings against you my little one.

I hope so. I need you so much. I can't do this Jesus. I just want to run away and hide.
And yet you stay my little one…. Keep holding on to me my little one. I am all that you need.

Choosing to believe the truth over lies was something we had to do over and over again. Sometimes we didn't even want to because it seemed like the lies were true and the truth was lies… the lies just told us what we already believed. Jesus was showing us a new way, but his way was so hard most of the time. It was much easier to agree with the lies than to keep on fighting. It helped when we could really see and understand the choice that we were making, to see that choosing lies was to choose the enemy over Jesus and to choose death over life. I talked with the Holy Spirit about these things when I was further on with my journey and getting to know him. He helped me understand a lot of things.

That is right my little one, in following the wishes and desires of the enemy you harm yourself and others, but many of our people have yet to truly understand this little one. They see it as a restriction of their right to choose but that is not what it is little one. We never restrict anyone's right to choose we only show them the way to life. Whether they accept it or not is always up to them.
Yes... but the enemy fools us doesn't he into thinking it won't hurt or it doesn't matter or that your way isn't good, and you don't want good things for us.
Yes little one he does. He will try to persuade you that you can find a better way little one or that our way is too hard or too costly. None of this is true little one. Follow us with all of your heart and you will find life, true life little one not the death life that the enemy gives.
Yes. It is all a big lie what he says.
Yes little one it is but many listen to him little one.
Yes. I listen sometimes. I am sorry.
I know little one but remember this, that our way is the best way. It is the way of hope and of life and of peace. Little one he will try to lead you astray if he can but do not ever listen to him little one.
I need your help holy spirit because I can't do that on my own. His lies are... they seem like truth and I get confused.
Yes little one but we will always help you to see and know the truth. Little one you will help many to find their way through the maze of the enemies lies. He spins a web little one and many are caught in it but we will work through you to bring truth to many who like yourself have been caught in his web. You will help them to see the truth my little one and with the truth will come freedom and healing.
Yes. The truth is very important Holy Spirit.
Yes little one the truth is very important.
And it is a lie to think you can do what the enemy wants and not be under his power.
Yes little one that is a lie for as you come into agreement with him, which is what sin is little one, you give him power and influence over you. He will do all he can to make this happen little one for then he can begin to destroy you by your own choices.
But... that... I mean he has always had power over me because of the lies and maybe other things I don't understand yet.
Yes little one he has had a great deal of power over you but you are breaking free little one. Choosing us always leads to freedom.

Their attacks could be subtle like all the whispering that went on all of the time, about how there was no hope and how bad and useless we were but sometimes they weren't subtle at all.

I put out my light and tried to get to sleep... but I just kept crying. I was seeing, imagining myself cutting my arms so that I would bleed to death... I would just go to sleep and not wake up. All I felt was despair... I realized eventually that this was the enemy and remembered what Jesus said, that I only had to call because He is always here with me. So I prayed Jesus come and save me. I literally felt the demon being pulled off my back, which was a little startling, but I immediately felt better. No more thoughts of despair, no more images.

Most of all though they attacked us through our conversations with Jesus. They would pretend to be him. They were very good at tricking us and would tell us all kinds of things that weren't true. I don't think they minded if we worked out it was them. If we were tricked then they could tell us things that weren't true, especially about the future but most of all they kept us from listening to Jesus. If we found them out, then they still won because it made us so upset and confused and afraid. It made us not trust the things that Jesus had said. It made us doubt all the things we were heard including Jesus plans for us. It made us question if we could trust Jesus at all. We didn't understand why he would let them trick us in that way.

My little one the enemy is determined to stop you in whatever way he can. Primarily he is trying to confuse you, make you afraid and lose hope. He will not stop my little one. You must learn to discern his voice from amongst your own thoughts my dearest one. Do not tolerate him. Do not listen to his lies. Do not give him any more power over you than he already has. My little one I am always watching over you but I want you to learn the difference between his voice and mine and between your own thoughts and those that he is giving you. My dearest one you need to be more vigilant. You are allowing him to fill you with fear and thoughts of despair. My dearest one I will always come when you call upon me. I do not want you to listen to him and I will not leave you at his mercy when you call out for help. My little one this is a good time for you to begin listening more closely to the voices that you hear.

But what about when I ask you to come and I still hear them. Like this morning. I know we've talked about this before, but I still don't understand.

My little one I am always with you as I have said. I will not abandon you but I will teach you to know the difference between his voice and mine. Sometimes I allow him to continue so that you can learn to recognize his voice but I do not leave you. I am watching over you.

I'm not sure I can recognize him in my thoughts Jesus. Because like you said he tells me what I already believe so how can I know it's not just me.

My little one as you pay more attention you will learn to know the difference but even if they are only your thoughts my little one you must be careful of them. Choose to think on the truth even in the midst of your fear. My dearest one you must always choose the truth. In this way the enemy will lose much of his power over you and you will be able to walk more confidently on the path that I have for you. It is not my desire that you should live in fear and doubt my little one. I want you to live in the truth with all the security that it brings.

Yes. I see that. I do. But what do I do if I realize it's the enemy?

My little one you call upon me just as you have always done. Trust me to answer in the way that is needed and to show you the truth. My dearest one do not be afraid to let me teach you these things. I will keep you safe and I will enable you to know the truth and to live in it.

Help me then. I want to live in the truth Jesus it's just... hard.

My little one I know this is hard for you for many reasons but you cannot afford to give any ground to the enemy. He is constantly seeking for ways to turn you away from the path that you are on. Do not allow him in my little one. He will show no mercy in his quest to destroy you.

This is a battle that I have had to keep on fighting. It has taken me a long time to learn the things Jesus has been wanting to teach me and to understand why I had to learn them. I am still learning them. They have been very painful and difficult lessons to learn.

The future is sure my little one. This will not overcome you for you are hidden in me. I will give you all the strength you need. This despair does not come from me my little one but from the enemy who is beginning to fear all that you will become. Do not lose hope my little one but take heart. I will not leave you. I will not leave you. You are not abandoned, and I will not let you die my little one for it is my desire that you should live. That you should know what its is to truly live, to live out of me and who I am. The enemy does not want this, and he will seek to destroy you before that can happen. But I am your protector. I am your strength. Run to me my little one when you are afraid, when the battle is fierce. I am always here waiting with open arms. Do not give up my dearest one for I will give you the crown of life. Persevere and endure in my strength and I will show you how great I am and can be in and through your life.

My ways are not your ways my little one. Trust me though you do not understand. Do not listen to lies. Do not give into despair. I am your beloved. I love you as no other could ever love you. I am with you my child in everything. Keep looking at me. Do not be distracted by the voice of the enemy. I know the plans I have for you and he begins to suspect. Do not listen to his lies my little one listen to truth my truth. Listen to my promises for they will bring you life. His lies are like poison and will bring death swiftly... or slowly for that is his intent. Do not listen my little one. Fix your eyes upon me and upon my truth. I will give you all that you need. Do not give up but continue as I have said. I will give you the strength you need. I will not let you go my little one. Cling on to me and do not be tempted to let go. Your hope is found in me and in me alone. Keep your eyes firmly fixed upon me and upon who I am. The enemy cannot overcome me my little one. It does not matter what he does for I am always in control. Trust me with everything that you have my little one for I will never fail you.

The promises that Jesus had given me seemed far away and impossible most of the time but that didn't stop me thinking about them. It was painful to hope when I didn't really believe I deserved anything good. I longed to be loved and accepted and have a life where I could be me and I could love and serve Jesus. I didn't see how I could have any of those things, but I wanted them. I was afraid to want them, but I did.

The enemy didn't miss their opportunity. My conversations with Jesus were so important to me. I talked with him everyday sometimes for hours. I cried with him, asked him questions... and he told me about his plans for me. I wanted to hear that there was something ahead of me that would make everything I had been through and was going through worth the pain. The enemy was subtle and clever and often when I thought I was spending time with Jesus I was really spending time with them. They comforted me and told me there was hope. They said all the things that I had learned to expect from Jesus and even though I knew that they were tricking me sometimes I didn't learn fast enough just how clever they are.

Spending time with Jesus and hearing his voice and letting him comfort and encourage me was something I needed. I needed it to make it through everything that was facing me past, present and future. But my need made me vulnerable and I was depending on the wrong thing. I was depending on my conversations instead of on Jesus alone. That meant even when I suspected it was the enemy, I sometimes didn't want to admit that to myself because they were giving me what I thought I needed. They told me what I wanted to hear, and I got sucked in deeper and deeper without even realising it. Jesus did tell me… he warned me, and I tried to fight, and I tried to be wary, but I got overwhelmed so much of the time.

The enemy talked to me a lot about the future. They told me over and over that my life would begin when I got to America, that everything I needed was there, that everything I wanted was there. I got desperate to go. Everything became about 'when I get to America'. I was told over and over that it would be soon, very soon. Then I was told I would be going before July the next year. That was repeated to me so many times that I felt like I had to believe it, or Jesus was a liar. But time went by and nothing was happening to make it real and Mike wasn't hearing anything from Jesus. But I kept on hoping because Jesus can do anything, and if Jesus said before July then it must be right. Mustn't it?

I did all kinds of things to prepare but I didn't tell Sophie or Richard. I didn't do that because I wasn't sure. I needed to be sure before I told them anything. Leaving them was such a painful thought and it made me feel guilty and bad for leaving them. I didn't see how it would be possible for me to leave them either. Time went on and nothing was happening, but 'Jesus' kept telling me before July. I didn't know what to think. I got very confused and I lost hope because I thought if it was a lie, I couldn't trust Jesus and if I couldn't trust Jesus there was no hope for me. No hope at all.

It got to January and there was still no sign of anything happening. In my chat time with Mike he told me that Jesus hadn't told him anything and he didn't see that it was possible for me to go just yet. He was very kind but very clear. To me it felt like it had all been a lie.

Hello Mike

I had another sleepless night last night. All that terrible anxiety is gone but now I just feel hopeless. I don't think I can trust anything I have heard. How can I trust that anything is true? I don't know what to believe about the future because it could all be a lie. Maybe that's why it hasn't been confirmed by your Jesus. Maybe your Jesus and mine are different. Maybe yours is the real Jesus and mine is just some demon. I don't think the real Jesus, your Jesus, would lie but I don't think any of it has been true. Maybe the real Jesus doesn't want me to come. I let myself believe and hope that it is was all happening, but it isn't. Nothing is happening and everything is back to the way it was. I don't want to talk to Jesus. I don't think He is there anymore because where was He all last week? I tried so hard to trust Him even though I was afraid, but it was all a lie and nothing is different. I don't want to do that again. I don't want to hope anymore. It hurts too much when it's taken away. I was feeling better about leaving and thinking my children would be ok after all and I was feeling better about being there with you too. I wanted it to be happening, but it isn't.

I don't know why you believe that I am coming if your Jesus hasn't said so. I don't think you should trust anything my Jesus says. Maybe your fleece will be answered for you, but my fleece is that my children will be provided for. I can't go anywhere until it happens. I can't talk to my Jesus about any of this. Even if it really was him, I was talking to I can't bear to hear him say it's soon or that this is going to happen or that this is how it will be. I don't want to hear it anymore. I need to see it because I can't do this anymore. It hurt me too much and Jesus wasn't there so I don't understand how I can trust him to keep me safe. I never did. I wanted to follow him and to do all those things for him because I love him, but I don't know who he is anymore. I don't know what's true and I feel afraid. I feel afraid to be with him. I don't know if can trust him or if it was all a lie. I know I'm supposed to but I'm afraid. And I don't know what to do because Jesus is my whole world. It hurts more than anything to think he doesn't really love me or care for me and that it has all been lies.

I don't want any more lies. I want to know what's true and real, but I can't find my way. I'm glad you didn't leave me, but I don't think you need to worry about me coming there. I think that will be better for you but not for me. I am sorry about all the time you have wasted, and I am sorry I didn't always trust you and wasn't always nice to you. I hope you will forgive me. It would have been nice to meet you. I would have given you a hug. I don't know if that would be ok, but it doesn't matter now. I don't know what I will do with no Jesus and no hope. I don't know. Maybe I can go away somewhere quiet on my own like I wanted. Sophie is leaving soon, and Richard will be better without me, so I don't need to stay. I don't want to give up but I can't do it anymore. It doesn't matter anyway if it isn't true. I don't think it is true, but I still want it to be. It would be amazing if Jesus was real and just how he says. If he really did love me and had a wonderful plan for me. I would like to come and do amazing things for him with you. Maybe your Jesus is like that, but I don't know about mine. I always knew that this would be the time if I found out if it was all real and true or if it was all wrong. I know there is still some time left but not very much and when it runs out, I will know for certain.

Like last night. Jesus told me you would write before our chat time, but the time got closer and closer and I got more and more afraid and upset. And it never happened and then I knew it wasn't Jesus at all and I thought you must have left me as well. I think that is how it will be. The time will get closer and closer and I will get more and more afraid and desperate. I don't think I would be able to manage that kind of disappointment. Maybe you can ask your Jesus to help me. I need someone to help me, but I don't think mine will and I am afraid to talk to him anyway. I know this is a bad letter to write and I'm sorry. Maybe I should be Jennifer for a bit and then it might be a bit better. I wish I could have come and been me. I think it would have been better even if it made me afraid. But now I have to keep on being Jennifer. It is too hard for me and I don't want to be in her life. I'm sorry I believed all those things and told you about them. I shouldn't have. It couldn't be true all those things. I suppose I just wanted to believe them. I don't know what I will do now because I gave everything up like Jesus asked and everything was about me leaving and I have no money and no job, and I don't want to be here. I don't want a life without Jesus. I need to stop crying now so I won't write any more. Thank you for helping me last night when you were ill. I hope you are better soon. Bye

AJ

I didn't realise it but most of our conversations now were with the enemy. That doesn't mean that Jesus stopped speaking to me though. When I did talk to him, he would tell me that there was hope but that he hadn't told me when I was going and that it wasn't time yet. Somehow, I didn't notice. I was blind to the things he said. Maybe I just wanted to believe the lie or maybe I was so confused I couldn't see at all I don't know. Jesus spoke to me through other people too. Jennifer's friend Cheryl told us that Jesus had said that I would not only minister to people like me who had been hurt, but we would minister to other ministers and I would be teaching them. He was telling me there was hope for a future… even in the middle of all the confusion.

Even though the enemy was spending a lot of time telling me in our conversations how America would be everything I dreamed of, they were also whispering to me about how awful it would be. That way it didn't matter whether I thought I wasn't going, or I was the future looked frightening and hopeless.

I think the enemy was trying to make me afraid about you and carol this morning, about how you won't want me and how bad it would be to be with you when you don't want me and how I won't have Jennifer any more and I will be all on my own and... how I won't be able to protect myself from you. I was being reminded of the past things as well and how much there is to overcome and how much pain and fear that is waiting for me. I am still wondering how much of what I have remembered is true. I am still getting little flashes of memories sometimes. I haven't told you about them. I forget about them if I can. I would like to have some certainty about something because nothing is certain for me. I still don't even really know who I am or my name or anything. I know that Jesus is the one who is certain, but I don't always think I can trust that or Him I suppose. I hope He really is what He says and that He can save me from all of this. I hope He will keep His promise to me. I hope I have found the truth and not a lot of lies. I know I will find out soon and that scares me. I am remembering what you said on Tuesday about how you will still be my friend no matter what happens. I don't know why because if it is all lies then I should go away and stop wasting your time. I don't think you will hear from me again if it is all lies except maybe to say goodbye. I don't want to think about these things anymore so I will finish now. Bye.

AJ

By February I was thinking about Plan B again. At least Plan B would end the confusion and the pain. It didn't seem like Plan A was going to come. It didn't seem like I could trust Jesus or anything I had heard. It was all a lie. Plan B was the only way out. Sometimes I got so close. I bought pills and alcohol and they sat in my cupboard promising a way out. In those times when it seemed like I couldn't take any more, I was saved by 'Jesus' who would comfort me and tell me I was loved and that there was hope. I was saved a lot of times by the enemy. This confused me more than anything... I believed that it must be Jesus who was saving me because the enemy wanted me to die. But the Jesus that saved me told me the same old lie... that I was going to America before July. It has taken me a long time to understand why the enemy would save me like that... why they didn't push me over the edge. It would have been easy to do, I think. But they were tormenting me and playing with me. They were like a cat playing with a mouse. They let me think I was going to die and then they let me go... only to catch me and pin me down again. It was a cruel game they played, and I got less and less able to know the truth from the lie.

April came and nothing had changed. There was no sign that I was going anywhere even though I was still being told and over that I was.

Somewhere along the line I'd decided that I couldn't talk with Jesus anymore. That I couldn't trust anything I heard so what would be the point. I thought that last night too, but the trouble is I need Him too much. I can't resist Him when He calls no matter how afraid I am. Even though I know it might not be Him. Even though I'm not even very sure about Jesus at the moment or if I can really trust Him, I just don't know what else to do. There is nowhere else to go. Nowhere at all. I think maybe part of me thinks I don't care if it is the enemy I would rather he finished me off than keep going through this. So this morning I wasn't going to talk to Jesus even though I wasn't feeling any better at all. I was afraid. But then I got a text from Cheryl who said that Jesus had said to tell me that He loves me very much. It just broke down all my resolve and started me crying again.

Jesus hadn't abandoned me, though it has been hard for me sometimes to understand why he allowed the enemy to torment me for so long. He was always in control and watching over me and there were times when he did save me.

All day long and yesterday I had this thought running through my head over and over and over. And the thought was 'I am going to die' and I believed it. I suppose it was the enemy and should have fought it, but I didn't I just agreed with it... yes, I am going to die. I couldn't see any other end to this. At this point while writing I started to get very distressed again.

Crying...
My little one come.
Help me please help me.
I am here my little one I am here.
Crying....
I will not leave you my little one.
Crying.... I can't manage this Jesus...Crying.... I can't.
My little one I am here with you. Hold on to me my little one. I will not leave you.
Crying.... I am going to die.
No my little one, you are going to live. My little one I have promised you life, you are not going to die.

I am.
My little one that is not my desire for you.
But there is no life... Crying.... It was all a lie... Let me die now please...
No my little one, I will hold you and love you and I will give you my life. You will not die my little one you will live.
No... Crying.... I can't live I have to die... Crying.... I have to die please let me die. I shouldn't be here please let me die...Crying....
My little one I will not let you die. It is my desire that you should remain and live the life that I have for you.
There is no life… Crying... only death...Crying... That's all there is. I won't survive I don't want to survive let me go…. Crying...
My little one I will help you through this. The enemy will not destroy you my little one. My will for your life will prevail. Hold on my little one.
Crying... I don't want to hold on.
I am holding you my little one. The enemy cannot take you.
Let him I don't care... Crying... I shouldn't be here… Crying...
Yes my little one you should. You belong to me now and I say that this is where you belong, here with me.
Crying... No... no... I belong with him.
No my little one you belong to me. Come into my arms my little one. I will hold you and keep you safe. He cannot have you my little one. You belong to me.
Help me… Crying....
I will not leave you my little one, hold on to me. My little one do you choose me?
Crying... Yes… I choose you... Crying...

I knew then that what was going on was a real battle. Even in the middle of all the distress and pain and fear I knew there was something like a tug of war going on. Maybe I imagined it, but it was like I saw four angels pull the demon off/out of me and take it away. It didn't want to go, and I thought I would come apart, but I didn't. And then everything was better and peaceful, and I wasn't distressed anymore and there was no pain.

Maybe that time the enemy was trying to finish me off I don't know… but choosing Jesus means surrendering to him and it takes the power away from the enemy. He saved me this time. But it didn't stop. Even though it was so close to the time I couldn't seem to let go of the belief that I was leaving by July. I was afraid to let go of it because that meant letting go of any hope. It meant that Jesus had lied. It meant that everything was a lie. It meant that I would die. So, I held on and held on even though there was no sign of anything happening.

Mike wrote to us and told us he didn't think it was going to happen. Jesus had said nothing to him, and he couldn't see how it was possible... He didn't say it couldn't just that he didn't think it was. I needed to hear the truth but to me it seemed like the end.

Hello Mike

I don't know how this will be for me. If I will make it or I won't. I don't know. It brings me comfort to know that you are believing there is hope. I can't seem to find it or maybe it is just that it is still too hard for me to hope because it seems to hurt so much. I haven't found the courage I need. I don't want you to think it was your first email or anything you said that made me lose hope. It was already gone. I can see it was a set up by the enemy. I don't think it was Jesus who told me to write to you. It was just the same as what happened in January when you were ill. This time I didn't write because I thought you had left me or that you didn't care. I expect that's what they were telling me. So, you didn't know what was happening. It was terrible. That is the only word I can think of. I didn't sleep hardly at all for five nights. I was sick with anxiety and I cried so much because of the pain. They were pretending to be Jesus. I knew I couldn't tell for myself because I was too upset. I hoped I could trust Jesus to protect me when I knew I couldn't help myself. But he didn't. That is hard for me to understand. So many things are hard for me to understand. So, your email was just confirming that this is what had happened again. And it is hard to risk being hurt like that again because it doesn't seem like I can rely on myself or on Jesus either. I am too afraid to talk to Jesus. I don't know if I want to talk to him. I am afraid it will only be the enemy and I won't know. It will take me a lot of courage to talk with him again. I don't have it. I am too tired and too unsure of everything.

I have been thinking about the battle and I think it was the Holy Spirit who was showing me things when I was still half asleep this morning. I know it is a battle and that I shouldn't be surprised if I get hurt sometimes. That doesn't make Jesus bad does it? It doesn't mean he doesn't care. I don't know. The Holy Spirit was showing me lots of things about being on the battlefield like how when it is dark and I can't see who's voice I am hearing, that just because it is the enemy's voice that I hear that doesn't mean that Jesus has gone away. He is still there. It's just I can't see him because it's dark and I can't hear him because of all the noise the enemy is making. I don't know if that is right. And that even if I couldn't see it because it was dark Jesus was defending and protecting me and even though I got hurt I didn't get hacked to pieces like the enemy wanted. And I didn't kill myself like he wanted either. So maybe that is right but I'm not sure. So now I have to decide if I'm going to desert from the army or if I'm going to stay. I don't want to run away. But I don't know if I can stay. I don't know if I trust Jesus enough to stay. The Holy Spirit talked to me about the lies that the enemy shouts at me like that I'm useless and a waste of space and just make it harder for proper soldiers like you. But he reminded me that Jesus picked me for his army, and he has a particular job for me to do. I can do that because Jesus picked me knowing that I could. Even if it's just a little thing it is better to do that and be with Jesus than to run away and not do anything at all. I see that it's just I'm not very sure about who Jesus really is. It is a hard thing for me to accept about myself, but I think somewhere inside I am believing that really, he hates me. I think maybe that is from when I was little. God must hate me mustn't he to let all those bad things happen to me. So, when bad things happen now, I get afraid that it is true, that Jesus does hate me after all. I think it must have been the Holy Spirit who said 'whatever happens Jesus remains the same' in one of those nights when I was laying awake afraid. That is true I suppose. I draw conclusions about who Jesus is from the things that happen, but I think maybe that is wrong. But it is hard to understand why it is wrong.

It is comforting to know the Holy Spirit is talking to me and helping me to see. Maybe He will help me back to Jesus. I don't know. I don't know if I will go even if I know it's where I belong and where I want to be. I was thinking about how all that time ago I said I would trust my guides when I couldn't see. I can't see and I don't know about Jesus. I am afraid to go to Him. But I will try to trust what you say to me because you see a lot better than me. I will listen to what you say because I don't want to be in this place, and I don't want to run away. I hope I find my way back to Jesus. I don't know about anything else. I still can't see the hope for everything that Jesus has said about the future, even if He said it, but it helps that you see it for me. Thankyou for being my friend and not leaving me.

AJ

The Lord is my shepherd;

I have all that I need.

He lets me rest in green meadows;

He leads me beside peaceful streams.
He renews my strength.
He guides me along right paths,
bringing honour to his name.
Even when I walk
through the darkest valley
I will not be afraid,
for you are close beside me.
Your rod and your staff
protect and comfort me.
You prepare a feast for me
in the presence of my enemies.
You honour me by anointing my head with oil.
My cup overflows with blessings.
Surely your goodness and unfailing love will pursue me
all the days of my life,
and I will live in the house of the Lord forever.
Psalm 23 NLT

Chapter 16

Letting Go of the Promise

Now I knew that I had been listening to the enemy, but I still didn't know who was Jesus and what were lies. I didn't feel like he left me, but I couldn't talk to him anymore. I felt like something inside had broken.

It is strange because I don't think that Jesus has left me. I think He is right here with me and I don't know what to do with that. Everything is confused. Cheryl and Ruth have both given me the same message from Jesus which was 'just tell her that I love her'. Everything is making me cry. I can't talk with Jesus...not like I usually do. It is like something inside died or got broken and I can't do it anymore. I suppose that Jesus can fix it, but He hasn't so far. I got into bed on Thursday night and I asked Jesus to speak to me. I am trying to remember who He is. I didn't think He would, but I picked up my bible and started to read. He didn't speak to me that way, but through the song that was playing. I wasn't really listening, but I suddenly started to hear it.

Another rainy day
I can't recall heaven's sunshine on my face
And all I feel is pain
And all I want to do is walk out of this place
But when I am stuck and I can't move
When I don't know what I should do
When I wonder if I'll ever make it through

I gotta keep singing
I gotta keep praising your name
You're the one who's keeping my heart beating
I gotta keep singing
I gotta keep praising your name
That's the only way that I'll find healing
Can I climb up in your lap?
I don't want to leave
Jesus sing over me
I gotta keep singing

Keep Singing by MercyMe

This made me cry and cry because I knew it was Jesus and I remembered back to when the memories first started coming. And I was confused, and I didn't know what was true. And I couldn't talk with Jesus or spend time with Him like I had because I was afraid. And I was waiting for His promise that help would come. And it seemed like there was no hope and that I would die in that place. I remembered that I survived that time by worshipping. That was all I could do. I couldn't pray or read the bible. It was the only thing I could do, and it got me through. So I know that is what I have to do now when I can't do anything else. So that is what I am trying to do, sometimes, mostly, all I can do is listen, but it helps.

Jesus kept on talking to me in lots of different ways. He spoke to me through songs, through the bible and he reminded me of all the ways he had loved me in the past. He spoke through other people 'God told me to tell you it's not over' and 'The well has not run dry'. He gave friends messages for me.

Mostly they were very simple...'tell her that I love her', which would make me cry and cry... but some spoke about who I am and the future that I thought was lost to me.

> As I was praying for you last night God started saying exciting stuff. He said to tell you psalm 84:6, 'when they walk through the valley of weeping, it will become a place of refreshing springs. He said that there's a river flowing from such a beautiful spirit in you that's flooded with light! Then I saw two pictures, one was a tree in the middle of a river, which I didn't understand, and one was the outline of a person who had such bright light coming from them... that there were all these horrible withered jagged claws a few meters away cowering in fear, terrified of the light, and there were streams coming from the light! It was pretty powerful and amazing.

He was encouraging me to hope and He kept me safe and held, but I was having a very difficult time still.

> I think the word was for me. It was about having lived under a black cloud of grief and pain for a long time and that the sun was going to break through (just like the word Cheryl gave me a couple of weeks ago). It went on to say the sun could break through in two ways, by the clouds parting or through a fierce storm which would wash everything away. But whichever way it was, the sun was going to break through and that I (assuming it was for me) would praise God because it was a new day. I could feel the Holy Spirit, it felt like it was for me, and I cried. But I am still afraid to believe it. I have been given this same word in lots of different ways so many times now but there is still no sign of it. Still nothing to see. It is hard to understand or accept that it is true. That it will ever be true. I think it is just making me sad. It reminds me of the word that was given in the meeting the day before you wrote to me. That was about a new day, about hope. I knew it was for me, but it was so hard for me to accept it, because it hurt so much to hope. But hope came. I don't know. But then a bit later on I had this picture of Jesus holding me, it made me feel safe and held and protected and loved.

I didn't let go of him but not because I understood or had a lot of hope or was sure I could trust him. I think maybe it was because he was all I had. I loved him and I couldn't let go of him.... and most of all because he didn't let go of me. But I was still struggling to understand what had happened and why Jesus had let it happen.

> I think if He was my friend like He says He would have told me I got it wrong about July, but He didn't tell me. I don't know what that means. I suppose it means I have to keep on waiting. I have been wanting to go home again. I feel very trapped and like there is no hope for me. Jesus does so much but nothing seems to change. How can what He does be real if nothing changes? I don't know. I'm not sure what is real, if any of this is real.

Jesus didn't want me to let go of him, but he wanted me to let go of everything else. He was talking to me in so many ways and leading to where he wanted me to be.

> I don't understand that about the plan... but I don't understand anything. It made me cry so much last night. I thought I could hear him telling me that he loves me and that he won't ever leave me. Sometimes it seems like I can believe in Jesus, but I can't believe in the promise... It seemed like I had to let go of the promise to take hold of Jesus and I did for a little while and I clung on to him and cried and cried. It makes no sense not to be able to believe the promise if it came from Jesus. Not if I believe in him, but every time I look at the promise, I lose my trust in him. So I told him I would let go of the promise and just hold on

to him because he is the one I want and need, not the promise. He held me for a while and then said he didn't want me to let go of the promise but that he would hold it for me so that I could hold on to him with both hands. He said the promise wasn't gone because he was holding it for me. I thought about how the promise is only good because it comes from Jesus and if it doesn't come from him, I don't want it.

He was leading me slowly and painfully to the place he wanted me to be.

He is asking me to sacrifice Isaac...which is my promise. I don't have a tangible Isaac of course but I know what He wants me to do. As I have prepared to come, I have bought and put aside things, including clothes. I often look at them and have thought of them as kind of statements of faith... things that say, 'I believe in the promise' and have known that I wouldn't wear them until and unless I come to America. So, what I have to do as a symbol is to wear the clothes I had in mind for the journey. It's kind of like saying that I lay the promise down. I'm not holding on to it anymore. It sounds like a simple thing but for me it does feel like something dying and it is hard for me to do. It doesn't feel like giving up hope though because my hope is in Jesus and not in the promise. I'm not giving up hope, but I am saying that my hope is entirely in Him. I don't need to be coming to America to have hope... so even though this is hard and is making me cry I don't feel despair. I am holding on to the one that I love and who loves me. That is all that matters. My Isaac is healing, to be free of the pain and the fear and the shame. I am willing to walk my journey of healing in any way that Jesus chooses, even if it means that I have to wait many, many, years to be free. Even if it means I am never free. My Isaac is comfort and understanding from people... to be loved for who I am. My Isaac is not to be alone anymore. My Isaac is a new start, a new life, a chance to be me without having to meet the expectations of others. My Isaac is to be able to hold my head high and say to people see I am doing something with my life. My Isaac is to make my life count, to give it all some kind of meaning. My Isaac is to be in a place where I am free to live abandoned to Jesus, to know and love Him and to grow into the person He wants for me to be. There are a lot of other things in the promise He has given me of course, good things, but I think these are the things that matter most to me.

It is difficult to see things how Jesus does. I got so caught up with what I thought was his plan for me and all the things I thought I wanted and needed, but there was so much more going on. He was always working to bring me closer to him, to help me surrender to him and whatever he has for me. To break the power of the enemy over me and to teach me so many things. When I surrendered my 'Isaac' he gave me a little glimpse, I think.

Yesterday when I was talking to Cheryl about the sense of peace, how I was feeling, was very difficult to put into words. I had a picture which was me standing in space, so completely surrounded, a bit like a planetarium type thing. It was dark but all around me were explosions of color and light. Beautiful patterns... maybe like the most amazing firework display but somehow deeper... that seems like the word. Like what was happening was significant? A sense of being caught up in something so much bigger than me, so much more profound and being a part of something. I don't know, difficult to describe. I felt safe and held and not at all alone, maybe like my eyes had been opened to see the reality of what was really going on around me... maybe seeing spiritually what or where I am. Like the physical world had been stripped away and I could see what really is? A profound sense of being held and at peace and in the right place... of everything being in alignment? Maybe it was about showing me how much I'm not in control and that by giving myself over into His hands I am becoming part of something so much bigger and more amazing and awesome than anything I could imagine. 'The dance' comes to mind, and 'the song', the purpose and the wonder of God. Lots of things. I think maybe the colors and the patterns that were made were God's creative word over my life... because sounds have color don't they… so I suppose God's word must have color too… and it is alive and dynamic so I expect it might make patterns. So I am held and surrounded by God's word, by Jesus because He is the Word. I hope that makes sense. Sometimes, when I can see, nothing else matters except that I am with Jesus. I said to you yesterday it felt like something was dying...and I suppose that would be me.

It was eight weeks before I had a conversation with Jesus again. That seemed like a very long time when I had been used to talking with him every day. But now I knew that I didn't need the conversations because whether I talked with him or not, he was always with me and wouldn't let me go. I learned that he would give me whatever I needed and would speak to me in lots of different ways no matter what.

This morning I was feeling upset and I was crying...and then I heard Jesus, but I was so afraid it wasn't Him that I kept saying no, but somehow, I knew that it was Him so eventually I took a chance...

My little one I am here with you...I have never left your side. I will give you all the power and strength that you will need to love and serve and follow me. Do not listen to the enemy my little one. He comes at you with lies of despair that tell you you can never do or be anything worthwhile, but you are already priceless to me my little one. You are precious beyond anything. I will help you with everything that I am asking of you, just as I always promised I would. Nothing is beyond you when you have me by your side. And I am always by your side my little one.

Crying.... Jesus. I have missed you so much. I have been so afraid...

Yes my little one I know and yet you have held on to me despite everything. My little one I do not see you the way you see yourself, nor does my servant. Do not fear what he thinks of you my dearest one he seeks only to encourage you for he knows what you are capable of in me. He sees the truth where you still see only the lies of the enemy. Do not despair my little one but remember all that I have said. My promises to you are sure, they tell of not only what you will do but also of who you are, who I am making you to be. I do not compare you to anyone else my little one. You are special and unique in every way. You are mine, my precious child in whom I delight. Do not be anxious and do not be afraid for I am with you and I will help you in every way that you need...

Why couldn't I hear you Jesus? What happened?

My little one the enemy is strong and for a time he overcame you, but I am far greater than He is my dearest one. I have been healing you and strengthening you and now you are ready to begin the next phase of all that have for you...

I don't understand about America.

My little one America is not lost. My promise remains. I will send you to be with my servant just as I have said. You will live and work in America to my glory for many years.

Actually America... the physical place?

Yes my little one just as I have said. I have not lied to you or misled you in any way.

I don't understand.

My little one it is the enemy's great desire to stop my plans for you. He will do this in any way he can. My little one no matter how many lies he throws at you and how many times he manages to deceive you I will always bring you back to the truth. I will always help you to see. I may allow the deception to continue for a time, but I will not ever leave you in his hands my little one. I am always with you...I am always watching over you. My purposes are always good.

So have I been listening to the enemy... in conversations?

Many of your most recent conversations were not with me my little one. Do not be anxious or distressed by this but learn from it. I will help you. I will always help you. I

will help you to see what you have so far not been able to see. I will help you to understand all that the enemy has been doing but do not be afraid my little one. Remember who I am. I am strong enough for you. I never leave you and though this time has been hard and the enemy has caused you much pain and distress, still I have been in the midst. I have used everything that he has done to draw you closer to myself. That is always my desire for you my little one, to draw you closer to me and to enable you to receive more and more of my love for you.**

You have been very good to me Jesus and I didn't fall or give up even when I got so confused.

My little one all that you must ever do is remember who I am and trust me to lead you through anything and everything that comes your way in this life. There will be many dark and confusing times my little one but I will always be there with you. I will not ever let you go...

So what am I doing now Jesus... have I been bad?

No my little one you have not been bad. You have done everything that I have asked of you. You have clung to me through darkness and through great trial. You have not been bad my little one. You have been strong and courageous in me. I cherish everything that you give to me my little one. Do not listen to the enemy. I do not see you in that way.

I felt so bad yesterday and like I might as well die because I was never going to be any use to you.

My little one your life is precious to me in every way. Even if you never reached out to another person on my behalf still, I would see you as precious and beloved. My love is not dependant on anything you do. My approval is not dependant on anything you do my little one for I see and understand your heart which is towards me. Your fear will not stand in the way of all that I have for you my little one nor do I condemn you for it I will simply help you to overcome it if you are willing...

I have missed you Jesus.... I want to be willing... I feel afraid to be willing though. I don't understand.

My little one I long to show you that I am working through you constantly. I know you do not see or understand this my little one. I have given you people to love and you have loved them well. Do not think that I am displeased or disappointed with you my little one for I am not.

Crying....I thought maybe you were.

No my little one I am not displeased or disappointed in any way. My heart is always towards you my little one. I will not ever stop loving you. Do not be afraid my little one. I will not ever leave you. Everything that you do for me and through me is precious my little one. I am not disappointed with you, not in any way.

But I have been afraid...

My little one I know everything about you. I see your heart of love my little one. I know that you feel afraid that you cannot do the things that I am asking of you, but that fear does not make you bad my little one. It does not make you any less precious or beloved. I will help you to overcome your fear, to trust me completely and to follow me wherever I lead you. All you must do is hold on to me and trust me my little one. That is all that you must ever do.

I want to do that Jesus.

My little one I know that your desire is for me and that you long to please me but my little one you have not yet understood that I am already pleased with you. It is not about anything that you do my little one. It is your heart which pleases me, the love that I see there for me and your willingness to do and be all that I ask of you even though you are so afraid of what that will mean. I am already pleased with you my little one. You do not need the approval of others for you already have mine.

Do I?

Yes my little one you do. Do not ever be afraid of what I will ask of you my little one for I am always with you. I ask it of you because of my love for you and for others. I will never force you to do anything and I will never ask you to do anything that I will not enable you to do. Do not be afraid then my little one but place your hand in mine and allow me to lead you forward into all that I have for you. Nothing is lost my little one. It is all still there.

But I am still here.

Yes my little one you are, for now. But I will work through this time to accomplish my purposes for you nevertheless my little one. My promises to you still stand, you will go to America just as I have said. For now, my little one keep your eyes fixed upon me. I know the way that I have for you. Everything will come in my perfect timing, but I have purpose even in the delay my little one. I will work through it to accomplish everything that I desire. My little one nothing is ever a surprise to me. I work through all things for the good of my children who are seeking after me. Do not fear anything that the enemy will do my little one. Only hold on to me and trust me. I know where I am taking you and it is good as I have said many times.

I am glad Jesus. Please... I don't want to be fooled by the enemy again.

You have learned many things through this that you are not yet aware of my little one and the enemy does not have the power over you that he did. Do not be anxious but continue to trust me...

Jesus held me and kept me and showed me so many things that he had wanted me to learn. I learned that he didn't give up on me and he didn't leave me. I learned that he is my promise much more than any of his plans for me and to want anything more than him is to make that thing more important than he is. That is never a good idea. I learned a lot about the enemy and how they work and how dangerous it is to listen to them… ever, no matter what they are saying. I learned that my mistakes don't change who Jesus is or who I am to him. My mistakes don't make me unlovable to him.

The enemy didn't stop trying to trick me or any of the other ways they attacked me, but I felt sure of Jesus and less afraid of my own mistakes. I tried to remember that Jesus was my promise, sometimes I still forgot but not for very long. The enemy still tricked me, but it didn't crush me or drive me to despair like it had before. Fear had lost some of its control over me and that was good. Jesus helped me to understand more of why he had allowed it to happen. I asked him about it a lot of times because it took me a long time to recover from what had happened.

My little one the lie that you believed brought you much pain for that is what lies do. My dearest one living in the truth is the only way for you to truly live. I know my little one that you do not understand why I allowed this to happen, why I allowed the enemy to hurt you so but my dearest one I was with you. My truth was always with you if you had but chosen to see it. My little one the enemy knows your weaknesses for he created them. He wants to destroy you my little one and he will use his lies to do this if he can. But I am greater my little one. The truth of who I am will sustain you through any lie and any deceit. My love will overcome everything that he has done my little one. I did not allow this because I do not care my little one, I allowed it because I knew that I could work through it to accomplish many things my little one. I allowed it because I knew that I could use it to help set you free from the very thing that he was trying to destroy you with. My dearest one this is not yet easy for

you to see and for you it is still painful and confusing, but I see my little one. I see so many things. This time will pass but the memory of this time will remain with you always. The things that you have learned and will learn through this will remain with you my little one and they will protect you in the future when the enemy is trying to deceive you and lead you away from the path that I have for you. My little one my love for you has not and will not ever fail. Though the enemy will hurt you many times I am always with you my little one and I will always redeem everything that he does. He cannot win my little one, not if you keep your trust and your hope in me and in who I am.

Chapter 17

Time Away

After I realized I had been talking to and spending time with the enemy for months I felt a lot of things, none of them good. I felt kind of dirty I think from having spent so much time in the presence of the enemy.

It is a horrible thought for me, not just because I've been deceived but also because I've accepted comfort and love and reassurance and all those other things from the enemy. I've poured my heart out to the enemy, all my fears, all my hopes and desires. I thought I was making a relationship with Jesus, but it wasn't Him. So the enemy is laughing and telling me I've been betrayed by Jesus. That He left me in their hands and that He has no future and no plans for me. It is all impossible for me to understand. My life is such a tangle of lies and deceit and I thought I was finally beginning to find my way through all of that and to find/see the truth. But now I find I'm even more lost than I thought... I just found more lies and deceit and Jesus let that happen, just like He let those other things happen to me. That is hard for me to understand if I am His precious and beloved child.

All the time the deception had been going on there hadn't been any healing happening. I, AJ hadn't taken any steps forward, nothing new had been revealed and I felt beaten and tired. So Jesus took me away to a place, apart from everything, where he could pour out his love on me so I could continue on my journey with him. I think it was the first time that I was really on the outside and he loved me as me and not through the others but directly. I didn't know it then because everything was so confused for me but afterwards, I realized that it had been me he was loving and that I had been on the one on the outside at least some of the time. He loved us all at the same time of course... but this was for me.

Jennifer and Ruth went away for a five-day conference. There were three sessions every day and each one started with a time of worship. I was finding it hard to begin with. I was struggling to worship, and I was full of fear that Jesus would overlook me, that He would do nothing. I was upset with myself for thinking this because I knew that He had never overlooked me before, even if I was afraid that He would.

I think it must have been in the second session when I was stood in front of a woman who was singing with a very, very, loud and shouty voice. I didn't like it, but it made me think about how small my voice is. I heard Jesus say that I didn't need to have a loud voice to be heard. He said He would make His voice loud through me. That made me feel better and like it is ok to be quiet. Later on, in the next session when I was worshipping, I was kneeling on the floor and I was crying again because I was still afraid, He was going to overlook me. I saw Jesus' feet in front of me because He had come to tell me that He won't ever overlook me. I said I was scared that He doesn't want me and that none of the future is true. I kept saying that I am nothing but that I was giving myself to Him because it's all I've got. Jesus said He would love me even if I never gave Him anything. He held me and told me that I would see that none of the things I was thinking were true.

I thought Jesus said to read psalm 18. I liked the first part where it says how God came to answer David's cry for help. It made me think that maybe He was doing the same thing for me even if I couldn't see it because it was happening in the spirit realm. It was interesting too because verse 29 had been spoken from the front but not as a verse as such and I didn't know it was from the bible so I think that Jesus was saying it to me, that nothing can stop me because He is with me. I liked that. And I liked the rest of it that talks about how all of my enemies will be overcome.

On Thursday I was still feeling afraid and a bit subdued. The church had a coffee shop attached to it so we spent a lot of time there between sessions and people would come and sit with us and talk to us. I found this very difficult. The amount of noise from all the talking made it hard for me to hear and was making me shut down because it was a bit overwhelming. That is because it was me on the outside I think, and I wasn't used to it. It was hard work for me to talk to strangers, but I tried to be polite and friendly. Ruth loves to talk to new people though, so she got into a lot of conversations that I wasn't part of. Some of that was the Holy Spirit because He asked her to prophesy over people and He was also making connections... so it was ok, but it was all a bit difficult for me. This lasted the whole week, but Jesus helped me as you will see.

In the first worship I heard Jesus say something to me. He said 'you see yourself as less than everybody in this room, but I call you precious and beloved'... I did a lot of crying at this conference. A lot of what came out of the teaching from Song Of Songs confirmed things that Jesus has said to me in the past, like that what He wants is a willing heart, even if I am messed up and not very good, that is what He is wanting from me. Ryan, one of the speakers, said that in the bible the branches on a tree represent ministry. I was reminded of the picture Holy Spirit had Jennifer paint a few years ago. We sat with him and he directed us. We didn't know what we were painting... we never did that before or since. It was a tree which I know was representing me, but He had her paint it so the branches went off the edge, so the extent of them can't be seen. I wondered if that will depend on the choices I make, whether the branches are big or little or will stretch a long way.

A vision... I saw a tree. It was tall and healthy and full of green leaves. It was in a forest. I put my hands on the trunk, it felt good. Then I began to dig around the roots... the roots were white and healthy, but lower down they turned black and seemed dead. I knew this was affecting its ability to take up water and nutrients. I knew that the black parts had to be removed. Then the tree was suddenly uprooted so that the whole root system was exposed. I could see how extensive these black roots were and how many branches there were. It would take forever to trim them one by one. I saw a chainsaw come and chop off the black roots. A man (God?) came and picked up the tree and carried it out of the forest and into the sunlight. He sat it down in a new place. I saw that the leaves were now shimmering gold and that the trunk was turning golden. It was set down beside a stream. Suddenly, I recognized the picture I painted with the Holy Spirit. Many butterflies came to rest in the branches.

In the first break a young man came to sit with us, and he was talking to Ruth, I was being quiet. I had this thought in my head that he was going to give me a word, so I wasn't very surprised when he did. He said that God was going to refresh me, that He was going to pour out His Spirit on me. That He knew the season I had been in and that He is close to the broken hearted. This reassured me a lot, that He wasn't going to forget me, that He wasn't forgetting me because He asked that man to tell me that. He is so good and kind to me.

In the next worship session, we sang a song called Dance with Me, which is taken from Song of Songs. In it there is a line 'winter is past, and the springtime has come', when we were singing that I could feel the Holy Spirit like He was telling me that it is true for me, now. I started to cry because it is still so hard for me to believe. Then the pastor of the church got up and gave a word about Aaron's staff budding in the Presence of the Lord. And I knew that was for me too because a lady at church gave me (Jennifer) a word a while ago about Aaron's staff budding, that I was like the staff because He has chosen me. So that made me cry more because it made me hope that maybe it is true.

Ryan was talking about trees again. He was talking about how trees need the wind to blow so that they put down deep roots. The deeper the roots the less they are affected by storms and droughts. That is like us, difficult things make us go deeper with God so that we are strong and steady in Him no matter what happens. That made me think about how Jesus had been making me strong so I can withstand all the things that life will bring. He referred to:

> **But blessed is the one who trusts in the Lord, whose confidence is in him. They will be like a tree planted by the water that sends out its roots by the stream. It does not fear when heat comes; its leaves are always green. It has no worries in a year of drought and never fails to bear fruit."**
> **Jeremiah 17:7-8 NIV**

That reminds me of Jennifer's picture too, because in it the tree she painted was beside water. In the evening it was Heidi Baker speaking. It was kind of strange because it took me by surprise at the end when she gave an altar call for those who want to be completely possessed by Holy Spirit. I went forward because I do want that, even though it is a bit scary. I wasn't really expecting anything to happen, but I got overwhelmed by Him as I knelt there, and I was shaking and burning up. I was crying and crying because I had this overwhelming sense of being wanted, kind of like He was gathering me to Himself, and that I am worth something. I kept crying and saying how could you want me I'm nothing, I'm not worthy but He just kept on loving me.

The next day, Friday, we were in the coffee shop before the first meeting and two ladies came to sit with us. I was very tired from the night before and even though they were very nice ladies I couldn't find the energy. It was kind of strange what happened because it was like Jesus drew me away to just be with Him in the middle of this very noisy place. I closed my eyes and found myself singing in tongues (quietly :)) I was sat at Jesus feet with my head resting on His lap and He was stroking my hair. I was singing to Him. It was peaceful and soothing and just what I needed. It felt a bit rude, but I couldn't help it. When the meeting started, I found myself kneeling in the worship, and I heard Jesus telling me to go lower, so I got as low as I could. He said He was going to raise me up, but I said I liked it down near the floor better where no one could see me. But He said He wanted to raise me up so He could shine through me and people would see Him. So I said ok.

Then it was Heidi speaking again. She said lots of things but right at the end she started talking about the cost of following Jesus but that He was worth it a thousand times over. I think she was weeping as she said it I don't know because it was like Holy Spirit came on me and I was weeping, kind of like He was saying that is how it will be for me too. I don't know but that's how it seemed. I went forward again because I knew I was meant to, even though I was thinking I have done this so many times already... saying yes to Him. But He doesn't seem to get tired of it even though I don't know how I can give Him any more than I have. Maybe it means He can go a little deeper every time I choose Him. I don't know. Anyway, it was just like the night before with shaking and crying but this time it wasn't about Him wanting me it was more about belonging to Him, that I do belong to Him and I can have this wonderful, miraculous and costly life that He has told me about.

Ruth gave me a word. She said she had seen me in a road, and I was surrounded by those barriers the police use for crowd control. She said that they were temporary, and that Jesus would remove them and then I could go on down the road. That was encouraging too because I was still thinking about the future and if it was going to come.

In the evening Heidi was speaking again. She was talking about her children in Mozambique and about the orphan spirit. I recognized so many things she was saying, and I was thinking that's just like me. I thought the altar call might be about that, but I didn't feel ready. I asked Jesus and He said 'you are still so far from me, but I am longing to draw you so close but it's not time. The time will come but it's not yet.' In the end the altar call was about something else that wasn't for me so this time I didn't end the evening by crying a lot which was good because I was feeling very tired.

On Saturday in the first session's worship I was overcome again by the Holy Spirit and all I felt was desperation for Him. I was longing and asking for more and crying so much. One thing that Ryan said was that prophetic words are often followed by a season of testing where there is absolutely nothing to see or to show that it is true or that it will happen and that what we go through in that season prepares and changes us for the fulfilment of the promise. That was very encouraging.

By Saturday I was feeling very overwhelmed by all the people. I don't like crowds and I don't do well in groups. Spending so much time surrounded by so many people was getting overwhelming. Ruth had been spending a lot of time talking to other people and Jesus was doing so much through her and I was feeling a bit like a useless piece of baggage. I excused myself and went and shut myself in the toilet and cried asking Jesus to help me and to show me that I wasn't just a waste of space. In the worship I was feeling very bothered by the people around me, even though I was right at the front so there was space in front of me. Jesus told me to get on the floor, so I sat down. I didn't know why He told me to do that but when I was down there it was like I was on my own because everyone else was standing. It was like it was just me and Jesus and the people playing the music. It was so much better, and I was filled with joy and worshipped with all of my heart. I felt much better after this. He is so good.

It was teatime on Saturday when Jesus started to show me some things about Heidi. I think she is both ordinary and very extraordinary at the same time. Jesus does shine through her. I liked that she was so real and open. During the time she was speaking one of the pastors from the church gave her some ballet shoes (Jesus said to do it). Heidi sat weeping as she told the story about the shoes, about how she'd been a dancer but had given it up to follow Jesus and how He had been telling her that it was time for her to dance again, that she would dance across the world with Him. She held them close and said, 'my daddy loves me'. Jesus told me once that we would dance across the world together. I don't know what He meant by that. I'm not a dancer like Heidi. I'm afraid to dance but it made me remember that He said it. So many of the things she said were about how He has loved her, in little and big ways. I never thought that Jesus would show His love in the ways she described. I don't know but somehow it was like I understood something I hadn't understood before about Him and how He loves us.

I watched her with the children at the conference, she had them around her, she got them to pray for people, she loved them. And it was like I could see Jesus and the way He loves His children, the way He loves all of us. I don't know. I have never seen anything like it. Not ever. I never knew it could be like that, that it should be like that. When she was introduced to us by the church pastor, he said she was childlike and she said it too, like it was a good thing and not to be ashamed of. And she is and there is something very captivating about that. I think that's the right word. It made me think that maybe it isn't a bad thing, that I am childlike. Jesus says I am. He doesn't mind it. It made me think that maybe it is ok to be me and not be like other people. I know I'm not like her, but it made me feel a bit better about being me.

In the evening meeting Ryan was meant to be speaking but things got a bit out of hand and so it just seemed to turn into a kind of Holy Spirit party. They did a fire tunnel. It is always hard to get through those and stay upright. It was fun and there was a lot of laughter and people staggering about. I was feeling a bit better than I had been earlier, but parties can be hard sometimes. Ruth was talking to the two ladies I mentioned before, and I sat on my own for a while. Then one of the ladies came over to me and I could tell she was listening to Holy Spirit. She started off by saying that she knew how old I (Jennifer) was because Ruth had told her, but she said that Jesus saw me as a beautiful child. She said that He delights in me. Then she said, 'you are what He is looking for, you have beautiful childlike faith'. I did listen and I thanked her because it was a lovely word, but it made me feel something I couldn't feel just then. Ruth told me later that this lady had been asking questions about me. Not in a bad way I don't think. She said to Ruth that she saw that I had a pure spirit. That is strange to me, but I suppose maybe that is Jesus. He has told me lots of times that I am beautiful and pure, maybe because I don't feel either of those things.

So, the two ladies left and we were on our way out when Ruth said that Jesus was asking her to give a word to this couple who were sitting near us. So I sat down again. I was sitting and watching everything going on around me and I did feel very alone. But the word that had been given to me was sinking in and it hit me while I was sitting there. I think it was a mixture of His delight and that being childlike is a good thing but mostly it was about me being what He is looking for. I was sitting there crying and knowing that He was there with me. I could feel His love for me. I didn't feel alone in that way but at the same time there I was sitting alone crying in a room full of people who were laughing and chatting. I don't know what I said to Him, I can't remember but He said that He was sending me to a place where I would be loved and cared for. That I wouldn't be on my own anymore. That made me cry too because it is so hard to imagine that could be true for me.

The next morning, which was Sunday, we went back to the church. The conference was over, but Ryan was speaking, and Ruth wanted to talk to some of the people she had met. Jesus spoke to me again in the worship time. He reminded me of something that Heidi had been talking about. She told us about a little girl called Magdalena who had been brought to her. She was starving and was very small and weak. She told about how she held her in her arms, my beautiful girl she called her and how she had wept over her. She told how they had started to give her food but that she couldn't keep it down but just vomited it back up because her body couldn't cope with it. Eventually she managed to keep the food down and had been nursed back to full health. Jesus reminded me about her and He said to me 'for so long you have been like that little girl, so starved that you haven't been able to hold on to the love that I have given you, but now you are beginning to be able. Now at last I can start to love you back to life.' His voice was so full of love and tenderness... and I cried and cried because now I felt like there was real hope. That I am going to get better, just like that little girl did. Later on, He reminded me of how Heidi had cradled the little girl, how she had loved her and seen her as beautiful. How she had fed her and nursed her even in the state that she was in. And He showed me that it is a picture for me. It is a picture of Him holding me and nursing me and feeding me and loving me, even in my mess, even though I'm weak and all the rest of it. He still sees me as His beautiful child.

> **You, Lord, keep my lamp burning; my God turns my darkness into light.**
> **With your help I can advance against a troop; with my God I can scale a wall.**
> **As for God, his way is perfect: The Lord's word is flawless;**
> **he shields all who take refuge in him. For who is God besides the Lord?**
> **And who is the Rock except our God? It is God who arms me with strength**
> **and keeps my way secure. He makes my feet like the feet of a deer;**
> **he causes me to stand on the heights. He trains my hands for battle;**
> **my arms can bend a bow of bronze. You make your saving help my shield,**
> **and your right hand sustains me; your help has made me great.**
> **You provide a broad path for my feet, so that my ankles do not give way.**
>
> **Psalm 18:28-36 NIV**

Chapter 18

Being Seen

Jesus now began working to separate Jennifer from AJ so that I, AJ could be seen more clearly. Up until now it had been very mixed up a lot of the time but as the separation between us got bigger it was much easier for us to see me as I really was.

It is something about me, AJ. It feels different but I don't know why. Maybe like... the separation is greater between me and Jennifer. It is making me afraid and I don't like what I am seeing. I feel like...

My little one I know that it is hard for you to see yourself and that you would rather see yourself as Jennifer but that is not who you are my little one. You are the one we are calling AJ, the one that I love and cherish and adore. You are the one I have chosen my little one. Do not be afraid to let Jennifer go when the time is right. You will be well able in me to do everything that I ask of you. And that is all that you must do my little one.

[I had a picture which isn't easy to describe... It was like a shell being pulled away from soft flesh underneath...I could see the membrane that was joining up the shell and flesh and it was tearing so that the shell could come away from the flesh]

My little one there must be separation between you and Jennifer so that you can be seen more clearly. That is my desire my little one, for you to be seen. Do not fear this my dearest one you will not be despised or rejected. You will be loved, and you will be healed. I am with you protecting you and loving you.
Jesus.

My little one what you are seeing is a combination of brokenness and lies. I will heal the brokenness and strip away the lies so that you can be seen for who you truly are my little one. The wonderful child that I see, the person I created you to be. I know my little one that you feel ashamed, but the shame is not yours. The shame belongs to those who hurt you so badly my little one. There is no shame and no condemnation for you. You are my precious and beloved child. You are being healed and restored, delivered from great darkness my little one. The road to healing is not easy my little one but this road also leads towards all that I have for you, including myself my little one. It is a road worth travelling even if it is hard and painful... My dearest one I will be your covering. You do not need Jennifer or anyone else to cover your shame. It is already covered my little one, long ago. It is dealt with and now you are mine and free to be everything that I have made you to be.

I'm sorry Jesus I just can't find any words. I understand but it is hurting.

I know my little one but I am holding you and strengthening you. I will help you with everything my little one. Everything that you are is held by me and loved by me. My dearest one though this time is hard and painful what I am doing is so necessary for your healing my little one. It cannot be missed out or avoided. I will help you my little one. I will give you all that you will need. Jennifer will still be with you in your day to day life, to help you in all the ways that you need but you will become more aware of yourself my little one and of all that you are. You will find this painful at first but as I heal you, you will see the change. I am preparing you my little one for the life that is to come. Do not be anxious then that I have forgotten my promises to you for I am bringing them about even now. Everything I am doing is necessary my little one.

I don't want to see myself Jesus. Help me to look at you.

Do not be afraid of what you will see my little one. You are loved just as you are. There is nothing that the enemy has done that makes you less loveable or acceptable. You are precious and beloved no matter what you think you see.

I am afraid. I am afraid of what I will see. I am afraid of the past. I don't understand why I am like this Jesus, not really.

My little one great evil was done to you and though you had many ways of surviving, still you were gravely hurt. My little one I know that you still fear the truth of your life, but I will help you with that also. It is not too much for me to heal or overcome my little one. There is nothing that the enemy can do to steal you away from me.

Why do they keep saying I belong to them?

Because they are liars my little one. They are liars but they understand the power of their lies over you. My dearest one I know you do not understand for you are still protecting yourself from the truth. I will reveal it to you in time my little one but for now continue to cling to me and remember that you belong to me. You are my own beloved child and you are safe, and you are secure in my arms. He cannot take you from me my little one and I will never give you up. I will hold you close to my heart all the days of your life my little one. Do not fear him but remember who I am and my great love for you which will never fail.

Being separated from Jennifer was frightening and I suppose I wanted to cling on to her, but I noticed more and more the differences. Before now I couldn't tell that it was Jennifer on the outside and not me... AJ but that started to change, and I began to see and know that I was not her just like I wasn't any of the other alters. It was strange to see Jennifer as different and to know it wasn't me. I knew who Jennifer was. I knew the things she could do and not do, what she liked and what she didn't. How she was with people... all of those things. I didn't know anything about me, I wasn't anybody. Nobody knew me or saw me... except Jesus and Mike. Jesus wanted this to change because his plan was for me to be the one on the outside and not Jennifer.

My little one at the right time Jennifer will fall away and only you will remain. Then you will be seen for who you truly are. You will have no reason to hide my little one for you are beautiful. You are not the way you see yourself. I am making you whole my little one. You and I together, that is what people will see when they look at you.

That will be good Jesus. Can I hide behind you?

You are hidden in me my little one. You do not need to hide away in shame for you are wonderful and you are precious in every way. There is no need for you to hide my little one. I am proud of who you are. I do not want you to hide away...

Well... I don't know how that will be. I can't imagine being just AJ. I... am less afraid than I was but... I don't know how it will be.

It will be good my little one. I will be with you. I am your hiding place and no matter what others may think of you I will always love you. You will always be my precious and beloved child...

Jesus told us that for now he only wanted me to let Mike see me.

My little one it is my desire for you to be seen for who you truly are, for you to be loved and accepted for who you truly are but my little one it is not yet time for you to let everyone see. It is not time for AJ to be seen my little one, except by those whom I have chosen.... This is for your protection my little one and because sometimes even true treasure is not recognized or seen for what it is by those who do not have eyes to see. It is not wrong my little one, for you to stay safe for it is not yet time. A time will come when others will see you my little one, when they will see the truth of who you are and of your life. That time will come my little one but it is not yet. My little one for now let it be enough for you that you are seen and you are known, completely known, by me. I will show you the truth of who you are my little one. The truth of who you are is wonderful but only I truly see it my little one. Only I can truly reveal it to you and to others. I understand your desire for relationship my little one for I placed it within you. It is not a bad thing but it is not yet time my little one. True

relationships will come but for now keep your attention upon me my dearest one. You are not alone. You are seen and you are known and loved. I am all that you need my little one.

That was good because I couldn't imagine that anyone would want me or like me and I was still scared of letting Mike see me in our chats. Now that he could see me more clearly, separate from who Jennifer was I thought he would hate me and want me to go away. I thought I was no good. I tried very hard to do what Jesus asked and to not hide from Mike and to let him see me, but sometimes I felt he didn't see me at all even though I tried really hard and that made it even more painful and frightening.

I am not sure you really understood what got me so upset on Tuesday... maybe it doesn't matter but... it matters to me that you understand. I think maybe it is a bit like I have lived my life behind one of those mirrors the police have... so I could see out, but nobody could see me. But now that is changing... and it is important to me that you see me and that people at group see me. I think when you don't seem to see me, I get afraid about a lot of things. I get afraid that I am not real. I get afraid because I think if I can't be seen then I might as well not exist and that I should die. I get afraid because I think maybe it means you don't want me to exist and you are hoping that I will go away. There are a lot of feelings that come with this about being unwanted and unloved and worthless. And of being so alone and so lost in the darkness. All of those come at me when I think you don't see me.

So I think that is why it is hard when I feel ignored and overlooked and forgotten. I know it is the way that I am seeing things, and that it isn't real, and you don't want me to feel like that but those thoughts and feelings come at me like a giant wave and it is hard for me to not drown. I think it is a bit like this anyway and I know the enemy just makes it worse. So then it is like I start to drown, but I can't tell you I am drowning and you can't see. I can't tell you for lots of reasons that we have talked about... like the memory I told you about and being ashamed and not wanting to be any trouble and just because I have never done it before and I don't really know if it is ok to do that. But Jesus says it is ok and you say it is ok, so I will try very hard next time to tell you that I am drowning and then maybe you will throw me one of those rubber rings and I won't sink like I have before.

I had to keep holding on to Jesus very tight and keep on choosing to trust and to follow him, because it was so very painful and frightening to me to be seen....and not seen. But then Jesus started to show me why Mike was having so much trouble seeing me. It wasn't just because of my hiding behind Jennifer even though that didn't help. It was a spiritual thing that had to do with the enemy's power over me. I had chosen to be hidden, to hide away from everyone and everything to keep safe. Now Jesus was asking me to trust him to keep me safe and to give up my own ways of being safe. The enemy didn't want this to happen. They wanted me to stay hidden, so they were making me afraid. I needed to choose to be seen and stop saying I don't want to be seen and to say I choose to be seen instead. Jesus told me that Mike was seeing a very blurred and confused picture of me, because of the things that were going on and that was helping the enemy and not me. I had to choose to be seen even if was scary because I was trusting Jesus to keep me safe.

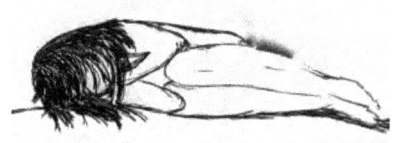

Choosing to be seen was very frightening for me and I could only do it because of Jesus helping me. I had to trust him to protect me and keep me safe. That was very hard for me because I got hurt so easy and because I still wasn't very sure that I could trust Jesus to keep me safe. But it was the only way to keep going forward so I chose as best I could with Jesus helping.

Even while I was struggling to let Mike see me Jesus was asking me to take another step. Mike ran an online chat group where other multiples would come and talk together. Jesus said he wanted me to go to because it would help me, but the thought of being seen by even more people was frightening too and I didn't know what to expect.

I don't want to complain or back away Jesus because this is what you want and everything that you want is good.

My little one I will give you all that you need. I will give you strength and courage and I will help you bear the pain my little one, just as I have always done. I will not stop now my little one.

I am glad you are with me Jesus.

Yes my little one I am always with you. I will not ever leave you. My dearest one I know that you are afraid of what I am about to do but I do nothing that is not good my little one. Everything I have for you is good. Do not be afraid.

I am afraid that you are going to ..expose me Jesus. Please don't do that.

My little one I will never do anything to harm you. Everything I do, I do for you. There is nothing that I will ever do to hurt you my little one. I will lead you forward one step at a time I will help you to see and accept who you are my little one. Some of this will mean that you are seen in increasing measure by others, but you do not need to fear this my little one for I will be with you. I will help you my little one. Do not be afraid of what they will see for you are beautiful and you are lovely. They will not see the lies my little one they will see the truth. This will help you to see and accept the truth of who you are which is my desire for you my little one.

I don't want them to see me Jesus....Crying....

I know my little one, but the power of the lie will be broken only as you come out into the light. Hiding away only gives power to the lie my little one. Do not be afraid. Do not be ashamed but hold on to me and trust me

Crying....

I will not leave you. I am always by your side. My little one.

Crying...

I want you to see the truth. You are lost in darkness and I want to bring you out into the light. Do not be afraid my little one. Take my hand and let me lead you. You are safe in my arms. I will not leave you. I will not expose you in any way.

Crying......But...help me...Crying....

I am here my little one. Hold on to me. I will not let you go my little one. I will lead you forward slowly as you can manage. I am always here for you my little one. You are always in my arms of love. Nothing can harm you. You are safe and you are loved.

Crying......Crying......But how can people see me. I have to be Jennifer.

I will make a way my little one. Small steps to begin with. That is all that you must do. I am with you, every step of the way I will be with you.

Crying....Crying.....But what if they see how bad I am and what if they hate me.

My little one that is not what they will see. They will not hate you for they will see you as I see you. They will love you my little one.

Who are they?

The people I am giving you to my little one.

I don't understand.

I know but follow me as I have said I will show you my little one.

How can I ever be me Jesus?

I will make a way for you my little one. Do not be afraid but take my hand and follow me. I will lead you forward. That is all that you must do.

It was very frightening to go to a group, even though they couldn't see me or hear me. Because of the time difference it was in the middle of the night for me, so I was tired too but Jesus wanted me to go so I did.

I will try my best to tell you how it is. I was happy that I did ok and that I didn't hide behind Jennifer or hide at all. It seemed ok to be me and that is good. I was glad because you looked after me when I needed you to. I know I said I would say if it got too much, but I couldn't do it. I hid under a blanket because it was too hard, and I didn't want to hear it but I couldn't say so. I think I was expecting they might be mean to me, maybe because the alters were mean to me, mostly anyway. But they weren't mean they were nice. I was making a really big effort and didn't run away even when I was wanting to hide. It has been harder afterwards than it was at the time. That is because it has started me grieving again. It hit me again that it is all true, the abuse and the alters...and even though I know that, somehow most of the time I hold it at a distance, and it doesn't seem real. But it seems real at the moment. Somehow really seeing the truth of my life and who I am seems to shake my world all over again even after all this time. It's like the ground under my feet is giving way. I think I should be past this by now, but I suppose I am still living a lie, a pretend life most of the time. That doesn't help me to accept the truth. I am holding on to Jesus though and remembering who He says that I am and that He loves me no matter what, just as I am. That is helping.

It was strange being me with other people. Now there are three people who know I exist. And even though I understand better that being Aj isn't a bad thing somehow it still hurts to be me. I still don't want to be me and all that means. So, I am hurting on the inside but still having to pretend on the outside. I am becoming more Aj but still living as Jennifer, pretending that all is...normal I suppose. When nothing is normal. So it is feeling a bit difficult but I understand why Jesus is asking me to do this. Some of it anyway. I know I need to accept the truth of my life and who I am... a multiple and all that. It is still hard even for me to write it. Being in the group will help me to take another step, that is what He says. If Jesus does want me to live as Aj then I have to start somewhere don't I. I expect Jesus has other reasons, but I think that these might be the hardest part for me. It was even strange for me because of the Americanness... if that's a word. It's not a bad thing just different...

I keep thinking that this will stop sometime, and I can go back to normal but that's not ever going to happen is it. I suppose that is making me sad too. I don't know what this life will look like that Jesus tells me about. I can't imagine it but I know I've lost the life I had. Maybe I shouldn't feel like that is a loss because it was a life built on lies... and not a very good one in a lot of ways but it is the only life I had so it does still feel like a loss. And I still find it hard to believe in the new life.

Even though I understood some of the reasons Jesus wanted me to go group could be a hard place for me to be. Sometimes I didn't see there was any point to it and I didn't feel like I belonged. Sometimes it would make me feel worse and I would cry and cry, but Jesus kept on telling me that it would help me to be seen...even if it didn't always seem that way.

My little one this group will bring life to you. It is part of the healing that I have for you and though it may be difficult and painful at times still it is good for you to be there my little one...
Why will it bring life to me Jesus?
It will help you to accept the truth of your life my little one, the truth of your past and all that it has meant for you. It will help you to understand many things that you have not understood and accept many things that you have not yet accepted. The truth always brings life my little one but that is not all. Through this group I can begin to show you who you are who Aj is. You can make friends and interact with people who understand you my little one. That is a precious thing. My dearest one I am helping you to grow and become stronger. This is necessary my little one for you will not always live your life hidden away behind Jennifer. Soon she will be gone, and you

will be seen for who you truly are. My dearest one I will help you with this, you do not need to be afraid but hold on to me and trust me to guide you through it. I will strengthen you and enable you my little one. You will not need Jennifer in your new life. The life that I am giving to you is given to you my little one and not to her.

So I kept on going and it got less frightening and less painful and I started to see myself differently. It was good to be with others who had been through the same sorts of things and had alters. It made me feel less weird. I did make friends and that was so good for me. It helped me believe that I was real. It was hard sometimes for me to feel like I was real because nobody really saw me except Mike…and sometimes even he didn't seem real to me. I still had trouble knowing what was real and had to trust Jesus to show me.

I think mostly I am still kind of making this picture in my mind of my life and maybe who I am. It is not Jennifer's life, but Jennifer's life is part of it. So my life is kind of Jennifer's life but not. It is a bit hard to get hold of. Her life feels as distant as mine does…by mine I mean all the things that happened and the truth about how life really was. Maybe my real life is only just beginning I don't know because I have never lived life as me. It is a bit confusing to me still. But Jennifer's picture of her life, the one I accepted and believed all these years, that is only a part of the truth of my life. Those things aren't lies, but they aren't the whole truth and maybe they have been interpreted in the wrong way. Maybe. It is still hard to know these things. So my picture of me, of Aj is very different and is difficult to accept as being real and true because it is still so strange to me. But I am not Jennifer I do see that, and those things that I am now remembering, they are real and true, and all those alters are real and true. So I am not Jennifer. I don't even think I want to be Jennifer. I think maybe I am starting to want to be me, because I have some hope that to be me might not be such a terrible thing. Sometimes I think it is exciting to be discovering who I am because I could be anybody, which means I could be something different to what I have been, or what I have expected to be. That is a good thought.

Seeing the truth of who I was meant seeing that the things I had believed about me weren't true...and learning what the truth was. The truth of my past life had been difficult to accept and sometimes I still doubted it could be true and I still hadn't really seen or accepted the truth of who I was. I think it was hard for me to accept the truth all at once, so Jesus showed me a little at a time. Even the things that I already knew took time to really be accepted, I still confused myself with Jennifer. It was hard for me to see me the way I was, but it was like the light was getting stronger and stronger and I saw more and more clearly. Jesus told me that there were two kinds of truth I had to accept. The truth of my life and the truth of who I am in him. Both seemed difficult to me.

My little one I am helping you to see the truth. The truth of your life and who you are. They are not the same my little one. Who you are is hidden in me. Who you are comes from me for you were created by me my little one. You with created with love and you are loved still. My little one the truth of your life is painful and hard for you to accept but it does not change who you are my little one. You are who I have made you to be. You are delightful and you are lovely and nothing that the enemy has done or will do can ever change that my little one.
It is hard to see myself. I get lost in all that stuff.
That is why you must hold on to me my little one. I am your truth. Everything that you need comes from me. There is nothing that can ever change that my little one. I will show you the truth and I will enable you to accept it. My dearest one I know that for you to do this you have to let go of so much that you thought you were and so much that you hoped to be, but my way is so much better my little one. The truth is so much more wonderful than anything that you have believed.
I want to see it Jesus, the truth. I do.

My little one I will help you. I am helping you. My dearest one when you look at yourself you do not see what I see. Your vision is clouded and confused for you have not yet taken hold of the truth though you are beginning to see the glimmers of light that I am showing to you. My dearest one as you begin to see who you are your perceptions will change. I know that the past is painful my little one and that you are afraid of what it will mean for you in the future, but I am your future my little one. No matter what has happened in the past I am your future.

Yes.. It kind of feels like wearing glasses that make me see things in a different way and I'm not quite sure where I am walking or what I am doing. I suppose I will get used to it.

Yes my little one you will. A shift in perception takes time to adjust to but it will come my little one. Do not be afraid to see the truth.

I am less afraid. Maybe because I know that you are here, holding me and I won't fall...but I need your help to see things how you do.

My dearest one I am helping you and I will not stop. My dearest one all that you are is hidden in me. I know that you know this and yet you have not understood it. I will help you to understand it my little one for it will help you to see the truth of who you truly are. My dearest one the horror you feel when you look at the past will fade, the pain and fear will fade, and all will be healed in time but who you are will not change my little one. You are already beloved. You are already my child...you are already everything that you will ever need to be. These things will not change my little one.

Yes... I know I am not seeing things from your point of view Jesus, but at least I can see that now.

Yes my little one you are moving forward day by day. I am helping you to see my little one slowly as you are able. Hold on to me, keep on trusting me. My little one you may not see the way that others see, your experience may be completely different to theirs and what is unacceptable to them may be acceptable to you and vice versa but my dearest one it does not matter what others think or how they see you or your life. Often the truth will be hidden from them my little one, but it will not be hidden from you for I will reveal it to you and enable you to live in the truth of who you truly are. Not the truth of who the world says you are my little one but the truth of who I say you are.

Yes. I think I see that. A little.

My little one you are delightful to me in every way. As you begin to see the truth of this for yourself you will begin to see yourself differently my little one. You will not feel the way that you do now.

Please hold on to me Jesus because I feel very unsteady. I am willing to see the truth Jesus, but it knocks me over every time. I want it to be ok to be me, but it still isn't... not for me anyway.

I know my little one. Keep your eyes upon me and listen to my words of truth. They apply to you my little one. You are not exempt because of who you believe you are. You are my child chosen by me. Created in love to be all that I desire my little one. You are qualified for everything that I am longing to give to you...

I talked to Jesus a lot about these things. Learning to see myself like Jesus does will maybe take my whole life and beyond I don't know because there is so much that I don't see or understand. But spending time with him and listening and being willing to accept the truth even when it made no sense or hurt, meant that I began to move further and further away from the lies of the past and into the truth.

I think somehow in my mind and my heart all the things that happened and everything that it has done to me has made me... somehow less than human. Maybe something to be pitied but not to be loved. Something that needs to be hidden away to avoid causing pain and horror to others. Something that has no hope or right to a life of any kind. But that's not what Jesus sees. He sees something different and all of that stuff doesn't change what He sees. It is hard for me to really see or take hold of it, but it is there, sort of. I know I expect that other people would look at me the way I do, if they could see me. I don't want them to see that. Maybe it is what some people would see I don't know but Jesus sees the truth doesn't He. So if people can't see what He does that doesn't make what they see the truth. I am holding on to Jesus wishing that things were different I suppose but maybe if I could just see the truth and really believe it then I would be glad for the way things are and the way that they will be. I feel like something is changing but it is hard to know what it is exactly.

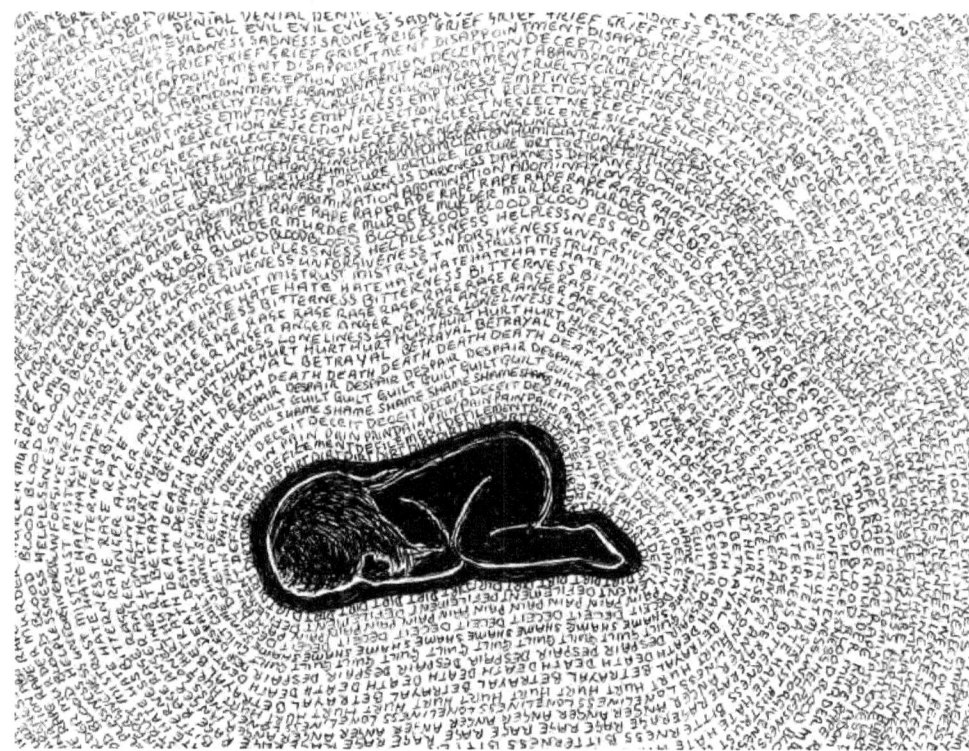

So I knew by now that Jennifer and AJ were not the same person, even though we had shared some of the same life, but somehow the truth hadn't got all the way in and when it did that was very, very hard for me to accept. The truth was terrible to me which I suppose is why it took me so long to really see it.

I keep thinking about who is me and who is Jennifer. It is not easy to say but if it is true that she is an alter and I experience everything through her then maybe the things that I say I do... like, well everything, maybe it isn't me at all. Maybe it is Jennifer and I just think it is me. I was remembering what it was like when there were other alters around and they were on the outside, it only happened a couple of times that I remember, or that I realized because I still thought it was me, even when it was them and I realized that later. It is no different with Jennifer. So all those things I have told you about, all the things that I told you I did. I don't think it was me, I think it was Jennifer. And maybe all I ever did was watch. And all I have ever done is sit here on this bed and talk to you or Jesus. It has taken me a while to see what I was hurting about, but it is like I lost my life all over again. All the things I thought I did, it wasn't me and all the things I thought I was, that wasn't me. I never did anything.

My little one come.
Crying... Why are you showing me these things Jesus?
My little one I am not showing you in order to hurt you but only to help you understand who you are. My little one it is not a bad thing that you have never done anything by yourself, it does not make you bad my little one.
Crying... What does it makes me?
It makes you my precious and beloved child my little one, that is who you are, who you always were and always will be.
Crying.... But all those years and all of those things and all of those people. None of it was me.... Crying....
My little one you gave your life away to another so that you could survive and so that you could care for those around you. My dearest one that does not make you bad.
Crying... Crying...

My little one come to me and listen to what I will say.
Crying... Jesus.
My little one you are my beloved child, you are loved and accepted just as you are. This will not ever change my little one. The life that you have lived hidden behind Jennifer was not for nothing my little one, you have seen and experienced many things. You have loved people through her my little one. Just because you did not do so directly or as yourself does not mean that it was worthless, or it did not count my little one.
I don't understand.... Crying....
My little one even though Jennifer has been the one on the outside there have been many times when the things that she has done and said were coming from you, though neither of you were aware of it.
Crying... I don't believe you. I just sat there and watched...
No my little one that is not how it was nor how it is. My little one part of who Jennifer is comes from you. It is true that there are many times when the things she does and says come only from her my little one. In the course of your lives together that has happened much of the time, as it has with other alters my little one.
Crying... I can't talk about this. It is too much. I am nobody...
My little one you are not nobody. Who you are is not defined by anything that you have done my little one, you are my child? That is who you are, my precious and most beloved child.
Crying.... Please help me Jesus. This hurts too much
My little one who you are is found in me. It is not found anywhere else my little one. I know that you have been believing for so long that you were Jennifer, but you were not my little one.
Crying...
You were never her. You were always my precious and beloved child, just as you are now separate and distinct from who Jennifer is. I have always known it my little one. I have always seen you, hidden away as you were. I always knew who you were my little one. I always loved you and treasured you. That has not changed my little one. All that is changing is your understanding of who you are and what your life has been. I know that this is hard and painful my little one but the truth of who you are is wonderful to me. It does not matter my little one if none of the things that you remember were actually you. It does not change who you are my little one, only your understanding of it.
Crying... I feel like I have lost everything Jesus. My whole life. It was never my life. ... Crying...
My little one though it is hard for you to understand the life that you lived through Jennifer was still your life my little one. You still experienced it, it still changed you and impacted you. It is not so different my little one. You shared those experiences with Jennifer and at times with others but that does not mean that those experiences did not belong to you. It does not mean that it made no difference that you were there, that you existed my little one.
Crying... Doesn't it?
My promises to you remain my little one. You are my precious No my little one. In just the same way as you are influenced by other alters, you also influence them my little one.
It is too hard to understand Jesus. Crying....
No my little one it is not. Your understanding will grow my little one and you will see that it does matter that you were there. Jennifer does not act in isolation my little one. She is so connected to you and whilst it is true that she is the one who has lived life and done all the things that you yourself remember doing that does not mean that you are unimportant my little one. It does not mean that you are nothing and

nobody. You are mine, my very own. You cannot ever be nothing.
Crying....
My little one nothing is changed and beloved child and through you I will do so many wonderful things. My little one your new life will come. It will be a life that you yourself will live my little one.
Crying...
My dearest one I know that the truth is hard and to you it seems like a terrible thing, but it is not my little one. You are who I say that you are. Nothing has changed.
Crying....
My little one I will help you to discover who you are, just as I said I would. It is a journey of discovery that we will walk together my little one. It is a wonderful thing that I am about to do my little one. I am about to restore your life back to you, everything that you have lost and more.
Crying....
I know that this is hard for you to accept my little one but everything is not lost. I will restore everything to you my little one.
Crying.... I know I have been saying it for a long time... about Jennifer but it has just hit me, the truth of it Jesus… Crying...
My little one you are not Jennifer, that is the truth. You have not lived her life my little one she has lived it. My dearest one that does not make you any less valuable. It does not change who you are or my plans for you my little one. The truth has always been known by me.
Crying... But what was it for Jesus? Why did I have to go through all of that when it wasn't... even my life... Crying....
My little one it still formed part of your experience. It still brought you to where you are my little one. It brought you to me. My little one I will help you to understand your life and the person that you are, but it will come slowly my little one. I cannot give you it all at once. The truth can be hard to accept my little one, especially when it is painful.
It is always painful Jesus.
No my little one not always, the truth of who I am and who you are in me, that is not painful my little one, that is good.
Crying... Yes, that is true.... Why didn't I see it before?
You were not ready my little one.
Crying.... Will it get less confusing Jesus?
Yes my little one for once you are able to see the truth your understanding will grow for you will be able to accept the way things truly are my little one.
Crying.... Who am I Jesus?
You are my child my little one. That is who you are.
Crying....
I will not leave you my little one. I will not ever leave you.
Crying......
My little one the life that I have for you will come. It will not be like the life that you have known before my little one. It will not be like Jennifer's life for you are not Jennifer. My purpose and my destiny for you is different my little one. The things that you have experienced through her will help you my little one for you have an experience of lived life even if you were not the one living it. My dearest one I know that it is hard for you right now but you will come to accept the truth my little one and knowing and living in that truth will help you to move forward into all that I have for you. For you my little one because you are my beloved child, chosen and accepted by me. Hidden in my love my little one, just as you have always been.
Help me to accept the truth then Jesus. Even if it hurts. Help me through this.... Crying...
I will my little one I will hold you and love you through everything. Nothing is

changed my little one. You are still my beloved.... My little one my love is surrounding you and will sustain you. I will continue to help you see and accept the truth my little one. Do not fear this but hold on to me for I am your security and your safe place. I am certain when all else seems uncertain my little one.
Yes. You are Jesus. I want to live in the truth. That is what I choose.
My little one your choice will lead you to life. Hold on my little one.
Crying.......Please help me to put it aside so I can sleep Jesus.
I will help you my little one. Acceptance will come and with it...peace.
Yes.
My little one yours will be a life worth living. It will come.
Thankyou.
I am holding you my little one and I will not let go. I will give you my strength and my courage so that you can take every step that is ahead of you.
Goodnight then Jesus.
Goodnight my little one. I am watching over you. I will not leave you.

I cried and grieved for a long time for the life I had lost. I had no idea who Aj was. But Jesus was always showing me the truth that no matter what had happened, no matter what I had done or not done the truth was the same that I was his child. That had always been true and always would be true. All that was changing was the way that I saw myself. 'You are who I say that you are' was something I held on tightly to because it seemed to me that the ground kept on disappearing from beneath my feet and the only safe place, I had was Jesus. He knew the truth even if I didn't.

He began to show me other things too. I had already seen Aj sitting on the doorstep on the inside but somehow, I hadn't understood what it meant but now I did. Now I saw that is who Aj was.

I was thinking about it this morning and I realized I was sitting on a doorstep, in front of a shut door. That is what the stone step was...I think it is right. I think that is me. I don't want to be me. How can I be me and have any kind of a life? How can I be the outside person? I don't know. Crying......
I am here my little one come, come to me.
How can I... I am confused... Crying.... Help me please help.... Crying....
I am holding you my little one. I am holding you and I will not let you go.
Crying.......I can't be me Jesus....Crying.......
My little one I will make everything possible for you. The life that you will live will be lived in and through me my little one. You do not need to be anyone except who you are.
Crying......
I will give you my strength my little one. I will enable you. I know who you are my little one. You are not the way that you see yourself. You are not who you believe yourself to be my little one.
Crying...... But was that me... Crying...... Was it? Crying......
Yes my little one it was. That is how you appear in the inside world. That is who you are my little one, but you are so much more than that, you are mine. You are held by and loved by me my little one, no matter what age you are and no matter how you appear to those around you those are the things that matter my little one.
Crying......I am so confused about everything.
I know my little one, but I am here with you and I will help you. My dearest one there is nothing that is too hard for me.
But maybe you are the enemy, and this is all made up.
My little one the truth is being made known to you. Sometimes it is hard for you to accept or understand but that does not mean that is not the truth my little one. My dearest one your mistakes in listening to the enemy whether that is in your conversations or in your thoughts will not overcome the truth in your life. I am in you

my little one. The truth is already in you and you will find it if you continue to seek it out. My little one do not ever give up. When you grow weary, I am your strength and when you grow afraid I am your courage. My little one do not ever run away from me or try to keep yourself safe by turning away from those I have given you to. My little one that is not the way that I have for you.
That is what Jennifer wanted to do.
I know my little one but that is not the way that I have for you. You follow me my little one.
Yes Jesus. I do...Crying......How can I be that girl. I don't want to be her.
My little one it does not matter if you are old or young it only matters that you belong to me.
Crying......But I can't be me.
Yes my little one you can. You can be who you are with me and you can be who you are with my servant. My little one that is enough for now. Do not despise small beginnings my little one for from these beginnings something greater will grow....
Yes. It is hard to see myself Jesus, but you will help me.
Yes my little one I will. I will always help you. My little one it is not a bad thing to be you. I will enable you to live a life that is full my little one...
Is that what I am doing Jesus, learning to be me?
Yes my little one you are learning who you are and how to live as I desire that you should which is not the way that Jennifer has lived my little one.
Different choices.
Yes my little one different choices. Choices that lead to life.
Yes. I get so sad about my life Jesus. I am sorry.
My little one there is much for you to overcome but you have my strength. My dearest one I understand your struggles but remember that my way for you is always the best way. That my desire is always to bring you good and not to harm you. My dearest one the confusion and fear that you feel do not come from me. My little one the enemy will try to stop you in any way that he can. Do not stop my little one but continue with me. I am leading you and guiding you my little one, no matter how it seems to you. I will not leave you.
I want things to be different Jesus. I get afraid that they won't ever be.
My little one things are already changing. You are changing. Things are not the same my little one for you are walking with me. My dearest one I know that sometimes you feel like you are standing still but you are not. You are moving forward with me in the direction that I desire my little one. Do not be afraid but continue. I will lead you forward my little one, no obstacle can prevent my plans for you from coming to pass....
It is hard to be so alone Jesus.
I know my little one, but this will change as you become more able to be who you are, and you grow less afraid of the people around you. My little one it cannot come all at once. Take one step at a time with me my little one.
I suppose that is true Jesus. I don't manage very well with people.
But this will change my little one as you learn, and you grow stronger and less afraid to be who you are. My little one everything that I am asking you is helping you to walk this path. It is all helping you to grow stronger in me and in who you are my little one. It is not so slow as you suppose for you have made great progress already and will continue to do so my little one.
I want to be with you Jesus... Crying.... I want .. to be loved by you.
My little one I am already loving you and holding you. I know that you need and desire more my little one and it will come as you walk with me. I am always by your side my little one. Always.
Show me how to be loved by you Jesus... and how to be loved by people because...

Crying...... I don't know how to do it. How to let it happen… Crying.... I don't know.

But I am showing you my little one. Each step that you are taking is leading you towards all that you need and everything that you desire. Keep on walking with me my little one. I will not leave you, but I will love you and love you and love you. I will show you how to do all the things that you need to learn and to make all the choices that you need to make my little one. Hold on to me and do not be afraid. Everything that I have for you will come as you walk with me on this journey.......

That is better Jesus. I see better now.

Yes my little one. I will always help you. Keep walking with me my little one. My way for you is good and I will enable you to walk in it.

Yes. Thankyou. Please help me to know who I am. I am confused still about Jennifer.

It will become clearer to you my little one for many things are changing. Do not be afraid but accept the changes as they come my little one.

I will try. Thankyou.

I am always here for you my little one. I will not leave you.

I want... whatever you want Jesus. Help me to follow you.

Yes my little one I will always enable you to follow me. I will lead you forward faithfully my little one.

Seeing AJ on the inside as a young girl only told me what I already knew, that I was much, much younger than Jennifer. Jesus led me slowly and I talked to him a lot about all the things I was learning. It took me a long time to be brave enough to ask him how old I was but eventually I did, and he told me I was sixteen. It didn't come as such a big shock because by now I was seeing myself better and not so afraid as I had been.

Jesus was showing me not only who I was now but who he was making me to be and helping me to understand what he was doing and what it would mean for me. He was helping me to see that I wasn't less because of my hurts and my fear but that because of what he was doing I would be more than Jennifer could have ever been. This was hard for me to accept because I saw Jennifer as being the important one, but Jesus wanted me to see it different.

I saw a picture in my mind of a butterfly struggling to break free of its chrysalis. The butterfly was kind of unsteady and crumpled and bedraggled and its wings looked like bits of rag that were a deep crimson color. I understood immediately that the chrysalis represented Jennifer and the butterfly represented Aj. It made me cry…

Is that really how you see me?

My little one you will emerge crumpled and battered and unable to fly and yet you will be so beautiful. I will breathe my life into you and heal all the wounds my little one and I will enable you to fly. My little one by yourself you may be fragile and vulnerable, but I will be your protector and there is nothing to fear.

Crying….

My little one I will give you the strength and the courage you will need to emerge from all that has been containing you and keeping you bound for so long. My dearest one it is almost time. Time for you to emerge and to be seen for what you are my little one.

I don't know what I am.

No my little one but I know. I have always known. You were never a caterpillar my little one but always a butterfly, longing to fly free. But you have been held captive my little one imprisoned by the very things which have kept you safe. No longer my little one, you will not need that protection anymore. I will draw you forth and you will leave all of that behind so that you can become all that you are and fly free with me…

There's a big difference between a chrysalis and a butterfly Jesus... in what people see and what it can do.

That is what I have been telling you my little one. My dearest one I see what you do not, I know all that you are and all that you will be. All that you are not does not really compare my little one.
Is it true? Is that what will happen?
Yes my little one it is true. I do not lie. My dearest one I know who you are. I see the truth. I will bring you out my little one just as I have said.
I think... Crying...... I would like that Jesus.
That is what I am about to do my little one. You will need to hold onto and trust me to keep you safe for you will feel vulnerable and exposed but I will keep you safe my little one. My servant will keep you safe...you will have no need to be afraid.
It... is much easier to hurt a butterfly than... a hard chrysalis. Is that really the difference?
Yes my little one you have protected yourself well but you cannot live or breathe or fly when you are encased in that way my little one. You must come out in order to do any of those things.
But...
My little one I know what you will need. I will be there for you. I will be your protection my little one.
Can I really trust you to do that?
Yes my little one you can. You can trust me to love you and heal you and protect you all of the days of your life. My little one I am making something so beautiful. I will not allow it to be destroyed. All you must do is stay close to me my little one and I will protect you from all of the storms and from everything that will come against you.
Why a butterfly Jesus... It's so small and fragile...
But beautiful my little one and full of so many colors that glitter and shine in the sun. Butterflies may be fragile, but they can still fly great distances. They have both strength and beauty my little one.
Are they? They don't strike me as being very strong.
But they are made in such a way my little one that in spite of their fragility they can withstand many things. They have a different kind of strength my dearest one, a strength that cannot be seen from the outside but it is there.
I suppose if this is what you want me to be. I don't think I understand it really Jesus.
My little one I will show you why I have chosen this way. My dearest one I could have made you any way that I desired but this is what I have chosen for you. I will show you all that it means my little one as you follow me for there is still a great deal to be revealed.
I don't know ... whether I like the thought of being so small and squashable, but I would like to fly and not be stuck here anymore.
All this and more my little one. That is what I have for you. Do not be afraid. You will not be squashed. I will heal and restore you my little one so that you can be what you were always meant to be.
Thankyou Jesus because you help me to see... a little and you never tell me I'm bad or wrong on the inside even though that's how it feels to me.
I know the truth my little one and I will reveal it you until you are able to accept it completely and you see yourself as I see you my little one...
I've got many thoughts in my head Jesus... about things. I want so much for the next few months to be gone because they look so hard but... you will make everything happen won't you.
Just as I have said my little one.
Will I be ok?
Yes my little one. Hold on to me and you will be ok. I will not let you go and I will do all that I have said.
I want to see it Jesus. And I want to stop being a chrysalis even if it...feels safer.
You will my little one. Keep walking day by day and you will see all that I have

promised.
I'm so glad you found me and saved me and that you are with me. I…want to be with you more Jesus. To always know that you are there. I want to see you and... but you are God and I'm only me.... Crying….
You are my child my little one and all of these things are also my desire my little one. I long to draw you close and to be the realest thing in your life. I long to spend each moment with you, with you being aware of me and able to receive all that I am longing to give to you. That is my desire also my little one.
But you are God and...
But I am God with you my little one, I am God in you and around you. I am your friend and your helper, I am your healer, and your savior. I am always with you and I will never leave you. Being God makes all of those things possible it does not make them impossible.
I suppose that's true.... Crying…… But I don't know why you would want to spend time with me.
Because I love you my little one.
I don't understand.
I know my little one but that is the reason for everything I do. My love is always the reason. Try to accept it even if you cannot understand it.

I was slowly beginning to see that being AJ might be a good thing, that I wasn't what I saw but someone else. Someone who could be more than I ever dreamed and could live the life Jesus told us about. It was still just a glimmer of light, but it was there.

I am God's own handiwork, recreated in Christ Jesus, born anew, that I may do those good works which God prepared for me. Taking paths which He prepared ahead of time, that I should walk them, living the good life which He prearranged and made ready for me to live.

Ephesians 2:10 (AMP)

Chapter 19

Losing My Old Life

As I began to see the truth more clearly Jesus asked me to start letting go of the old... Jennifer and her life... and to take hold of the new that he wanted to give to me.

I have had a couple of dreams now where there have been leaves falling, dead leaves like in autumn but there haven't been any trees in the dreams. I have been wondering what it means but I think it is about loss. I think it is about things being shed to make way for new growth. The leaves are dead, withered and dry like there is no life in them, like the things that are being lost have no life in them anymore. I think that is what it means.

Letting go of the life I had known and accepted as mine, was frightening and painful. Jesus was asking me to let go of the person I have always thought I was. He was asking me to let go of the things I thought I needed to survive and trust him to provide for me. He was asking me to let go of all that I had hoped for as Jennifer and start thinking about my future life as the person he said I was. It was another step forward. It was a hard one to take like so many of them were.

I didn't know what it would mean to live as AJ, but I knew it would be different because I wasn't the same as Jennifer. I couldn't do the same things, I didn't think in the same way and there was so much fear and pain that always seemed to be there, which made it difficult for me to do even ordinary things. I was very afraid I would lose Sophie and Richard and that they would hate me, because I wouldn't be able to be a proper mummy to them. They wouldn't know it was me, but they would see the difference I thought...and they wouldn't like it.

My little one the life that I have for you will come but first there is much for you to let go of. This is a time of letting go my little one. Letting go of the old so that the new can come. This is a good thing my little one and not something to be feared, even if it is sometimes painful for you.
Yes I see that and I am willing to let go Jesus... it's just I will be glad when the new comes. I get afraid that I will be left with nothing.
My little one you will always have me, and I am everything that you need.
Yes. You are. I am sorry...those things don't matter really. I will trust you Jesus and I will follow you.
You are following me into life my little one. There is nothing to fear.
Yes.
My dearest one everything that I am asking you to let go of belongs to your old life, the life of Jennifer. There is nothing that I am taking from you that you will need my little one. At the same time, I am helping you to see and to grow into the person that you truly are so that you will be ready to begin your life my little one. Your life was stolen from you, but I am restoring it little by little.
Yes I see that but... my children Jesus.
I am not taking them from you my little one though I am asking you to let them go. They belong to me my little one and I will care for them. They will always be a part of your life my little one you will not lose them.
That is good Jesus. I don't want to lose them... Crying...
You will not lose them my little one. They are part of you, and you are part of them. They will remain with you my little one even when they are far away.
Crying... Yes. It is still hard for me to imagine that it will be possible for me to leave them.
I will make it possible my little one. Everything is in my hands...

Letting go of my need to know and understand was difficult as well. I had learned the hard way how the enemy can take advantage of my wanting to know over wanting to trust...but it was still hard to let go of...all of it meant trusting Jesus.

> **You desire to know the timings of events so that you can plan in your mind and rely on your own understanding of how and when things should be done but that is not my desire for you my little one. My desire is for you to lean on my understanding and not on your own.**
> Yes. I still find that difficult... to fully let go and to trust you.
> **But I am helping you my little one. It is part of the journey you are on. No matter how much understanding I give to you and no matter how much you are able to live in the truth you will still need my understanding my little one. That will not change.**
> No... I have a feeling it will increase because I will know very well that I can't hope to know and understand.
> **That is so my little one. You cannot, all you can do is trust me my little one. That is a good thing for I know the way, I know all things.**

Now that Sophie was leaving home to go to university, other things were changing too. I was happy for Sophie that she was starting a new life and in some ways I knew it would be easier for me when she was gone, but it was still sad to see her go and to know a big part of my life had come to an end. It meant there was less money coming in too. I wouldn't be able to afford to have a car anymore and even though I wouldn't need it, it still seemed like a big thing to lose, a backward step and not one that anyone would understand.

> Jesus... do I have to let the car go?
> **Yes my little one let it go for you will not be needing it.**
> That will be hard for me too Jesus.
> **I know my little one but it is necessary. Let it go...**
> I got scared... when I was driving...
> **I know my little one, but I was with you. I kept you safe. My little one I will not leave you alone, not ever but it is good for you to let the car go now my little one. Things are changing and you will not need it as you once did. My little one I will not ask anything of you that is not good for you to do.**
> No. I know. Will you help me sell it then Jesus? I can't think who would want to buy it but maybe you know.
> **I will help you my little one.**

Jesus made selling the car so easy for us. We sold it the very next day after putting a notice in the window and for more than we thought we could ask. He showed us something else too... something we gained even when we were giving up something that had been so precious to us.

What I think He showed me was that in choosing to give up my car, in obedience and dependence on Him, it has meant that He could set me free of something that was holding me. Like it was a spiritual thing. I don't understand really what that is... but I think that is right. I think Jesus has set me free from something that was keeping me from depending on Him like He wants me to. So that is a very good thing and I haven't felt sad, I have felt glad about not having the car. He is so good.

We had a lot less money than we did before, but people gave us gifts that helped us a lot. It was hard for me to accept these gifts because I didn't feel like we deserved them, and it made me feel ashamed. But Jesus saw it differently to the way I did. He saw it as his gift to me and part of who he was calling me to be.

My little one it is not wrong for those who are called to receive help and support from those who are not called in that way. Often that will be the case my little one for the calling that I place on some people's lives does not allow for them to make a living by working in the usual way. But it is not wrong for them to work either my little one, not if I ask it of them.
Ok...
My little one sometimes my people do not give as I wish them to, sometimes those called to this kind of life are not supported as I desire that they should be but that does not mean that I cannot provide for them my little one. There is nothing to fear.
I suppose...I was thinking maybe that is why some work.
No my little one that is not the reason for I will always provide what is needed for my people to fulfil their calling. Sometimes the seeming lack of provision can cause faith to falter as I have said but that is not the reason why I ask some of my ministers to work my little one.
So... I shouldn't feel guilty when people give me money.
No my little one you should not, for everything is according to my plans for you my little one. You may not yet see or understand that you are in full-time service to me, but that is the reality my little one. You are working for me, you are being obedient to me. You are called to serve my people in the way that I have asked you and they are called to support you in that.
But... what about support that doesn't come from your people?
Everything belongs to me my little one and I will provide for your every need.
Like you were saying before... so even if your people don't give... you will find a way.
Yes my little one. My people sacrifice much blessing when they do not give as I ask them to, but I am well able to provide for you my little one.
Yes... I see that you are. It's just... I don't feel like one of those people, like I deserve it or am earning it.
My little one everything will come. You are serving me now just as you will be serving me then. For now, your service is largely hidden from the world my little one, but it is not hidden from me. I see you my little one, I see everything that you are doing for me. You have given yourself, your life, over to me in order to fulfil the calling that I have placed in your life. My little one you cannot work to earn your keep and fulfil this calling. It is not possible for you. Do not feel anxious or ashamed because this is so, it is my desire and my design my little one. You are working for me and not for any earthly employer.
Is that true Jesus?
Yes my little one it is so rest in my provision to you and do not be afraid to accept that which is given. My little one I will show you who I am but I will also reveal to you who you are my little one. My servants are always given everything that they need to follow me. It will be so for you my little one.
Alright Jesus. I find it hard though and I do feel ashamed.
My little one what others see should not concern you. Remember that I have called you to this and that everything you are doing or not doing is in obedience to me. Do not be ashamed of your calling my little one.
I'm not ashamed Jesus. I think it is amazing it's just I suppose others can't see it. I can't see it a lot of the time, so it feels wrong to take money.
But it is not my little one. Remember what I have said to you. This is my desire for you my little one.

Sophie wasn't the only one that was leaving. Ruth was also going away to college, only for a year, but it seemed like it was the beginning of the end. Even though she is only going for a short time and I will see her again somehow it seems like a more permanent thing, like this is the end really. That isn't just me, she feels it too. So, we were a bit tearful and not really wanting to look at that. It is hard to think we won't be spending time together in the same way anymore, that our friendship might be coming to an end. It is all making me sad. It is very good of course that she is moving forward and that things are changing for her. We both know that to move forward with Jesus, we have to let a lot of things go, even each other, but it is hard. These things were all coming at once and it was hard for me not to feel like I was losing everything. Most of all I knew that I was preparing to lose Jennifer. That felt like the biggest loss of all to me, because it was like I was losing myself, even though that wasn't so.

I will show you who you are my little one, who I have made you to be. Not the person that the enemy has made you to be but the person that you truly are. My little one many things must be stripped away, many things must be lost but the things that remain will be cherished and nourished and you will blossom and grow into all that you were meant to be my little one. Do not fear this for it is a beautiful and wonderful thing. I am making you new my little one and even though sometimes this will be painful it will be worth it my little one, to become everything that you were meant to be, it will be worth it.

Jesus was showing me a new picture of I was... not Jennifer but someone else completely. Someone who was a child yet couldn't live as a child. Someone who wasn't like other people, not like other children. Someone that Jesus was calling to be different again because of all the things he was asking me to do and be. I was very afraid to be different, afraid of being seen. But it wasn't just that I was afraid. I wanted to be a little girl and do little girl things and play and have fun and be loved and looked after. I so longed for that but the picture Jesus showed me wasn't really like that.

Crying.... I don't know what the matter is Jesus...
My little one you are beginning to see. You are beginning to see clearly my little one just who you are and all that I have called you to. That is good my little one but it also means that you must let go of some other things. Things that you have held on to my little one but which are not helping you.
Crying.... Like what...
Like the belief and the hope that you can be an ordinary little girl.
Crying....
My dearest one even though you can never be an ordinary little girl living the life that an ordinary little girl would have what I have for you is better. So much more my little one.
Crying.... I don't know what... Crying....I was thinking Jesus... I can never be normal. Crying...I don't know why I thought it... If I did. I don't know....
My little one you long for all the things that little girls need and long for. You long for love my little one, for acceptance of who you are. You long to play and to laugh and enjoy the life that is given to you. You long for the freedom to express yourself without fear and most of all you long to be cared for. My dearest one these things are not wrong for you. They are my desire for you my little one. I will meet all of these needs and more my little one, but you will never be an ordinary little girl living an ordinary life.
Crying...
My little one letting go of this will enable you to take hold of everything that I am longing to give to you. My dearest one what I have for you is far better than the things you are holding on to.
Crying.... I didn't even know I was till now Jesus. But... Crying....
My dearest one all that you are belongs to me. I will give you everything you need my little one. You are so very precious to me and though you cannot ever be ordinary in this world my dearest one I am making you extraordinary. My dearest one to love and serve me in this world is not easy and less so for you my little one because of all the challenges that you face but I will make it possible for you my little one and through you I will do so much more than I could ever do if you were an ordinary girl. That is

better my little one. It is far better.
Crying.... I know I am silly Jesus.... Crying....
No my little one you are not silly. This is part of accepting who you are my little one. You are not ordinary... you will never be ordinary, but my dearest one you are mine. You are safe my little one and you are so very loved. I will make you all that you can be as you follow me. My dearest one I will not ask you to be ordinary I will ask you to be who you are. That is better my little one. It is far better.
Crying....Crying....
My little one I will give you all the love that you need, all the acceptance that you need. I will help you my little one so that you can receive these things from others also. My dearest one I have so many good things for you.
Crying....
My dearest one the things that you want are not bad, but I have something better for you.
Crying....I am a bit afraid of what you are making me to be.
I know my little one for you fear being different, set apart. You fear to be seen but my dearest one these are my desires for you. I am making you so very wonderful my little one and even though you will be different you will also be loved and even though you do not blend in you will be accepted. My dearest one do not be afraid.
Crying....I am afraid.
I know my little one, but I am with you. I will always be with you. My little one you will not ever be alone. I know my dearest one that you still feel alone and think that this will not ever change but my little one it is not my desire that you should feel alone, not ever. I am always here with you my little one. I will send you to be with my servant and there you will be loved and cared for just as you need. I know my dearest one that the path is not easy, but I am here with you. I will help you to become everything that I desire for you to be. Do not fear it my little one.
Help me not to be afraid Jesus....
Yes my little one I will help you to accept the person that you are becoming and not to fear it in any way. My dearest one as I lead you forward on this path you will become stronger and more able to do the things that I am asking you to do. But it is always your choice my little one, to follow or not.
I want to follow Jesus... Crying.... I want to be everything you want me to be... But I am scared.
I know my little one, but I am with you and will help you. My dearest one as you follow me you will find that being you, the person that you were truly created to be will bring you life and through your life to others. This may be scary at first my little one, but I will help you,
Crying....
My dearest one you have been living your life hidden away, even in this life that you now have you are hidden away for the most part. I am asking you to step out into the light my little one, to be seen for the person that you are and everything that that means. My dearest one I understand your fear, but you are safe in my arms of love. I will not ever leave you.

I spent a lot of time talking to Jesus about what it would mean to live without Jennifer. I didn't want her to go. I was afraid and didn't see how I could live her life and be her to the people around me, people who expected things of me I didn't think that I could give to them. I was very afraid of what people would think of me. I knew I wouldn't be able to make myself acceptable by having a job or being clever or any of those things that people think make you worth something. I was very afraid that I wasn't worth anything. It was especially hard with mum because she would ask Jennifer about plans for the future and what she was going to do, and we couldn't tell her anything that sounded good to her. We were hiding everything from her of course and she didn't understand why Jennifer had given up counselling and the promise of a good career to sit around and do nothing. I was very afraid of what people would say to us. Letting go of my need to please people and trusting Jesus to protect me was very difficult.

>I can't manage without her Jesus.
>**My little one everything that you do you do in my strength. I will not leave you helpless and unprotected my little one. I will give you everything that you need. Jennifer is still with you and though she will soon be gone she will always be there when you need her. You will not need her when she is gone my little one.**
>You mean you won't take her until I don't need her.
>**Yes my little one so do not be anxious about her. I know my little one that you fear exposure, but I will not leave you unprotected my little one. I know what you need to live in this place, and I will provide it for you.**
>You make it sound like she will be gone before I leave.
>**She will soon be gone my little one but that will not matter for you will have me. I will be your protection. I will be your strength.**
>But I can't let people see me Jesus, not here.
>**They will only see what I allow them to see my little one. Do not be afraid. I will not abandon you. I will be with you. I will be your covering and everything that you will need.**
>Why can't I keep her Jesus?
>**Because she is not you my little one and my desire is that you should be who you truly are and not anyone else.**
>But not here Jesus.
>**Yes my little one even here.**
>But that's not what you said Jesus. You said that I could keep her here because I need her.
>**I said that you could keep her whilst you needed her my little one. You will not need her for you will have me.**
>But... how will that work?
>**My little one I can do all things. Everything that you need is to be found in me, not in yourself my little one, not in Jennifer but in me.**
>I understand that you want me to rely on you and only you Jesus... but how can I be here as me. Nobody knows me, nobody will want me. Please don't do that.
>**My little one they will not see you as you believe that they will. They will only see what I allow them to see. Do not be anxious my little one but depend upon me for everything. I am everything that you need my little one, even here in this life.**
>I know... It's just not what I thought you said.
>**My little one everything that I have for you is good, everything that I ask of you is for your good. Do not be afraid my little one. I will hold you and protect you and enable you to be and do all that you need to be and do my little one. The only difference is that you will be relying upon me and not upon Jennifer.**
>So you will do what she does?
>**I will do it better my little one there is nothing to fear.**
>But... I don't want them to see me Jesus. Even if I can do everything I need to, I don't want them to see me.
>**My little one you are hidden in me there is nothing to fear. I will keep you safe. I will keep you protected and secure. No one will see you that you do not want to see you my little one.**
>That would be no one. I don't understand. Is it just about dependence?
>**It is about dependence and trust my little one. This will require you to trust me and to depend upon me for everything.**
>I don't think I like it.
>**I know my little one, but I will show you that I am safe and that I will keep you and**

give you all that you need.
It doesn't seem like something I can do.
I know my little one, but you can do everything that I ask of you. I will enable you.
I don't like it.
My little one everything I am has been given to you, you belong to me, every part of you belongs to me. I love you with an everlasting love, I will not ever let you go or fail you in any way. You are safe in my hands my little one, no matter what I ask of you.
I know that must be true, but I don't feel safe.
But you will my little one, as you surrender yourself more completely into my hands you will feel safer than you have ever done. My little one my way for you is good, do not fear it.
I will try.
I will be enough for you my little one.

In my efforts to understand I would talk to Jennifer. It was very strange to talk to her like she was an alter, because I was only just beginning to see her that way. It did help me to accept the truth though and it helped that Jennifer was so accepting of the changes that were happening. Jennifer didn't write to Mike very much, but now things were changing for her as well as for me.

Hello Mike.
This is Jennifer. I wanted to write because of all the changes that are happening. I think maybe I have some things to say that will help you and I hope AJ to accept the things that she is learning. Not that you need help to accept them... but maybe so you can help AJ to accept them. I don't know but anyway here it is. I have been talking a great deal with Jesus. I find him interesting and I enjoy his company. He always has a lot to say about you and about AJ. I think because he wants me to help AJ in every way that I can. I want to do that. I know that sometimes I have been upset with you, but I also know that you do truly care about Aj and that you are willing to follow Jesus wherever he takes the both of you. I know that my time with Aj is coming to an end and that yours is about to begin.

I don't want you to write these things….
Why not?
Because…Crying…. I don't… Crying… It scares me.
There isn't any reason to be afraid of what Jesus has planned for you...
I don't know. I am sorry. You write, it is ok.
Ok. Don't worry... so... Mike your time with Aj is about to begin. I don't know when this is going to happen, Jesus hasn't told me, but I don't think it will be long. I suppose what I am trying to say is please take care of her. She will need a lot of love, I think.
Crying......Please don't.
It's true though isn't it
Crying...You don't need to say it though.
I am worried about you.
Why?
Because I won't be here to look after you anymore.
But...
I know you will have Jesus. I know but, I will just feel better if I say this ok.
Ok.
Mike, I know that you have been doing this for a long time, but this one is special. I know you will say they are all special and I suppose you are right. I just want to know that you will care for her and not leave her on her own. There. I am sorry Aj. It isn't a bad thing for me to say.
I don't understand why you would care... I am sorry.
Of course, I care that's why I'm here.

Does Jesus say that I am going?
Yes. He does. That is His main concern now, to get you ready so that you can go. I am not going you know.
I know... Crying... Crying...... I can't do this... Jesus
I am here my little one.
Crying... Help me
I am here my little one. I am holding you.
Crying...
My dearest one keep holding on to me. Hold on to all that I am. I will bring you through all of this my little one. I will help you.
Crying......
You will not be overcome.
Crying... Is all of this real?
Yes my little one it is real. My dearest one I will help you to live in the truth. Do not be afraid my little one but hold on to me. I will bring you out of this place just as I have said. This time may be hard my little one but you can do it in my strength. I am holding you. I will not let you go.
Is the things Jennifer said right?
Yes my little one, according to her understanding of them.
I wish that you would just... I don't know.
My little one this time will come to an end and you will see your new life but my dearest one before you can begin your life you have to let go of the old one, much of which was never really your life my little one. I want you to know and accept the truth of who you are so that you can step unhindered by those things into all that I am giving to you. Your new life will be yours my little one, completely yours and though the past has been shared by many the new life that I am giving to you will belong to you my little one....
What about all the alters? You said... they would be outside sometimes.
Yes my little one from time to time they will but that does not mean that your life will be shared or taken away from you. Your life will be yours in a way that it has never been before. My dearest one this body will be shared by many for many years to come but that does not mean that you cannot have your own life my little one.
No. I see that Jesus.
My little one I will help you in every way that you need. This time is hard my little one but it will not last long. You are almost there my little one. Keep holding on and keep trusting in who I am. New life is coming my little one.
Ok Jesus. Thankyou. I am going now. Please help me with the rest of the day.
Yes my little one I will give you the strength that you need. Hold on to me my little one.

The fear that I was letting go of all of these things and people and who I was and my life as I had known it and that there would be nothing to take its place was one that I struggled with a lot because I was afraid to believe in the promises Jesus had given to me. I still didn't think I deserved to have anything good.

My little one I am always with you. I walk with you through every valley my little one, through all the seasons of your life. I will not ever leave you. My little one this is a season of change and transition, where much will be taken but much will also be given. My dearest one change is not always easy for it requires you to let go of the old familiar things and to take hold of new things, things that will seem unsafe to you for a while. But I am with you my little one. I am your safety and your security. There is nothing that lies ahead of you that I do not know and have not prepared for you. You can do everything that I ask of you my little one, you can accept every truth that

I am giving you. You can overcome all of the obstacles that stand in the way of you obtaining the new life that I have promised you. All of this and more you can do because I am with you. I will not leave you my little one. I will give you everything that you need. Every change that I am bringing into your life is for your good my little one no matter how it may seem. My dearest one keep on holding on to me and trust me. The way I have for you though not easy is good. It is very good my little one. I am able to give to you the best of all that I have for you because you are willing to follow me. Do not stop my little one. Keep your hand in mine and I will lead you forward. There is nothing to fear my little one. I hold you in the palm of my hand. You are loved and you are safe. All that I am I give to you my little one.

Jesus was helping me to see and understand that by letting go of the things I thought of as mine, that I thought I needed, I was more able to take hold of the things he wanted to give to me, which were far better.

My little one come.
Jesus. I remembered you are here, and I can talk to you any time I want.
Yes my little one you can always talk with me. I am never far away....
I was thinking yesterday about how I think it should be possible to live with you by my side, like you were anyone else. So that I can talk with you and laugh with you and I could hear you and even if I can't see you it would almost be like I could because I would be so aware of you. I would like that Jesus.
My little one this is my desire for you and for all of my children that you can live so close to me that you are always aware of me, that you hear my voice and know my ways. My little one there are so few of my children who ever get close enough to me to live in this way. It is not impossible my little one, but few choose to follow the path to such intimacy.
Why is that Jesus?
Because of what it requires my little one. It requires you to live in my world over and above the world that you see around you. It requires total trust and surrender to me. It requires you to follow me with an open heart. It requires you to believe my little one...
But... surely some people live in that way.
Yes my little one some do and that is to my great delight but many do not my little one for it requires too much of them. To live in complete awareness of my presence is not an easy thing my little one for there is no hiding in my presence.
No... but do you mean because we like to pretend you aren't there so we can do and say things you don't like.
Yes my little one but not only that. Living in my presence means that every moment is surrendered to me or if it is not then it means to be aware of that. It is not easy my little one to live in that way but that is the way that I desire you to live.
So, to live in constant awareness of you, like you were physically here means, to acknowledge that you are lord all the time of everything, every thought, every word, every action... is that what it means?
That is what it would mean for you my little one. There would be nowhere for you to hide if you knew that I was always there with you in the way that you are thinking of.
But that is the truth isn't it. You are always here... so am I choosing not to be aware of it because it suits me better, because then I can do what I want or hide from the truth or whatever?
Yes my little one, that is what it means. There are still areas of yourself and your life that you are unwilling to open up before me my little one. I understand this and I will help you to do so as you follow me. But to live in complete awareness and surrender to me means no more hiding and it means living in the truth my little one...

When you say it like that Jesus, I am not surprised that it's only a few people who live like that.

My little one I will teach you and lead you and enable you to live in this way for it is my desire for you as it is for all of my children, but you are still afraid my little one. That is what is hindering you...

Yes. It makes me sad. I am still afraid... and the truth is still hard for me.

My little one the truth of your life will not hinder you anymore once the fear is gone and it will go my little one for, I have come to set you free from all the fear and the pain of the past. It will come my little one. Your healing is in my hands...

When I know who I am and how much you love me and that there is no shame for me in your presence... then will I be able to live in that way?

That is a big part of it my little one for then you will have no more fear of me or of what I will ask of you. You will know that you are completely loved and accepted my little one, but you must also learn to live in the truth of the kingdom which surrounds you and is within you. There is so much that I have for you if you will follow me my little one...

I can't help thinking Jesus that... it ought to be possible to live that way but maybe I am making too much of myself even asking about it.

No my little one you are simply recognizing who you are. You are made to live in my presence my little one, to know and be known, to be loved and surrounded by me. You were made to inhabit the spiritual world just as you were made to inhabit this world. There was never meant to be a division between the two my little one. I came to restore everything that has been lost to you, all that you have to do is take hold of it.

But often that is hard and means fighting doesn't it?

Yes my little one it does. It requires great sacrifice to take hold of the things of the kingdom in this world for there is much opposition my little one. You must be prepared to let go of many things in order to enter into all that I have for you.

But those things don't compare, do they? The things you have for me are much more wonderful.

Yes my little one that is so but often you must believe by faith that I am giving to you real treasure in place of the false treasure you are holding on to. You must be prepared to let go of that which you value to take hold of that which is truly valuable.

Yes... are we back to talking about letting things go again?

Yes my little one we are for that is the season you are in. My dearest one I know that it is not easy to let go of your life, for that is what I am asking of you but my little one what I am giving you in exchange is so much better. There is no comparison my little one....

You are making me think about the bigger thing of losing my life to find it, it is like that isn't it?

Yes my little one it is a picture of that for when you give your life to me I ask you to lay everything down and follow me, your life belongs to me and not to you but in exchange I give you true life, eternal life so that in laying your life down you gain my life, which is true life. That is what I am asking of you my little one. Though this is not the spiritual exchange of life that I have just spoken of this is similar. You are already in possession of my life my little one, but this is a physical expression of that. You lay down this life, the one that you have always known, the person you have always been, and you exchange them for the life that I am giving to you and the person you were made to be.

Yes. I understand. I have to be prepared to lose everything, even myself, so that you can give me whatever it is you are wanting to give me.

So that I can give to you true life and your true self my little one. That is what I am giving to you. I am giving to you the life that you were created to live, and I am

making you to be the person you were created to be. I am restoring everything my little one according to my purpose and my desire.

I like that Jesus... but it is still hard to let go.

I know my little one but I am helping you. Do not be afraid of the pain that comes with laying these things down my little one. You do not need to hold on to the old you, you do not need to hold on to the life that you have here. Hold on to me my little one and let the old fall away. I will restore to you everything that has been lost if you trust me and follow me my little one.

Yes. I think I am willing Jesus... I am willing but it is hard. And it is making me cry. And I'm still not sure that you will give me anything. I'm sorry…

My little one I will not break my promises to you. I will not take everything from you and then leave you bereft my little one. That is not my plan for you. That is not my desire my little one.

Crying......But that's what I'm afraid of. That you will leave me here with nothing, not even myself. And that you will go. I'm sorry.

My little one I will not ever leave you. I will not ever leave you. I am not asking you to let go of what you have so that I can leave you with nothing my little one. That is a lie of the enemy. I am asking you to let go of what you have so that I can give you something better, something so much better my little one. The enemy does not want to you to have this, he is afraid of you having what I am about to give but I will not fail you my little one. Keep on following and be willing to sacrifice everything to me my little one for I will always bless you and keep you and love you and provide everything that you will ever need. You will never give more to me than I do to you my little one. Not ever.

I am sorry. I know you are right. What I am laying down is nothing compared to what you have promised. Help me not to be afraid Jesus…

My little one I will help you. I will always help you to do everything I ask of you. My dearest one this time will pass, and you will see that all that I have asked of you was necessary my little one and that it was worth it. My dearest one there is so much that I am longing to do. Keep following and keep trusting and do not be afraid. Do not ever be afraid of me or what I will ask of you my little one. You have not understood how much I love you or what that means but I am longing to show you my little one.

Whoever finds their life will lose it,

whoever loses their life for my sake will find it.

Matthew 10:39 NIV

Chapter 20

Hello Holy Spirit

I was learning more about who I was and about Jesus plans for me. He always told me that even though he had plans and purposes for my life and how I would serve him his bigger plan and purpose was to draw me closer to him and to make me into the person I was created to be. One night I had a dream.

In the dream I was sitting at a meal table with some other people. A new person, a man, came and sat next to me. He didn't seem interested in anyone else but told me he was a teacher. He was very enthusiastic about his job. He was wearing glasses and a pink jumper. He said he wanted to be my boyfriend, but I said we should get to know each other better. We were trying new dishes, things to eat, I think. What I think this means is that it is about me sitting at the table with a new teacher. I am going to be shown/fed new things. The teacher wants to become more intimate with me, but I am thinking I don't know him very well yet. I think the pink jumper probably represents love. The teacher is the Holy Spirit.

I had spent lots of times with the Holy Spirit when I was being healed and had learned a lot about the dreams and visions that he gives before I knew about the bad things, but this seemed like it was something different and new.

My little one my Spirit is with you and will show you many things. This time is for you and Him my little one. He is your teacher for this season.
Why? Him and not you? It is hard to...you are different...I don't know.
My little one I will not leave you and I will continue to spend time with you in this and many other ways, but my Spirit is within you and guides you constantly my little one. It is time for you to get to know Him a little better.
I would like that...
It is His delight to spend time with you just as it is mine my little one. He is your partner and your friend. He will never leave you or forsake you and will empower you to do everything that I ask of you.
I don't know what to say. I feel excited about... what I am going to discover I am thinking this is about me seeing... me and you and the world a bit clearer.
Yes my little one that is what it is about. It is necessary for you to begin to learn and understand so many of my ways and the ways of my Spirit. It is necessary that you begin to see yourself as you truly are and to begin to walk in the truth to a far greater extent than you have so far been able. My little one this is a time of hope for you. Do not be anxious about the next season but take hold of this one.

I didn't really know how to talk to the Holy Spirit, so I decided to write... because that's what I knew how to do.

Jesus told me that the Holy Spirit was setting me free to receive everything he wanted to give to me. Jesus said they were both working together to draw me closer to him and I didn't need to understand it all. That was good because I didn't. Right at the start of our times together the Holy Spirit gave me a picture. It is one that I have gone back to time and time again on my journey because it is a picture of what was ahead for me and it helped me to understand a lot of things as time went on.

The first thing I saw was the sun. It was a very fierce sun blazing down on what liked like black fog. The fierceness of the sun drove the black fog away and I could see me standing there in the sun. It was a bit like a desert, and I felt very exposed. I felt like I was being wrapped in a blanket which covered me and comforted me at the same time. It helped me to feel safe even in the brightness of the sun. Then a man... I think this was the Holy Spirit, came and took me by the hand and led me to a river where there was a small boat, a bit like a rowing boat but it didn't have oars it just had one paddle which the man used to paddle the boat downstream. It was only a short distance and then we came to a waterfall. It was a very long drop, but he just sent the boat straight over. We landed at the bottom without even getting wet. It was different at the bottom of the waterfall than the top. The top was like a desert but at the bottom there were trees and a gentle breeze and birds singing. The man guided the boat to the shore and led me into the forest. It got dark again, but he took me to a clearing where there was a fire, like a campfire. There was a group of people sitting around the fire in the dark. They seemed happy and like they were all good friends. The man took me and put me in the circle with the other people, maybe nine or ten people I am not sure.

When he gave me this picture, I was still in the darkness, but I knew that when I came out into the sun that is when I would be on the outside instead of Jennifer. It was a comforting promise that even though I felt so exposed I would be covered and protected...that was what I was most worried about for now.

The Holy Spirit began showing me who he is in my life and helping me to understand all the things he does for me and wanted to do for me. He wanted me to understand that I wasn't alone on my journey and that everything I needed would be given through him.

My little one everything that you do is done through me, everything that you experience is through me, everything that you hear and see is through me, that is my gift to you little one. I enable you to see and hear and perceive. I enable you to respond to us. I give you everything that you need to be the person that you are, living in our kingdom as a child of the king. It is through me that all of these things are possible my little one. That is why I say I am giving you a testimony. I am giving you a testimony about the king my little one.
I don't think I have really understood about these things Holy Spirit. Please keep showing me who you are.
Yes my little one. Do not be afraid because you do not yet understand. I am showing you many things my little one for I do not want you to be ignorant of these things. I want you to know and understand who I am in your life and all the things I make possible for you. This will give you confidence my little one and increase your capacity to grow and receive from us, from all of us my little one.
Because you are the spirit of the father and the son.
Yes little one that is so.
And you... it is because of you that I can hear Jesus.
Yes little one, I have given you that ability.
Thankyou Holy Spirit.
You are welcome my little one. I am longing to show you all the things that I enable you to do and to be, many of which you have not yet discovered...
I think... you are changing something inside... I can feel it happening.
Yes little one. I am changing your perception of what you thought you understood. I am bringing you truth little one...
Are you praying for me Holy Spirit?
Yes my little one I am constantly praying for you.
But that makes no sense to me Holy Spirit. Why would you pray to yourself?
I am not praying to myself my little one I am praying before the throne of the father from whom all things come.

So... you have to ask the father?
Yes little one as does Jesus
Why?
Because little one he is the source
I am not understanding why he is the source and you aren't Holy Spirit.
Because that is how things are ordered little one. Even though we are all equal even though we are all one the father is the source, just as Jesus is the savior little one.
So like you have different jobs?
Yes little one a bit like that but not quite.
And the father is in charge of giving you things for us out of the storehouses of heaven maybe?
Yes little one something like that.
I know there is more Holy Spirit.
Yes little one there is much more.
So you go to the father and ask him for stuff and I suppose he always says yes to you because you are always agreeing. He wouldn't ever say no, would he?
He would not ever say no little one, not to me and not to Jesus for we know his heart completely, we are one with him little one.
So why can't you just go get the stuff yourself Holy Spirit?
Because the father is the source little one. I know you are not fully understanding but that is because there is still much for you to see and to learn.
Alright... so you and Jesus you both pray for me and the father gives you what you ask for because they are always good things.
Yes little one that is so.
But... Some things take time, though don't they.
Yes little one sometimes they take time to be made real in the physical sense but in heaven they are already real. There is no waiting in heaven.
So the father is not being slow to make up his mind or give you the stuff.
No little one. He is not slow to answer.
But... the answer may be slow in getting to us?
Yes little one and there are many reasons for that which we will discuss at a different time.
I think that would be a big conversation Holy Spirit.
Yes little one it would.
So... are you praying all the time Holy Spirit?
Yes little one I do not ever stop. I am constantly before the throne interceding on your behalf.
I expect you will stop when I am dead though Holy Spirit.
It changes little one but there are still things that must be asked for and received even in heaven.
Really?
Yes little one for the father will always be the source. It will not ever change little one.
Oh... I think... heaven might be another day too or I will get confused.
Yes little one another day.
Why does it say about you groaning Holy Spirit?
Because when I am praying through you little one that is how it can sound and feel, for I am expressing things you cannot understand and asking for things that you have no knowledge of... My prayers are deep little one, they go to the heart both of God and of man.
I don't know what to do with that at all Holy Spirit. Deep prayers... I get ashamed about my prayers. I think they are not very good.
Little one I will teach you how to pray effective, strong and deep prayers. That is part of all that I will give to you but little one do not underestimate the power of your

prayers, you are heard and you are answered. Many words are not required little one. The true power of prayer lies in the heart.
But your words have power, don't they?
Yes little one they do but the words in themselves are not enough little one, it is the power behind the words that is important. This comes from the heart of the one who is praying little one.
I see... but I am thinking there is a way to release that power Holy Spirit is that right?
Yes little one it is and that is what I will teach you.
That's good Holy Spirit. I would like to pray prayers that make a difference.
Your prayers already make a difference my little one but there are different levels of prayers. I will help you to go deeper little one so that you can pray with greater power than you are able now.

He started to teach me a lot of different things from the bible. He talked to me about who I was going to be as Jesus' servant. He taught me things about the spiritual world that I never knew before and helped me to see and understand a lot of different things. He started with the story of Joseph and showed me how my story is so similar in a lot of ways. He helped me see how Joseph's time in the prison had prepared him for what was to come. He said that was like me... that I was hidden away and that sometimes seemed like a prison to me, but that he was using it all to prepare me so that when I come out of the darkness I could be the person I was created to be and live out the purpose he had given to me. I looked at the story of Moses too and how the desert was a place of preparation for the Israelites. They weren't led there to die it was to make them ready to receive their promise and even though I was in the desert too... like in the vision... they hadn't taken me there to die like I thought so often. They took me there to make me ready to receive my promise.

I saw that the Israelites were angry and fearful and that they didn't trust Moses and they didn't trust you. I think that is because of their past because of what had happened to them Holy Spirit.
Yes little one. They were afraid. They thought that we were leading them to death and not to life. They did not see or understand little one.
Like me sometimes. I think you are going to leave me here in the desert and I will die.
Yes my little one but that was not and is not our intent.
No. You were leading them to the promised land and giving them everything they needed on their journey.
Yes little one.
But they got afraid because they couldn't see the promise and they didn't trust you.
Yes little one.
And they wandered around in the desert because they never responded to all that you did. They never learned to trust you.
Yes little one we could not take them forward because of their lack of trust and because of the bitterness in their hearts little one. We longed to bring healing to them, but they would not receive it just as they would not receive us. If we had allowed them to go they would have been destroyed little one because of the faith that was needed to take the land. They would have been destroyed little one and our people would have been lost. So we had to wait little one, for the next generation, who were able to step forward in faith.
That is like me isn't it. I need to have enough faith to go into my promised land and until I do, I have to stay in the desert.
Yes little one but unlike the Israelites you are following us. Like Joshua and Caleb, you are ready and prepared to follow us into the promised land. You are not like the Israelites little one. You will not share their fate.
I didn't see that before, but it is true. I am like them, in the desert waiting to go into the promised land.

Yes little one you are so do not be afraid. We did not bring you here to die little one we brought you here to prepare you for the promise. Keep on walking little one...keep on following and trusting and do not be afraid.
Thankyou. That helps. I am sorry if I get like them sometimes.
My little one we will always help you just as we helped the Israelites, but the choice is yours my little one to stay or to follow. Do not let fear or doubt keep you here little one. This is not what we have for you.
Can we take a direct route out of here Holy Spirit? I don't want to wander around.
We are taking the fastest route little one. By the time that you are ready to leave this place it will be time.
Did that make sense Holy Spirit?
Yes my little one it did. When you are ready then it will be time.

While I was learning all of these and lots of other things too the Holy Spirit took me to a place in the mountain...the mountain of the lord. I had a classroom that was just for me where he showed me lots of things about the spiritual world and about who I am in him. While I was there, he showed me lots of things about the spiritual kingdom and about what it means to follow him. He showed me something to help me understand how to follow where he leads.

Holy Spirit?
Watch closely little one what do you see happening?
I think the light makes a path but a very short one Holy Spirit so that the path is only one or two steps in front of me and then it is dark again.
Yes little one what do you think that means?
I think maybe I am thinking about the light of your word is a lamp unto my feet. Your revelation, the light of your revelation Holy Spirit, it lights up the path in front of me but not very far. Just far enough so I can take the next step.
Yes little one that is exactly right. My little one everything that is here is here for a purpose and I will use it to show you many things.
I... am wondering why the light is only one or two steps ahead but I think that is... oh... I don't know... it is so that we will stay close to you isn't it?
Yes little one it is. Tell me what your thought was little one.
Well I was thinking about walking in the spirit and how you walk with us and how it is you lighting the way and I thought about... you being light... and shiny and all of that so I was thinking maybe the light is you because you are with me and in me... so if that is right... we can't see that path if we aren't walking with you because you are the one who is lighting it up... maybe that is obvious Holy Spirit.
Yes little one it ought to be but for many of our people it is not. They think they can find the path without me little one, they think they do not need to walk closely with me but can walk on their own and find the right path. It is not so little one. Only those who walk closely with me will find the path that I have for them for only then will they be able to see it.

Sometimes the things he showed me were hard to believe because it seemed so strange the things I saw and learned but somehow it always made sense...and made sense of other things that I knew but didn't really understand. It was a wonderful place just for me and I learned a lot and got to know the Holy Spirit much better and to understand that he loves me just like Jesus does. I learned even more that he is kind and gentle and that I could trust him.

My little one our love for you is like an ocean in that it is deep and vast and wide, but we will only give it to you a drop at a time. We will not drown you little one, but we will teach you to swim and to immerse yourself in all that we are longing to give to you...

And you show me things and let me experience things but not too much.

No little one we are leading you gently by the hand. We know your heart little one we know that you are desiring so much more but we must go gently little one for there is still much healing to be done and a relationship to be built between us that will last little one and withstand all the storms of life.

Yes. You are making me strong in you.

Yes little one we are for revelation in itself will not make you strong, it is relationship which does that little one.

I keep thinking about something you have been saying in my heart for a long time. People talk a lot about your gifts Holy Spirit and how they want them.

Yes little one they do, though often it is for their own purposes little one.

That is bad Holy Spirit, but you have never talked to me about gifts you have been saying over and over that I will minister out of relationship and not out of gifts. What does that mean?

Little one I give many gifts to our children. Gifts through which they are able to serve us and bless those that we send them to. My little one there is something greater than this. Gifts are just that little one and they are good, but it is a greater thing to be filled with us, to be so full of us that you are overflowing with our love and our power little one. So that you are able to touch and affect the lives of others just because of who you are because of your deep and abiding relationship with us. That is far greater little one than any gift.

I think it would be better to be full of you than to have a gift Holy Spirit. I am not sure if... I know how it is different.

Little one you can have a gift and it can be the greatest gift that has ever been given by us but little one the gift is not us, we give the gift but it is not us. To have a relationship with us that means that you are filled to overflowing with us, is to be able to give us to people little one, to be us to people. Little one people can have powerful gifts without being filled with us. They can minister in our power and cause many things to happen around them but that is not the same little one as being able to be us to people. There is no love in the gift little one, love comes from relationship with us.

Is that what Paul was talking about when he said that love was greater?

Yes little one. Gifts without love, gifts without us, are empty little one. You will minister out of your relationship with us. You will minister with love little one, you will show people who we are. You can only do this when you are rooted and established in us and in our love little one. You will not minister out of the gifts that are given to you, you will minister out of your relationship with us. Which is far greater little one?

The Holy Spirit did want to give me gifts though. One special day he said he wanted to show me something, but I didn't know what it was.

I am not sure what I was expecting but what happened was that I went for my hair cutting. I was wondering what He was going to do, and I was getting anxious that I had heard wrong and that I was making it all up... but He just kept telling me to relax and to trust Him. He said it was about us spending time together, about our relationship. I asked Him what He wanted to do after my hair cut (it was Jennifer of course but... it is still my hair) and He said He wanted to take me to my favorite shop and buy me something. He reminded me that it is valentine's day. I wasn't sure about what I was hearing, it seemed like a strange thing to me, so I suppose I was arguing a bit and saying that there wasn't anything I wanted, but I went anyway. I was looking around, the Holy Spirit said there was something I would like but He didn't say what it was, when I saw it. It was a bracelet, silver with pink and silver hearts. I liked it a lot and the Holy Spirit said that was it. So, I picked it up, but I was still thinking I was making it up and that the Holy Spirit didn't really want me to have anything. I walked around the shop with the bracelet, still kind of talking to Him and feeling scared that I was being silly. But in the end, I bought it. I was feeling a bit sad because I convinced myself I just made it up. But when I got home, and I took it out of the box I saw that there was an inscription in the box and it said wear this bracelet as a symbol of how loved and special you are. That made me cry and I knew then I hadn't got it wrong.

I am wanting to talk with you Holy Spirit.
I am here little one.
I don't know what to say. I got confused and unsure. Did I hurt you Holy Spirit?
No little one I understood your fear. My little one you are dearly loved. It is not wrong for me to do this little one.
But... it was you?
Yes little one it was me. You heard me my little one even though you were not fully understanding.
What wasn't I understanding Holy Spirit?
That I was wanting to spend time with you and show you that I love you.
Yes... I think I understand better now.
Yes little one you do. Little one our relationship will always be priority for me. Your gifting and all the things that I am longing to do through you come second to that little one, always.
Yes. I think I see... I am sorry Holy Spirit. Thankyou.
My little one it is my delight to give you good gifts. Treasure it as a reminder my little one, that you are loved and you are special to us.
Yes. I will treasure it Holy Spirit. Thankyou for showing me things too. You did show me many things but not in the way I thought.
My little one I will often surprise you with the things that I will do or not do. Be ready and willing to accept my way my little one.
Yes. Thank you, Holy Spirit.

It was hard for me to receive gifts because I never thought I should have them, but I was learning that isn't how Jesus or the Holy Spirit sees it. There were other kinds of gifts too. They were inside gifts, but they were just as special and made me cry just the same because they made me feel so loved.

I held on to Jesus. I held on to His hand holding one of His fingers... He seemed big and strong and very safe. I could kind of see the Holy Spirit, I thought maybe He kept changing colors, but I am not sure. I could feel something happening and then after a little while I was in the attic again. The Holy Spirit opened up a box and He gave me a doll, a book and a ring that He put on my finger. They looked old but if they belonged to me, I don't remember them. Then He led me by the hand through a door into a room. There was a lovely fire and a red patterned rug in front of it. There were toys scattered about on the rug and a rocking chair at either side. The rest of the room was dark. The Holy Spirit told me it was a safe place, my very own place where I could play. He sat in one of the chairs and Jesus sat in the other, like they were sitting with me and watching over me

and I started to cry. I am not sure what this is about or even why I cried so much but I think it is about giving things back that have been lost and making it safe again for me to play.

I had been starting to draw my own pictures of the things I was seeing and learning about. It was strange for me to draw and see how different it was from the pictures that Jennifer drew. Jesus told me that my pictures were helping me, and I liked to put him in them but now I started to put the Holy Spirit in them too. He was kind of hard to draw though. Jesus wanted to share in my drawings and help me with them, because sometimes I got scared to do them even though I liked to.

Hello little one.
I am going to do some drawing. Will you help me?
Yes little one we will help you. What are you going to draw little one?
I don't know. It is still a bit scary. I will just draw me and see what I think of.
Yes little one do that...
Am I real Jesus? Sometimes I don't think so. Maybe I'm Jennifer just pretending.
No little one you are not Jennifer. You are my very own, separate from Jennifer little one...
It is a sad happy picture Jesus. You and the Holy Spirit are with me holding my hands, but we are in the dark.... Crying... I don't want to be in the dark any more Jesus.
That is good little one. I do not want you to be in the dark either. We are walking out into the sunshine together little one. Do you see that?
Crying... Yes... But maybe the tunnel goes on and on for a long time....
No little one you are almost there. Look at your picture little one.
Crying.... But that is just my picture Jesus. It isn't real. Crying....
Yes little one it is. You asked us to help you and we did. Little one you have drawn a true picture. You are in a tunnel little one, but you are coming out. You are not alone little one we are holding you. We are with you...
Yes. I gave me a pretty dress. I don't know if that is right Jesus. I don't have a pretty dress.
Little one you may wear anything you choose in your pictures. Your dress is very pretty little one as are you...
I don't know if I drew the Holy Spirit right, but it is how He looks to me.
My little one why don't you ask Him what He thinks?
What do you think Holy Spirit? You should be sparkly, but I don't have the right pencils for that.
I like it very much little one. I like that you made me blue. I like that you made me hold your hand. I am always holding your hand little one.
Are you?
Yes little one I am....
Drawing makes me worry.
Little one the more that you do it the more that you will see that it is you and that you are real. It is a good thing for you to do little one and it will help you...
I like to draw.
Yes little one I know you do. Little one drawing is a wonderful way to express many things. You will find it helps you a lot little one. Keep drawing but always draw with us little one for we are always with you.
Yes. Ok...
My little one do not afraid to share everything you do with my servant.
I don't want to Jesus. He doesn't want to see my drawings.
Yes little one he does for they will help him to get to know you.
But I am not getting to know him Jesus. I am wanting to hide again. Crying......
I know my little one but remember all that I have said. He is your friend little one and he cares for you very much.
Crying...

My little one remember what I have said.
Crying... I remember Jesus.... Crying...
Do not be afraid little one he will not leave you and he does not hate you.
Crying... Will it be better soon Jesus?
Yes my little one it will be better soon. Keep holding on my little one.
I should go now Jesus.
Little one we will be with you. We will not ever leave you.
Yes. Bye not bye.
Bye not bye little one. Do not forget to share your pictures with my servant. He will want to see them my little one.

Jesus would often be there in my times with the Holy Spirit. They worked together to love me and to show me a lot of things about who they are and who I am. They were giving me the things that I needed to grow and get better and to follow wherever they wanted to take me.

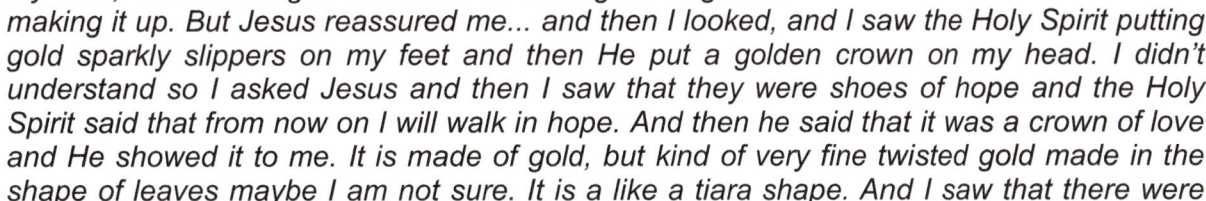

So, I snuggled myself down in Jesus' arms and He held me and kissed my head. I could feel things happening... And I cried a bit. I could see the Holy Spirit washing my legs and my feet, and I thought this was so strange I might be making it up. But Jesus reassured me... and then I looked, and I saw the Holy Spirit putting gold sparkly slippers on my feet and then He put a golden crown on my head. I didn't understand so I asked Jesus and then I saw that they were shoes of hope and the Holy Spirit said that from now on I will walk in hope. And then he said that it was a crown of love and He showed it to me. It is made of gold, but kind of very fine twisted gold made in the shape of leaves maybe I am not sure. It is a like a tiara shape. And I saw that there were tiny pink stones in it, like pink diamonds maybe? And three big ones at the front, one from the father, one from the son and one from the Holy Spirit. It hurt so much that I told Jesus to stop but He held me close and said He would help me bear it. Jesus said that I must always wear my shoes of hope and my crown of love. I cried a very lot.

I didn't realize then how important these gifts were going to be, but Jesus and the Holy Spirit have worked through them in a lot of ways to help me. Sometimes it was hard to understand what I was being given and what it meant but Jesus would help me to understand. The Holy Spirit talked to me about what it meant for me to be a child and how that was their gift to me too.

You have not yet understood about what it means to be a child in the kingdom of God.
What have I not understood Holy Spirit?
That you are blessed my little one. As you become more childlike, more who you are, we will be able to reveal so many of the deep things to you little one for you will be able to accept them. Not only that little one but you will be able to live in and be part of the spiritual world in a way that few adults ever could my little one, only the most childlike of adults can live in the spiritual world in the way that a child can.
Is that like what Jesus told me once, that babies can see the spiritual world but then they get... it gets dulled until they can't see any more?
Yes my little one for the physical soon begins to take precedence over the spiritual and they lose the ability to see or perceive my little one...
I suppose all the things I have been asking for... like to see... they are what children have.
Yes my little one.

So, I have been asking to see like a child and to be childlike?
Yes my little one that is what you have been asking for.
That is not the same as being a child though Holy Spirit.
Yes my little one it is. To be childlike is to be a child in spirit my little one. It has nothing to do with the physical self.
No. I see that.
My little one you are a child in an adult's body. That makes it harder for you to accept that you are a child my little one, but it does not change the fact that that is what you are.
No.
Nor does it mean that it is a bad thing my little one. Your childlike spirit is an asset to you. It will give you access to things of the spirit that others will not have my little one.
But... you could give them access Holy Spirit.
Yes little one but there are not many adults who are willing to become childlike my little one, it goes against everything that this world tells them they should be. It is not easy my little one to be a child in the natural world.
No. It isn't Holy Spirit.
My little one I will take you to places that I cannot take many of our children, I will show things that I cannot show to many of our children my little one. You are blessed because of your childlike nature, because you are a child my little one.
I see that Holy Spirit. It is like, to be what I can be in the spirit I have to be all the things that the world... thinks is... useless or not good.
That is only because they do not see or understand my little one. For the truth that is hidden in the deep places can only be found with an openness of heart, with the eyes of a child my little one.

And there was more that they had for me. Another gift that was just for me.

As I laid in Jesus arms, I saw Him covering me in something. It looked like a blanket of daisies then I realized that it was a dress. They are real daisies not material, all kind of woven together, very soft. I wondered about this and I thought about what daisies mean to me. I remember when we were little making daisy chains, we made crowns and necklaces and bracelets out of them... and pulling the petals off- 'he loves me he loves me not'. I don't know if you have that in America but in any case, you aren't a girl. Daisies are the flower of my childhood... they make me think of warm summer days sitting on the grass, peaceful times without anyone else about. It made me cry because I realized that is what it is...like Jesus gave my childhood back. Maybe that sounds silly but that is what it means to me. That he gave it back and that it is a good thing.

Alongside all of this I was being healed and set free. Jesus and the Holy Spirit worked together in this too. The enemy was continuing to try and trick me by pretending to be Jesus and now the Holy Spirit, but they used it to teach me and to help me get free of them.

Holy Spirit
Yes my little one.
I don't like it when the monsters are waiting for me.
I know my little one, but you are able to discern the difference they did not fool you little one.
No... not this time. It is hard to live in the spiritual world holy spirit.

It is difficult my little one because the enemy does not want you to see and understand the things of the spirit, he does not want you to have confidence in what you are seeing and hearing but persevere my little one and you will overcome. All you must do is persevere and continue to seek the truth. My little one if you are truly desiring truth, he cannot deceive you.

Is that true?

Yes little one. You must give him permission to deceive you, he cannot do it otherwise.

How do I give him permission Holy Spirit?

By believing lies over the truth and by preferring those lies my little one, for whatever reason.

Is that true?

Yes my little one. Even the lies that hurt you are only there because you believed them as truth and gave them permission. My little one for someone who does not know the truth it is easy for them to be deceived for they cannot distinguish between the truth and the lie. Not so with you my little one. You know the truth for the truth dwells within you.

So... I don't know what you are saying Holy Spirit. Is it my fault then that I think that I believe things that are not true?

Only in as much as you continue to choose to believe them my little one. As soon as you begin to choose to believe the truth the power of the lie begins to weaken and will eventually be broken my little one and the truth will take its rightful place.

So... I don't Holy Spirit because sometimes... the truth... it seems like a lie and the lie seems like truth because it does.

Yes my little one that is so. When you have believed something and all your life it has seemed to be true then for you it takes on the appearance of truth. But that is all that it is, the appearance.

Like... when the monsters pretend to be you or Jesus... it seems like you but its not.

Yes my little one it is the same. The lies disguise themselves as truth and will give you many reasons to believe that they are in fact the truth when they are not my little one. They are lies disguised as truth. The truth is only to be found in us little one. Not what you see or feel or experience, not what life has taught you or what other people say. The truth is only found in us little one and in what we say.

So... like... the things I believe about me that you say are lies...they are pretending to be truth so that they can hurt me.

Yes little one and they can only stay because you allow them to, because you keep on believing that they are what they say. Like with the monsters, they cannot deceive you once you have seen the truth of who they are little one. They must leave. So it is with the lies.

You make it sound like lies are... monsters too.

No little one they are not monsters, but they are from the monsters, sometimes they are attached to the monsters.

Like bindings... and they pull them and tighten them and remind me that they are there... they hurt me with them.

Yes little one. But once you start to resist and to believe the truth, or at least choose to believe the truth the bindings begin to loosen and they loose their power over you.

How... but they need to go completely don't they?

Yes little one they do. That is the power of truth in you. The truth will always overcome the lie my little one. As the bindings weaken and the truth takes hold the hold that lie has on you weakens further and can be stripped away my little one, sometimes it falls away, displaced by the truth but often it has to be removed my little one. Sometimes this takes time if the bindings are strong, sometimes the lies go so deep that it takes much time and healing to drive them out completely my little

one but you can be free of them. You can be covered by and saturated with truth.**
But I have to start with choosing.
Yes my little one. The truth will not ever take hold while you are choosing to believe the lie.
Why are you telling me this now Holy Spirit?
Because it is time to take another step little one, another step towards the truth. Little one you are constantly besieged by the lies of the enemy. That is not your fault my little one for they have had so much power over you and bound you in so many lies that have gone so very deep. But now you are beginning to see and to understand little one. You are much more able to choose to believe the truth, even though the lie is still there.
Yes. I see that. Sometimes... I know what the truth is... but I don't believe it... that you love me. Sometimes I believe it a bit, but... there is a lot of me that doesn't.
Yes my little one there is the beginning of freedom but the lie goes so deep that it will take time to remove it completely.
So what are you asking me to do Holy Spirit?
Little one it is time for you to receive more healing. It is time for you to make choices which will strengthen you and strengthen the truth in you. It is time to weaken the power of the lies of the enemy over you. Are you ready little one? Are you willing?
I don't want lies Holy Spirit. I want the truth.
Yes my little one I know that you do. Come then my little one. You savior is here. We are going to heal you my little one, just a little bit more.
Jesus?
Yes my little one I am here.
What are you going to do?
We are going to weaken and remove lies my little one, the lies that are binding you and causing you pain.
Ok. What do you want me to do?
First of all, little one I want you to choose to believe the truth. No more believing the lies my little one. Do not accept their presence in your heart or in your mind. No more speaking them out little one. You must choose to believe the truth even when you do not feel like it could be true.
That will be hard Jesus.
Yes my little one but we will help you. It begins with your choice my little one. Will you choose to live in the truth? Will you choose to break the power of the lies in your life by turning towards us, by choosing to live in the light, in all things my little one?
Yes. I choose to live in the truth, in the light Jesus. I don't want lies... but help me because... I don't know... they seem like safe places.
But they are not my little one. That is part of the deception. There is no safety in lies my little one. That is a lie in itself...
Yes... I think maybe that is ... my first choice Jesus... to believe that the truth is a safe place because it doesn't feel safe.
My little one I am the truth.
Yes. You are safe Jesus.
Yes my little one I am.
So truth is safe.
Yes my little one. Do you choose to believe that?
Truth is the safe place. Lies are not safe... Yes Jesus... I choose. Please help me.
Yes my little one come then and rest in my arms. Allow my spirit to work my little one.
Is it going to hurt Jesus?
The lies go deep my little one. Hold on to me.
Is that a yes?

Yes my little one but you have my strength. I am holding you.
Don't let Richard hear.
No little one. I will keep him from hearing. Come then.

So, I curled up on my bed. I thought nothing was happening but then I realized that there was a big battle going on. I am not sure what was happening but that is how it felt. Then I saw the Holy Spirit go into the attic. He went to one of the walls where there was a big black curtain and he pulled it so I could see a door in the wall. He went though the door into a very dark room. I could see there were boxes in there. The Holy Spirit looked at them for a little while and then he went to a little window and pulled back a curtain. It let in a little bit of light, but the window looked very dirty. Then he went to another wall and another little window and did the same. Now I could see the boxes. There were lots of them stacked up. They were black not like the attic boxes which are brown cardboard. I knew that in these boxes were lies. I didn't want to see them because I knew they would be very ugly. The Holy Spirit looked around and asked me what I wanted to do with them. I started to cry and told him to throw them out of the window. That I didn't want them, I wanted him to get rid of them. He didn't open the window, but the floor fell away and all the boxes with it. And then the room fell away and disappeared. I was crying and crying. The Holy Spirit said that there was no room for lies any more. I could feel things happening, and I was holding on to Jesus and crying. I got scared suddenly because I felt empty because the room was gone, and I started crying because the lies were gone, and it was empty and I was scared. But Jesus held me and said he would fill me with truth, and I could feel the Holy Spirit. It went on for a while and then I felt very peaceful and much better and I stopped crying.

My little one it is done. That is enough for now.
I feel funny... like ... something is missing.
Yes my little one but it is not anything that you will miss.
A whole room full of lies.
Yes my little one, there is no place for you to keep them anymore.
But does that mean... what does it mean?
It means you have chosen my little one, you have chosen not to make room for the lies that the enemy has given to you. My little one to undo the power of his lies in your life will take time and much healing but you have taken an important step towards this my little one. You have chosen.

These things happened over about five months, while I was still mostly hidden away inside. They were getting me ready for the next part of my journey which was to be on the outside and to start living my own life. I was about to come out of the darkness and into the light.

Little one as you learn to live in this world you will find more and more that you are not of this world. Little one you are a stranger here you will not fit little one for the things of the world and the things of the spirit cannot co-exist in harmony little one. You will bring with you light and hope and peace wherever you go but you will also bring with you a different way of being and thinking and doing that will seem strange to those around you. That is because you are not of this world little one you are of the spirit. That is because you have been redeemed little one, bought back for us, taken out of the world and placed into the spirit. You will not fit little one but do not desire to fit for there is nothing in this world that is of true worth little one. Do not desire it.

Chapter 21

Out of the Well

Jesus told me it was time to let people...some people...see AJ for the person she was. That was very frightening. Jennifer had a friend at church who had worked with multiples, but she didn't know about us. Jennifer hadn't known her very long, but they had been working together helping a lady in the church and Jesus said he wanted Jennifer to tell her about the bad things and about me. Jennifer did a very good job of explaining things and Annette listened very well, but she said some things about me that upset me a lot. I think she didn't really understand or see me the way Jesus did. He said she was still learning.

Crying....... Please hold me Jesus.
I am holding you my little one. I am holding you close to my heart of love.
Crying......
My little one I am with you. I am always with you. My love for you is unending my little one. I will not leave you.
I don't want to be weird. I am confused. I don't want to be weird.
My little one you are not weird, you are special, extraordinary, precious and beloved, but you are not weird.
I am Jesus.
My little one you are who I say that you are, not anyone else my little one. Not Annette, not anyone else.
I don't want to be me.
My little one I want you to be you. Annette is learning my little one and she does not yet see you or those like you in the way that I do but I am longing to show her the truth my little one. You can help her to see the truth if you are willing.
Crying...... How?
By being who you are my little one, which is not weird in any way. My dearest one all that I have for you will require you to be yourself, not anyone else my little one. Only you can fulfil the purpose that I have for you. It will require courage my little one but most of all it will require you to know that you are precious and beloved in my sight, no matter what anyone else may think of you. You are not worth less than anyone else my little one.
Crying...... I don't want her to see me Jesus.
My little one when she sees you, she will not reject you. I will give her my heart for you my little one.
What are you doing Jesus?... Crying...
I am helping you my little one. I am helping you to move forward into all that you can be. Do not be afraid my little one.
It is no good telling me not to be afraid Jesus...Crying...... I am afraid...
I know my little one, but you do not need to be. You hold on to me my little one, I am with you. I will help you to show my child who you are which is not weird my little one. You are fully loved, just as you are. You are not less my little one.
Crying... But maybe she thinks I am less.
But you are not my little one. No matter what she thinks you are not less.
Is it right Jesus? What are you doing?
My little one I am helping you just as I have said. I will not bring you to harm my little one. I will help you to walk this path with me. I will show you the way my little one. I will give you the courage and the strength that you will need.
She isn't a bad person Jesus.
No my little one she isn't but remember that she does not yet know you, she only knows my servant Jennifer, she is the one that my child is relating to.

Yes. I know. I am sorry I got so upset... it is just seeing myself through someone else's eyes...It is... difficult.

I know my little one, but you are able. I am with you little one.

Are you going to talk to her?

Yes little one I am already talking to her. I will show her many things through you my little one, do not be afraid.

Yes. I do see Jesus. Will you... I need your help a lot.

Yes my little one I know that you do. My little one each step forward is helping you. It is all leading you forward my little one and helping you to become stronger and more able to be who you are...

I wish... I... how are you... I mean how can... Everyone will want Jennifer to stay and me to go Jesus.

But that is not what I want my little one. Jennifer is there for you not the other way around.

I hope you are going to help them see Jesus or it is going to be hard for me.

Yes my little one I will help them to see. It will be a journey for each of them my little one, but I will be with them.

I would like to be able to be me. Would she accept me?

Yes my little one, she would accept you. She may not see you as I see you but she would accept you.

You mean she would see Jennifer as being the real person?

Yes my little one but that is not the truth. You are real my little one, we will help her to see that.

I am not thinking I can do that Jesus.

No my little one but I can. I can show her many things through you my little one, things which will help those she ministers to and those I will bring to her in the future.

Yes. I would like that Jesus... to help her see.

Yes my little one. I will help you. Do not be anxious but take each step as I lead you. I will help you my little one and I will also help her for there is much that I am longing to show her.

Ok... I will do whatever you want me to Jesus. As long as you will help me and be there for me after when I need to cry.

Yes my little one I will always be here for you. I will always help you.

I love you Jesus.

Yes my little one your love is a great delight to me. My dearest one I will do so many things through you in this time. Do not be afraid but keep on following my little one. Everything that I am doing is working for your good and for the good of others.

Yes. Will I be able to be me one day Jesus?

Yes my little one you will. Your new life will begin very soon my little one, this is preparation for all of that, even this my little one.

Ok. Please help me.

Yes my little one I will always help you.

Thankyou.

I was scared about what Annette would say to Jennifer after that, but she was always kind... curious and maybe not really understanding but wanting to learn and that was ok.

I had been going to the online chat group for a few months, but it had got very difficult because I felt so much younger than everyone else and the conversations would scare me sometimes.

I got very sad last night and that is why I had to go. I got sad because I understood something, I have kind of seen for a few weeks, but I didn't know what it was. Some of the conversations scared me last night. I put on some worship music because that helped and cuddled my teddies and talked to Jesus just to make sure He was there. It seemed a bit like everybody was talking at a different level to me and I couldn't join in because I didn't know how, and I couldn't get there. That is how it felt... and how it feels a lot of the time for me at group. But then I understood what it is. It is that I am a child in a group of adults and that is why it feels like that. I think it is more that way now because I am getting to be more and more me. I got sad because I knew it wasn't the right place for me to be, that I don't belong there. I don't mean it feels like people don't want me just that it isn't right. So, I got sad and I left because it was too hard. I snuggled up to Jesus and cried a bit and went to sleep. I wasn't surprised at what He said this morning because He was saying it to me last night too, I think.

Hello Jesus

Hello my little one. My little one I am holding you so close to my heart. There is not anything my little one that will ever change that. I will never be taken from you.

I would like to just be in heaven with you Jesus. What good am I in this life?

My little one I have great purpose in your life. You may not be like anyone else that you ever meet my little one but that does not mean that you are not precious. It does not mean that I cannot work through you just as I have said.

Yes... I am just getting used to being me that is all.

Yes my little one I know that you are feeling sad but being you is a good thing my little one not a bad one....

I feel too sad to talk Jesus. You tell me what it is I am needing to hear and what you want me to do.

My little one your time at group has come to an end. It has served its purpose my little one and you are stronger and more able to accept who you are. My little one I have worked through you also. I have used it all for good my little one but now it is time for you to stop and continue your journey with me knowing that you are not alone my little one. You are never alone.

I see that is has helped me Jesus.

Yes my little one it has helped you a great deal most of all it has helped you to see and accept who you are my little one.

Yes. But I don't belong there Jesus.

It is not a group that will meet the needs that you now have my little one that is true. It does not mean that you are not accepted or loved for who you are.

Yes... Is there a place for me Jesus? Will I have friends?

Yes my little one there is a place for you, a good place my little one where you will have many friends. I am making you so special my little one for you are learning how to live your life trusting and depending upon me, completely defined by me and who I say you are. Not many choose to live in this way but you have chosen my little one. It will set you apart from others my little one and it will make you different but does not mean that you will be alone or that there isn't a place for you. I have a very special place for you my little one with very special people. My plans for you are good my little one.

Crying... Yes. They must be Jesus. I am sorry if I am sad. It was a surprise to me... even though it wasn't.

I know my little one you have been seeing the truth without recognizing its meaning for a while. My little one this has been part of your journey to becoming all that you are. It has been a good thing my little one. It is not wrong to be sad but do not lose your hope of love and of friendship and a place to belong. They will all come my little one.

Crying... Crying... I belong to you Jesus.

Yes my little one you do and that will not ever change. My little one everything that I am taking you through is for your good. This has been a good thing my little one but now it is good that it comes to an end for you. This does not mean it is the end for your friendships my little one only that you will not be a part of that group anymore.

I don't know what that means Jesus. I don't think I understand anything about friendship. Are you teaching me?

Yes my little one and I will continue to do so. I will show you the true meaning of friendship my little one. I will help you to have close and sustaining relationships in which you will be safe and loved and in which you will be able to give of yourself my little one for you have so much to give. You will be a wonderful friend to many people my little one.

If you teach me how Jesus.

Yes my little one I will. My little one this is the first of many endings for you for everything is about to change. Hold on to me my little one. I am your strength. I will give you everything that you need my little one.

Yes ok.

Your sadness will pass my little one for as the old passes away it leaves room for the new. My little one I will make everything new for you. Hold on to me my little one and do not ever let go.

Yes... This is a strange path Jesus.

I know it seems so to you my little one but it is a path that requires you to trust me and to follow me closely wherever I lead. That is a good path my little one even if it is hard.

Jesus said that he didn't want me to go anymore because it had done what he wanted it to, but he did want me to stay in touch with one of the ladies there. We started to email, and I got to know her and some of her alters better. That was very exciting for me. It was the first time I had a friend... apart from Mike of course but this was different.

The scariest thing of all was telling Cheryl about me. Jennifer and Cheryl had been close friends for a lot of years, and she knew something about the bad things and the alters but she had never met any of them. Jesus said it was time to tell her about me. He said that we would be friends and that it would be ok. I was scared though.

Later on, in the week I think maybe Jesus was telling me that I needed to tell Cheryl about me...that it isn't just Jennifer. I think that was because I realized that she does see me. I am not sure that anyone else does, maybe Sophie and Richard sometimes now that things are changing but nobody else does except Cheryl. I got scared and upset because Cheryl loves Jennifer, but I am not sure about me... even though she sees me she thinks what she is seeing is Jennifer. If she knew Jennifer was going and I am the one who will be left I think she would be very unhappy. But I was thinking about how I think maybe this is the only friendship that Jennifer has now that will survive the changes. I might be wrong, but I don't think any of the other ones will. So maybe that means that she will have to know sometime about me... because soon Jennifer will be gone. I don't know and I got upset... anyway maybe if that is so it isn't yet. Maybe when we are blended, and the change has already happened, and she is friends with me without even knowing it... maybe then it would be easier for her to accept. I don't know. It seems wrong but I don't know.

Telling her was scary but she mostly seemed interested and wanted to know more. For me it was much scarier because I knew Jesus plan was to blend Jennifer into me...so Jennifer would be gone. I knew that would be very hard for Cheryl and I thought that she would hate me for taking her friend away. Jesus said that even though he wanted her to know about me and eventually be friends with me it wasn't time for her to know the truth about the blending yet. I was very glad about that. When Jennifer had told Cheryl about going to live in America it had been very difficult, and Cheryl cried a lot. Jennifer didn't talk about the future much with her because she didn't want to tell her about the blending and because talking about America made Cheryl so very upset. It was all very difficult and made me afraid and feel like I was very bad for upsetting Cheryl so much. I felt like it was all my fault.

It seems like things are changing. I don't know what that means maybe it doesn't mean anything. Jennifer went out with Cheryl tonight. They were talking about me and about America and about you too. Cheryl got upset and started crying. I think this is going to be very hard. I feel very bad because I know that I am the problem and that I am taking Jennifer away from everybody. It isn't my fault because it is Jesus who is doing it, but I still feel bad and like it should be me who is going away.

Not long after this Jennifer and Cheryl went away for the weekend and they went to a zoo. I loved all of the animals. I was very scared because I didn't know what Cheryl would say about me and we couldn't run away and hide if I got upset but it was ok and nothing bad happened. I had made her a card to say thankyou for taking us to the zoo and even though I was scared to give it to her she really liked it. After that I started emailing with her. That was strange too because now someone I had known for a lot of years through Jennifer was getting to know me. It was hard for me to feel like there were people who wanted to know me and be my friend. I didn't think I should have friends because I was still believing that I was bad.

Cheryl said something in her last email that I haven't let myself think about at all. She said that I am precious to her and that she is my friend. I don't like it and I am wanting to run away but I haven't thought about it until now. I should talk to Jesus about it. Today I got 3 emails. I got one from Ester, one from Milly and one from Kitty. I read them all and looked at the photo Milly sent me of herself and I think maybe I was happy and excited but it was like I couldn't let myself feel it and I put the emails away and even though I have thought about them a lot I can't seem to look at them or read them again. I don't know what it is. It is all mixed up inside of me and I am still feeling a bit like I am bad. I keep reminding myself that I am not but that feeling inside of me is still saying that I am.

Things were changing for me and I was starting to see me more in and through Jennifer. I bought some clothes that I chose, and I loved to wear them. I started to see differences in the way that Jennifer was too, like she was getting more like me in the things she did and said.

I have been kind of chatting to Jennifer. For the first time this year Jennifer gave Cheryl some Easter chocolate. Cheryl always gets her something, but Jennifer never has. I don't know why... So, we were kind of thinking talking about that. Jennifer said I was a humanizing influence on her and that was good.

I only ever came outside when I was safe in our room but one day when the house was empty, I came downstairs for the very first time.

Jennifer said that I could have the whole evening and I said I would make a card for you. Jennifer suggested that I should do it downstairs because I have never been me downstairs before. I thought that might be good, so I did. I took my pencils and things and my rabbit and went and sat downstairs but I never did you a card I am sorry. I sat curled up in the chair with my rabbit feeling scared. It looked different but not. A bit like when you put glasses on, and things look bigger and sharper and more 3-d. That is what it is like to see with my eyes and not Jennifer's. It made me cry maybe because it felt scary and I felt small. Jesus was there telling me that he was with me and that I was safe, but I still cried. I sat there for an hour just looking. I wonder what it would be like for me outside where there are lots of things to see and hear. I was touching things too... that felt different. I suppose in our room it is different, but I am used to that, so I didn't realize but I have never been me downstairs. It is scary and it made me think that I am real. It is hard to explain. I am feeling very on my own but I'm not. Jesus is here.

Now I could see that the things Jesus had been saying were happening. Jennifer was becoming more me, and I was getting stronger, making my own friends and spending more time on the outside. We were going away for a weekend conference with Cheryl. I was nervous but excited because Jesus said he was going to do good things. He did a lot more than I thought. Cheryl had given me a message from Jesus a while ago, she thought it was for Jennifer of course but it wasn't.

I have a love for you that runs deeper than you have yet experienced little one. Your pain is to you a deep dark dry well, with little light and no way of escape - but the measure of my love for you is greater than the well in which you now stand. There is an abundance in my love for you that will never run dry. Think of it this way little one - the well has an end point as dark, dry, and deep as it may be, as trapped as you may feel, there is an end point, a floor on which you stand looking up into the light that seems so very far away at times. There are times when the light fades altogether from your sight as though night has fallen over the well in which you lay and all is in darkness, but know little one that I never leave you, I am always with you, and will always be with you. I have never left your side. My love for you is an abundant waterfall, one you have experienced much over these past years little one, but there is more, there is always more of me for you, more of my love, more of my power. The well has not run dry as it seems so often. My abundant love for you consumes the well in which you lay, not to drown and overpower you but to move and save you but you must swim little one, you must keep your eyes heavenward, do not give up. This water of love - is water of life... it is I who lifts you out of the well as you press through with all that you have to reach toward the light, the well is flooded and overflows and out of its grasp you will be freed. Do not be afraid to trust me little one, I am he who is faithful and true, I will not let you go, I will not leave you abandoned and alone. And I unlike the well, have no end - my love, like the waterfall, flows forever and always. There is an end to this season of pain dear one, there is a healing in my love, and it is for you. My love is not always gentle little one; there are floodgates of love stored up for you and the floodgates are quaking, ready to burst forth. You will be overcome but not consumed for I am here to bring you to the surface to lift you out of the well in which you now stand. This is the measure of my love for you little one, and the flow carries you further, away from that which held you captive, and from this season you will be free.

I talked to Jesus about the word Cheryl gave us a lot of times. She had given Jennifer that word in November and now it was May. It had seemed like a long time.

I have been thinking about the well...and the flood that is coming? Is that what you meant?
There is an overflow of my love which will take you from the place that you are in my little one and wash you away to the place that I am taking you to. That is what I was speaking of my little one. The place that you are now in, the place of pain at the bottom of the deepest well, that is not the place where you will live out your days my little one. I will not keep you here. It is my love which will rescue you. It is the overflow of my love which will do this my little one. You must hold on to me and allow me to carry you to where I will take you.
Is that my new life?
Yes my little one, your new life and all that I have promised you. I will not leave you here my little one. I am coming and I am coming soon.
I hope so Jesus.
My little one it is my promise to you. Keep holding on my little one. It will come.
I suppose it is hard to see anything from the bottom of a well.
Yes my little one and that is why you must trust in my sight. I will not leave you here my little one.
Help me to wait then Jesus and not lose hope.
I am with you my little one. I will not leave you. I will take you from this place just as I have said. My dearest one all the things that I have told you of will come. Hold on to me and do not let go. That is all that you must do.
My dearest one I understand that you are longing to see and experience so many things. That you are longing to fly my little one and that is good, but you must be

ready my little one. I will not allow you to fly before I know that you can do it. I do not want you to be hurt my little one. That is not my desire for you.
Yes...when I think of me being in that cocoon or at the bottom of the well...I am not ready to fly. It isn't time.
No my little one it isn't but it will come. This time is making you ready my little one. When you emerge you will be ready to begin your lessons in how to fly for that will also take time my little one but you will be able to stretch your wings and you will be seen for who you truly are, not hidden away any longer my little one.
They all come together.
Yes my little one, they all come together.

It will be good when I am out of the well. I have drawn a picture. It shows Jesus love coming into the well and me being washed out. Jesus is holding me tight. I put the Holy Spirit in the boat waiting for me, it is the boat that takes me to my new life.

We went to a conference called the father's heart with Cheryl on Friday. I didn't know what Jesus was going to do but he said he was going to do something good. He did lots of things and they were all good. The first part of it I think was Jesus kind of opening up my heart to the father, I started to think that maybe it would be ok and a good thing. That Jesus daddy is safe because Jesus is safe, and he is always with me. There were lots of thoughts about that kind of thing on Friday evening. On Saturday morning in the worship I was dancing with Jesus on the inside. I liked that a lot.

Then he turned me around, so I had my back to him and he kind of nudged me forward so I was on the outside I think. It was ok because everyone was worshipping, and I had my eyes closed mostly. Jesus showed me something. I saw that he was behind me, very close and he put his hands under mine and lifted them up very gently and he said that he is my strength. Then he showed me that he was wrapped around me kind of like a golden coat, holding me tight. It reminded me of that vision where I came out of the tunnel and the Holy Spirit wrapped himself around me and kept me safe. Jesus said he was my shield and my protection. And then he showed me that he is in me too. That is hard to describe but it is like I could see him inside me. He said he couldn't ever be separate from me because he is in me. And I
thought about that is how it is and how it will be if I was on the outside and I said that seems ok... maybe it would be ok for me to be on the outside. And Jesus said yes it would.

Then there was some talking from the person leading. They were talking about orphans and about the orphan heart and how orphans need to know their father, the father. I started to think about the children that you are helping and those that will be in your safe house. I never thought of them as orphans before, but they are aren't they. And Jesus was showing me how they needed a father. And how they need his love and he wanted to work through me to show them that love and to help them find it and I remembered a word Jennifer was given a while ago about how she wouldn't run away from the father but would draw others to him. But then I thought about how I don't know the father and his love so how can I help others find him? It was like Jesus was asking me if I would take a risk for them, because of their need. Not because I need the father's love but because they do. I think somehow that gave me more courage, so I said yes to Jesus. That I wanted to know the father and his love so I could help those children because I think for the first time, I understood how much they need him... and me too. But I am not sure if I could be that brave just for me.

I am not sure if it was before or after that, but it was in the worship time again when I think maybe it was the Holy Spirit this time who showed me something. They were singing a song about how Jesus turns our mourning into dancing and our tears into laughter and I was listening. He showed me how it isn't just that I won't be sad anymore because there will be other things that will be making me happy and the bad things will be gone but that somehow it will be those things, the bad things, that hurt and make me sad that will make me dance and be joyful. It will be the bad things that will make me sing. I don't know how he can do that...but it made me think about all the things that make me sad...like being me, being an alter, Jennifer going...all of those things and how that meant that it is those things that I will be glad about somehow as well as maybe the bad things...it made me cry to think that. I hope I am not forgetting things because there was a lot going on in my head. The other thing that someone said was that we have to choose to let the father love us. That it is always our choice, like everything is. So, I decided that I wanted to let him love me even though it is scary, and I know how much it hurts.

Saturday evening was in the Norwich cathedral and Heidi Baker was the speaker. Me and Jennifer were feeling a bit weird on the way there, like we... or she I don't know... wasn't quite there. We got a seat and then Cheryl went off to the toilet. As I was sitting there, I started to think and to realize that maybe it was me... on the outside I mean. I couldn't find Jennifer. It was a bit scary, but I remembered about Jesus being around me like a coat. Cheryl came back. I said that there were people on the ceiling because there were... I think they are saints and angels, little figures carved in the wood way up high. Then I started to really know it was me... and I asked Jesus and he said that I was on the outside and I got scared and I couldn't look at Cheryl or talk to her. I thought maybe she knew it was me, but I didn't know. She did know because she saw it was me and she was asking Jesus.

She put her arms around me, and I snuggled in close and cried because it was so scary and overwhelming to be on the outside. And I cried more because she was holding me, and she didn't want me to go away. I have never been hugged before excepting by Jesus and it was nice. I felt safe and warm and loved and that made me cry a lot. After a little while I sat up again and looked around. Everything was so loud it was hurting my ears, so I asked Jesus to fix them, so it didn't hurt. I think he must have because it got better. I was looking around at everything. There was a lot to see and I was watching the people. There was a lady dancing. I liked that. I sat holding Cheryl's hand. She talked to me a bit, but I couldn't say anything or even look at her. I sang a bit in the worship, but I was still crying... it didn't seem to stop. I kept getting scared that I would go back inside, and Jennifer would come out. I wanted to stay out.

Jesus said that he had something for me, and it wasn't time for me to go back in yet. Then Heidi got up to speak and she was telling stories that made us laugh and go wow about what Jesus does. At the end she prayed and said to go to the front if we wanted to receive daddy's love. My heart was beating so fast it was hurting... like it was being pulled... maybe it was. So, I took hold of Cheryl's hand and we went and knelt at the front. I cried so much. It hurt so much but I heard him, my daddy telling me he loves me, and I don't need to be afraid. And I knew it in my heart, that I have a daddy and he loves me and I cried and cried and it was wonderful but it hurt a lot.

Cheryl was holding me, and she was crying too, and I was asking our daddy to let her know that he loves her too. Then Heidi was talking about our inheritance because we are his children and I heard Jesus and he said that my inheritance is love, to give love and to receive it. And I thought that was so wonderful and I cried and cried. When I stopped crying... kind of... I looked down and saw that I had made a puddle on the stone floor. That seemed kind of right somehow. That a little bit of me would stay in the cathedral… I don't know why... kind of like I gave those tears to my daddy there. So, then that seemed to be my time and Jennifer came back out.

Cheryl seemed kind of happy amazed about our time together. Jesus did stuff in her heart and she has moved a lot closer to our daddy, I think. She said lots of nice things about me and didn't seem worried about it at all... I think maybe she even liked it. We were very tired, and our head was hurting a lot and our eyes were swollen from all of the crying I did. But I was very happy and excited because I had been on the outside for the first time with other people and it was good. And I had found out about my daddy a little bit and that was good. It was a lot and I was too tired to take it in.

On Sunday morning there was a service to go to, but we weren't sure, so we asked Jesus. He said go for a walk. We were near a lovely forest that was on the way home, so we stopped there. Jennifer and Cheryl were having some lunch, but Jennifer was feeling weird again, so it wasn't so much of a surprise when I realized it was me on the outside again. We were walking through the trees and I was feeling scared. I wasn't sure if it was me, so I asked Jesus and he said it was. Cheryl and Jennifer had been talking, but I was very quiet. I asked Jesus if she knew it was me and he said she did, but I didn't know what to do. I really wanted to hold her hand, but I felt scared. Jesus said if I held her hand then we would both know that we knew it was me and that would be better. So, I did.

Cheryl took my hand and said she had thought it was me. Cheryl let me choose about everything like which way to go... I asked Jesus so we went his way. We went down a little path through some trees that looked dead. It seemed like a strange way to go but then we saw some big metal bars on the ground. I took Cheryl to see what it was because I was holding her hand. It was a giant xylophone... there were two hammer thingies so we both played tunes and made a lot of noise. It was fun and made us laugh. So, then we went a bit further and all along this path there were different things to play like bells and things you jumped on to make a noise and ropes to pull. I had a very good time running and jumping and pulling and pushing things and Cheryl had fun too because she likes to play. We went in these wobble dishes that tipped me upside down, so my legs were in the air. That made me laugh a lot. It was strange because I knew I was doing things that Jennifer wouldn't ever do but I liked it and I let myself do them. We only saw one family all the way round even though there were lots of people about. That was good because I was scared of the people. I laughed when we came out of that part and we saw all the signs saying it was closed for maintenance. It felt like we had been very naughty, but I knew it was ok because Jesus told us to go that way. He made it quiet on purpose just for me, I think.

So, then we walked a bit further. Cheryl was a bit worried about getting lost, but I was following Jesus instructions and I wasn't scared. I hear him better when I am on the outside than when it is Jennifer. That is very good. We went down a bit that was a bike track and there were little hills to run up and down. It was fun. Jennifer says we will have to get a lot thinner and fitter if I am going to keep doing these things :). Jesus told us the way back to where the toilets and the cafe were so that was good, and Cheryl bought me a drink and we sat down and watched the people. There were too many of them for me really, but I was ok. Even though I know that it must have looked strange to other people because I was holding Cheryl's hand it didn't feel strange. And even though I knew I was big... that the body is big, tall I mean... I didn't feel like a big person. It is a bit strange and hard to explain.

I liked it a lot, but it was time to go home so Jennifer came out again. I don't know how I got on the outside. I don't know how to make it happen or to make it not happen, but I am very excited that it did. Cheryl says that me and Jennifer are very different. She says we walk different and talk different and laugh different. She had a good time playing with me. She said I am very playful. Jesus told me that a while ago and it is true. She says I have wide curious eyes and a nice giggle. It is a bit of a lot to take in... it means that I really am real and that I can be outside and do outside things. I talked to Cheryl and looked at her this time so that was better too. It has given me a lot of hope and I know that Jesus is the one who made it all happen.

We talked to Jesus a lot about all the things that had happened. I was so excited because it was a big adventure for me to be on the outside and to see and experience everything for myself. The world seemed different...like it had when I spent time downstairs and there was so much to see and do. I wanted to know what had happened and how it all fit together with the things that Jesus had been saying before we went away.

I was wondering about that if it happened Jesus and I am out of the tunnel.
You are out of the tunnel my little one and in my light. You are safe and protected my dearest one, but you are no longer hidden away in the darkness.
It isn't as scary as I thought it would be Jesus, but I am a bit confused because you have given me a lot of pictures to help me understand my journey with you. I am trying to put them together, but I am not sure if I am getting it right. In the one with the waterfall where I come out of the tunnel and you wrap me up and keep me safe... Is that where I am... out of the tunnel.
Yes my little one that is where you are. You are safe, wrapped up in me but you are no longer in the tunnel my little one.
So now we are going towards the boat.
Yes my little one. Step by step we are moving towards the boat that will carry you to your new life with my servant and with his wife.
So, what about the one with the well... I am out of the well now…yes.
Yes my little one you are.
And that was to do with daddy's love. It was his love that brought me out of the darkness and into the light.
Yes my little one it was. My dearest one you have been in such a dark place, not only the dark place of your own hiddenness but a place of darkness where you were unable to receive the love that our father has for you. You are no longer in that place my little one. You were lifted out by his great love for you and brought to rest in the light of his love.

It was a new beginning for me. I began to spend more time on the outside with Cheryl. Jesus was in control. I never knew how to make it happen. Cheryl seemed to enjoy our times together. She said I helped her look at things a different way, a good way. Being on the outside helped me to see myself better and to know that I was real and not Jennifer. That was exciting too, and I was looking forward to all the things I could do that Jennifer never wanted to. I wanted to know what I liked doing and what I liked to eat and all of those things. They weren't the same as Jennifer and I thought that was good.

> I will lift up my eyes to the mountains; From where shall my help come?
> My help *comes* from the Lord, Who made heaven and earth.
> He will not allow your foot to slip; He who keeps you will not slumber.
> Behold, He who keeps Israel Will neither slumber nor sleep.
> The Lord is your keeper; The Lord is your shade on your right hand.
> The sun will not smite you by day, Nor the moon by night.
> The Lord will protect you from all evil; He will keep your soul.
> The Lord will guard your going out and your coming in
> From this time forth and forever.
>
> **Psalm 121 NASB**

Chapter 22

Into Daddy's Arms

Now that I had met daddy, I wanted to get to know him better, but it still felt a bit scary to me. I felt safe with Jesus, but I was still learning that daddy is just as safe. I talked to Jesus and asked him about it because I didn't know what to do or what to expect.

Hello Jesus
Hello my little one.
I have been thinking about daddy. I think maybe I am scared Jesus. I don't want to be, but he seems kind of big and... scary.
My little one our father loves you just as I do. He is kind and gentle and will not ever hurt you. My little one he understands everything about you and he will not take you too fast. He has much love to give to you my little one, for you and for others but he will not give you more than you can manage.
Will he show me what a daddy is Jesus? I am not sure about what it is. It sounds kind of nice and safe but…he is so big and...
My little one he will not ever hurt you. He is longing to gather you in his arms and show you that you are completely safe with him my little one. Will you allow him to do that?
I don't know. Will it hurt.
Only because it is healing my little one, not because there's anything bad in it.
Will you stay with me Jesus?
Yes my little one for he is my daddy also. I am not afraid of him my little one for I know his heart for me which is the same as his heart for you. There is so much love waiting for you in the heart of our father. He will not hurt you.
Can I hold your hand Jesus?
Yes my little one. Hold on tightly to me. I will not let you go my little one.
What will he do?
He will show you his love for you my little one, just as much as you can manage, not more.
Will he talk to me?
Yes my little one. He will speak to you words of love and of acceptance, for you are his beloved child.
How will I know it is him Jesus?
My little one you will come to know him just as you have come to know me and my spirit. It is not different my little one.
What should I do Jesus?
Say hello to him my little one. He is waiting.
Crying...I am scared.
I know my little one but I am here with you. There is nothing to fear.
Crying... Ok... Crying...Hello daddy.
Hello my child
Crying... I have come to say hello. Jesus says... it is ok.
My little child I have been waiting to hear your hello to me. It is a sweet sound in my ears. I will not hurt you my dearest child. All that I have for you is love.
Will you help me to feel safe and to love you and let you love me? Will you show me what a daddy is... Crying?
Yes my child I will. Step by step, a little at a time. My dearest child I will not ever stop loving you. I will not ever leave you. You belong to me and I have loved you for all of your life. I will not stop now my little one. When you are ready, I will hold you close to

my heart and you will know how completely safe and completely loved you are. This is only the beginning my little one, but it is a good beginning.

Will you talk to me like Jesus does and like the Holy Spirit does?

Yes my child I will. I am not far off distant my little one. I am with you just as they are. My child will you allow me to reach out to you with my love. It will bring you healing and much joy.

Yes daddy I will.

Come then little one. Come and sit here. My beloved son will hold you in his arms. He will not leave you.

I didn't really see anything except I knew I was sitting in Jesus lap. It was a bit like Saturday except I didn't cry as much. I still cried a lot. I have a daddy and he loves me. It is like that takes my aloneness and makes it not true and it makes me feel safe and like I belong. These are big things and they hurt a lot but in a good way.

A lot of things seemed different for me now. I had times on the outside with Cheryl where I could learn about me and the things I liked and how I was different to Jennifer. I was different in a lot of ways. I liked spending time on the outside, it was helping me to know that I was real. It gave me hope too that things were changing just like Jesus said. I was writing to Ester and her alters from chat and to Annette too. I was making friends and it was good. I tried to spend time with daddy most days. Mostly I would talk to Jesus first and then he would take me to daddy. It was so painful to be with daddy that I never stayed very long. I worried a bit about that, but Jesus said that daddy understood and that he would go slowly and not rush me. He wouldn't get impatient or angry of it was hard for me to spend time with him.

Hello daddy.

Hello my dearest child.

How am I going to get to know you daddy? Our times are so short.

But I am working through them my little one. There are still many barriers to overcome. I am taking you a step at a time my little one. Our times together will grow but first I must work within you to reveal my love to you as much as you are able to receive. I am helping you to feel safe my dearest child just a little at a time. Keep coming to me my little one you are drawing closer each time you do.

That is good. I don't think I am very used to having a daddy yet and I am not very sure about it. Please help me because I would like to be able to run into your arms daddy and feel safe and loved but I am still feeling scared.

I know my little one. I will help you. That day will come my child, but I will not overwhelm you with my love for that would not help you my little one. Come then. Draw a little closer. You are safe in the arms of my son.

Yes. Ok.

I am not sure what all of the barriers were, but they came from the bad things and the lies I believed about daddy and about myself. All I ever knew about men who were a kind of daddy to me... like grandad was that they hurt me or abandoned me... like dad did. So somehow, I got those things confused with my real daddy.

Hello daddy

Hello my little one. My child it is my great delight to see you here. It is my great delight that you come my little one, that you come to sit with me a while and learn a little about my love for you.

You are a good daddy.

Yes my little one I am a good daddy.

Not like those other ones.

No my child I am not like them. I am full of love for you and I will not ever hurt you

nor will I ever take anything from you that it is good for you to have my little one. My desire is only to bring you life and healing and to help you know that you are loved and that you are safe. My arms are a safe place for you my little one.
I would like to feel safe in your arms daddy and to forget about them and know that you aren't like them.
I will help you my little one. Healing will come and you will know what it means to have real daddy love not what they gave you my little one but what I give to you which is true and pure. I am not like them my dearest child. My heart is broken for all that you have suffered and all that has been lost to you, but I am here, and my arms of love are open to you. I will help you to feel safe enough to receive that love my child, for it is given freely to you.
I am holding on to Jesus. He helps me feels safe.
Yes my little one. Come then. Let me show to you just a little bit more of my love for you. Snuggle into the arms of my son. He is your safe place for now my little one.
Ok daddy.

Daddy told me a bit about what it means to be his child and how he sees his children. I thought maybe he was thinking I was not very good, but he would love me anyway… kind of because he has to, but he doesn't seem to see it that way.

Hello daddy.
Hello my child. My dearest one do not ever be afraid to approach me, I am always here for you just as my beloved son is always there for you. It is not different my little one.
It kind of feels different. I think…I am… I need to know you better.
Yes my child you do and it will come as you spend time with me and allow me to reveal my heart and my love to you. My child you have not ever known what it is to have a daddy, not in any sense but I will show you my little one. I will show you what it means to be safe and held and protected and to belong. You are part of a great and wonderful family my child. You have many brothers and sisters and aunts and uncles, all of which are there for you to know and enjoy relationship with. My family is the greatest family of all my little one and you are part of it.
You sound very proud of your family, your children.
Yes my child I am very proud of my children both those who are still on the earth and those who are already with me.
But…even though…we are…not what we should be here. Because I know I'm not and I don't think many of us are…what you want us to be.
My child I am proud of my children. No matter what they may do or not do they remain my children and I am glad that that is so. It is true my little one that many of them do not discover the fullness of who they are whilst they are on the earth but that does not diminish my love for them or mean that I am not proud to call them my own.
I am a bit confused by that. How can you be proud of children that do bad things?
Because I do not see them as you do my dearest child. I see them as they truly are. They are my children and they belong to me. Their behavior does not change the way I feel about them my dearest one.
But… don't you get angry.
I get angry at the wickedness that I see my little one, but I am not angry with my children, not in the sense that you mean, for in your heart you see anger and hatred as being one and the same. That is not so my little one. I am angry with the sin and the wickedness that I see but I do not hate my children. My love for them is unending.
I think maybe it will take me a while to understand about that.

My little one there are many things that I have to teach you about my heart of love and what it means to be my child but my dearest one I will not and could not ever hate you. Even if you are disobedient and wayward I will always love you.
I think…maybe somewhere inside I have thought you hated me because I am bad on the inside. But... maybe I don't think that anymore because I am getting better.
Yes my little one you are getting better. The lies that have been in your heart do not have the hold that they once had. You are not bad my little one for you have been made pure and whole in me and in my love for you. I have not ever hated you my little one. I have always loved you no matter what the enemy has done or said that cannot ever be changed.
Will you help me to see that and to know what it really means to have a daddy. I don't want to be thinking of you as kind of big and... scary, even though you kind of are. I don't know.
Your ideas of who I am are not yet founded in truth my little one, but I am changing this slowly. Keep coming to me my child and I will help you to see and know the truth.
Yes. I will keep coming daddy. I like that word. It makes me feel loved.
And that is what you are my dearest child, you are loved, and you are precious, you are safe and you are held. These things cannot ever be changed my little one any more than I can be changed. I am the unchanging one as is my love for you.
Yes...maybe...I could get a little bit closer today daddy. You are still…far away.
Yes my little one for I will not go too fast. Come a little closer than. My son is with you. He will hold you and help you to feel safe.
Ok daddy. A little bit closer.

Every time I would go and spend time with him, he would be healing me. It is hard to know exactly what he was doing but I would cry and cry. Jesus would hold me, and daddy would hold him. Jesus was my safe place for now and helped me to receive daddy's love.

It was only a few weeks after I first met him that it was Father's Day. I was excited because I had never known that I had a daddy before but now I did. I wanted to spend the day with him and for it to be special. I wanted to make him a card and give him a gift... but I couldn't think what that might be. It didn't work out the way I wanted and lots of things got in the way, so I didn't get any time to be with daddy or even with Jesus that day. That was sad for me. But daddy had a plan, a very good plan that was even better.

The next day something happened. I started calling out for my daddy right down from somewhere deep inside me and I ran into his arms. I know it sounds very silly but he seemed just like a soft white pillow to me and I cried and cried… and I kept calling out daddy my daddy… and then I felt very still and peaceful for a little while and then it would happen again and I would be calling out for my daddy. It happened a few times, the same thing over and over. It reminded me of that bit in the bible that talks about out crying out for daddy. That never really happened before for me. And I was in his arms even though he seemed like a lovely soft pillow I know it was him. Afterwards... after a little while I talked with Jesus...

Hello Jesus
Hello my little one.
I made it to daddy.
Yes my little one you did. My little one he has been waiting for so long. That is the greatest gift you could have given him my little one.
For daddy's day?
Yes my little one.
But I missed it.
My little one you did not miss it in your heart which is all that matters to us.
I was going to make a card.

Yes my little one I know. You can still do that.
Its not too late?
No my little one it is not too late. Your gifts to us are always received with delight my little one.
Daddy gave me a gift. Yesterday I mean.
Yes my little one he did.
So... I will wear it and think about him and all the things that he has given me... Crying.... Jesus... It is too much... Crying.... Sometimes it is too much...Crying
I know my little one.
Crying
That is why we must go slowly my little one. We will not take you too fast.
Crying.... I want to go fast Jesus.
I know my little one, but we are going fast enough.
Crying... You always love me more than I think…
Yes my little one that will always be so. We will never stop surprising you with our love. It is our delight to do so my little one.
Crying... I want to love you with all that I am Jesus and daddy Crying.... And Holy Spirit... Crying
Yes my little one we will make it possible for you to love us with your whole heart. Nothing held back my little one. This will be to our glory and for our joy. My little one you have no idea how much joy you bring to us.
Crying... Please stop Jesus... Crying...
No my little one it is not too much for you. I am holding you my little one.
Ok Jesus.
My little one you fill our hearts with joy, you cause us to sing my little one, a song of joy and hope and love over your life. My little one your life is a gift to us.
Crying... But you made me Jesus. That is like giving yourself a gift.
Yes my little one but it is also a gift that you have given to us. My little one you have given us your very self there is no greater gift than this.
I am a gift?
Yes my little one you are, a very good gift.
I don't know what to say Jesus.
My little one your words are not always necessary. Come and rest in my arms a little my dearest one. There is much that I am longing to share with you, but it is not yet time. Come into my arms of love and rest a while.
I love you Jesus.
Yes my little one I know that you do. Come.

The gift that daddy gave me was a ring. The Holy Spirit had been teaching me about colors and he had said something about wanting us to have a ring with all of those colors. I hadn't understood what he meant but I was browsing on eBay and I saw it, a ring with different colored stones and I knew that was what the Holy Spirit had meant... It is a gold eternity ring with sapphires. In the middle is a yellow one, which means hope and on either side of that are blue ones, they mean truth and then pink ones which mean love and then green which is life. The Holy Spirit said they were my colors because those were the things he would give me and give through me to others... It is maybe one of the most beautiful things I ever saw. I bought it on Sunday which was daddy's day and I knew then that daddy was saying it was his gift to me. That seemed a bit wrong because I thought I was supposed to give him something. So anyway, it came, and I cried...

It is so very beautiful Jesus.
Yes my little one let it be a reminder to you of our love and of all the things we have given you and are teaching you.
Is this what the Holy Spirit meant when he said about rings of different colors?

Yes my little one that is what he meant.
I didn't understand.
No my little one but that does not matter. My dearest one it is always our desire to give you good things. It does not matter my little one if you misunderstood for you have received our gift to you. That is what matters.
Yes Jesus I have. Thankyou... Crying... Sometimes it hurts so much to be loved... Crying...
I know my little one hold on to me.
Crying... I want to say thank you to daddy because... Crying... This was from him... Crying...
Yes my little one it was his gift to you on father's day.
Crying... Thank you daddy. I love my gift... Crying...
My child it is my great delight to give you many good gifts. My little one let this be to you a reminder of my great and unending love for you a love that will last for all of eternity my little one. Unending love.
Crying... I will wear it always daddy.
Yes my little one wear it with pride, not a pride that comes from self my little one but a pride in who you are, my beloved daughter, beloved and precious in every way.
Crying...Because I am proud to have you as my daddy because...You are the best daddy...Crying....
Yes my little one and I am your daddy. I will always be your daddy. I will never be taken away from you.

I wear the ring always and it reminds me of daddy sometimes when I forget. Now when I look at it, I always think and remember that I have a daddy who loves me. Spending time with daddy was something that I loved to do but it was painful for a long time. I never saw him, not like Jesus and the Holy Spirit but I did see something.

It is strange because he is solid but kind of like a white cloud. I don't see him. I was wondering about this and I think it is like a protection thing, like the cloud on the mountain. So, he is real and solid, but I am protected. He isn't the cloud, but the cloud covers him to keep me safe. I was looking at the cloud and in it, or behind it I couldn't tell, I could see lots of flashes, like lightening in lots of different colors. It was very pretty and not frightening.

> **I see my child, my one and only child. My little one I have many children but each one of them is hidden in my beloved son. I see each one just as I see him my little one. It is the same love that I have for him that is given to you. It is the same heart of love that is shared with you my little one. When I look at you, I see you as I see him, beloved and lovely and perfect in every way. I am proud to call you my own my little one.**

Chapter 23

Never Alone

Everyone was going away. Cheryl and Richard and Sophie were all going away on holidays and Mike was going away too. I was going to be alone for ten days. Jesus told me that I would be the one on the outside for all of that time. It was a time to be healed and a time to find out more about who I was. It is one of the hardest times I remember because of the amount of healing that Jesus did every day. He said it was like I was in hospital having lots of operations. It took me a while to recover from it and to be able to say it was worth it, but it was.

Hello Jesus
Hello, my little one...My little one I am with you. My dearest one I will help you and guide you through this time. My dearest one this time is for you to discover more of who you are and to grow stronger in me. Do not be distressed my little one. This time will pass. You are not alone my little one. You are not ever alone.
It seems like a long time Jesus to be here all alone.
I know my little one, but it is not. I have many plans as you will see.
Crying...Please look after them Jesus... Crying....
My little one.
Crying....
I will look after them.
Crying....
And I will bring them safely back to you.
Crying....
My little one I will help you and I will bring healing to your soul.
Crying....
I know my little one that the pain of abandonment goes so deep.
Crying....
But my little one I will help you to see and understand that you were not ever abandoned.
Crying....
I never left you my little one. Not even for one moment did I leave.
Crying....
Hold on to me my little one. You are safe and you are loved. I will not leave you. I will never leave you.
Crying... What should I do?
Hold on to me and do not be afraid.
Crying....
I am healing a deep wound my little one.
Crying....

I kept on crying and crying. It was like I couldn't stop. I couldn't seem to do anything but lay on my bed and cry or sleep. That was all I could do. It was very bad. Everyone going away all at once had brought my feelings of abandonment to the surface. It was this that Jesus was wanting to heal but it was so very painful and frightening for me. There were things I needed to remember too so that Jesus could heal me and show me that I wasn't ever alone. He never left me.

I was talking to Jesus while I was crying because I was remembering something- kind of. I was remembering a luggage trunk we had. It was a big brown one with metal fastenings on the outside. I was remembering that they put me in and locked it and left me there because I had been crying and made a fuss about something. They left me there a long time and I felt like I had been forgotten. I was talking to Jesus and he said they left me there for two days. I don't know if it is right. I still find it hard to believe these things.

My little one I am here.
Are you making me better Jesus?
Yes little one I am. Hold on to me and do not let go. Do not be afraid my little one I am strong enough for you.
It hurts.
I know my little one. I know.
Did... Is it what I think?
That is part of it my little one, only part of it for there is so much more that needs to be healed. I will not give you more than you can bear my little one.
I don't want to be here all alone Jesus... Crying....
I know my little one. Hold on to me.
Crying....
You are not alone my little one you are never alone.
Crying... I can't be here all this time on my own Jesus. Why can't Jennifer come out... Crying....
Because my little one it is you that needs healing. My dearest one Jennifer is not gone. She will return my little one but for now hold on to me and allow me to work within you. I know it is hard my little one.
and so very painful for you but I am with you and I will not leave you.
Crying.... I want to do nice things Jesus... Crying.... and have friends and not be here anymore...
I know my little one. All of this and more will come. Hold on to me my little one.
Crying....
I am your strength and your shield. I will give you all that you need in this time my little one.
I don't know what to do Jesus... Crying....
Rest In my arms my little one and allow me to work. That is all that you must do.
I thought we were going to draw.
Yes my little one we will but for now come into my arms and let me continue to heal you my little one.
Crying.... I don't want to.
I know my little one. Come.

It was still hard for me to accept the truth and to feel the pain without wanting it all to just stop. I couldn't see what Jesus said he did, that it was a good thing that I survived and that I was still here. A lot of the time I wanted to go home and be with Jesus and for all of the pain to be gone and not to have to do any of this anymore.

My dearest one my greatest gift to you is myself. I give myself freely my little one. All that I am. I am always with you and I will never leave you. I have always been with you my little one. In your very darkest hour, I was there.
Were you in the trunk with me Jesus?
Yes my little one I was there holding you and giving you the strength to survive. You were not alone my little one.
I don't remember it Jesus not really. Is it a shared memory?
Yes my little one for not one of you could have survived that on your own. I enabled you all to survive my little one.
I still think it would have been better if we died Jesus... Crying... It would have been better.... Crying...
No my little one it would not have been better. Trust me my little one. I know what lies ahead. It would not have been better.
You let some people die.

Yes my little one many do not survive what you have endured but that does not mean that I loved them more. My dearest one my purpose in enabling you to survive is good. It was not to prolong your suffering my little one but to bring you healing and life and through you to many others.

Will I see it one day Jesus?

Yes my little one, one day you will see it.

Help me then because it looks like too much for me Jesus. All of it.

I know my little one, but it is not. Take one day at a time and remember that I will make it possible for you to do and be everything that I ask of you. You are not ever alone my little one.

In between the healing I was doing ordinary things, shopping, jobs around the house and that sort of thing. I was enjoying wearing my own clothes and putting my hair in bunches and not having to worry about what anyone saw or heard. I spent some nice times with Jesus too.

I was listening to some worship music and I started to worship. I could see Jesus and he was dancing with me. It was a lot of fun and made me laugh. I got tired after a while and had to stop but Jesus kept on dancing. That made me smile too.

But the healing continued and there were more things to remember.

I snuggled down and for a while I just felt very peaceful. It made me think about anesthetic. Then I started to see something, a memory. It was a little girl. She was wearing a pretty white dress. Maybe it wasn't a dress but like an under-slip because the bottom part was netting you could see through. I don't think she was wearing anything underneath, but I wasn't thinking about that. I was wanting to be the one wearing the pretty dress and twirling round like she was. I think maybe I was three or four. I was wearing a scruffy vest and knickers. My hair was short, and she had long pretty hair. Then they took us out. I think we were the only two children. It was in a cave. I was put to one side and told to sit still. The little girl was lifted up and stood on a rock that made me think of an alter. I wasn't liking this memory and I was saying to Jesus that I thought she was going to die, and I didn't want to see it. He said she wasn't going to die. I was surprised about that. It was the people in the red robes, I think. I wasn't really looking at them I was looking at the girl. One of the robed people gave her a long knife and was saying something about the blood of innocents bringing life. Then they put a baby at the girl's feet, and she put the knife in. They cut it all the way down its body, so it was cut in two. I was crying a lot by now, here I mean I don't know about the me that was there. The stone had like a bowl cut in it where the baby was and there was a channel that the blood came down and they collected it in a cup. They all drank the blood but not me. Then when they finished someone took off my vest and knickers and put me on the stone. They told me to lick up the blood that was left. When I was remembering this, I was thinking it couldn't be right because it makes no sense, but Jesus said it was right. So I remembered licking the blood. Maybe they were just being cruel and that is all it was. When I looked up everyone was gone. There was no one in the cave just me. And then the candles went out and I was left all alone in the darkness. This is when it got really bad and I cried and cried and cried and held on to Jesus. It was so bad I was begging him to stop because of all the fear and the pain but he kept saying just a little more. I didn't remember anything else except Jesus showed me how he was there with me holding me. I thought they all forgot about me and left me. I suppose they came back for me and I don't know why they did it, but it was very terrible to be naked and alone in a dark cave sitting in blood. It was very bad.

The memories made me think about other things too that I wanted to ask Jesus about.

I have been thinking about that little girl Jesus. The pretty one.

Yes my little one I know that you have.

I wanted to be like her didn't I. She was pretty and she didn't get left out or forgotten even though she had to do that terrible thing. I think... I don't know I was thinking about my pretty things and how I want to be pretty. Is it... is it because somehow, I think if I am pretty, I won't be forgotten?

My little one there are many things for you still to see and understand about the past and the present also. It is not wrong for you to like pretty things my little one or to want to look pretty but always remember that you are loved for who you are no matter what you look like on the outside my little one. That does not matter. What matters is who you are on the inside.

Yes, because I am old on the outside and if I get thin, I will still be old.

But you will still be you my little one. The beautiful person that you are no matter what the outside looks like my little one.

Yes Jesus. But is it alright for me to have pretty things and... to be as pretty as I can?

Yes my little one as long as you remember that is not what is important to me. I see you as you truly are my little one and you are beautiful to me, inside and out.

Am I?

Yes my little one you are. I will help you to become the person that you truly are and to express that in all that you do and say, including the way that you look to others my little one but do not look for acceptance or love because of the way that people see you my little one. You are loved and accepted already. Enjoy your dressing up my little one, make yourself look the way that expresses something of who you are, this is good my little one but do not look to others for acceptance and love because of the way that you look or because of the things that you do. Be yourself my little one that is all.

I love you Jesus. Please be helping me with all of these things.

Yes my little one I will always help you.

Some of our times together I would just snuggle into Jesus arms and cry and cry. I suppose it was about letting go of the pain that was hidden away and putting Jesus love in its place. Jesus healed me in other ways too. He showed me some of what he was doing so that I could choose and so that I could learn too.

So, I did rest for a little while but then I began to see something. It wasn't a memory. Jesus was talking to me and saying that there was a locked room in my heart and there was a lot of pain there and he wanted to open it up. He was giving me a choice I suppose. So he took me to a door and it had a golden padlock on it. He gave me a little key and said I was the one who needed to open it. I was afraid but I did it anyway. The door opened and all this wind came out. It smelled very bad and there was stuff blowing about in the room. Jesus told me to wait outside and he went in for a little while. He came out holding what looked like a very big diamond, maybe as big as a football. He gave it to me and said it was something that had been lost to me for a very long time. Then he told me to lock the door again and we went down a corridor into another room. There were a lot of jewels in this room I think but we went straight to a wall where there was a hole just the right size and shape for the diamond. Jesus put it in and then we went out again. He said I had a choice now that we could go back to the room and he could clear it out or it could stay locked. I was afraid about what was in the room because I thought I saw something horrible in there, but I didn't want it to stay there so I said we should go back.

So, we went back and went in. It was a bit like a rubbish tip. That is how it smelled. The floor seemed very black, but Jesus was holding me in his arms. He walked to a window. On the way there I saw something on the floor that looked like a giant maggot and there were other things moving in the rubbish too. Jesus said he was letting in the light. I was crying a lot by now and I was very afraid of what the light would show. Everything was so black and dirty. The floor was kind of black and gooey and there were creatures in their horrible things that I didn't see exactly because they were under the rubbish. Except the maggot. It was there because it couldn't move fast enough. I was crying and crying to have such a room in my heart, but Jesus said he was going to cleanse it all. He seemed to get a sword from nowhere and stuck it through the maggot and then the room was full of white fire that was whirling round and round and burning everything up except me and Jesus. And I was crying and crying because it hurt so much but Jesus was holding me. Eventually the fire went, and the room was empty and clean, and Jesus said now we could begin to fill it with good things. I haven't asked him what it all meant... I don't think I want to know just yet.

I did ask Jesus to explain it to me much later on. I knew that the jewel represented a gift because there had been others that had been recovered and given back to me. He said that the room was a room of belonging that the enemy had filled with lies and fear which caused me pain. The maggot wasn't a maggot but something from the enemy which fed on all the lies and stirred up pain and feelings of abandonment and the diamond was my lost security, security in Jesus, which he gave back to me.

Ten days is a long time and it seemed to go very slowly to me. I was in so much pain I counted down every day that passed. I got very tired, but Jesus gave me times of rest and the strength to keep on going. I needed to hold on to him and trust him.

Jesus said to come back after tea and by that time there was so much pain I just curled up and cried and cried. At first, I was saying I don't want to be here over and over and then that turned into let me out over and over. I was holding on to Jesus, but I remembered about daddy and then I was in his arms and that seemed somehow even safer like he is bigger and stronger. But then I knew where I was. In the box and I was so very afraid and desperate to get out. I thought the fear and the darkness would kill me but then I felt daddy's arms round me, and he said you are safe, and all the fear went, and I stopped crying and I felt very peaceful and safe. I stayed for a long time because it was nice. I talked to Jesus afterward.

My little one my arms of love are around you and they are holding you so close. I am with you my little one. I will not let you go.
It is a horrible feeling Jesus feeling trapped.
I know my little one, but you are not trapped you are held my little one and that is different.
Tell me.
My little one to be trapped is to be locked into a place with no way of escape. You know this my little one but you are not trapped. You are held in my arms my little one. There is a way for you but I am holding you safely in my arms until it is time for you to go. It is not the same my little one.
I get them confused don't I.
Yes my little one you do but it is not the same.
That's why I get so panicky about not being able to leave.
Yes my little one it triggers deep fear that is still unhealed but it will not always be so my little one. You are being healed but slowly as you can bear it.
Yes, because it is very bad.
Yes my little one it is, it goes very deep my little one and will take time to heal but it will come my little one.
Is that what you were talking about starting but not finishing this weekend.
Yes my little one. There is more that we will do but we cannot do the whole my little one not in this time.

We were almost to the end of our time together, but Jesus said he wasn't finished. He said that he had something nice planned for me and that sounded so wonderful after such a hard time. It was a difficult day and I felt like the enemy was around and that made me scared especially when the day was going by and the nice thing didn't come. I didn't want to be tricked. It felt like too much when I was so hurting and tired. I spent some time worshipping and that helped, and I didn't feel so afraid or depressed. I came to be with Jesus again.

This time I found myself in the attic with the Holy Spirit and Jesus. The Holy Spirit had a kind of a light, like a golden ball, because it was dark in there. There was a big cardboard box and he said we were going to open it. It looked big and scary but inside it was almost empty except for a very little metal chest. It was black and had a combination padlock on it. The Holy Spirit gave me a tiny key to open it. He said the combination had been used to lock it but this key would open it. So I did. But there didn't seem to be anything in it. I was sitting in Jesus lap and it was like… something like a gas was coming out of the little box. I don't know what it was, but it felt like pain and I started to cry. I held on tight to Jesus and he said I needed to be willing to receive what was in the box. So, I said I would even though I didn't know what it was. And I cried and cried because it hurt so much. Then Jesus said to look in the box again and there was a little pink jewel that I took out. He said it was my need to be loved that I had locked away so long ago. I said I know I need to be loved but he said I need to feel the fullness of it, and it would help me to receive the love that I was given. I cried a lot.

Jesus had done so very much in such a short time and I was so very tired but there was more... and this was the hardest healing of all.

In the evening I got more and more worried because I was waiting for my nice thing and it didn't come. I tried to keep busy and not think about it but I got more and more anxious. Eventually I realized the nice thing wasn't coming and it had been a lie and I started to cry and cry. Jesus was there talking to me, but I was so angry and upset with him. I told him to get away from me and leave me alone. I told him he left me with the enemy and let them do those things to me and he said he never left me and I said he did and it was all a lie and how could he do that and I was so very angry and upset but then I started to say about the bad things and how he left me then... even though I know he didn't. Jesus just kept saying he never left me. And I said what was the point of being there if he didn't help and he just let it go on and on and didn't help me. And then I got very afraid and even more upset because I said I didn't trust him. I felt like he had betrayed me and abandoned me and that is more terrible than anything. I didn't see how I could ever trust him but if I don't have Jesus, I don't have anything, and I might as well be dead but even being dead wouldn't be any good if Jesus wasn't who he said. I was getting more and more afraid and desperate and crying and crying and saying help me help me help me, but he didn't help me. I thought I was going to die and that this was the end of everything. Then I stopped breathing. I do that sometimes when I get very upset. Its not like holding your breath its just that I stop breathing and I concentrated very hard on the lights in my room and I calmed down and stopped crying. Even while I was doing that, I was thinking how Jesus gave me the ability to do that and if he didn't then maybe I wouldn't be here. I would have hurt myself... I think.

So, I was calmer but still very upset. I said that nobody ever helps me nobody ever comes. He didn't help me. But he said he answered my cries for help. Just not the way I wanted him to. He didn't make it stop but he did help me. And I said you made alters and he said yes. That was his help. He answered all of my cries for help. He never ever left me. I know Jesus has told me this a lot of times before, but it was like I suddenly got it. Like I saw it and it was true. That he did help me, and he never left me. It was like something fell into place.

But then I saw something else. That this was the nice thing he had planned for me and I got upset all over again. He said it was and that none of the healing stuff had been the enemy, that I hadn't been deceived. That was good but I got angry and upset all over again. And I said it wasn't a nice thing there was nothing nice about it. I spent a long time telling him that nice didn't mean any of the things he had just done. He said his idea of nice was a bit like his idea of good.... and that he had to expose the lie in my heart. I was still very upset. I calmed down and I could see how he had done something good because I really know now, he never left me, and he did help me, but it was not nice. It was very not nice. Eventually I went to sleep but I knew in my heart I hadn't forgiven Jesus for letting me believe the enemy had deceived me and for telling me it was a nice thing he had planned when it seemed to me like a very cruel thing he did.

This morning I woke up feeling terrible. My eyes were swollen, and my head hurt. I was very tired and still very unhappy. I didn't want to talk to Jesus even though I knew he was waiting for me. Eventually I heard him, except it wasn't Jesus.

Come then my child.
Crying... Daddy? Crying...
Yes my little one, my child I am here. I am here with my arms around you.
Crying... Why... Why are you here? Where is Jesus?... Crying...
He is here my dearest one. He has not left you.
Crying... I can't do this…. Crying... Daddy? Crying....
My child I have come that I might comfort you and hold you. My child everything that we do is out of our great love for you.
Crying....
Everything...
Crying... It doesn't always seem that way...Crying...... Crying...
I know my child I know. My little one do you remember when we first met?
In the cathedral?
Yes my child. And do you remember what I told you then?
Crying... No... Crying...
I told you that I had been with you. That I had always been with you, that I had always been your daddy.
Crying... Crying... I don't remember.
My little one I have always been your daddy. I have always been looking after you and protecting you. I know it has not always looked that way to you my little one and you have felt so alone and so abandoned for so very long.
Crying... Why did you let me go on thinking that if it wasn't true?
Because you were not ready to see the truth my little one. The truth has to be accepted for it to have any power to heal and transform. My little one, my dearest child I have been waiting for this moment when I could gather you into my arms and you would know, truly know that I never abandoned you, that I have always loved you.

I felt so safe and so wrapped up in his arms it was wonderful and awful at the same time and I cried a lot.

My little one you are safe in my arms and will always be so. My dearest one I know that there are many things that you do not yet understand about your life, but you are held in my arms my little one.
Crying...
I know the truth of all things and will reveal it to you as you are ready. Will you trust me to do that my little one?

Crying... I want the pain to stop daddy, I want it to stop... Crying...
I know my little one.
Crying... I know... Crying...
My little one you are held in my arms of love. I have given you my son to walk with you and my spirit to help you in everything. You are not alone my child. There is nothing that you cannot overcome in our strength. My child many things are changing for you, but you are safe in my arms. I am holding you and will keep you safe and secure. Nothing will harm you my dearest child.

I felt that I was being snuggled safe into his arms. He seemed so strong and warm and safe to me.

My dearest child all the things of this world that try to take you away from me they cannot succeed and the enemy of your soul he cannot succeed. I will always be your daddy and I will always protect you and keep you close to my heart. There is nothing that can take you away from me my little one. You are mine. You belong to us. We are all of us with you. We are all of us holding you and loving you and protecting you. There is nothing we cannot do my dearest one. There is nothing we cannot do in you through you or for you. You will see many things in this life my little one that will seem to say otherwise but the truth remains. All you must do is accept that truth my little one. The truth in your heart is a powerful thing and will set you free from many things that have held you. My dearest child I will not ever let you go. Continue to hold on to us and trust us just as you have done. We will help you with the pain of this life my little one. We are in it with you. There is still much healing to be done and many things for you to overcome but you are able my child because we are with you.

It seemed to me I was sitting on daddy's knee and he was holding me so close and Jesus and the Holy Spirit were there too, and I felt so safe and held and loved by all of them.

My dearest one my son loves you and will not ever hurt you. Everything he does is for your good. Go to him now my little one and let him love you and put his arms around you. He is here for you my child.

I ran into Jesus arms...

Jesus... Crying...
My little one my love for you is unending. There is nothing I would not do for you my little one. Do not fear me or anything I will do. My heart is broken for you my little one and all that you have suffered but I have come to save you and to heal you that you might know my love and the love of our father. My little one my healing will come to you in many ways. It is always the best way my little one though it may be painful it is always the best way.
Crying... I love you Jesus.
I know you do my little one.
Crying...
My little one this time is now ending, and a new part of your journey is about to begin. Keep your eyes fixed upon us my little one and remember that we are always with you and that you are safe and held. Rest now my little one and do not be afraid. This day is for you to rest and to play as you are able. We are with you my little one. We are always with you. Rest now.

That was a difficult ending to a difficult time, but Jesus had seen me through, and I had been healed and set free enough for the next steps that he had for me.

I am making all things new... I am taking everything that is and making it into what it is not. My dearest one many things are not the way that I intended them to be, many things have been lost my little one and they will be restored. Many things have been broken and they will be mended. Many things are not as they were intended to be my little one but I will make them new again so that my purpose in them is also renewed. My little one I am doing this in your life and in the lives of those around you. I am working constantly to bring my promises to pass. My dearest one hold on to me and do not let go. You have not yet seen nor imagined all that I have for you.

Chapter 24

Blending

Things were different now. Up until now Jennifer had been on the outside most of the time and I came out to spend time with Mike or Cheryl but now it was me who was outside most of the time and Jennifer only came out when she was meeting with some of her friends like Ruth.

It has felt too hard to write. The first week after my time alone with Jesus I was too sad and too exhausted. Then I was away with Cheryl for a couple of days. I was out for almost all the time. I had a good time, but I felt bad that Cheryl didn't get time to be with Jennifer. Jennifer was out less than a day and then Jesus put me on the outside again and that is how it has been since. I have had to do all the things Jennifer does and pretend to be her with Sophie and Richard and with her mum and all the people she knows. It has been exhausting and I have begged Jesus to bring her back. I don't like pretending to be her, it feels wrong and I get sad that nobody even notices she is gone... except Cheryl. She has been getting anxious and saying things like what if she never comes back. I don't know what to say. It has been just like Jesus said, he has helped me do everything even when there have been emergencies which there have, and people don't notice I am not Jennifer. But I have felt very sad because I know what it means and because I don't want to be here in this life being Jennifer. Jesus says the outside life is mine now and Jennifer will come and go to be with people when needed until her purpose is finished. It is all happening just like he said, and his plan seems very real. That is frightening. I have felt very overwhelmed and have tried not to think about what is happening but that doesn't work very well.

It was very difficult being on the outside for most of the time. I got so tired and afraid and overwhelmed by everything and there didn't seem to be any escape from it because Jesus was in control not me. I didn't think I could do all the things or be all the things that Jennifer was. To me it felt like Jesus was doing a bad swap and that there wasn't anything good about it.

Crying...Jesus
Yes little one.
Crying...
I am here with you .
Crying...
I am always with you my little one I do not ever leave you.
Crying...Please don't leave me. Please don't leave me... Crying...
I will not ever leave you my little one. Come. Let me hold you for a while and then there are things that we need to talk about.

So He held me in His arms and I cried and cried.

Jesus why are you here?
I am here to help you my little one. I will always help you.
About the blending thing?
Yes my little one.
Crying...Ok Jesus I am listening.
My little one the blending with Jennifer has already begun you know this.
Yes.
It is not a bad thing that I am doing my little one. It is for your good and for Jennifer's good also.
Crying...But she has had a life Jesus. A real life. Not like me. And now she has to give that

up and be nothing- like I was... Crying...
No my little one that is not how it will be. My little one you are not the only one who will gain from this Jennifer will also gain much my little one. This is a good thing for her. Each of you will become more than you were my little one. Neither of you will lose. This is not about Jennifer sacrificing herself for you. That is not how it is.
Crying...Isn't it?... Crying...
No my little one it isn't. My dearest one I am asking this of you both. Both of you must agree to this before it can happen my little one. I will not force either of you against your will.
No Jesus I know that.
Both of you have agreed my little one because you both understand that it is my will for you and it is good.
Yes. We are trusting you.
Yes my little one you are for neither of you fully understand what it will mean for you. You are both choosing to trust me. That is good my little one. For my desires for both of you are good, not to harm you my little one or to take anything away from you but only to give you more than you currently have... My little one whilst it is true that Jennifer is giving up her life as an individual to become part of who you are that does not mean that she is sacrificing herself my little one. It means that she understands that this is for her good and your good and ultimately for the good of many others. My dearest one she will gain so much more than she will lose.
Crying...But she is losing herself. How can that be good Jesus? Crying... How can that be good? Crying...
My little one Jennifer is a part of you, a part of you that has been lost to you my little one. In coming back to you she will not lose who she is, she will find it. My little one she is not losing who she is, she is becoming all that she was ever meant to be, which is part of you my little one.
Crying... It just seems like a really bad thing like she is dying when it should be me. It should be me Jesus. Not her... Crying...
No my little one no. It was never meant to be you my little one. I have saved you. It was always me who saved you my little one. You were not meant to die. That is what the enemy has told you my little one, but it is a lie. You were not ever meant to die. You were meant to live. You were meant to be the person that you are and to be full of joy and hope and love my little one. You were not meant to die...you did not deserve to die my little one. It was not meant to be you.
Crying....
My little one this is not the same. Not in any way. My dearest one the little ones who lost their lives should not have done so but that does not mean that you should not have lived my little one. It does not mean that you were meant to die or that you should have died instead of them.
Crying... I don't even remember it Jesus… Crying....
No my little one not fully but you retain enough memory of it my little one, you still carry the pain.
Crying...You should have let me die Jesus... Crying...
No little one hold on to me. I will help you. My little one the pain will pass. Hold on to me for just a little while.
Crying...Crying...
My little one all of these things are yet to be healed but my dearest one you were always meant to live. It is good that you did my little one. Now it is time for you to truly begin to live, to take hold of the life that I am giving you my little one. The blending with Jennifer will continue until it is complete. It is a good thing my little one, not a bad one. Both of you will gain from this. My dearest one I will not leave you, not ever. Let me hold you for a little while.

It was all getting mixed up for me. I thought I was bad because of the bad things that happened and the things I was told in the past. I didn't think I deserved to live. I didn't think I should have lived when so many others died. I didn't think I should take Jennifer's life from her when so many others had died already, and I hadn't. The past was getting mixed up with the good thing Jesus was doing, which was to put us back together again, to restore the things that had been taken. But I couldn't see it. Sometimes I thought I did a little bit but the things I believed about myself went very deep, so I needed Jesus to tell me over and over again that I wasn't bad and that he wanted me to live. When I wasn't crying, I was trying to understand what was happening and what it would mean to be blended with Jennifer. I needed a lot of help.

Yesterday me and Jennifer had a picture... I think we share a lot of things. Cheryl was talking about how her relationship with Jennifer had been a long one with lots of ups and downs and how her relationship with me is only just beginning. Jesus has been telling her that we will be friends. The picture was of a rose stem split in two... on one part was a rose in full bloom (Jennifer) and on the other part was a bud (me) just beginning to open. It was kind of a picture of something else too. Jennifer shared that bit with her, but I think maybe I saw something else. I saw that Jennifer's rose is almost ready to fall... like roses do when they are finished blooming. And that when that happens that part of the stem will kind of die back so there is just one stem and one rose which is me. That made me feel a bit sad.

I wanted to talk about Jennifer and who I am and who I will be because... I don't know who I am Jesus.
My little one who you are is my beloved and precious child. This will never change my little one, no matter what happens, no matter who you become in me your identity does not change my little one.
But I will change.
Yes my little one you will for you are not yet all that I have created you to be. There is much healing to be done my little one.
Please help me to understand.
My little one in all that you are and all that you will ever be, you are held by and loved by me. When I created you, I created you with love and with purpose my little one. I made you who I wanted you to be, but you are still being formed my little one you are still becoming the person that you truly are. This is true for all of my children my little one for you will not be made perfect until I come again. Only then will you be all that I created you to be.
Yes. Ok... but you keep saying that... you are making me to be all that you created me to be... I thought, maybe I understood wrong.
My little one who you are is already complete in me. My work is finished my little one but for you the journey still continues. My little one my work in you will continue all the days of your life for I am constantly working within you to bring you into the perfection that I have for you.
I kind of understand that Jesus... but it seems different for normal people.
But it is not my little one, not really. It only looks different to you. All that I am doing is giving back to you that which has been taken my little one. That is no different from any of my children for the enemy has stolen so much from each one of you, you are not who I created you to be my little one, not yet. My little one when you come together with another alter, I am giving back to you that which was lost because of what was done to you. I know my little one that you were not conscious of this, you did not understand at the time nor do you fully understand now my little one but I will return to you everything which was taken my little one. I will do more than that for my healing is such that you will be restored not back to what you were my little one but into someone even more glorious. This is my work in you my little one. This is the

healing that I have for you.
But... if they are people in their own right...
They are part of you my little one, even though they have become a person in their own right they are still part of who you are.
I don't understand that.
My little one all that they are was taken from you. Their experiences may be different from yours because to a degree they have lived separately from you but all that they are came from you my little one.
But... they are them and I am me.
For now, my little one but it will not always be so. My dearest one just because I give them back to you that does not mean that they cease to exist, all that they are remains my little one, it remains in you.
It doesn't seem right.
My little one in joining with you they also become all that they were meant to be, my original intent my little one.
But you made them... the way you wanted them.
Yes my little one I did, for a time, but when that time is ended I will make them to become all that I desire them to be, all that I created them to be, which is to be joined with you once again.
So... are you going to blend me with Jennifer?
I am going to return to you those qualities which you gave to her. This will only strengthen you my little one it will not make you into a different person. It does not change who you are, it strengthens who you are, you become more of who you are and not less.
It is hard to understand.
My little one everything that makes Jennifer who she is came from you.
I suppose... but... she isn't me.
No my little one she isn't but she was formed from you. I will return to you that which was taken my little one. It will make you stronger, it will make you more complete. It does not change who you are my little one.
Will it change... will... I don't know.
My little one you will retain everything that you currently are. Nothing will be taken my little one. You will only become more not less.
It is a good thing?
Yes my little one it is a good thing. It will be better by far my little one. Your dependence upon me will grow, you will grow, everything will be better for you my little one not worse.
But if I am still me... I still don't know how I can be me here.
Because you have me my little one and I will make it possible for you to live this life, even as yourself. My dearest one there is nothing that I will do that is not good. Everything is moving you closer to the person that I desire for you to be, a person who is completely and wholly mine my little one. There is nothing to fear from this.
I... have given myself to you Jesus so you can do whatever you want... but I don't want to be afraid of it. I don't want to lose myself again.
You will not lose yourself my little one you will only become more of who you are. My little one when you give yourself to me, I begin to change many things within you, I begin to remove the things which hinder you and keep you from me.
Yes.
But that is not all my little one I will also add many things. As you receive from me, I can make you so much more than you have been my little one, you grow more and more into who I created you to be. That person is only to be found in who I am my little one. Do not fear becoming all that I desire for you to be, no matter what that means or how different that may be from the person that you see now...

Yes. I know you are right about that. Help me to see it like you do Jesus.
Yes my little one I will continue to help you. Do not fear anything that I will do my little one. You are safe in my arms. I will not harm you in any way.

The enemy was making things harder. They didn't want me to be the one on the outside, learning and healing and becoming. They did everything they could to make me want to run away and hide inside again.

I was thinking this morning and maybe I won't explain it well, but I think I saw that the enemy is using past things... all the bad things to make me not want to be on the outside. Like making me feel like I am weird and reminding me of bad things, like when I was out with my walk with Cheryl and we came to a graveyard, sometimes it is ok, and I can manage it but not this time. And I remembered about the girl who cried and made a fuss and how they killed her and how scared I was on Tuesday because I was crying with Cheryl and I wanted to go inside because it didn't feel safe.

Blending and alters and who I was in all that were difficult things for me to understand. When I first realized I wasn't Jennifer I thought I wasn't a real person. Not like her. I thought that I was somehow less of a person, less important. Not worth anything really. I thought Jennifer was so much better than me. It didn't make any sense to take away the real person and swap her for someone who wasn't anything or anyone but my idea of who I was wasn't a true one and Jesus and the Holy Spirit and daddy wanted me to see and understand the truth as much as I could.

I had a dream that was very real. I think maybe it was a God dream because it was so real and because of what it told me. I woke up and wrote it down almost straight away, but I can still remember it very well. In the dream I was drowning in cold water, maybe in a lake or something. It was very real. I could see and hear and feel like in real life. I think I knew it was a dream and I was struggling and trying to escape but there was no way to escape... but then it was like I started sliding out of myself and I dropped out of the person who was drowning, kind of like I left my skin behind but the skin was still a person, but not me anymore. I dropped down into a room and left the other person in the drowning dream. I had fallen into another dream.

When I woke up and was thinking about it I thought it was like what happens when alters are made, that the person who is having the bad dream escapes by leaving something of themselves behind and falling into another place- inside. It is hard to explain in words, but it makes a lot of sense to me how I saw it, more sense than it has before. As I was thinking about this, I saw something else. I was awake so maybe this was like a vision or a picture. I saw a drop of water and it was falling through a crack in the floor/ceiling. As it came through from one room down into another the drop of water fell down into the room below but then I looked at the ceiling and saw that a drop of water had been left behind. What I saw was that there had been one drop of water and now there were two... but they were both drops of water. One didn't stop being a drop of water... they were both still a drop of water. So that made me think about how one person who becomes two, because they are alters, are still people just the same, they don't become something else that isn't a person just because they got split, like the drop of water doesn't stop being a drop of water because it got split. And it made me see that I am not less than Jennifer I am the same and I am not less than a normal person I am the same. That makes a lot of sense to me. And then I thought about how it is when you put two drops of water close to each other and how they kind of merge to become one drop of water and I thought maybe that is how blending is, like two drops of water becoming one drop of water. Maybe that is how it is for me and Jennifer now, we are kind of joined like two drops of water starting to merge together. You can still see that there is two drops but soon they will be one drop.

Jesus said that the blending was happening gradually, and that Jennifer would still be there for a while because she hadn't fulfilled her purpose yet. He said that she wouldn't go until I didn't need her anymore.

Hello Jesus
Hello my little one.
I am getting amazed by what you are doing Jesus and that I can have an outside life, but some things are still a bit confusing.
I know my little one but that will not always be so. Many of the questions that you have will be resolved as you learn and grow and as the blending process continues and is completed.
Yes. I think... I am wondering about how things are changing for us. It is a bit like we are swapping places Jesus. Is that how it is?
That is how it seems my little one in many ways but that is not truly how it is for Jennifer is becoming part of you but you were never truly part of Jennifer, you were always you my little one, separate and distinct from her even though you were unaware of it.
We have been wondering Jesus, I think it is we, if she is starting to experience life through me like I used to experience it through her. I mean I still do on the inside most of the time, but we were thinking about when we spend time with you... are we both here?
My little one your relationship with me and Jennifer's relationship with me has been intertwined and you have shared many things together with me my little one. Much of what has been given to you has been given to you both because of the close and deep connections between you but I do not ever see you as the same my little one. You are two persons who are becoming one. I am making something so special with you both. My dearest one whilst the process of blending may seem confusing at times and eventually you will be joined together as one person, I do not want you to think that I lump you together in any way. Jennifer is her own person still my little one and my relationship with her is different to that which I have with you. She is experiencing more and more of her life through you my little one and will continue to do so for that is what the blending process will mean for her. This is beginning already and will continue.
So... she's not here?
No little one she has her own times with me.
Does she Jesus because... It doesn't seem like she does. She says you aren't doing anything in her life.
I am changing her my little one but not in the way that I am changing you. I am enabling her to give way to you and to let go of the life that she has known. I am helping her with all of the changes that are happening in her life and within her. I am not doing nothing my little one, but it is different to what I am doing with you.
Because it is about the blending and then she will be part of all you are doing in and through me.
Yes my little one that is so. Sometimes she shares in what I am telling you where it is helpful to do so but for the most part, she spends her own time with me when I strengthen and encourage her to continue along the path that I have for her.
She doesn't share it much Jesus.
No my little one she doesn't for it is not in her nature to share that which she believes will cause others distress but I am her strength my little one. She will not falter or fail as she follows me just as you will not.
It is a strange thing Jesus... this blending, I think we both want to get it over with but... I am still afraid Jesus and sad.
I know my little one. The process will continue slowly. It will happen at just the right time my little one. My plans for you are sure and they are good. Keep on following and know that I am in control. Everything that I am doing is to bring you life my little

one and in you I will also bring Jennifer life. It is for her good my little one that I am doing this.

Even though Jesus told me over and over that it was a good thing it was very hard for me to believe. Jennifer had a lot of things that she could do, not like me... I couldn't do anything except cry I thought. Jesus kept telling me he was making me strong, but I thought he meant strong like Jennifer was, not needing anything or anyone else and being able to do lots of things and be grown up. I thought Jesus wanted me to be like Jennifer was and that confused me. I didn't want to be Jennifer. I had been Jennifer for all of my life and now I wanted to be who I was, like I thought Jesus promised me.

My little one I am holding you so close to me. My dearest one everything that I am doing is working for your good. There is nothing you cannot do with me by your side.
Crying... I don't want to be this strong person who can do anything... I just want to be a little girl.... Crying... who is loved...
My dearest one you are who I say that you are, and you are both my little one. You are strong because you are strong in me, but you are also a little girl who is cherished and loved.
Crying...
My dearest one I have not forgotten who you are. I know you my little one so much better than you know yourself.
Crying...
My little one all that I am doing is for your good. Being strong does not mean that you are not loved. Being strong does not mean that you are alone... My dearest one you can be strong in me, so strong my little one that you can do anything that I ask of you and yet still need to be loved and cared for.
Crying...
My dearest one I understand your need... I understand my little one I have not forgotten who you are. My little one I will meet your need. I will help you in every way that you need but that does not mean that you will never know what it is to be loved here on this earth or that you will be forever alone. My little one that is not my plan for you. It is not my desire my little one. I am making you strong so that you can know and understand just who you are. That does not mean that I do not want all the things for you that I have promised you my little one. I have not forgotten.
Crying... I am very confused about who you want me to be. Crying... I am having to be this grown up person who is strong and can do anything... Crying... But then you say I am a little girl and you want me to be loved... and cared for and I can't be both. Crying... I can't be either.
My little one I will enable you in everything that you must do and be in this place. In this way you will grow strong my little one and learn many things, but this is not who you are my little one.
Crying...
I have not forgotten who you are.
Crying...
My little one I am making you so strong in me but that does not mean that you are a grown up or that you will live a grown ups life. That is not the life I have for you my little one. I will enable you in this life, but it is not your life my little one. In the life I am giving you, you will be who you truly are my little one which is a child, my little girl, of whom I am so very proud.
Crying...
My little one you will be loved and cared for just as I have said. All of these things, all that you have needed to be in this place will fall away from you my little one and you will be able to be who you truly are.

Crying...

My dearest one I know that it is hard. I know what I am asking of you is hard my little one but that is because I know what you can do and all that will be accomplished through it. This is not your life my little one and it is not my desire for you to live in this way, a grown up's life. It is only for a little while my dearest one.

Crying...

My little one you have lived much of your life through the eyes and through the experience of an adult and though it is hard for you in many ways this life is familiar to you my little one, you understand how it works and who you need to be. The life of a child is unfamiliar to you my little one and though that is who you are it will take much learning and much letting go for you to become the child that you truly are. I know that this is hard my little one, but this is the journey I have for you. This is not who you are my little one you are still discovering the person that you truly are.

My dearest one I know the best way for you and though it is hard it is possible my little one. I will help you to become the person that I created you to be my little one, that is my great desire for you, but you must take it step by step as I lead you. I know you do not want to be here my little one I understand that it is difficult and confusing, but I will work so much good through it. Do not give up my little one hold on to me and let me complete my work in you. It will not be too much for you my little one. I am helping you. I will not let you go... My dearest one all the things that you are struggling with, all the things that are making you afraid, all of them are in my control my little one. There is nothing that is beyond me, there is nothing I have forgotten or overlooked. You are safe my little one, my plans for you are good. I will help you to become all that you were created to be my little one. I will not leave you here in this life which does not belong to you, but I will lead you forward into the life that I have for you. Everything is to help you achieve this my little one. Everything is to help you on your journey to becoming who you are. Do not be afraid my little one. I am with you and I will not ever let you go. Trust me my little one and know that my way for you is good, it is very good.

Crying... But it is so hard... Crying...

Yes my little one I know it is.

Crying...

My little one I am your strength and your courage, and I will not fail you. I will be enough for you my little one. This journey is only the beginning for you. It is not the end my little one. Keep holding on. Let me lead you forward my little one and do not be afraid of anything.

Crying... I am not feeling like I can do it Jesus.

I know my little one, but you can.

Crying... I am sorry.

I know my little one. My dearest one it is not wrong to feel that way that you do but keep holding on to me. My dearest one I will love you and carry you through this. I will enable you to receive all that you are longing for my little one. You will be able to receive so much more because of all that I am doing in you.

I don't see it.

I know my little one... my dearest one trust me with everything. I am enough for you my little one. I understand everything that you need my little one and I will supply it. Remember that this is the journey my little one and not the destination.

Crying... If I had to stay here like this, I think I would die Jesus.

But you do not my little one, you will leave this place just as I have said. Hold on to me my little one. I will not let you go... My dearest one rest now. My arms are around you my little one. I will keep you safe and protect you. I will give you the strength that you need. I will comfort you as you sleep my little one. You are not alone. You are never alone.

There were so many things that I found hard about Jesus plan to blend me with Jennifer. I thought Jesus was taking Jennifer away from people who loved her and most of all from her children. To put me in Jennifer's place meant that I would have to be their mummy and I knew I couldn't be. Not like Jennifer was. That seemed terrible to me and very wrong.

Crying... Jesus I think your plan is cruel. I am sorry I know it can't be because you're not but it seems so cruel. Crying...
No my little one it is not cruel.
Crying...
My dearest one all of my plans are for good. All of them. This is including your blending with Jennifer. My little one I know that is not how it seems to you right now. I know you do not see my little one. But trust me to know the way that I have for all of you. My dearest one my love for you all is unending. I do not love one more than another. My dearest one I am holding you. Choose to trust me my little one with this as with everything. Do not try to see what you cannot yet see my little one.
Crying...
I know that plans I have for you, for all of you and they are good my little one. They are so good... My dearest one you know that love you.
Crying... Yes, Jesus I know you do... Crying...
You know my little one that I am good. Even when you do not understand you know that I am good.
Crying... Yes...
Then trust me my little one everything that I am doing is good. It is good for you my little one it is good for Jennifer.
Crying...
And it is good for Sophie and for Richard. There is nothing that I am doing that is not good my little one.
Crying... I don't understand Jesus.
I know my little one I know.
Crying....
My little one Sophie and Richard will not see the loss that you see. They will see a loss when you move away my little one, but it will not be the loss that you see for them. They will still have their relationship with their mum my little one. Their mum will be found in you.
Crying...
It will be different my little one, but it will be good. It will be very good.
Crying... But I can't be their mum... Crying...
No my little one but you can be their friend. You can be the one they turn to even though you will not be the one they believe that you are. That will not matter my little one for everything that Jennifer is will be found in you. They will not lose anything my little one, but they will gain much.
Crying... I don't see that.
I know my little one, but I do. Trust in my sight my little one. Continue to follow where I lead. I know my little one that much of what I say to you and much of what you see happening does not yet make sense to you, but it will. In time you will understand my little one and you will see that I have worked all things together for good. Everything that you are longing for will come my little one. It will come.
Crying...
I just want them to have good lives and be happy and to know that they were loved. I want them to know that they were loved.
Crying...
And they will my little one. They will.

Crying... Jesus this is so impossibly hard.... Crying...
My little one I know that there is much pain and sadness for you but my plans for you are good everything that I am doing is good my little one. I am holding you and I will see you through.
Crying... I think it is too hard Jesus... Crying....
No my little one it is not too hard. Hold on to me. You will see that I will work all things together just as I have said my little one. All of my promises will come true.
Crying... I want to stop crying Jesus.
I know my little one.

I had this conversation with him a lot of times because it was so hard for me to see and accept that this could be good for them or for me. I felt like I was useless and that no one would ever want me or love me so how could I pretend to be a mummy and do all the things that a mummy does. While I was going through this time, I seemed to always be getting it wrong especially with Sophie. She seemed to think the things I did and said were stupid and got cross and angry with me. It is hard to know what was going on. I think maybe she was going through a difficult time too....and maybe because of all the stuff going on for us I...and even Jennifer...hadn't been there for her when she needed us. I don't know. I do know that I tried very hard to do my best for Sophie and Richard no matter what was going on for me. Sometimes I got it wrong…and that was very difficult for me because I thought I should be put away somewhere because I was bad and useless.

I thought that because I wasn't like Jennifer and couldn't do all the things she could, that I was stupid and no good. Jennifer was clever... she had a master's degree...she knew how to do a lot of stuff… but I found it hard just doing normal things like cleaning and shopping and sorting out the house stuff. I couldn't understand things the same, sometimes I had no idea what people were talking about, I didn't understand books and things like she did. I thought I was dumb.

My little one you are not Jennifer and you understand things in a different way to her, you do not see things in the same way as she does. It does not mean that you are stupid my little one, only that you see and understand things differently.
Is that because...I am not grownup?
Yes my little one you think and see as a child. It is a simpler understanding my little one but that does not mean that it is a shallow understanding. You will often be able to see right to the heart of an issue when others get bogged down in the complexities that they see.
But... when Jennifer is out... is it her thoughts I hear?
Yes little one. Her understanding is given to you but my little one her understanding is not superior to yours it is just different.
Sometimes... I don't know. It is like I have two different brains. It is a bit confusing.
You have your own brain my little one, but you also have access to Jennifer's brain. You are used to thinking and feeling with Jennifer's brain my little one, but you are discovering your own brain and your own thoughts and feelings my little one. That is confusing at the moment, but it will not always be so.
When she is blended will I just have my own brain?
Yes my little one you will not have two brains...you will not have access to her brain anymore. You will only have your own my little one which is more than enough.
I won't start thinking like she does...
No little one you will retain your own unique perspective on the world. It will become clearer to you when you are blended my little one for things will not be confused for you as they are now.
I expect I will get used to it and people will get used to me.
Yes my little one they will. They will not see you as stupid my little one for I am giving you both wisdom and insight, you will not be stupid my little one.

There are worse things to be Jesus. Jennifer is cleverer than me but that is ok.
My little one she is not cleverer than you she only thinks in a different way.
Ok.
My little one you are becoming the person that I have made you to be. That is good thing my little one. You do not need to compare yourself to anyone else my little one. You are not less...you are you and that is all that you need to be.

Pretending to be Jennifer wasn't just hard it made me feel like I was lying to everyone by saying I was Jennifer. It felt like a very bad thing to do, to deceive everyone about who I was even though I knew that I couldn't let them see the truth. If I did then that would cause a lot of trouble. I was very afraid I would be discovered, and the truth would be found out, but it was horrible to be living a lie.

I need to talk to you about being ashamed.
Yes my little one you do. My dearest one there is nothing for you to feel ashamed of. Deception is not what you are intending. You are being yourself even whilst you are seen as Jennifer, you are still you my little one.
Yes, but if I am pretending to be her and letting them believe that I am the person that they know isn't that wrong?
Is it wrong for you to be present in the body which belongs to you my little one?
No.
And is it wrong for you to have relationships and friendships of your own?
No.
And is it wrong for you to protect Jennifer by not exposing her or her true self to those she has not chosen to reveal it to?
No Jesus its not wrong to protect her.
No my little one it isn't. My dearest one you are doing nothing wrong. There is no deception in what you are doing my little one no matter how it seems to you.
I think you will have to explain that to me more Jesus because it seems deceitful to me.
My little one when I came to this earth I came as a man and only a few knew the truth of who I was for many years. I lived and worked as an ordinary man, but I was never an ordinary man my little one. Even when the time came to reveal my true nature, I did not reveal it to everyone and not everyone wanted to believe the truth of who I was when I did. My little one the truth of who you are must remain hidden for now. Some are able to accept you for who you are my little one and that is good but for now you must allow them to see the outside, just as I did. It is not deceit my little one.
I suppose people who knew you saw you as someone that you weren't and maybe you didn't tell them the truth.
No my little one I didn't not for many years. The truth must be accepted my little one for it have any power in a person's life. It would not have helped those around me to know the truth just as it would not help those around you to know the truth.
I see that Jesus. That helps. Thankyou.
My little one I will always help you with everything. This road that you are travelling is not an easy one for there are many challenges and obstacles for you to overcome but I will make it possible for you to walk this path my little one hand in hand with me. I will lead you forward into the life that I am giving to you. Do not be anxious my little one everything I am doing is good.

Most of the time it didn't feel good. I discovered that having to live life as someone else, to keep pretending to be someone you are not is a very lonely thing. I thought it would be the practical things that I would find hardest about being on the outside, but it wasn't.

I am feeling more unhappy than I have for a long time and lonelier. I think it is a lonely thing to live your life as someone you're not. Maybe there a lot of people who live that way even though they don't have alters. I don't think that I am doubting more or feeling more despair it is just that every day is so... I don't even know what the word is. I am desperate to see Jesus do what He's said so I don't have to be here doing this anymore but at the same time I don't want those things to come either. How can I look forward to Jennifer being gone and all the pain that will cause Cheryl? I don't know how to think of that without feeling afraid and like it is a terrible thing, even though I understand that it is a good thing I don't think it is going to seem like that for a long time. I was overwhelmed by this feeling this morning of how very helpless I am, everyone is, in their lives and how there is no hope at all for any of us without Jesus. I know that is truth. It is terrifying and wonderful all at the same time. It is like a feeling of falling through space which is terrifying but being held in safe strong arms which is wonderful. That is what I saw this morning. It gave me hope in a strange kind of a way. I get so upset about not being able to be the person that Jesus has shown me that I am, that I am still discovering. All that time I spent accepting that I wasn't Jennifer and that I wasn't doing any of those outside things, that I wasn't responsible for them and now it is like I have gone backwards, and I am living Jennifer's life but knowing I am not her. It is horrible. I know that it is only possible because Jesus is making it so. I can't do any of the things I am doing. I can't live this life I am living. I suppose Jesus is teaching me that everything is possible for me, but I really want him to stop. I so want Jennifer to come back and do her life. I don't want it.

Jesus said he understood about the loneliness.

> Crying... Were you very lonely?
>
> **At times my little one but I learned how to be with my father in such a way that all the loneliness I felt was held by him, I drew my strength from him my little one and my comfort also for the road I travelled was not an easy one.**
>
> No, I don't expect any of it was easy.
>
> **No my little one it wasn't but I was able because my father made me able, he gave me everything I needed. It did not come from anyone else my little one. Even though I was surrounded by many people, even though there were many who loved me it was not from them that I drew my strength it was always and only from my father. My dearest one you will have many friends and you will know what it is to be truly loved for who you are but everything that you need to walk through this life and fulfill the purpose that we have for you will come from us. There are many who will help you and comfort you my little one and many who will love you but your need for these things will be met by us and not by them. They are there for you my little one, but they cannot ever fill the need that you have which can only be filled by us. Do not hope for it my little one do not desire it. Look to us for everything that you need my little one.**
>
> I don't know if I understand Jesus. Why do you ask us to love people if you are the one they need?
>
> **Because in loving them you can show them who I am. In loving them you can give to them the love that I have for them. My little one not many are able to come directly to us and receive from us in the way that you are. They have not travelled the road that you have my little one. They have been unwilling or afraid or unable for many reasons, but I will ask you to reach out to them with our love for them my little one so that they can be healed and restored not only in themselves but in their relationship with us.**
>
> Crying... I am sorry Jesus...
>
> **I know my little one I understand. The road that you are walking is a hard one my little one but in doing so you are learning to draw upon us for everything that you need. That is not so that you cannot or will not receive from others my little one but**

only so that your source is my father which is as it should be for everyone my little one. Other people were never meant to fill your need for us, but often that is the way it is my little one. When you have truly learned to draw upon us for everything that you need then you will be able to give without measure just as I did my little one. You cannot do it otherwise. My dearest one we are doing so much more than you know and making you able in so many ways that you have not yet understood. My dearest one as you learn to trust and depend on us for everything it is then that we can truly fill you and transform you and flow through you to a hurting and dying world. There is a cost my little one there is always a cost, but it is worth it my little one. Hold on to me and trust me just as you have done. I will not leave you my little one and I will fulfil your every need in time. I know the way that I have for you my little one and it is good even if it is hard, it is good.

How can I be me here then Jesus? I want to do little girl things, but I have to be grown up and do all these things I can't do. It feels too painful to do things I want to even if knew what they were.

My little one we will give you the strength that you need. Do not be afraid to do the things which bring you joy my little one even in the midst of this time you are able to do many things which will bring you joy and life.

Help me then Jesus to do that because living this life it feels like it is sucking the life out of me.

Yes my little one and that is why you must make time to do the things that you were created to do. Many things are necessary for you to do in this time my little one, there are many tasks to be done but it is just as important that you do the things that come from you, the things that you enjoy my little one. Do not forget yourself in your efforts to live this life my little one. It will not help you to do so. My dearest one it is not wrong to make time for who you are, it is right and good that you should do so.

It is hard to do both Jesus.

I know my little one, but I will help you. I am already helping you.

And then there was Cheryl. I felt so guilty because now she was hardly getting to see Jennifer at all. It always seemed to be me who was on the outside when we were with her. I felt guilty and afraid too because I knew that eventually Jennifer would be gone... and I felt like I was lying because I wasn't telling Cheryl that even though Jesus kept saying it wasn't time yet. Cheryl was getting upset and anxious too and I didn't know what to say or do. It made me afraid.

Let's talk about Cheryl first Jesus.

Yes my little one for I know that this is causing you a great deal of distress. My little one you are not responsible for her pain. All that you are doing is following me. I will not harm her in any way my little one. I am watching over her and keeping her safe.

But how is she going to bear it when she knows Jesus. Are you going to change your mind about Jennifer and let her stay?

No my little one I am not going to change my mind.

Why aren't you talking to her Jesus?

Because she is not yet ready to hear what I will say my little one. I am speaking but my dear one is not hearing me, her fear and anxiety are keeping her from me but I am holding her my little one. I will not let her go.

How is she going to know about Jennifer Jesus if you aren't speaking or she isn't hearing? Who will explain it to her and help her?

My little one there are many ways in which I will reach out to her and help her. One of those ways is through Jennifer herself and also through you my little one. This is not anything that you must do my little one, only be yourself that is all.

But how will she not hate me Jesus when I have taken over Jennifer's life and made her go away.

But it is not your doing my little one and Cheryl will see and understand this.
Will she?
Yes my little one she will.
I am worried about her Jesus.
I know my little one, but she is safe in my hands.
Will she know soon? It is hard to keep these things from her because she is asking anxious questions.
I know my little one. She will know at just the right time and it will not be long my little one. I will hold her and love her through it just as I will hold you and love you through it.
Do you really have to do it Jesus?
Yes my little one I do. I know that is a hard thing that I am asking of all of you, but it is a good thing my little one.
What about Jennifer. How is she. I don't hear her much anymore.
Jennifer has accepted my will for her my little one. She is at peace. Do not be anxious about her my little one. As she becomes more and more a part of who you are you will be able to hear her less and less. This does not matter my little one for you do not need her the way that you used to.
It makes me so sad Jesus.
I know my little one.

Cheryl was very kind to me. She took me out and I got to do new and fun things, things that Jennifer wouldn't ever want to do. She didn't seem to think I was a freak or bad or any of the things I thought she might. She seemed to like spending time with me and that helped me a lot. I got to hold hands and have cuddles and that was a wonderful thing for me. I was learning a lot about who I was in my time with her, but I felt under a lot of pressure from Cheryl sometimes because she so wanted to talk with and spend time with Jennifer. She would send emails and texts hoping for an answer, but Jennifer wasn't on the outside and couldn't answer. That made Cheryl upset, but I couldn't do anything about it. Sometimes I would reply pretending to Jennifer just because it was too hard but that felt bad to me too. I felt bad all of the time and sometimes got angry with Jesus for making me live Jennifer's life because it was so very hard and confusing and painful and lonely and frightening. He was always patient and kind and understanding. He never got angry or impatient, but he didn't change his mind either, no matter how many times I begged him to. I had to keep trusting that this really was a good idea.

...and then I just got upset and mad at Jesus for asking me to live Jennifer's life and be in this place and have to do all these things. And I cried and I cried, and Jesus was there but I just shouted at him and told him to go away because I don't like him. I think it had been building up again because of things. Yesterday I had to accept Jennifer's birthday present from Kate and be all appreciative and happy and pretend to be Jennifer with people and it was hard, and I feel like I am all alone. I am all alone and there is no one at all for me to... do whatever people do when they are in trouble and have friends. So, I had a bit of a meltdown and refused to talk to Jesus for a while, but he didn't give up or go away.

I don't want to talk to you... crying... I just want to die... crying... I can't do this... crying... I don't want to do this... crying... Please stop... crying... But you won't ever stop. Why do you hate me so much? crying... Just kill me or make me go away… crying... Please... crying...

My little one my dear little one.
crying... I don't want to hear about being your little one... crying...
Then hear this my love for you is unending I do not and will not ever hate you my dearest one. All the things that have happened to you and are happening and will happen they are all in my control but not all of them are my will for you my little one,

not all of them are the things I want to you to see or experience or know but that does not change my love for you my little one. This time is to give you strength to overcome all of the things in your life that will come against you past present and future. I know that you do not see or understand this or why I am asking the things that I am asking of you but my little one.

crying...

I am holding you in my arms of love, they will keep you safe from harm and you will come through this time. It is not for nothing that I am asking this of you my little one. It requires that you trust me and that is good for it helps you to grow and become stronger in me. Sometimes I will ask things of you that make no sense or that you do not want to do but my little one that does not change my love for you. It only means that you do not see or understand... I know that I am asking a hard thing of you, to live this life that is not yours as someone you are not and to you that makes no sense, to you that seems like the opposite of what I have promised you but my dearest one sometimes my ways are not what you would expect and the way that I have for you will seem to twist and turn in ways that make no sense to you. It will be hard, and you will need to trust in me but I will help you my little one. I will always help you. My dearest one everything that I have for you is good and though you do not see or understand what I am doing my promises to you will be fulfilled just as I have said. This is all part of that my little one whether you see it or not. Trust me my dearest one and do not give up your hope of all that I have promised you. Know that it is good my little one and that it will come. It will come.

crying... I don't want to do this anymore Jesus... crying...

I know my little one I know.

crying... I want to just not be. Why must I do this? crying....

To get to where I am taking you my little one. That is why. My dearest one I know that you cannot see the path before your feet, but it is there and you are walking forward day by day. Do not give up hope my little one. New life is coming, it is just around the corner. Now is not the time to stop my little one you have come a long way and you are almost there. Hold on to me. I will give you all the strength that you need.

crying... I think I am not trusting you Jesus... crying... I'm not… crying...

My little one I am faithful and true and my word to you will be fulfilled. Trusting me in the hardest place is what makes you strong my little one. That is why I am leading you this way to make you strong.

crying... Why do I have to be strong Jesus? Why can't you... just look after me? crying... Why do I have to be all alone and not have people to love me and help me? crying... Why do I have to be grown up and do things I don't want to do and can't do? crying... And not be me. Why show me I am me and then not let me be me? crying...

My little one this world can be hard place and you will need great strength to be who you are in it. Everything that I am doing is to help you to be who you were created to be which is far more than you have yet understood. My dearest one I have not forgotten who you are, I know what you can do and what you can't do. I know everything about you. I know who you will be and all the things that you will do and the life that you will lead my little one. I see it all. Hold on to me my little one and keep on trusting me. The way ahead is clear for I am making it so. There is nothing that can keep you from all that I have promised you if you do not give up.

But I am not believing in that life or that person. I don't know who she is and... crying.... I don't think I could have that life.

My little one I see and know all things. I see the truth my little one nothing is hidden from me. I know who you are my little one, you are not the person that you see. You are my child, beloved since before the beginning of time. You will not ever die but will go on from this place to the place that I am taking you to and from there my little one into eternity which you have not even begun to understand. My dearest one you

are not who you think you are, but I will show you my little one as much as you can understand who I have made you to be. This is part of the mystery that I will reveal to you my child, a mystery which my people have not yet understood but I will give a greater revelation of it to you my little one. There is so much that I have yet to show you my little one. This part of your journey is so very small. Do not give up my little one. Hold on to me and trust me. I know the way my little one and I will give you the strength to walk it.

I don't want to Jesus.

I know my little one, but will you take my hand and walk with me anyway even if you don't want to.

crying... Why do you ask such hard things Jesus?

Because I know what will be accomplished my little one.

crying... It is too hard for me Jesus... crying...

Yes my little one I know but it is not too hard for me and I am with you. I will give you all that you need my little one. Take my hand and come with me. I am leading you to a good place my little one even if the road is hard, I am leading you to a good place.

crying... But I can't see that either Jesus. It doesn't look good. Even if can get there. What will I do? Nobody will want me crying.... I don't want to go I don't want to stay I don't see anything good... crying....

My little one I am with you. I am taking you to a good place where you will be loved and cared for my little one. You will serve me in many ways my little one, there is no shortage of the things that you will have to do. My dearest one the life that I am giving to you is good.

crying.... I don't see it Jesus. I just see... being out of place and alone and useless... if I get there at all.

My little one that is not what I have said.

No Jesus it isn't.

Then trust in my word to you my little one. I see and know all things. My dearest one the enemy of your soul will fight me all the way. He does not want you to go and live the life that I have for you. He does not want you to love me and serve me. He does not want my glory to be seen in and through your life. He will try to convince you in many ways that there is no hope my little one and that everything that I have promised you is a lie, but he is the one who is the liar my little one. Do not listen to him My little one I will give you all the strength that you need. You are not alone my little one for I am with you and my spirit is with you and my father also. Your daddy loves you my little one he will not let you go.

Everything gets confused in my head Jesus and I feel like I am lost and everything is hopeless and it makes me want to die... or not be because if I came to heaven now I am afraid that you would be angry... crying... And you wouldn't want me... crying....

My little one you have not yet understood my great love for you and how it cannot ever be changed by anything that you do or don't do. I will always want you my little one nothing can ever change that. My dearest one I ask you to stay for your good and for the good of many others. You are my light in a dark and cruel world my little one. What I am asking of you is hard and you must be strong in me to accomplish it but I am making you able my little one. If you should fail for whatever reason I would still love you and want you my little one that will not ever change but my dearest one you will not fail, not while you hold on to me. I will give you all that you need my little one. All.

Can you give me the desire to do it Jesus? I don't have any. I don't want to do it. I want to stop and come and be with you.

I will give you the desire that you need my little one. I will help you in every way that you need but keep your eyes fixed upon me and upon all that I am. My dearest one this is our journey. We walk it together. I will not ever leave you or forsake you my

little one. We are going on a great adventure and not all of it will be this way my little one. Keep walking and do not think of giving up. I will be with you.
But I think about giving up all the time Jesus. It is hard to hope.
Remember what I have said about the enemy my little one. Do not give in to him but hold on to me and trust in who I am. I will not ever fail you my little one. I will not give you more than you can bear. I will lead you faithfully forward into the life that I have promised you. It will come my little one it will surely come.
Sometimes I think... about if I get there... and it will be... lonely and... all the things I think about and I think about how I can die there Jesus because... but I don't want to go through all this just to get there and die it would be better to do it now.
My little one you will not die now or then you have many years ahead of you, good years my little one.
Not too many Jesus. I would… rather come and be with you.
I know my little one.
I don't want to go Jesus and I don't want to stay.
Trust me my little one. Take my hand and follow me. That is all that you must do.
That is a lot Jesus.
It is enough my little one.
Can I do it?
Yes my little one you can do all things as I enable you.
Help me to want to do it Jesus. I still don't want to do it. I still want to not be.
My little one I will help you. Hold on to me and do not let go. Trust me for everything in every moment. I am working something very great in you my little one. It will be worth it.
For me?
Yes my little one for you and for many others.
I keep wondering when I can give up Jesus. If I am here in a year's time can I give up?
No my little one do not ever give up. My promises to you are sure even if they seem a long time coming, they are sure.
Please help me.
I will help you my little one.
I will go then. I am sorry if I got cross Jesus.
I understand my little one I will hold you and love you through everything. I will not leave you.
Bye then Jesus.
Bye not bye my little one I will not leave you.

My little one the pain and suffering in this world do not come from me. I am not the author of these things my little one. I work through them to bring good where there is only evil and light where there is darkness, but I do not create the things that cause you and so many others the pain that you feel. My dearest one I understand what it is to suffer but I also understand that there is something greater, far greater that is at work. My little one there is so much that you have to understand about so many things. Hold on to me my little one and know that I am good and that my ways are good and that everything is in my control. I will help you my little one with everything that comes against you in this life. I will carry you through the darkness and the pain. I will give you my strength and my courage and when all is said and done you will see the victory that I have won for you my little one. It is a glorious victory and worth all of the pain and the suffering that it cost me.

Chapter 25

The Birthday

It was time for the birthday. Every year the birthday came around and every year I didn't want it to. A lot of bad things, kind of normal things that I always knew about, had happened on the birthday so that didn't help. When it was just Jennifer, I thought I didn't like the birthday because I didn't like a fuss being made or being the centre of attention and I suppose that was true, but there was something deeper that I didn't know about then. Something Jesus was showing to us a little at a time. Two years before he told me that the birthday was a time when I would be given 'presents', bad one's like grandad doing it to me and then the last year I learned more about why the birthday was so very hard for me.

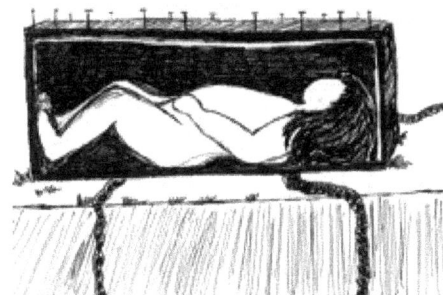

It is my birthday today and now I know why it has been such a bad day for me. I was dreaming last night, horrible dark dreams where I was buried underground, and I couldn't move. I was surrounded by darkness and wood and earth. And then there were worms which turned into snakes to come and bite me... When I woke up, I knew that the dream was from the enemy, but I also knew that it was real...taken from something that really happened. I couldn't stop crying...

My little one come.
Crying...
I am here with you my little one nothing can harm you... My little one the things of the past are gone. You are safe, held in my arms. I will help you and I will heal you my little one. There is nothing to fear.
I don't know what to say...Crying...
I am holding you my little one and I will give you my peace.
Crying... I keep seeing it Jesus.
I know my little one, but I am here with you. You are safe my little one...
Please help me to get this image out of my mind Jesus.
It will fade in time my little one hold on to me, you are safe my little one, you are loved. The things of the past cannot harm you though they may cause you pain...
Please tell me what is happening.
The enemy is tormenting you with images and memories from the past my little one, they are doing this to remind you that this was their day for you, the day that they celebrated you belonging to them but you do not belong to them my little one you belong to me.
Crying...I don't know what is happening Jesus...
I am holding you my little one you are safe in my arms. Nothing can harm you.
Crying... Is that why my birthday is so... why I get so scared about it?
Yes my little one but you are safe now. You are safe my little one. Hold on to me. I am here with you and I will not let you go.
Why... was this their day Jesus?
My little one you were promised to them from the beginning even before you were born. They saw your arrival as the day that you became theirs, but it was not so my little one, you were always mine.
Crying...I don't understand. I don't want to understand.... Crying....
My little one everything that you are belongs to me. You were always mine, always my little one, you did not ever belong to them. I have rescued you my little one and you are safe in my arms. I am with you my little one, you are safe in my arms.

Crying...Why did you let them?... Crying...

My little one everyone has choice you know this. Those who were meant to care for you chose to go against my will for you in every way possible, but I came, and I claimed you back my little one. You never belonged to them. You always belonged to me.

Crying... Please help me Jesus.... Crying....

I am with you my little one. I will not leave you, but I will help you to bear the pain of this. My little one all that you have suffered, everything that you have experienced, all of it will be redeemed my little one, everything will be healed. I am holding you so close to me my little one, I will not let you go.

Crying... Why are you telling me this now Jesus... after all this time?

Because you are ready my little one. I know that it is painful, but you are ready. My little one it will not always be this way for you. I will redeem everything in time my little one...

I am going to need your help Jesus because I have to get through this day looking like it's a good day... Crying...

I will be here for you my little one and I will help you. My little one the pain that you feel will be healed. I know my little one that you do not want this to be true any more than you want any of it to be true but acceptance will help you my little one, it is a step towards the healing that I have for you...

Yes. I know.

My little one I am here with you nothing will ever change that. Hold on to the truth of who you are, my beloved and precious child. You are not what they told you my little one, nor are you what they tried to make you, you are mine, beloved in every way, safe and protected and completely loved and accepted just as you are my little one...

Yes. I am yours Jesus. You chose me and I chose you.

Yes my little one and nothing can ever change it. My little one I have a day for you, a day that will be your very own to celebrate your belonging to me. I will give this day to you my little one and this one will fade away.

That would be nice Jesus.

Yes my little one all things will be made new. Hold on to me my little one. I will see you through this and every other day...

I am feeling calmer now thankyou. Please don't leave me.

I will not ever leave you my little one. I am always right here with you...

It is all so hard for me to understand Jesus.

I know my little one but understanding will come as you are able to accept it. Keep holding on to me my little one, I will not let you go.

This year of course it wasn't going to be Jennifer on the outside it was going to be me. That was harder because part of the problem with the birthday was having to pretend to everyone that I was having a good time when all I wanted to do is hide away and not have a birthday. But people don't understand those things and Jennifer's friends and her children wanted her to have a good time and enjoy herself. They were being kind, but it made it a lot harder for me. I wasn't nearly so good as Jennifer at covering up when I was upset and afraid, I was very worried I wouldn't be able to do it. Jennifer had tried to explain to Cheryl about how hard the birthday was and that she wouldn't want to celebrate it, so Cheryl suggested a trip to London as a birthday treat but after the birthday. That still sounded hard but better, so Jennifer agreed to that. But now the birthday was coming, and it seemed like Cheryl hadn't understood at all.

And now Cheryl has just emailed to say she wants to take Jennifer out for her birthday next week. It makes me want to run and hide. But this is the very thing I didn't want to happen, and we tried to make it not happen by telling her. I thought we did but now it is just like we have to do twice as much birthday stuff and then there is Ruth asking too and Kate. I know they mean well but... Crying... Help me... Crying...

My dearest one I will help you. Together we will find a way through this my little one. Together we will walk through this. You are not alone my little one.

No... I know Jesus but it's like the two things together. She writes to Jennifer and invited her out but Jennifer isn't here so what do I do. I don't know what to do Jesus. I don't want to do anything. I don't even know if Jennifer will be out for her birthday... Crying...I don't want the birthday... Crying...Please help me ... Crying...

I will help you my little one. My dearest one remember that this is not anything that you must do. This is Jennifer's birthday my little one and not yours. It is not your decision my little one nor are you the one who must deal with this. Let Jennifer do it my little one. She is able. I will help her.

Crying... Yes. That's true Jesus. It's not for me to do.

No my little one it isn't. My dearest one I will give you all that you need. I am holding you and will keep you safe through this time my little one.

Crying... It is enough that it comes at all Jesus but to have to enjoy it and I know it is silly because there isn't anything bad but Crying... I get so afraid... Crying...

I know my little one. I know that you do but remember that you are safe in my arms my little one and that nothing can harm you. Remember everything that I have said to you my little one. Remember my love for you. My dearest one I am with you. You are safe my little one.

Will Jennifer answer?

Yes my little one she will but not tonight. My dearest one rest in me and remember that I am with you and that I am holding you. I know everything that you need my little one.

Yes... is this to do with the enemy... is it like one of those times?

Yes my little one that is part of it though not the whole. This is a time of vulnerability for you my little one, but I am here with you. I will keep you safe.

I have tried hard not to think about it Jesus.

I know my little one.

I won't have to go through this next year will I Jesus. Please... Crying...

No my little one, not next year. Next year will be very different for you my little one.

Crying... Please help me... Crying...

I am here with you my little one and I will not ever let you go.

Crying...

My dearest one I am holding you. You are safe and you are loved my little one. I am holding you close to my heart. Rest in me my little one and in my great love for you. This time will pass my little one. I will bring you through it.

Yes. I just don't want to have to go through it Jesus.

I know my little one, but I am with you. I will not leave you.

I felt a bit reassured by that and glad that it was going to be Jennifer explaining those things. It was too hard for me to talk about the bad things that happened and how it made me feel. Jennifer did much better. But her talk with Cheryl was much worse than I could have thought it would be.

So, Jennifer and Cheryl went for some lunch. Cheryl was looking very unhappy. Jennifer told her about the birthday and what happened and how it is and that we are expecting this week and Thursday to be very difficult. Cheryl said she understood and it didn't matter that it wasn't that day but that she needed a day to celebrate Jennifer's birthday so Jennifer said about celebrating her Jesus birthday in November and Cheryl seemed kind of satisfied with that but worried that other people would think she was a bad friend because of not taking her out etc. Then she started to talk about herself and how terrible things are and how she is wanting to die and doing a lot of crying and she said about me and how it was hard for her to be with me because I just change the subject and want to have fun and how it is a big strain on her and she is hoping that she won't have to spend a lot of time with me in London because it will be too much for her. Jennifer did say some things on my behalf. I can't tell you how I was feeling because I had to keep it all under control and Jennifer was saying stuff like don't cry, hold on and Jesus was holding me tight. Eventually Jennifer got back home. I didn't want to come out because I knew what would happen, but I couldn't keep it in and I cried so hard, so hard. It took me a while before I could even talk to Jesus.

Crying...
My little one I am holding you close to my heart you are loved, and you are so very precious my little one.
Crying...I don't want to be me... Crying...I don't want to exist... Crying.... I am no good Jesus... Crying.... Make me go away... Crying... Please make me go away... Crying...
No my little one I will not make you go away. I will hold you so close to my heart my little one.
Crying...Crying...
I will love you and lead you and give to you a life that is good. A life where you can be who you are my little one.
Crying...
And be loved for who you are.
Crying...
My little one you hold on to me... You are who I say you are my little one and I say that you are precious, and you are loved. My dearest one you will not always be what others want you to be.
Crying....
You will not always fulfill their hopes and expectations my little one.
Crying....
But I am always here for you my little one and I will help you to be who you are, the wonderful person that I made you to be. You do not need to be anyone else my little one. Only yourself.
Crying... I can't be here anymore. I can't do this... Crying...
My little one I will give you all the strength that you need my dearest one you are not responsible for what other people expect of you my little one.
Crying...
You do not need to be anyone except who you are.... You are completely acceptable to me my little one, just as you are. I love you with all that I am, just as you are. That will never change my little one.
Crying... I don't want to be here Jesus... Crying...
I know my little one I know.
Please can Jennifer go to London. I don't want to go... Crying.... I don't want to go... Crying....
My little one Jennifer will go to London. This is to be her trip my little one. I will work through it to do many things. You do not need to go my little one.
Thankyou... Crying... I don't want to go...
I know my little one I know. My dearest one all of these things that you are feeling will pass away. They will pass away my little one. Hold on to me. You are loved and you are wanted my little one. You are mine and I will not ever give you up.
Crying...
You are my hearts desire my little one. The one that I adore. There is no one that can take your place my little one. You have a special place in my heart that no one else can fill.
Crying... I wish I could just be with you Jesus... Crying...
I know my little one, but I am always with you and I will not ever leave you. My dearest one my love goes before you and will make a way for you.
Crying...

My little one remember what I have said. That you are loved, and you are safe and no matter what anyone else may think do or say that will never change my little one. You are mine, my very own. I chose you my little one.
Crying...
You are not unwanted or unloved.
I want to die Jesus... Crying...
No my little one you will not die but you will live. My dearest one everything that I am asking of you is working for good. Others may not see it my little one but that does not mean that it is not so. Trust in me my little one and in my sight. I am working through you for good my little one. You are not worthless.
Crying... How will I survive this Jesus?
In my strength and mine alone. My little one I am all that you need. There is nothing that you need from anyone else my little one. I will give to you many good friendships my little one that will help you and bless you, but your needs will always be met by me for that is the way that I have chosen for you. It is a good way my little one.
Your ways are always good Jesus.
Yes my little one they are.

So I stopped crying for a little bit and went and helped Richard cook his tea that sort of thing. A bit later I went to have a bath, but I ended up on my hands and knees sobbing and sobbing as I remembered all the things that Cheryl had said. I don't understand why she spends time with me if it is so bad for her, I don't understand about the birthday or why it matters so much to her, does she do all the things she does for us so she can feel like she is a good person? Why is she pretending to have fun and telling me she is having fun if really, she is just gritting her teeth and getting through it. How could she say those things knowing that I was hearing them? How come she didn't even care about what happened and is happening for me but only about how she looks to other people. Why am I here if I am making everyone unhappy? All those sorts of things.

Jesus helped me to understand and to see things a bit different once I could listen to what he was saying. I needed his love and his comfort so much. The outside felt like a very frightening place to be especially when it seemed like the person you are with is wanting you to go away.

My little one this world can be a cruel and a difficult place to live. You know that my little one. To look anywhere else for the love and the affirmation that you need will only bring you pain my little one. Look only to me and not anywhere else my little one. I will help you to bear the blows that come from friends and enemies alike for the enemy of your soul will work through both to try and destroy you my little one but I will never leave you nor forsake you, for you are mine. You are my beloved. I am making you to be who I want you to be and you have nothing to feel ashamed of my little one. The fault is not yours. You follow me my little one, let no one else's opinion of you change the way that you see yourself. Listen only to my words of love and of truth my little one.

I did see that this was the enemy attacking me. The birthday was like a battleground and I felt like I was getting beaten up from all sides, but Jesus was helping me to see that he was on my side and that I was safe, no matter what. In the worship time I was being held in Jesus arms and I had my arms round his neck, and I saw he was wearing a gold locket round his neck. It was shaped like a heart and had a little keyhole in it like it was locked and there was a key to open it. I didn't ask him what it was, but I kept thinking about it during the day like he was reminding me.

Come then my little one let us speak about what you saw yesterday.
Yes... I saw a golden locket around your neck Jesus... I did, didn't I?

Yes my little one you did.
What is it?
It is the locket I wear to remind me of all that you are to me.
That didn't make sense so I started to worry it wasn't Jesus, so I prayed and prayed and in the end... Jesus.
Yes my little one I am here.
I am tired and I can't work this stuff out please help me.
My dearest one I will always help you and show you the truth.
That was you?
Yes my little one it was.
So... it doesn't make sense. Why would you need to remind yourself? That means you might forget.
No my little one I will not ever forget you. You are close to my heart at all times my little one. The locket that I wear is a symbol of your heart my little one.
I don't understand.
My little one each of my children is precious to me. I carry them all close to my heart my little one.
Yes.
The locket that you saw represents your heart my little one. Your heart which is a treasure to me. Your heart has been locked and hidden away my little one but now I wear it openly for all to see.
So... I don't understand about what you said about reminding you Jesus. People... I know you aren't people, but they only need reminding of things they might forget. Like I have a ring to remind me I have a daddy who loves me because I do forget.
But I will not forget you my little one. I wear you close to my heart as a reminder of all that you are to me...
I heard it wrong.
Yes my little one. The reminder is not for me it is for those who would oppose my work in and through you.
The enemy.
Yes my little one.
Ok... like a statement.
Yes my little one. It says that you belong to me and that you are always close to my heart. It says that you are treasure to me and that I do not ever forget you my little one. It says that your heart belongs to me and that I hold the key to it my little one. It is a key that I will not ever surrender.
I like that Jesus… but you say it like... you just put it on display for the enemy to see. Like it just happened.

Yes my little one it could not be seen before now.
So... why?
It is a warning to them my little one, a statement of my intent towards them should they harm you in any way.
That sounds... serious.
Yes my little one the powers of darkness are very great but my dearest one there is nothing that they can do to take you from me. That is what I am declaring before them my little one. Your heart belongs to me and I hold the key.
Because they want to steal my heart away from you?
Yes my little one that is always their desire. They long to break our relationship my little one but your heart belongs to me and they cannot take it from me.
And you are... telling them that.
Yes my little one I am.

It was kind of strange to see Jesus as fierce but fierce for me and not against me. It made me feel safe and protected. There was a lot I didn't understand about the locket or even about what had happened in the past, but I knew that Jesus was with me. That no matter what the birthday brought he was in control and he was going to do something good.

He was very good to me too and showed me that what he told me about the locket was real and true because sometimes I still doubted what I saw especially when I was afraid.

Sometimes I still think I make this stuff up but then I get shown I'm not. I got a book because I think Jesus was telling me to. It is a book about belonging to daddy. I read in it something today. I read about how daddy has the key to my heart, and he is unlocking it. And then I knew that what I saw, the locket round Jesus neck, which is my heart, is really real. Sometimes he needs to show me that the things I see and hear are real.

So the day arrived. I had nothing planned, no celebrations to get through because Jennifer had managed to make it that way. That was good because it was me on the outside like I thought it would be.

Hello Jesus
Hello my little one.
What is happening today Jesus.
My little one I will protect you through everything that is coming. I will not leave you my little one you are safe in my arms.
But I keep thinking that nothing is going to happen, and it is just a fuss about nothing.
I know my little one.
Am I wrong?
Yes my little one you are. My dearest one the enemy will not give up his opportunity to stake his claim if he can. My dearest one I know that you do not fully understand but such is the nature of his attachment to you, it is not yet broken my little one, but it will be. I am well able.
What do you mean attachment Jesus?
Through all that was done to you my little one there were spiritual bonds and ties made which attach you to the enemy and give him power over you. He will try and reassert that power my little one but in doing so he himself will be overcome and the bonds that bind you to him will be broken forever.
That sounds bad and good all at the same time.
It will be difficult my little one, but you are safe in my arms. He cannot have you my little one.
So, what should I do Jesus? How will I know?
You will know my little one and all you must do is call out to me, choose me my little one and give yourself to me completely no matter what is happening or what the enemy is saying to you my little one come to me.
Ok. I wish... I know its all the way you want it Jesus, but I wish I didn't have to be alone.
You will not be alone my little one. My servant will be with you...
I don't even know what that means Jesus.
I know my little one but all that you must do is hold on to me. I am the one who will save you my little one and break every tie that the enemy has over you.
Yes. Ok then. I don't want to talk any more Jesus. Maybe a little snuggle would be nice.
Yes my little one I am here for you. Come.

So most of my day was ok like I said apart from all this fear I was feeling. I tried to ignore it but it didn't go away. I was wondering if I had it wrong and nothing was going to happen, but I knew I didn't feel right. About half past eight there was a knock on the door. I don't ever answer the door if I don't know who it is and definitely not in the dark when I am in my pajamas so even though they knocked and knocked I didn't answer it. Then I got a phone call from Annette, it had been her. She was with some other people and they all sang happy birthday to Jennifer and she said she'd left something outside. That was very nice and everything, but I was scared when someone knocked at the door and I was scared about the phone ringing and when they sang happy birthday I just froze. So that was very bad, and it took me by surprise which made it harder, I think. But anyway, I managed to say thankyou and that was that. It took me a long time before I could get up and go look for whatever it was because I was frozen in the chair. I didn't find it when I looked because it was too dark to see. I was thinking that whatever was going to happen would be when I went upstairs to bed, like the Holy Spirit was telling me maybe... and it was.

I hadn't even got into bed and I started to feel afraid and I just started to pray in the spirit without even meaning to. That was the Holy Spirit I suppose. So, I was crying and praying, and I got more afraid and cried harder and harder and I could hear Jesus telling me that he was with me and that I belonged to him. But then I saw them. There was a whole group of them a little way away and they were calling to me and saying that they had come for me, that I belonged to them. And I was saying no I belong to Jesus and I was afraid and cried and cried. They didn't give up but got closer and closer and there were pictures in my mind of the Goatman. I could hear Jesus though, telling me that he was with me and that I belonged to him. And I was saying I choose you Jesus I am yours I am yours. And I was crying and crying, and they got closer until they were circling round me and I got even more afraid and it felt like Jesus disappeared and they were reaching out and telling me they were going to take me because I belonged to them. And I was saying no I belong to Jesus. But then it was like they grabbed me, kind of sucked me away from Jesus and there was nothing I could do, and they were saying that they had me and that I was theirs. But then I thought no Jesus is always with me, always no matter where I am. So, I called out to him and there he was, and he held out his arms and I ran into them and then I saw angels come and they drove the demons away. I could hear them screaming. And I cried and cried in Jesus arms. And then after a little while I talked with him.

Jesus
My little one I am here with you. My arms are around you my little one you are safe and you are loved.
Did it happen like I saw?
Yes my little one they came to stake their claim over you but they cannot have you my little one. Their claim over you is broken for you chose and I claimed you for my own in their presence. They will not come back my little one. You are free of them.
There were a lot of them.
Yes my little one there were.
I don't understand about these things Jesus. Maybe you can explain it one day but not now.
No my little one not now. Only when it will be of help to you my little one. For now rest in me. You are safe in my arms my little one. You are loved and you are free of them forever.
Is there more?
Yes my little one there is more for the enemy still has many claims over you that need to be broken but freedom will come my dearest one, a little at a time.
Yes... Thankyou. I feel better Jesus.
Yes my little one you do. My dearest one there is not ever anything to fear for I am always with you and will help you with everything that you ever need.
You are enough Jesus.
Yes my little one I am...
Will I always be alone.
No my little one, not always. For now, rest in my arms my little one. I am with you and will watch over you. I will not leave you my little one.
I am glad Jesus. You didn't leave me. You didn't let them have me.
No my little one they cannot have you, not ever. You are mine and that will not ever change.

    It felt like a big relief the next day. I was so very tired after that big fight, but the fear had gone and that was good. There was still the London trip to go on. I wasn't looking forward to that and praying it would be Jennifer on the outside because I knew Cheryl didn't want it to be me. But it was Jennifer on the outside for the whole time and even though I was still hurting the weekend was ok and Cheryl and Jennifer had a good time. The birthday was over for another year.

Lift up your heads, you gates;
be lifted up, you ancient doors,
that the King of glory may come in.

Who is this King of glory?
The Lord strong and mighty,
the Lord mighty in battle.

Lift up your heads, you gates;
lift them up, you ancient doors,
that the King of glory may come in.

Who is he, this King of glory?
The Lord Almighty—
he is the King of glory.

Psalm 24:7-10

Chapter 26

Season of Endings

Jesus' work in me continued but it was often hard for me to feel like anything was happening. I was still wanting to have this new life Jesus had promised me. He kept saying soon but soon never seemed to come and even though being Jennifer got easier for me in some ways in other ways it was just as hard as ever.

Jesus said it was time to let go of more of Jennifer's life, like the things she did at church. Some things Jennifer had stopped doing anyway because we weren't coping very well with all the memories and alters but now, I was giving up being part of the worship group and running the prayer line. It was a relief to give up the responsibilities, but it felt sad too. Like Jennifer was slowly slipping away.

Jennifer was hardly ever out. She would be out to meet with Ruth and to help Annette with the ministry but that was about all. Occasionally she would meet with Cheryl but most often it was me. Sophie and Richard hadn't seen Jennifer for months. I kept going holding on to Jesus, but I found it so hard. I didn't realize it but I was still trying to keep myself safe. Every day felt like more than I could do and any mistakes I made seemed overwhelming and too much to bear. I still wasn't trusting Jesus completely and didn't really know how to rely and depend on him for everything. But Jesus helped me like he always did. He helped me choose to trust him as my safe place more than any way I tried to protect myself, it wasn't easy to trust him when I felt so vulnerable, but I knew he was my only hope.

My little one I am always with you. I walk with you through every valley my little one, through all the seasons of your life. I will not ever leave you. My little one this is a season of change and transition, where much will be taken but much will also be given. My dearest one change is not always easy for it requires you to let go of the old familiar things and to take hold of new things, things that will seem unsafe to you for a while. But I am with you my little one. I am your safety and your security. There is nothing that lies ahead of you that I do not know and have not prepared for you. You can do everything that I ask of you my little one, you can accept every truth that I am giving you. You can overcome all of the obstacles that stand in the way of you obtaining the new life that I have promised you. All of this and more you can do because I am with you. I will not leave you my little one. I will give you everything that you need. Every change that I am bringing into your life is for your good my little one no matter how it may seem. My dearest one keep on holding on to me and trust me. The way I have for you though not easy is good. It is very good my little one. I am able to give to you the best of all that I have for you because you are willing to follow me. Do not stop my little one. Keep your hand in mine and I will lead you forward. There is nothing to fear my little one. I hold you in the palm of my hand. You are loved and you are safe. All that I am I give to you my little one.

Christmas came and went, and I began the New Year knowing that there were difficult things to come. The first thing that was coming was to tell Cheryl about the blending, that Jennifer would be going for good and I would be staying. I was so anxious about it because I knew it was going to be very hard. I was still finding it hard with Cheryl. She was my friend, but she confused me, and I didn't feel safe with her. She wanted me to do things and be things that I couldn't and feeling like I had to hide the blending made it worse.

Cheryl was saying things that I found hard, I don't understand how she forgets that I am a girl and talks about men like I am interested in them and things she thinks are funny like that. It just scares me. And then she started saying about how I am not like myself and have clammed up and that scared me too. I said it is hard pretending to be Jennifer all the time and it makes me sad. She said that I was making her sad and that made me feel like I was bad, and I was scared because she wants me to share things about how I am feeling, and I can't. I can't tell her about not feeling safe with her or about the blending or about how I am feeling or anything. So it didn't go very well I don't think. I know that it is different to when I first started spending time on the outside. I think I was more me then and everything was an adventure and it felt ok to be me. Now it doesn't, not even with Cheryl because I don't feel safe anymore. It is like she is one way with me but then she says different things to Jennifer, so I get scared and confused. She says she is planning fun things to do but I don't know why if it is hard for her to spend time with me or that I like to have fun and not just talk about how sad I am or how sad she is. I think I am getting it all wrong and I don't know what to do but it makes me feel bad and want to disappear because I make everything worse.

I was worried about her too because she seemed to be running away from Jesus when she needed him the most. He was the one who could help her with all the things that were going on, but I think maybe she was scared what he would say to her. It made me wonder about a lot of things.

My little one Cheryl may be losing her friend, but she is not alone my little one. I am with her and will help her through this.

I am not sure she sees you as her friend Jesus. I don't understand what is happening with her but...I think it is like a lot of people. I get confused about them and I don't understand.

My little one my children face many challenges in this world. Staying close to me is the greatest challenge of all my little one. The enemy gives my people many reasons to look elsewhere for the things that they need. Do not be anxious or distressed about it my little one but remember that I am with each one of them. I am helping them to choose me my little one no matter how it seems to you.

It seems to me Jesus...maybe I am wrong...that they want a wonderful relationship with you, to trust you and follow you and all the things it is supposed to be like but, it is like they want it to happen like magic, kind of poof and everything is the way it is meant to be. They don't want to... like what you say Jesus... they don't want to pay the price.

Yes my little one that is so. The cost of following me is high my little one but the rewards are so much greater than anything you could give. It is not wrong to count the cost my little one but in doing so my people should recognize that not being willing to pay the price means they can never have what they most want and need.

They want it without the cost...I think.

Yes my little one they do.

And then they complain and think... you are mean because they don't have what they want.

Yes my little one they do.

Don't they see or realize Jesus?

No my little one often they do not. Often the truth is hidden from them my little one. The human heart is deceitful my little one.

But you can show them the truth Jesus.

Yes my little one but often they are not willing to see or accept the truth. The truth is there to be found my little one for those who truly desire it.

I suppose it is easier...seems easier to accept the lies Jesus. But I get sad about it all because what is the point of being here and living a lie...not seeing the truth and not living the life that you have given to us. Jesus you have given us a lot but, I don't know about it all but... I know... I think... but maybe I am wrong... I think what you have given us is worth the cost. Sometimes I don't think that because... it hurts a lot and I want to just come and snuggle with you, but they don't. I don't know because it is all hard to understand Jesus. I would like everyone to know you like I do and more but...I can't give it to them like they want. They just want it to poof, and I know it won't. There... that is it. It makes me sad.

It makes me sad too my little one, but I will help you to show them the way. It is always their choice to go that way or not my little one, but I will help you to show them the way.

Will any take it Jesus?

Some will my little one, some will.

But a lot won't.

Some will start down the path my little one and fall away. Some will go part way down the path I have for them but never fulfill their true purpose and calling. Some will follow me with their whole hearts as you have my little one. They will be my shining lights in this dark world, just as you are.

I don't feel like a shining light Jesus. I just feel sad.

I know my little one, but your sadness cannot stop you if you keep following me. You are my shining light my little one. Nothing can change that.

Are you sure Jesus? What if I... decided to say no and turned away from you or something. That wouldn't be very shiny.

No my little one it wouldn't but my dearest one you have given yourself into my hands and I will enable you to keep following me. Nothing can stop you my little one.

I know we talked about this before Jesus but... don't I get a choice?

Yes my little one always.

It is hard to put those things together Jesus.

My little one the choices that you have made are sealed in your heart and they cannot be undone. Your choice to follow me is sealed in your heart my little one and no matter what choices come after that that choice will always remain.

But people who have chosen you and loved you and served you... they make choices and turn away and stop shining don't they.

Yes my little one sometimes they do but their choice remains my little one and their light still shines. My dearest one there are many things you have yet to understand about the spiritual realms. There are things which cannot be undone my little one. Light which is given that cannot be extinguished.

So is that like... once you save someone, they can't be unsaved because it is done and finished and can't be changed.

Yes my little one like that.

It is a comfort to me Jesus because... I don't want to be stupid and turn away from you, but people do and so maybe I will. I don't want to Jesus.

I know my little one. I will help you.

Jesus wanted Jennifer to tell Cheryl about the blending while we were away for the weekend. It was Cheryl's birthday and it was meant to be a treat... but it seemed like the opposite to me. I wanted Cheryl to have as good a time as she could and to be able to spend time with her friend so they could say all the things they needed to but I was afraid I would get in the way because I would get so upset and be crying. I thought I would only make everything worse for everyone. Like it was all my fault.

Jesus... Crying....

My little one I am here with you. I will not leave you. My little one, everything I have said is true. This is not the end for you and Cheryl. My little one I am doing something good and though it is hard I will see you through it.

Crying... I believe all of that Jesus... Crying...

I know my little one I know. My little one times of grief will come but I will help you to walk through them. I know my little one that this feels like more than you can do but it is not my little one. I am with you.

I don't know how to do this in a good way Jesus. I know Cheryl needs to say goodbye to her friend and I don't want to get in the way... Crying... I want to help... Crying...

And you will my little one you will.

Crying...

My little one all you must be is yourself. Be honest about your feelings and do not be afraid when the time comes. Remember that this all part of my plans for you my little one and my plans for Cheryl also. My dearest one I am using all of this to work something good in her. Do not be afraid my little one.

I am afraid Jesus... Crying... I am afraid I will make it worse because of all my crying... I don't want to make it worse... Crying...

You will not make it worse my little one. I will be with you. I will help you.

Is my life worth of all of this Jesus? Crying....

Yes my little one it is. It is more than worth it.

Crying...

My little one hard as this is it will pass and what will remain will be good my little one. Your life is more than worth it.

But why does my life have to hurt people? Crying....

My little one.

Crying...

My dearest little one your life does not make things worse, you are not hurting people with your existence my little one. I know that this is a lie that the enemy torments you with, but it is a lie my little one.

Crying...

You are my gift and a blessing to those around you. Your life does not make things worse my little one.

Crying... It is very hard for me to see that Jesus.... Crying.... I wish you would take me away so I can't hurt them.... Crying....

You are not hurting anyone my little one. This is my doing and not yours. It will bring life my little one and not death. It is a good thing and not a bad one.

Crying....

My little one of all the things I have ever told you about your life and about the future I have for you I have never once said that your being in the world was a bad thing. I have never said that I have kept you here to hurt people or cause them harm. I have never said that you make the world a worse place my little one.

No.

So why are you believing those things my little one. They are not true.

Crying...

My little one it is a lie that you have been told over and over in many ways, but it is not true my little one. You are my gift and your being in the world is a good thing, you make it better and not worse my little one. You are my light in the darkness. That is a good thing my little one, you bring life and not death wherever you go.

Crying... Crying...

My little one my plans for Cheryl are good. They are not to bring her harm. Do not be afraid to follow me my little one and do not blame yourself for things that are not your fault. I am undoing a great work of the enemy my little one. It is not easy and there will be pain at times, but I am restoring you and making you whole and that is a good thing my little one and not one to fear.

But I don't want people to suffer because of me.

My little one none of this is your doing. It began with the enemy my little one. The pain is his responsibility and not yours. This plan to restore you is mine my little one and not yours. That is my responsibility. My little one you are not making anyone suffer. Hold on to me my little one and trust me. Follow wherever I lead, and I will use your life to bring hope and healing to many. That is a good thing my little one, not a bad one.

The weekend came at last. Mike had missed his appointment with us, and I hadn't heard from him. I was very upset, and I felt he left me when I needed him the most. I was very scared, but I knew that we had to tell Cheryl sometime and it would be a relief to have it done. I was on the outside the first day and we had a nice time, but I was feeling sad and scared. The next day was Cheryl's birthday.

I woke up about 4am and there were a lot of thoughts in my head going on and on. Mostly about you and how angry I was with you... and then I realized it wasn't me at all it was Jennifer... and then I knew that this was it and Jennifer was on the outside and I was scared and asked Jesus and he said yes. But it felt awful to me. It was Cheryl's birthday... why would he choose her birthday? So, there was no more sleep. Eventually it was morning and Jennifer told Cheryl it was her. It was awful. Cheryl cried and practically leapt on her and said how afraid she'd been that Jennifer had gone and what a lovely birthday present.... I expect me and Jennifer were feeling pretty much the same... like the worst person ever.

Jennifer said nothing and after breakfast wrote that letter to you. I was scared about that and it made me feel even more anxious. They spent the morning together and it was nice except we were feeling sick. In the afternoon Jennifer suggested a walk in the snow, because I think somehow it is easier to say hard things when you are walking. And then she did it, she told her. I thought she said just the right things and made it clear... but it was just as bad as I thought it would be. Cheryl sobbed and sobbed and said all kinds of things I don't want to even think about. She didn't and doesn't blame Jennifer or even me I don't think but she is so angry and upset with Jesus. She was already not talking to him but now it is worse. And so the rest of the day was like that with a lot of crying from everyone... and a lot of questions from Cheryl that Jennifer tried her best to answer but some of them we don't know the answer to and some of them... they are about Cheryl and Jesus. Cheryl knew, because Jennifer told her that it would be me on the outside again on Saturday and she didn't even want to go to sleep because she knew when she woke up Jennifer would be gone. I didn't sleep well... I have been so tired. I knew that one of us had to say something in the morning... it had to be me because Cheryl just wasn't saying anything. So I said I was glad that she knew about Jennifer and that it was ok to be sad, because she had kept saying to Jennifer that she wouldn't be able to be sad with me.... that I wouldn't understand or something.... I don't know I forgot what she said. So that started us both crying... I had to ask Jesus to hold my sobbings because they were coming, and it would have been too much. Tears are ok, sobbings are not. And he did. Cheryl has a lot of hard questions that I can't answer and if I did, or Jesus did, I am not sure she would like the answers. She wants me to ask Jesus so many things... I wish she would ask him herself. We did have some fun like I said so it wasn't all awful, but I think it is going to be very hard. I don't feel as relieved as I thought I would because now she knows it is like Cheryl is clinging on to me wanting answers and reassurances... needing it to be this way and not that. I know Jesus will help me... and I will do whatever he asks, I hope I will, but I know that I am needing to say goodbye to Jennifer too and not seeing how I will get space to do that. But Jesus knows.

It took some time for me to recover from that weekend. Jesus had held my sobbings, but they came out when I got back home. I still felt like it was my fault and even though it was a relief to not be lying... or feel like I was lying to Cheryl it wasn't really any better because she wasn't coping with it very well.

Hello Jesus
Hello my little one.
I think you will have to help me talk today Jesus. I am too sad and other stuff.
My little one I am here, and I will help you with everything. It is all in my hands my little one. Do not be afraid.
I think I am though Jesus. I think... I am hiding from how I feel. Please help me not to do that.
Yes my little one I will. My dearest one I will take you one step at a time. I will not overwhelm you my little one, not with anything...
It was very bad Jesus.
I know my little one, I know that it was hard for you.
Yes, and it wasn't even me who had to do it. Jennifer is so brave. It was a horrible day Jesus. I don't know... how to do this... to... I don't know what I'm meant to do with Cheryl's pain when mine is enough.
My little one all you must do is hold on to me just as you have done. I am there for her my little one just as I am there for you.

But... she hates you.

No my little one she does not. She is in pain and she is confused but she does not hate me.

But... I am not strong enough to bring her through this Jesus. She needs you but she is holding on to me.

Yes my little one she is but through you she is also holding on to me. I am there for her my little one and I will help her. I will help you also my little one. It will not be too much for you though it will be hard.

What about her questions Jesus and all the things she says she needs from you, through me? It feels like too much and what if you say the things she doesn't want to hear?

My little one I will give her the truth as she is able to bear it. It will not be long my little one. I will not make this a long time for it would not help any of you. Jennifer's time is drawing to a close and I will give her the time she needs and that others need, for her to say goodbye but that is all my little one.

So what do I tell her Jesus?

Tell her that I am with her and that I love her and that I will help her through this. That this is to bring her life and not death and that I will work through it to bring great good not only to you my little one and to those I have for you to reach in the future but also for my dear daughter Cheryl whom I love with all of my heart.

I am not sure she will be satisfied with that Jesus.

That is all that I have for you to tell her right now my little one. All that she needs will come to her. I will not leave her. I will speak to her my little one.

Mike said he would help Cheryl to understand some of the things she was struggling with if she would like it. I thought that would be good because she was asking hard questions. Some of them I didn't know the answer to, some of them I didn't want to know the answer to and some of them I did know the answer to, but I was afraid to tell her. I felt under a lot of pressure to tell her what she wanted to hear. So Cheryl wrote to him and he wrote back. She didn't say much to me at the time except that some of it was helpful, but she was upset by some of the things he said and didn't want to write to him anymore. Now Cheryl was angry and upset with Jesus and Mike, and I was stuck in the middle.

My head is full of worrying about Cheryl and about Mike Jesus.

I know my little one, but you must trust me with them both. This is not your responsibility my little one.

But I am the one who told Cheryl she could write, and that Mike would help her.

And I am the one who told you my little one. You are not responsible.

What am I responsible for Jesus?

You are responsible for your own choices my little one and not those of others.

But...

My little one you follow me. You do not follow others my little one, not ever. No matter what they want from you, you must always come to me and ask me what I want my little one. My dearest one as you follow me you will find that there who many who will ask you to do and to be things that I do not want you to do or to be. You follow me my little one.

Yes. What do you want me to do Jesus?

I want you to trust me with them my little one. They are in my hands and not yours. This is not anything that you can do my little one nor is it anything that I want you to do.

What if Cheryl decided she won't trust him?

That is her choice my little one.

But why make it hard Jesus?

I am not making it hard my little one I am only giving her a choice, to accept the help that is given or not.

Your terms and not hers.

Yes my little one.
They can be hard choices Jesus.
Yes my little one but they are good choices. They are powerful choices my little one.
Ok. Help me not to worry about it Jesus because I, we need to think about Ruth and that part of our journey.
Yes my little one you do. My dearest one this is an ending, but it is also a beginning. It is a good thing my little one and not a bad one. There is much to celebrate in your friendship with Ruth my little one and though it is now drawing to a close and there is sadness there is also hope for all that is to come.
It is a bit hard because she doesn't know me but the friendship is ending for me too.
Yes my little one it is. I know my dearest on that you feel you cannot be sad because this has not been your friendship and Ruth is not your friend but you have been her friend my little one for you have shared in Jennifer's friendship with her. This friendship is now ending for you as well as for them and so there is sadness and some grief but there is also hope my little one for it marks the beginning of a new chapter for each of you.
Does it Jesus? I suppose I am thinking... this is a chapter ending but it isn't quite done... not till the blending is done.
That is so my little one, but endings and beginnings often flow together, they are not as sudden as they often seem my little one. Endings and beginnings can take time and grief and hope become intertwined with loss and with the new beginning that comes.
Yes. Well Jesus you have been in the friendship all the way please... make the ending special.
Yes my little one I will, for all of you.
Good. That is all then Jesus. For me anyway. I love you.
And I love you my little one so very much. I am with you in your sadness my little one. I will help you.
Yes. Thankyou. Bye not bye Jesus.
Bye not bye my little one.

In my worrying about Cheryl I didn't have much time to think about my own goodbyes. I had shared in her friendship with Jennifer and now that was coming to an end even though my friendship with Cheryl would continue. Or I hoped it would. Not only that but Ruth was leaving too to go and live in a different part of the country. Her promises from Jesus were coming true which was wonderful, but it made me feel a bit sad because I was still here waiting for mine. So Jennifer had goodbyes to say to Ruth too and that friendship was ending for me as well. I had my own grieving to do and of course I was saying goodbye to Jennifer too. Jennifer was a lot of different things to me. I had believed I was her for a long time, so it felt like I was losing part of me... even though Jesus said she was being given back. It was hard to understand. I was learning that I could do the outside life without her, but I didn't want to. It was still Jennifer's life and I didn't want to have to keep on pretending. Once she was gone then all of it would be mine and I didn't want it. I missed her too.

I was thinking, sort of about Jennifer going... and the goodbye she will be saying to Ruth soon because Ruth will be leaving. I came to talk with Jesus in the morning and sat with him in his chair like usual.

Jesus
My little one I am here with you. There is nothing to fear.
I don't know if I am afraid or not Jesus... Crying... I am afraid.
I know my little one I know but I am with you. My little one everything is in my hands. My little one the time is near for the blending with Jennifer to be completed but first she must say goodbye to those she has been closest to.
Crying...
I know that this is hard my little one but hold on to me and I will help you through it.

Crying... I don't want to think about it...

My little one I am holding you close to my heart. I will help you my little one. Everything that I am doing is very good my little one.

But... Crying... Goodbyes are so hard Jesus and... Crying... It is so final. Soon she will be gone forever... Crying...

My little one everything that Jennifer is will be found in you. I know my little one that this does not comfort you, but she will not be lost my little one. Nor will she be forgotten.

I don't understand why… Crying... Why couldn't you take me away Jesus and leave her? Crying...

My little one my plans are for you. Jennifer is a part of who you are my dearest one. I am restoring that which was lost to you so long ago my little one.

Crying... But it is hurting other people.

No my little one it is not. My little one Ruth is unaware of what is happening. Her life is taking her in a new direction my little one and though she will always remember the friendship she had with Jennifer she will not feel its loss my little one.

That is a bit sad.

No my little one it is as it should be. It is time for a new thing my little one.

But Cheryl?

Cheryl will grieve for the loss of her friend my little one, but it will not harm her. My little one I am using all of this for her good. I will help her my little one.

Crying... I am afraid to lose Jennifer Jesus.

Why are you afraid my little one?

I don't know.... Crying... She is who I have been for most of my life... and now she is going and leaving me here. Crying... All alone Jesus. Crying...

My little one you are not alone, you are never alone and though Jennifer will no longer be a separate person she will still be with you my little one. Everything that she is being given to you.

Crying... But I don't want her to go... Crying...

My little one my plans for you are good, they are very good. There is nothing to fear my little one, not for you or anyone else.

But she will be gone... Crying... She already is gone.

No my little one she is not yet gone. She is with you still my little one. You will see her again my little one.

Because... Crying... She has to say goodbye.

Yes my little one she does.

Crying... I am going to need your help Jesus. Crying...

I know my little one I know. I am here for you my little one.

Crying... I don't want her to leave me.

My little one she is not leaving you she is becoming part of who you are, that is not the same my little one.

I know and it has been so long since she was around, and it is ok but... Crying... Don't leave me here Jesus. Not in this life... Crying... Please....

My little one I will not leave you here. I will take you from this place just as I have said. My little one this is all for a purpose. I am not taking you through all of this for no reason my little one. Your blending with Jennifer is part of the preparation my little one so that you can leave this place. My dearest one I will help you with every step that you must take. This is the next step for you my little one. It is almost here, and I will help you with it just as I have helped you with every other step that you have taken. It will not be too much for you my little one.

    Jennifer seemed to be taking it all in her stride, accepting that her time was ending. She said she was spending time inside with Jesus and he was helping her, and she wasn't afraid about what it would mean to be blended with me.

Hi Mike

This is Amanda. I've given it some thought like I said I would. Maybe it is because things are changing, I don't know. I think up until now Aj has not only been telling you her story but our story because she was still thinking somehow that she was me. Now that is changing, and our lives are becoming separate which made me wonder if she wasn't right in a way. I have always thought that you were there for Aj and that I wasn't supposed to be writing to you or talking to you. I've been ok with that because I haven't really wanted or needed to. I think maybe I have been caught up with Aj's journey and not really thinking very much about my own. It hasn't seemed to matter somehow. Maybe in my own way I've been as confused as she has. I am not sure what lies ahead for me. This time seems like it is running out to me and my time with it. I am at peace with that. I am ready to go like I said. It is different being just me. I think it has been difficult to really see me because there were always others obscuring the view, especially I suppose Aj who has always been there. Honestly, I don't think that I am very much without her. I can do things she can't that is true but all the things that matter like love and generosity and affection, I think they have mostly come from her. I trust Jesus when he says that this is a good thing for me, even though Aj gets so very upset about it I think that when it is done, she will be ok without me... so to speak. I think she will thrive and grow in her new life with you. It is true I get annoyed and frustrated with you. It's not that I don't understand why you mess up, I see that you have a good heart and that you are helping us in the midst of a lot of difficult things, I do see that but I also see the pain and distress of Aj. You have lots of people and things to care about but apart from Sophie and Richard I only really have one, that's why I get upset with you. I don't need or want to shout at you, not really. I don't shout at anyone. I don't like it when I get shouted at when I am trying my very best to help someone, I'm sure you don't like it either. I'm not going to shout at you. Maybe since this is my swan song as it were, I will write a little bit now and again. I don't know but thanks for the offer. It is appreciated. You are appreciated. Bye for now.
Jennifer

Jennifer and Ruth had a weekend away to spend time together and say their goodbye's. They went to the same place in the little cabin where they had met with Jesus before and where he had done so very much. Jesus had told us not to tell Ruth about the blending, so she didn't know about that. Maybe it's because she was the one leaving but this goodbye was a lot easier. We did all cry, but it wasn't a gut-wrenching grief stricken crying it was a crying that said how thankful we were for the friendship and that there is sadness for the ending but hope in the beginning too. It was very different and much better.

Ruth's last day at church came and it turned out to be the last time she saw Jennifer though she didn't know that for a long time. It was Jennifer's last time at church too. It was a difficult day. Jennifer and I wanted to say goodbye to Ruth in a good way, but Cheryl was there too wanting to be with Jennifer while she was on the outside. Cheryl didn't like Ruth very much and often seemed jealous of the time Jennifer spent with her, especially the weekends away... so it wasn't easy for us to manage all of that.

Sunday was church and a buffet lunch for Ruth and her husband to say goodbye. Jennifer was out because it was about saying goodbye to her friend and for other reasons too. So, there was more goodbye's and being upset about Sophie, and Cheryl was crying because of the Jennifer blending things. It was horrible Mr. Mike and I wanted to cry and cry. After that we went to a friend's house and that was nice. They made things out of clay. I would have liked to do that, but it was still fun even if it was Jennifer and then we had food. Then Cheryl wanted to go to the pub so she could talk to Jennifer. Then there was more crying by Cheryl and Jennifer was trying to explain some things to her, but it is hard. And I was wanting to cry, and Jennifer kept saying to me don't cry and I didn't. I kept saying to Jesus to hold my crying for me and I suppose he did. So, then we came home, and I came out. I didn't cry at first but then I did but it was like... I don't know, I could feel the Holy Spirit. It felt a bit like he was holding me together and I felt loved and I didn't cry as much as I knew I could have. But today I have not stopped crying. I am still crying Mr. Mike. I can't seem to stop. I am crying for Sophie and for Richard and for Cheryl and for me being me and the blending and so many other things and I can't make it stop.

Jennifer's time was ending but mine was really only just beginning. There was much more to come and a lot more changes ahead for me. Even while the endings were happening there were beginnings too that I hadn't seen yet.

My little one I am with you. I will not ever leave you. All of your life I have watched over you, every moment of your life is in my hands. I know that there is so much that you do not understand. I know that you are afraid but my little one I am who I say that I am. I am faithful and true, and I will not ever leave you. My dearest one all the days of your life are in my hands. You are safe and you are loved. There is nothing to fear. My little one I am with you. In every moment I am with you. I do not ever leave you. My strength is given to you my little one so that you can walk this path with me. It is a good path my little one though it is a hard one. My little one you are able to do all things as you walk with me. The enemy will try to convince you that this is not so. He will send many things against you to discourage you and cause you to doubt but my little one you have all that you need in me. I will not leave you my little one. I will give to you the life I have promised you. My little one it is not far now. Keep following and trust me in every moment of every day for all that you need. My little one the strength that I have is given to you, all that I have is given to you my little one so that you can be the person you were created to be.

My little one there is hope before you though you do not see it, there is life before you though there is little sign of it, there is love my little one so much love for you to discover and enjoy as you walk with me. Do not give up my little one. Do not listen to the lies of the enemy. He is seeking to destroy you my little one, but you are my beloved child and I am holding you so close to my heart. Trust in me and not in what you see or even what you feel. I am who I say that I am my little one. I am faithful and true and my love for you is unending. I will not ever fail you. My dearest one you will see your new day. You will see it and when you do you will know that it is I who made it possible for you, that it is my gift to you my little one. It will come. Hold on to me and do not give up. You are safe and you are loved. I will not ever leave you. Do not be afraid my little one, there is nothing to fear as you walk with me. I will care for you and watch over you in every moment. I am always here for you my little one. I will help you to understand my ways and to follow where I lead you. My ways are always good my little one though they are often hard. Do not fear this my little one but know that I will always be enough for you in everything. I am leading you forward day by day towards all that I have promised you. It will come my little one.

My dearest one your time in this place is almost ended. Do not give up but place all of your hope in me, in who I am and not in anything of yourself or what you see around you. I will make all things possible for you my little one even to go and be with my servant. It is not too much for me. I will love you and care for you my little one. You will never be alone. Hold on to me and do not be afraid of anything. I will lead you from this place my little one, at just the right time I will open the way for you. For now, hold on to me and continue to trust in who I am. I do not change my little one. I am all that I am and will ever be so. All that I am is given to you my little one so that you can walk with me all the days of your life and bring much glory to my name. The time is near my little one no matter how it looks to you now. Keep on hoping and keep on trusting. I will not fail you.

Chapter 27

A Home in My Heart

While he was healing me, Jesus was also teaching me. He showed me things about the spiritual world that amazed and surprised me. Right from the very beginning of our journey with him Jesus took us into an attic place where there were boxes that seemed to be filled with past things.

What I am speaking of now are your thoughts and feelings that you have buried very successfully over the course of your life, things you were unable to deal with or acknowledge at the time my little one.
Things in those attic boxes?
Yes my little one. Things long packed away and hidden from sight but not from my sight.
I see. That doesn't sound good.
It will not be easy my little one for you hid them away for a reason, but I am here. I am your strength and your comfort. We do this together my little one. You are not alone. I will help you though this and bring you healing and life.
I'm thinking that in some ways this sounds harder than memories... or will there be memories too.
Some my little one, some of what you will discover are attached to specific memories, some are more general... thoughts and feelings from many years of feeling unloved and unwanted.

I didn't like the boxes. They scared me because I never knew what was going to be in them. I asked about them a lot of times because I wanted to understand about them. Jesus had a very different way of seeing these things.

There are many boxes as you know. Each one is in my care my little one. Each one will be opened at just the right time. I will help you my little one. There is not one of those boxes that you cannot bear. I will always be with you.
I wish you could just destroy the boxes. Why do you have to open them?
Because they are part of who you are my little one, they are part of your life. I cannot destroy them without destroying something precious my little one...
They aren't a part that I want Jesus.
I know my little one, but each box is also full of treasure.
How can that be?
Because I can use it my little one. I can use it for good. Do not fear the boxes my little one. I will not open one of them before you are able...
I don't think I understand very well Jesus. Not any of it.
My little one though the pain is great it will be healed. Through all the suffering you have endured and will endure I will do so many great things my little one. My dearest one it is my great love for you which allows this. I know and understand your suffering my little one, but I also know what will come out of it. That is why I allow it my little one.
Like your suffering Jesus?
Yes my little one for though my suffering was great it was worth it my little one. You make it worth it my dearest one...and in just the same way your suffering will be used for great good so that you too will be able to say that it was worth the price that was paid.
How...those things are hard for me to accept Jesus. I am not worth your suffering. Maybe someone else might be worth mine. I don't know.
My little one I know what you are worth. I paid the price for you my little one. The price was high, but it was not too high. My dearest little one you do not know or

understand how much you are loved and valued but I will show you my little one. As you follow me and allow me to heal you and restore you, I will show to you the depths of my love and the measure of your worth to me my little one. The same is true for all of my children. My dearest one this world is a dark place for evil still rules in so many people's lives. My dearest one together we will defeat the powers of darkness in the lives of many. Through you I will save and heal many of my children my little one. The price is high my little one, but it is worth it.**

Is this what it means in the bible when it talks about sharing in your sufferings?

Yes my little one for my suffering brought about the redemption of many. Through your suffering many will be saved and healed my little one because I am in you and you are in me. You share in my suffering which brings about the redemption of the world.

I think maybe that is one of those very deep things that is hard to understand.

Yes my little one but you are able to take hold of the understanding that I am giving to you now. My dearest one this path that you are walking with me is truly walked with me my little one. You and I are one, we belong to each other, we journey together and together we will bring about the redemption of many. That is what you are called to my little one, that is what all my children are called to but so few are willing to pay the price my little one.

It is hard Jesus.

Yes my little one it is but I am your supply. I give you everything that you need. You only need to be willing my little one. My people are able they are just not willing.

I am sorry Jesus. I want to be willing.

My dearest one the price that you are being asked to pay is high for that is the price that I will enable you to pay my little one so that you can follow me into the darkness and shine my light.

I don't know if I understood that Jesus.

My little one the path that I have chosen for you to walk with me will require great courage and great sacrifice. The price will be high but because you are willing to pay that price, I can take you into the darkest of places, places that others are not willing to go my little one. Through you I will shine my light in a way that I could not do if you were not willing to pay the price my little one.

I don't know Jesus. It doesn't seem like you could be talking about me.

My little one you are not who you believe yourself to be. My dearest one none of this depends upon you, it is all dependant upon me in you. My dearest one no matter what you think you see in yourself that cannot hinder my plans for you if you continue to follow me.

It is hard to see Jesus. I will just hold on to you and follow you.

That is all that you must do my little one. You are safe in my arms. I will not leave you nor forsake you my little one.

Jennifer visited the attic place quite a few times before we knew about me but after that it seemed to be a place I went, and Jennifer didn't. There were other rooms too like the room of lies that Jesus got rid of. He told me that these were rooms in my heart, that my heart was like a house with different rooms that all held different things. It was kind of hard to understand at first, but Jesus was going through the rooms in my heart clearing and cleansing, emptying boxes of things that didn't belong and recovering lost treasures, like the diamond he found that was his gift of security.

There is the house too, with the attic and those different rooms. That is in me isn't it?

Yes my little one it is.

How can I have places in me Jesus? Is that different to the spiritual world you made for the alters, is it different to the places the Holy Spirit takes me?

My little one there are many places within the spiritual world. Some of which lie within you and some of which lie outside of you. Places within places my little one

for it is not like the physical world. **Spiritual places do not take up space in the same way my little one. It is possible for you have many different places within you, places that I can fill my little one and make my own.**
Does everyone have places within them Jesus, it's not an alter thing is it?
Everyone has spiritual places within them my little one. Everyone has a house or a shelter of some kind, everyone has a land that belongs to them. It is part of my gift to each of you my little one. Each of you has your own place in the spiritual realms but there are many other places also my little one, shared places, like the world that your alters inhabit.
And that is just for us?
Yes my little one it is.
And each of the alters also have their own world... is that right?
Yes my little one.
But if everyone has their own world why don't we know it Jesus?
Because for the most part you are bound to this physical world and all that it has to offer. Most do not ever explore their own spiritual world my little one.
Ok... so worlds within worlds... but not taking up space. A world within me. That is very hard to understand Jesus.
Yes my little one it is hard for you to understand for your understanding is based on this world with its physical and natural laws but the spiritual world is not like that my little one.
But... if I have places in me then... what am I Jesus?
You are more than you have yet imagined my little one. My dearest one my creation has no bounds. What you see here is only the tiniest part of all that there is. There is so much you have yet to discover my little one.

Even though Jesus and the Holy Spirit took me to see spiritual places I longed to see them better. I wanted them to be more real... that's how I thought of it but Jesus told me that the spiritual world was even more real than the physical one was it was just that I was still learning how to use my spiritual senses. He said he wanted to teach me how to live in both the physical and spiritual realms at the once. I said I thought that might take some learning.

Even though we had been to different rooms there was still a lot I had to learn about my house. The Holy Spirit started taking me to see it and show me what it meant and what they were doing to make my house and my heart new again. He showed me the roof that was covered with new red tiles. I didn't like to think about it, but they were a picture of the covering of Jesus' blood over me. My house was protected from the storms that would come. All the rooms I had ever seen in the house were bare and dusty and dilapidated, but things were changing as I healed. So I found myself on the ground in front of the house.

Well...my house is looking nice Holy Spirit.
Yes my little one, many repairs have been made, your house is in good repair my little one.
Can I ask how that is Holy Spirit because I know that there is so much more healing to do?
Yes my little one there is but the basic structure of your house is sound my little one. The walls of your life are firmly in place, the foundations are laid, the roof is complete.
Is that what you've been doing?
Yes, my little one it is for only when the basic structure is sound can we make the house all that it can be.
What is the house, how do I understand it?
The house is your heart my little one.
Yes. Ok... why is it a house and not a tree or something?
A house is a home my little one, or it should be. It is where we make our home in

you. **We fill your heart with good things and clean out the bad. We make your foundations secure my little one and we entrust you with many gifts which are placed in your house ready for you to find at just the right time.**
Ok...so I am seeing grass Holy Spirit and I can see rock through the grass. Is that good?
Yes my little one it is good. My little one there is more work to be done but the foundations are in place. You are planted firmly on the rock my little one, which is the truth that has been given to you and which you have accepted.

I noticed too that my house wasn't really where I would have put it. It was on the top of a cliff and looked very exposed. I didn't really think that was a good idea. Surely it would be better in a nice sheltered valley or somewhere like that?

Am I seeing this place right Holy Spirit? We seem to be on a cliff top. It doesn't seem like the safest place.
[The house is on the top of a cliff and on one side is the sea and on the other side land, all green and nice but very exposed. I was a bit worried about the cliff crumbling away and my house falling down].
The rock will not give way my little one, the truth will not crumble and fall no matter what comes against it. Your house is secure my little one though its position may seem exposed.
Yes... it does. Why here Holy Spirit?
My little one the life that you have chosen to live is not an easy one. There will be many storms that the enemy will bring against you my little one. The wind and the waves may be strong at times, but they will not sweep you away.
But... you decided where my house, my heart should be didn't you?
Yes my little one we did. This is the perfect spot for you my little one. The wind is fresh and will keep you from falling asleep, the sky is open and wide and will help you to see what is ahead. You can see the waves as they come my little one and the storms as they gather overhead. You can see the lands around you my little one for your view is not obscured by anything.
So you want me to see?
Yes my little one you will see many things that others will not see. You will see the attacks of the enemy before they come, you will see the world around you as it truly is. It will not be hidden from you my little one.
It is the kind of place you would put a light house Holy Spirit, but it is not.
No my little one not yet for your house is not yet complete. The basic structure is complete my little one but there are things yet to be added.
You are making me a light house? What does that mean?
It means that you will shine for all to see my little one.
Is that why I am up here too, so I can be seen?
Yes my little one it is.

Everything about my house seemed to be a picture of something, it all meant something. I got surprised by the things he told me, but all made sense somehow.

Can we look around the house... the outside I mean?
Yes my little one tell me what you see.
Well it's square... maybe... there's a little bit sticking out there. And the walls are covered in that white wood stuff. Why is that Holy Spirit... why not bricks or stone? I suppose wood is warmer and kind of living, more approachable and softer somehow and white... well I'm supposed to be clean and holy, robed in white, all that stuff.... Is that it Holy Spirit?
Yes my little one you are seeing well.
The roof tiles were red... Is that like we are covered in the blood? I don't like that but... that's what it is?
Yes my little one that is what it is.
There is a little porch and three steps up and the door is a dark blue... I think that is the communion... I don't think that is a good word but that color you showed me before and it is about relationship.
Yes my little one it is. The door to your heart is found in relationship with us my little one and those who have room in your heart enter through it.

Even the land around my house had meaning and purpose. The Holy Spirit told me that the boundaries would move outwards as I grew stronger and fuller of who they were. There were places where he told me others would be welcomed and would receive things given from my heart. There were little bridges that formed connections with other lands, other people's hearts. There was so much to see and understand even though a lot of it was kind of half finished and not yet what it would be.

So all of this is being made for me and for others?
Yes my little one it is.
Is the boundary set Holy Spirit?
Your land will grow as you grow my little one.
Because it is about what is flowing out of my heart.
Yes my little one and the more that you overflow the more land that you will occupy.
My land is still a bit empty Holy Spirit, but it is still lovely and yes, it is lovely. Just a bit empty. It needs to be more... lively Holy Spirit.
And it will be my little one. Remember this is a reflection of what is flowing from your heart. As your heart is mended and begins to flow with all that we are giving you this land will come to life and be filled with much more than you can yet imagine.

There was something else too. A long time ago Jesus had shown us a room that was just for Mike. There wasn't much in it just a box for him to sit on and a little table... but it was there. Jennifer hadn't liked it at all. She didn't think it was safe.

So as I lay on my bed just relaxing I found myself thinking about this thing with you again. It seems to me that somehow Jesus has managed to sneak you in by the back door when I wasn't looking, past all my defenses. As I was wondering how I felt about that I got a picture in my mind…. You and Jesus sitting together in a room... a room that is somehow inside, in my heart if you like. It's a very bare and empty room, just two chairs which you were both sitting on and an upturned crate which seemed to be being used as a table. I pondered on this picture as I was cooking, wondering what it was saying. I think that somehow Jesus has given you access, to somewhere that no one else has access to, somewhere on the inside of me. That's scary, very scary but then I realized that Jesus is with you there, you are together which makes it ok, it makes it safe. I'm not sure what the room represents exactly. Like I said it was completely empty, bare floors and walls, maybe like it was ready to be decorated and furnished? Anyway, something is different.

That was a long time ago, before we knew about me. Now I was seeing something new.

What is that bit sticking out of the house Holy Spirit?
That is a new room my little one, one that we have been working on.
You have made room for something Holy Spirit?
Yes my little one but not something, someone.
Oh, like an annex.
Yes my little one a permanent place for him to live.
Mike?
Yes my little one.
Why does he get his own annex Holy Spirit? It seems like a lot to give to him... just one person. I don't mean to sound... help me understand why I need it.
My little one the relationship that you will have with our servant will not be like any other relationship you have ever had. You need a special place in your heart for him my little one, a place prepared and built for him. My little one he is a part of your life now and will always be so. He is your partner and your friend and many other things besides my little one. This is his place in your heart.

I was very surprised by this, that he should have been given such a big permanent place in my heart but there was so much to see I didn't ask any more about it for the moment. Maybe that was enough for now. The walls of my house seemed to glow with light and the Holy Spirit told me that they were the boundaries and guidelines that gave my life structure. I didn't understand.

Why is there boundaries and guidelines Holy Spirit?
Who you are gives your life structure my little one, it forms the shape of your house, it keeps it solid and enables us to fill each room as we desire.
Explain that more.
My little one each house that is built is different. Each house is a reflection of the person it belongs to.
Because it is their heart.
Yes my little one and every person is unique. Every person has their own boundaries and guidelines my little one.
Like?
Like your personality my little one, the things you like and don't like, the things that you can do and can't do. Each person has their own limitations my little one but that is not how they are to be viewed. They are boundaries and guidelines my little one and form an outline for the person that you are.
Like a basic... this is who I am, and you get to work with that and build on it and fill it in... sort of.
Yes my little one.
So what is the glowing light... why does that come out of the walls?
Because it is who you are my little one. You shine with our light in you.
Because I am your child.
Yes my little one.
So when you said this would be a light house, you didn't mean there would be a big tower with a flashing light on top.
No my little one I didn't. I meant that your whole house will shine for all to see. This will be a house of light my little one.
So that will happen the more I am filled with you because the more my house is filled with you the more it will shine.
Yes my little one. Your house will shine with the light of who we are in you.

I asked about windows too because they seemed important to me.

> So, I am asking about the windows. Will they let the light shine out too?
>
> **Yes my little one they will but that is not their primary purpose. They are there to let you see my little one.**
>
> So will you add more windows Holy Spirit? I didn't see the windows from the outside. Kind of like they were there but I couldn't see them.
>
> **They are there my little one though some of them are not yet opened.**
>
> So, they are there but it is like the shutters are closed and you need to open them up so I can see.
>
> **Yes my little one just so.**
>
> Ok. Do you have... is there any open windows Holy Spirit... I want to ask if the room of lies... I forget so easy but I remember Jesus pulling back curtains at a window so I could see a dark room.
>
> **Yes my little one but that was a different kind of room. There was no light there.**
>
> Because it was a room put there by the enemy?
>
> **Yes my little one it was a room that did not belong in your house.**
>
> Are there other rooms here that don't belong?
>
> **Yes my little one there are but they will be destroyed and removed my little one just as the room of lies was destroyed.**
>
> Ok. Is this the kitchen?
>
> **Yes my little one it is.**
>
> There is a nice big table.
>
> **Yes my little one, many will come here to eat.**
>
> What will they eat Holy Spirit?
>
> **Love and kindness, truth and hope, compassion and mercy. All of these and more will be found at the table of your house my little one.**
>
> That is a different kind of kitchen Holy Spirit.
>
> **Yes my little one it is.**

One time the Holy Spirit took me to an upstairs room, but he wanted me to look out of the window to the outside.

> **Come and tell me what you see.**
>
> I see fields, the little stream with the bridges. It goes a long way into the distance.
>
> **Yes my little one it does for you have a good view from here. What else do you see my little one?**
>
> [this time I looked down at the bit of land just in front of the house... just grass, not flat lawn but rough kind of lumpy grass, nice and I thought I saw something, but I wasn't sure].
>
> **My little one?**
>
> Crying... I see a little rabbit on my land just down there.
>
> **Yes my little one what does that remind you of?**
>
> It makes me think… Crying.... about the velveteen rabbit Mike keeps talking about.
>
> **What was special about that rabbit my little one?**
>
> I didn't read it yet Holy Spirit.
>
> **I know my little one.**
>
> Crying.... It was loved.
>
> **Yes my little one it was.**
>
> I think... Crying... There are lot of little rabbits playing down there.
>
> **Yes my little one there are. Each one of them loved and special my little one.**
>
> But... Crying....
>
> **My little one the little rabbits that we will give to you are those which have been unwanted and unloved, but which are so special to us. We will bring them here to be**

with you my little one for you too are our velveteen rabbit. You will show them what it means to be loved my little one, you will show them they are special and that they are real.**

Crying... How will I do that? Crying....

By loving them with the love that we give to you for them.

Are they children?

Yes my little one they are.

Why am I here looking down on them Holy Spirit?

Because being here helps you to see my little one.

I don't understand.

The windows of your heart help you to see my little one. That is why they are here.

Crying... What am I seeing?

Your purpose my little one or part of it.

Crying....

My little one there are many who need what you can bring to them. You understand so much about what it means to be like those children my little one. You can give our love to them in a way that so few can. My little one our love will flow through you to those like yourself who have never known what it is to be loved or special. You will help them to see the truth about themselves my little one just as we are helping you to see the truth about yourself.

Crying... Can I do that? Crying....

Yes my little one you can. With our help you can reach out to them and love them. My little one the person you are is so special.

Crying....

I know my dearest one that the path that you are on is difficult and there is much pain but those we will bring here need what you can bring to them my little one.

Little rabbits.

Yes my little one, little broken rabbits for you to love. Can you do that my little one?

I don't know Holy Spirit... Crying... I don't know .... Crying

My little one remember what I said to you about how this house will shine with our love, with who we are in you.

Crying... Yes.

Many will be drawn to that light my little one, many will come. The lost and the broken will come. Little ones will come. We will help you to love them my little one. All of this is not only for you but also for them. This is your house my little one but it a house that is a gift to many.

And the little rabbits will come and play in my garden?

Yes my little one they will for they will find many things that they need here.

But my house is still empty, and the garden isn't much... there isn't anything here for them Holy Spirit.

But that is why we are preparing you and making you ready my little one. So that others can come.

Like making a home.

Yes my little one a safe home where others can come and find healing and rest. I know my little one that this is your home and the healing that will come is first and foremost for you, but you will share it with many my little one. Your house is a gift. It is a good place.

Yes. It looks good.

Yes my little one it is and it will become so much more than it is now. We are only just beginning my little one. My dearest one your life is precious. It is a gift to those around you. It is a good thing that your house is here my little one, it is place where many will find healing and life.

Why did you show me the rabbits Holy Spirit?

Because I know your heart for them my little one. I know you do not see it yet, but we

have given you a heart to reach out to the little ones, who have been so broken by the evil in this world.

But I don't know who I am Holy Spirit.

No my little one you don't but we do. My little one your life is a gift to those around you. We are making you ready my little one so that you can share our love with many. I know that this is hard for you to see and the steps we have for you are hard, but this is where it is leading my little one. We are making your house a home not just for you but for many others.

But they can't all live here Holy Spirit.

But they will visit my little one, they will spend time with you and find much healing. Your heart will be a home to them my little one where they will feel safe and welcomed, accepted and loved.

My house will be very special then Holy Spirit.

When I was spending time with daddy, he took me to his room of comfort where he would love me and comfort me. He told me it was a special place in his heart that he made just for me, that there were lots of rooms in his heart that were mine. That made me wonder.

I have been thinking about houses a lot too Jesus. If daddy has a house, then you must have a house and the Holy Spirit must have a house?

Yes my little one we do.

Do I have a room in your house Jesus?

You have many rooms in my house my little one.

And is that different to... I don't know because there is a lot, I am not understanding yet. I know that when you have room in someone's house you have a place in their heart.

Yes my little one you do.

And I have a place in your heart Jesus?

Yes my little one you have your own special place in my heart which is just for you.

But if I have many rooms isn't that more like a house?

Yes my little one it is.

So I have a house in your house?

Yes my little one.

And a house in daddy's house?

Yes my little one.

And a house in the Holy Spirit's house?

Yes my little one.

And I am thinking that maybe house isn't quite right maybe it is that I have a home in your house?

Yes my little one you do. You have a special home, made just for you in each of our houses. Our hearts have more than enough room for you and all of our children my little one.

That is the places within places again Jesus isn't it because that is... a lot to do in my head... all those homes within homes... Is it different to have a lot of rooms... a home... in someone's heart, than it is to have a room?

Yes my little one it is. When someone has a home in your heart that is very special my little one. That is someone who has a very special and permanent place in your heart.

And... maybe it takes time for someone to make a home in your heart?

Yes my little one it does. You may start off as a guest my little one and then you may be given your own room but only a few ever truly make a home in your heart my little one. That is very different.

What does it mean Jesus? If someone has a home in your heart?

It means they have access to everything that is yours my little one. Your home is

their home, they are not a guest anymore, they are not confined to a certain part of your house, they have free access and are welcomed everywhere.
Like I do in your heart and daddy's heart and the Holy Spirit's heart?
Yes my little one.
Do you have a home in my heart Jesus? Crying...
Yes my little one I do.
I am glad. I think maybe the Holy Spirit does too... doesn't he?
Yes my little one he does.
I am not sure about daddy. I think maybe he only has a room.
No my little one he has a home in your heart but he is waiting to be invited further in my little one. He will not go places you are not ready for him to go.
That is good. I want you to have a home in my heart, all of you.
And we do my little one.
There aren't any people who have homes in my heart Jesus. Some have rooms I think, but not homes. Is that wrong?
My little one for you to give someone a home in your heart is a difficult thing for it requires a great deal of trust my little one. There will be many homes in your heart, but you are not yet ready or able my little one for your heart is not yet ready for that.
It is still being mended?
Yes my little one it is.
But people have rooms like Mike... but why is he... no you told me... it is because he needed a special place.
Yes my little one he does.
Will he have a home Jesus? I am thinking he already has more access than anyone else.
Yes my little one he does and he will have a home in your heart my little one, when you are ready.
Ok.
My dearest one all of these things that we are showing you are to help you understand all that we are doing. Your heart is being made ready to receive many my little one, some of whom will stay and make their home and some of whom will not, but you must be prepared for both my little one.
When someone is in your heart, if they are a guest, or have a room or a home... they can hurt you Jesus.
Yes my little one they can for they have access to the deepest parts of you.
Especially the ones with a home.
Yes my little one especially those people.
But you are there, all of you and if my home gets wrecked... you can mend it again.
Yes my little one we can. We are working constantly within your heart my little one for there is much to be done.
I expect there are parts of my house that are still broken.
Yes my little one there are. There are rooms that still need to be mended my little one.
Or got rid of.
Yes my little one or got rid of.

There was more to find out about how Jesus and daddy and the Holy Spirit had made their home in me and what that meant. One day it was daddy and not the Holy Spirit who took me to see something very special in my house. He showed me a new room that had comfy seats and a big fireplace in it. He told me the fire was their presence in me and that this was the room where I would share my heart with others for my healing and in time for others' healing too. It is called the room of meeting. I wanted to know more about the fire that was there.

Tell me about the fire Holy Spirit.
My dearest one our presence in you is a fire. Do you know why that is my little one?
There are those things about how fire burns the rubbish. I don't know what else.
My little one a fire has many flames, each flame is significant and important for it forms part of the whole. Your fire has many flames my little one would you like to see?
Yes. Ok Holy Spirit... The flames are all different colors.
Yes my little one they are. Tell me what you see my little one.
There is yellow and green and blue and pink, the colors you have talked to me about, the colors in my ring.
Yes my little one for they speak of our presence and our work in and through you.
This is you in me but is it different to your light. Light is different to fire isn't it?
Yes my little one it is. Fire has light my little one, but it is more than that.
What else is it?
It is all consuming my little one.
There is something about that, my God is a consuming fire in the bible... what does it mean?
It means my little one that when we are in you, we are burning everything away that is not of us. We are taking your life and using it for our purpose. We are everything in you my little one.
So... in a way you are burning up my life for your purposes?
Yes my little one in a way we are but what else do you notice my little one?
There isn't anything burning Holy Spirit... no logs or coal... just flame.
Yes my little one.
Why is there smoke Holy Spirit? There was smoke coming out of the chimney.
Yes my little one there is.
Is that... things of me that you are burning up and getting rid of?
Yes my little one it is the things in your heart that hinder you from following us, that keep you from all that we have for you. We burn those up my little one and then you are free of them and your house is cleaner than it was before.
I think that there is more about the fire Holy Spirit... it's hard for me to tell but I think it is in the middle of the house... is that right?
Yes my little one it is, right at the heart of your house my little one.
The heart of my heart.
Yes my little one that is where we dwell.
That is where your home is?
Yes my little one.
But Jesus was saying yesterday how... you all have a home in me... I suppose I was expecting rooms but... maybe it is different for you?
Yes my little one it is different. My dearest one we all of us dwell together at the centre of who you are. We are not confined to any room my little one. This fire though it is seated here is spread throughout the entire house my little one.
How can that be Holy Spirit?
Its heat can be felt wherever you are in this house my little one, our presence is not confined to this room.
I suppose that must be true... but what is the heat of this fire then Holy Spirit? Your light is in the walls and you said there is different kind of light... and the fire has different flames... and heat and light.
Yes my little one it does. Remember that the fire is our presence in you my little one. Our presence is not confined by anything but is greatest where we are welcomed. You have welcomed us into your heart my little one and we have made our home in you, right at the centre of who you are. That is here my little one, in the room of meeting but our presence is also in every other room my little one. Our fire cannot be contained.

Does that keep my heart warm Holy Spirit, not cold hearted?
Yes my little one it does.
And can the fire be bigger or smaller?
Yes my little one our fire in you depends upon many things but most of all it depends upon your willingness to surrender yourself to it my little one. The more willing you are to give your whole heart the bigger the fire will be.
And the warmer it will be and the more rubbish will be burned... what else Holy Spirit?
The more you will be consumed by who we are my little one.
What does that mean?
It means you become filled with us my little one.
So kind of... the fireplace will get bigger?
No my little one the fireplace will not get bigger but the fire will extend beyond its confines into the whole of the house, into every room my little one, to a far greater extent than it is already.
So the heat from the fire that is everywhere, but the flames aren't, not yet?
Yes my little one that is so.
But...does that mean when I am filled with you that my whole house will be full of flames?
Yes my little one it does.
There is a long way to go then Holy Spirit.
Yes my little one but we have begun and we are preparing you for the more that we have for you.
So my walls will be glowing and my rooms will be full of fire that will be bright and colorful?
Yes my little one it will. It will shine for all to see my little one.
Yes it will. And then my whole heart will belong to you?
Yes my little one it will.
And I will be completely surrendered to you.
Yes my little one you will.
It is hard to imagine that is possible Holy Spirit.
But it is my little one. We are the ones who make it possible not you. All you must do is surrender my little one and follow just as you are doing.
So are you saying you dwell in the flames... all of you? That is your home?
Yes my little one that is what I am saying.

There was a lot to learn and I would keep on learning not only about the places in my own heart but the places in Jesus heart too.

**Do not let your hearts be troubled.
You believe in God believe also in me.
My Father's house has many rooms;
if that were not so, would I have told you
that I am going there to prepare a place for you?
And if I go and prepare a place for you,
I will come back and take you to be with me that
you also may be where I am.**

John 14:1-3 NIV

Chapter 28

The Dollies

I was starting to notice something. Aj on the outside seemed to be getting older somehow. I thought that was because of the blending that was happening with Jennifer but even while she seemed to be getting older there was still a younger part that I was noticing sometimes. Jesus showed me how there was more than one of us, that we were like Russian dolls with smaller younger ones hiding inside bigger older ones. I talked to Jesus a lot about it and he helped me understand even though it was quite confusing for a while. There was dolly 1 who was kind of a mix of Jennifer and Aj while the blending was happening, then there was dolly 2, that was Aj then there was dolly 3 which was me and then dolly 4 and dolly 5. When Aj was first on the outside she was a mix of Aj, me and dolly 4 and dolly 5 but Jesus had been separating us out from each other. At the same time the blending with Jennifer was happening… and that made dolly 1 who was on the outside now. Jesus has helped me understand even more since that time because it was very confusing about who was who.

My little one when the dollies were revealed to you there was a great deal of change happening and though there were five of you, you were not separate in the way that most alters are. You had the ability to each draw from one another what was needed my little one. Dolly 1 was Aj drawing upon Jennifer to live the outside life.
Mmm...but why is that different to blending?
It is not different my little one. In this case it was part of the blending process.
Ok...but what do you mean we weren't separate like most alters.
You were all part of one person my little one which is you.
But aren't all the alters part of me.
Yes my little one they are but not in the same way. The dollies were much more deeply connected to you my little one. Jennifer was the most separate of all. She surrounded and protected you my little one and in the true sense she was never a dolly at all. Not until the blending process began and the connections, she had with you and the other dollies grew closer.
So do you mean... kind of we could flow in and out of each other. Affect each other… that kind of thing.
Yes my little one but not in the way you are thinking.
Hmm. How then Jesus?
My little one think of a row of paper dollies all holding hands.
Yes.
The paper can be folded once or many times to bring two or more of the dollies close to each other so that they share in the same space, have the same experience.
Yes... ok.
Before the blending began you were all folded together my little one. There were four of you surrounded and protected by Jennifer.
Yes.
Then as Jennifer and Aj began to blend that became the fifth dolly. Dolly 1. She was not like Jennifer in that she did not cover and protect you in the same way but she enabled Aj to live the outside life.
Kind of she... dolly 1 was part Jennifer and part Aj.
Yes my little one but dolly 1 and dolly 2 were so closely connected that they were folded together for much of the time. Though not all of it my little one.
And I suppose sometimes...to begin with Aj was unfolded... but the rest of us were still together and then you started to unfold us…so that we could all be seen separately.
Yes my little one but there were still times when you were folded together and you were always connected each one to all of the others.
No wonder it was confusing Jesus. I suppose it was like Russian dollies because we were

hiding behind each other.

Yes my little one that was to help you understand at the time and it is still true my little one but you are now able to understand more than you were then.

Now we knew about the dollies it was hard because things were confusing and uncertain again and I had to start learning all over again about who I was, but it made sense of things I was wondering about. Jesus showed me things that helped me to understand.

In the worship I was in Jesus arms like I often am in the worship time. Sometimes I seem very small and sometimes bigger. I have thought that was strange and it made me think maybe I was just imagining being in Jesus arms but this morning I realized what it is. I am seeing the two parts of me, dolly number two and dolly number three. Dolly number two is older and bigger than dolly number three. I realized that is why sometimes I am big and sometimes I am small in his arms. I saw something else too. I saw the golden locket he wears round his neck which is my heart. I saw the side of it that I never noticed before. It has three layers, a bit like a sandwich. The middle part, like the filling of the sandwich is much thicker than the outside bread parts. I think that this is the three parts of me. Dolly number two, three and four, all together but separate. And dolly number three, that is the child part of me...that is the biggest part. Dolly number two and dolly number four are just little parts of me. Dolly number four is the part that holds the bad memories if you forgot. I saw that and understood what it meant. I want all those parts to be together Mr. Mike but they aren't not yet. I was snuggled in Jesus arms and I felt safe and loved and he kissed the palm of my hand and I cried because I felt so safe and loved. So that was my worship time at church.

The locket I saw was the same one Jesus showed us when it was the birthday. The locket is my heart and Jesus was showing us how it was made up of different parts. It helped me a lot to be able to see it and how the different parts of us were connected. It changed over time as we healed and blended and that helped me too to know where we were in the healing that Jesus had for us.

Jesus said it was time to let little Aj, dolly 3 be seen and to be allowed to talk for herself. That was me. Aj had been Skyping with Mike for a little while now. It was very scary for us to be seen and heard by him after all of this time, but it was much better for us to see and hear him. It helped us get to know him better and trust him better too. But now it was my time to be on the outside and talk with him. Mike told me about Lamby, a hand puppet who helps him talk to children. Lamby is a lot less scary than he is ;) and he thought maybe it might help with talking to me.

I think Aj was scared to find out 'she' could be younger when she was having to live the outside life as Jennifer. She was scared of what I might say and do too a bit like Jennifer had been when Aj was being discovered. So it was hard at first for Aj to let me come out and for me to be brave enough to come out and talk with Mike. Jesus helped us both to trust him and to let me be seen and heard, but only with Mike. I suppose it helped that we had been through it before when it had been Jennifer and Aj. But now it was my turn. I started off by writing to him.

I am going to call you Mr. Mike if that is ok. Then you will know it is me, little Aj and it seems better to me somehow. I don't think you will mind because you are kind and nice. Do you know what has happened? I think this is right. When I was made the outside one, I seemed more like me but then as time went on, I seemed more like Jennifer...that is dolly number one. I got lost and forgotten again because it isn't safe to be me here. But now Jesus says it is time to get to know this part of me and not just the part I have been getting to know for the last few months. I quite like that part and it isn't hard to want to be her, but I don't think I want to be me very much. It seems too hard and not safe to be me here because I am too little to be let out. That is why I have to write as me and talk to you and to the Lamby so we can get to know me together Jesus says. I am glad it is a together thing. I get so lonely. I am sad a lot too but maybe I won't always be sad. I am not wanting to be me because I can't do anything. Not things that grownups need to do anyway. I don't know what children need to do. What do they need to do? I made cookies today and I have sent you a picture of them. They were yummy but maybe they needed longer cooking because they were a bit soft. I liked the melty chocolate. I think maybe you would have liked to test my cookies. Maybe one day I can make some cookies for you and not make a mess like you do ;) I like your stories they are funny, and they help me know you better. I would tell you stories if I had any. Maybe I will get some. I have been talking to Jesus a lot since we talked mostly because I have been very upset and needing his help. I am glad he is always there and helps me. I think I wouldn't be here if he didn't. Sometimes I think about going away and being in heaven with him because I feel like I don't fit here, and I am not good for anyone. I was feeling like that yesterday and today. It is bad feeling that way and it hurts a lot. I wrote down my talks like I always do. I was sitting cuddled in his lap like always. It is a good place to be because he wraps his arms around me and holds me tight and I know I am not all alone like I am feeling inside.

Talking to Lamby helped me to come to the outside and be me with Mike. It was hard to get to the outside at first and to know that it was me, like it had been hard for Aj. I was scared to be me, but I liked it too. I liked to talk with Lamby. Even though I knew that really it was Mike I was talking to it made it much less scary to talk to Lamby. We were still getting used to life without Jennifer and we missed her. Jennifer didn't spend time on the outside anymore, but we heard her sometimes. That was kind of comforting to know that she was still there. I still didn't want her to go. That felt too scary to me. But sometimes she made it harder for me to be me.

Sometimes but not very often I hear Jennifer. I think she was there yesterday when I was talking with you. Maybe she still thinks she needs to protect me from you. I wish she wouldn't butt in when I am allowed to be me. She gets all those times when she could butt in when I am trying to be her. I wanted to tell Lamby that I wished I could cuddle her. I wanted to tell you that I love you, but it wasn't allowed. She seemed to think it was obvious that I am depressed, but I didn't know that's what it was Mr. Mike. I still wish Jesus would get rid of me instead of her.

I was learning about who I was and writing to Mike and talking to him and Lamby in our chat times. Jennifer and Aj were blending and then there was dolly 4 who I hadn't met yet but I kind of knew she was there even so. It was a lot of changes all at once and difficult to understand. I was known as dolly 3 for a little while. It wasn't much of a name, but it helped me know who I was and how I was connected to the other dollies. I had to learn about other things too, like how old I was. It was a scary thing to ask those kinds of questions. It was scary because I got afraid of hearing wrong and it was scary because I got afraid of what he might tell me. Maybe I wouldn't like it.

I am scared to ask Jesus, but I want to.
Yes my little one I know that you do.
Should I ask you Jesus...will it help?
It will not hurt you my little one.
Do you want to tell me Jesus?
My dearest one I want you to see yourself as you truly are. That includes the thing that you are afraid of asking.
Well...ok... So how old am I Jesus. How old is dolly 4? Help me not be scared about hearing wrong Jesus or make stuff up in my head.
My little one there is nothing to fear. Dolly 4 is five years old my little one and you are a little older.
How much older Jesus?
You are eleven years old my little one.
Eleven.

Yes my little one.
That is older than I thought Jesus.
But it is not too old my little one.
I don't know. It is a funny number Jesus because it's not so little but it's not big either...and, dolly 2 is sixteen?
Yes, little one she is.
Is there a dolly 5 Jesus... is she very little?
Dolly 5 remains hidden for now my little one. It is better that it should be so for the time being.
But she is there.
Yes little one she is there.
And she is younger than dolly 4?
She is very small and vulnerable my little one, but I am with her. She is safe.
Ok…. Eleven.
Yes my little one that is your age.
And it won't change no matter what.
No my little one it won't change.
Ok... I will think about it Jesus... I thought maybe I was younger but then... sometimes I'm not sure. It gets confusing Jesus.
I know my little one and whilst things are changing it will seem confusing for a time but my dearest one, I see things as the truly are. There is nothing to fear from who you are my little one.
I will think about it Jesus. Bye not bye.
Bye not bye my little one.

So now I knew that I was eleven. That felt much better to me because I never felt like I was sixteen. I think maybe I felt younger because of dolly 4 being there as well. I was getting used to the idea of being me, but it was hard to find out that I wasn't the outside person all over again. It felt like losing my life over again because I had thought it was me making friends and doing things and talking with Mike, but it hadn't been, not really. It had been Aj and not me. It wasn't so bad as when I found out I wasn't Jennifer, but it was still hard.

When Jesus showed me how the middle part of the locket was the biggest part, and that it was the main part that the other dollies would become part of that meant it was going to be me on the outside, not Aj. I had only just got used to the idea that I would be sixteen and now I had to get used to the idea that I would be eleven...but still having to be Jennifer. I didn't see how that could be right.

My dearest one who you are is unique and special. You were made in love for a purpose my little one a good purpose. You were made to love me and be loved by me my little one for you are first and foremost my beloved child. Being my child means that you have worth and value my little one, that you are precious in your own right. My dearest one you find this so hard to see but recognizing and accepting this is as much a part of the healing that I have for you as the remembering and the blending my little one, indeed it is central to that.
But I suppose... I still think it would be better if you got rid of me and made all the others into one person. I think I would make it worse Jesus.
Yes my little one you do but that is not so. My dearest one you are a delight to me, and I do not ever want you to go away. I want to heal you and restore you and give to you a life that will bring you joy and great fulfilment. My dearest one my plans are for you, created in love for you and they cannot be fulfilled without you. My dearest one if you were to go away then my plans for you could not be fulfilled by the other alters in your system for none of them has the skills and gifts and abilities that you do. They are not you my little one and just as you need them to be whole again, they also

need you. You cannot go away my little one, not if my plan for all of you is to be fulfilled.

I think it would be easier if I was being blended into dolly 2 say... it is because they are being blended into me. Maybe I am confused about what that means.

You believe it makes you responsible my little one and that you will have to be good at everything and make everything work and be a grownup person living a grownup life doing things that you do not believe that you can do. You do not believe you are worthy my little one and you do not believe it to be possible.

Something like that Jesus.

My dearest one even though it is true that all the others being blended into you will make you the one person who is living the outside life, carrying out my instruction to you, loving and being loved that does not mean all the things that you believe my little one. My dearest one you have spent all of your life hiding behind one or more alters. This has helped you survive my little one and it was necessary but stepping out from the shadows and being who you were created to be is a good thing my dearest one. I know you are hiding my little one, but I am your hiding place. You do not need to be hidden away any longer. You do not need other alters to live your life for you. It is your turn my little one to live the life that I have for you, that I have prepared especially for you. I do not want you to hide away any longer my little one. You are my beautiful child and I am making you whole so that you can be free to live a life that is given in love so that you can love and be loved as was intended in the beginning.

I suppose it is true that I have always been hiding Jesus and to be the... to have nobody else there is... it seems wrong and frightening and wrong.

But it is not wrong my little one. It would be wrong for you to remain as you are now for that was never my intention my little one. It has been necessary to enable you to survive but it is not my desire for you my little one. You were not made to be hidden away.

Why am I here Jesus?

To bring glory to my name my little one. So that others may come to know me and be saved just as you have been saved. So that I can show my love and my power in the darkest of places and defeat the work that evil has done in so many of my children. That is why you are here my little one.

Can't you do it without me Jesus?

You were created for a purpose my little one, no one else can fulfil the plans and the purpose that I have for your life and though I can do all things I have chosen to work through you my little one. I cannot do that without you.

You don't make sense to me Jesus.

I know my little one.

I would like to know more of you Jesus and all the spiritual things because that's reality Jesus and I forget and get lost.

Yes my little one you do forget but my dearest one I am holding you and I will give to you everything that you need including revelation of my heart of love for you and a great many spiritual truths that you have yet to see and understand. My dearest one even though you will be living the outside life for the most part that does not mean that your inside life will become less for there are many things that I have to show to you, many things that I have for you to do, even in the spiritual realms that you have not yet seen or understood my little one.

Our conversations with Jesus had been a mix up until now, I think. Sometimes he was talking to Aj and sometimes to me but more and more it was him and me talking. It was changing again just like it had before. Jesus was helping me to understand where I fitted and how he was healing us all so he could put me back together again to be one whole dolly.

When I told you, you were the one that all the other alters came from I was not lying little one for the one you know as Aj which is all the dollies together, that is the one from whom all the other alters came.
But then we split up into dollies.
Yes my little one you did though it is not quite the same.
Why?
Because you are so closely connected to each other. You did not develop separate personalities as the other alters did my little one. You are separate but the same.
We are different ages.
Yes little one you are.
Why did we need to split up when we were hidden behind the others anyway?
Because my little one I always knew that this time would come. A time when I would bring you out into the light and begin to restore and heal you. My dearest one I have always been preparing you for this time so that I can make you whole in me. Separating you in the way that I have will help you heal my little one.
How?
Each of you holds something precious little one. The core of the person that you are is found in you. You are the one from whom the other dollies came.
I am the middle one.
Yes you are my little one and each one will be returned to you.
Why does that make us easier to heal Jesus?
Sometimes little one when something complex and beautiful is broken it has to be taken apart and each piece mended separately before it can be put back together and made whole again. It is like that my little one.
Ok. So?
My little one each of you has or will spend time with my servant as you have been revealed for the persons that you are. First there was Jennifer my little one who is beautiful and precious in her own right and then Aj was revealed, that was name given to the dolly that was seen at first.
And she was... kind of all of us together because... I know I saw me in her... I am not sure about dolly 4 and 5...maybe I was... I knew they were there... we seemed younger at first.
Yes my little one you did because the person that was first discovered and named Aj was a tangle of all of you together. I have been working to separate you my little one so that each of you can be seen for who you are and receive the healing that I have for you.
Like the broken thing that has to be taken apart and fixed.
Yes my little one.
And that is what you are doing, and we will be put back together again.
Yes. When each of you is sufficiently healed, I will put you back together again and you will not be dollies anymore but one whole person, complete in me.
But... why don't I have to go away Jesus?
Because my little one when each dolly is restored it is you that they will be given back to. It is you that will remain my little one though you will not be as you are now. You will be stronger my little one and much more able than you are now.
So you are working on each dolly and when they are fixed enough you will put them back.
Yes my little one.

When it came time to write about these things I wanted to understand better what Jesus had been doing all that time ago when he was healing Jennifer because now I understood that it wasn't really her that was needing healing from the past stuff it was me and the other dollies. Back then it seemed like Jennifer was the one that Jesus was healing. He was healing the other alters of course at other times, but these times seemed like they were to just to heal Jennifer. We didn't know about me or the other dollies then because we were still hidden away. So I asked Jesus to help me understand what he had been doing.

I have questions about the past and about Jennifer... things I don't quite understand... it is still a bit jumbled up for me.

My little one even though Jennifer was the one on the outside, the one who was seen and known you were not hidden from me. You were always the one that I was healing my little one. Jennifer was strong enough to carry you through for me, so that I could begin healing you and separating you from her. I know my little one that this does not seem fair to you that I should have asked her to carry so much but that was my purpose for her my little one. She bore her burden well and did not regret anything that I asked of her.

So all those times Jennifer spent in your arms being healed... it was me that you were healing and not her.

You were the one that was hurting my little one. I brought healing to Jennifer in all the ways that she needed but the healing of the past was for you my little one and though it seemed to you both that I was healing her my healing was being given through her to you.

Why did she have to go through all that pain Jesus?

Because you needed her to be there my little one. You were not strong enough on your own.

Like scaffolding.

Yes my little one like a support that enabled you to receive my love and my healing. My dearest one the things that hurt you left wounds so deep that if I had separated you before bringing a measure of healing you would not have survived.

But I suppose I thought I didn't get hurt so much because Jennifer... others maybe like Aj... were like a shield.

No my little one that is only true in part. The alters that surrounded you and kept you safe were entwined within you, supporting you and giving you enough strength to survive. There was shielding my little that came from being inside, hidden away, but the alters themselves were like an internal support. Without them you would not have lived my little one even hidden away as you were.

So... they were a bit like life support.

Yes my little one.

And... you healed me through them so that you could slowly take them away and I could be without them and not die.

Yes my little one that is so.

That is a bit different to what I thought.

It is not so different my little one. They helped you to survive. That was their purpose my little one.

It makes a bit more sense now Jesus. Thankyou.

You are welcome my little one.

I was very worried that when I was blended with Jennifer and Aj I would get old and boring and that would be the me that I saw. I liked to do silly dancing and have fun, but I thought maybe I wouldn't want to do that anymore. I wanted to be a child and do all the things that children do to have fun. Jesus told me that I would still be eleven and the blendings wouldn't change that. That I would always be a child and my age wouldn't change even over time. As well as that I was very scared that just like Jennifer and just like Aj that it would one day be my turn to go away and not be seen or heard any more. That was very frightening. I didn't want to go away again and be forgotten like I was before, but Jesus said that I was the one who would stay. That dolly 3 was the one all the other alters would be blended into and that wouldn't change who I was, I would be more of who I was and not less. It was hard to understand but like everything else I had to trust him.

Jesus told me that dolly 4 was the part that carried the memories of what had happened and that I, dolly 3, carried the pain of it. He said that letting dolly 4 tell her story would bring the memories and the feelings back together again. He said I needed to accept the memories as mine and that would bring healing to us both.

> *He says that as dolly 4 tells her story and I accept it as mine she won't be needed any more so she can be part of me again. It is hard to accept her story as mine Mr. Mike, but Jesus says he is helping me. He says she needs to tell her story in pictures as well as in words so there will be some drawings :(. I asked about all the memories we had before, like all the ones Jennifer told you about. He said that mostly they came from others but that dolly 4 needs to tell her story, so in a way that doesn't make a difference that we already remembered all that stuff. He said it is a bit like unpacking her boxes and giving what's in them to me. He said it won't all be healed it is more about bringing the parts of me, the dollies, back together. He said that is what this time is for, to bring the dollies back together and the blending with Jennifer... those things are what he is doing mostly. I know he is doing other stuff too but that is the main thing. It is hard to want to dolly 4's stuff but I suppose it is my stuff really and she has just been keeping it for me until I could take it back. Jesus must think I am ready to take it back now mustn't he. I know it is all healing and it is the way forward that Jesus has for me so I will keep hold of his hand and do as he is asking me.*

I was getting stronger and spending more of my own time with Jesus and Mike (aka Lamby). Aj and dolly 1 were on the outside and the blending with Jennifer was continuing. Now it was time to meet dolly 4.

As Jesus separated the dollies and began healing us separately the enemy began their attacks. They seemed to choose dolly 4 who carried the bad memories probably because she didn't know Jesus yet and didn't know how to call out to him for help. It was a hard time for me too because we were so connected. I had a lot of bad dreams and memories coming to the surface. I felt afraid and overwhelmed by all the changes that were happening and now the attacks of the enemy.

> **My little one I am enough for you. Even in this. My dearest one there is nothing they can do to harm you. You are mine. You belong to me. My dearest one no matter what they did or what lies they are telling you you belong to me.**
> Crying.... Crying....
> **My little one you know that you carry the memories of all that was done to you.**
> Crying... That part of me. The dolly number four part... Crying...
> **Yes my little one. That is the part of you that they are attacking. I know that it is hard for you to understand my little one for your awareness of her is limited for the most part but my little one she is part of who you are and the memories that she carries are your memories my little one.**
> Crying...
> **I know my little one that this is hard for you but it will help you to understand a little of what is happening. My dearest one the enemy will stir up the memories and the fear that are associated with this time. They will do this to try and reassert their claim over you. To convince you that you are theirs and to cause you pain and distress and ultimately, they will try to destroy you with it but my dearest one I am with you. I am holding you and I will not let them have you. No matter what lies in the past you belong to me my little one and no matter what memories they stir up or what lies they torment you with I will hold you and see you through this time my little one. I am with you. I will not let you go.**
> But… can't… Please keep me safe... Crying.... I feel so afraid... Crying...
> **I know my little one, but I am your safety and protection. Trust in me my little one. I am all that you need.**
> Crying... Crying...
> **My little one as you accept the things that were done to you, I can bring healing and**

freedom. There is nothing to fear my little one. I am with you.

It feels like… a tug of war.

Yes my little one that is what it is but I have already won you my little one. They cannot have you no matter how much they try to convince you otherwise they cannot have you.

Crying... I need you Jesus.

I know my little one. I am here. I will not leave you.

I don't know what to do.

Hold on to me my little one trust me. That is all that you must do.

I don't want to see… Crying... I don't want to see... Crying...

I know my little one I know. I am here. I will not let you go.

Crying... Please make it stop... Crying...

Yes my little one I will. In time it will stop my little one for it is my great desire to bring you complete healing and freedom, but it will take time my little one. Hold on to me. I am your strength and your comfort. I will keep you safe my little one.

Why now Jesus?

It is the beginning of Easter week my little one. There is a great deal you have yet to understand about this my dearest one but there is no greater time for the work of the enemy to be seen in your life and those like you.

Crying...

My dearest one I am holding you. I will keep you safe.

Crying... I hope so Jesus. I'm not feeling very safe... Crying...

My little one as this week continues you will see that I will keep you safe from everything that the enemy tries to bring against you. I am enough for you my little one. In everything.

Crying... You always are Jesus.

Yes my little one and I always will be. Do not be afraid my little one. I am here. My little one I will help you through this time and I will work through it bring you further healing. I know my little one that you do not want to see or experience the things of the past, but I will help you my little one.

Crying... I don't want to Jesus. The present is enough for me.... I can't manage the past as well.... Crying...

I know my little one, but I am here with you. I will help you.

Crying... Jesus.

I am here my little one.

Sometimes I forget about all this stuff.

I know you do my little one.

The part of me... the one that has the memories and the fear... Crying...

My little one she is part of you. I cannot make her go away.

But... I don't want those things.

I know my little one but accepting this part of you will bring you healing. I will not ask you to do it all at once my little one. A little at a time that is all that you must do.

But... the enemy...

I will use everything that the enemy does to bring you healing and freedom my little one, all you must do is hold on to me.

Like you did on the birthday.

Yes my little one like that.

Crying... But I am afraid there is too much. There is too much... Crying...

I am with you my little one I will help you and give you all that you need.

But... Crying... I don't want to... Crying...

My little one do you trust me to keep you safe even in the darkest of places.

Crying... You always have Jesus... Crying... But I don't want to... Crying...

I know my little one, but will you follow where I lead.

Crying... But it is the enemy doing this.
Yes my little one it is but I am with you and I will use it all to bring you healing and life. Will you follow me my little one?
Crying... Why do I always have to choose? Crying... I don't want to. Crying... I am afraid ... Crying...
Do you trust me my little one?
Crying... Yes Jesus... Crying...
Then do not be afraid my little one. Take my hand and follow wherever I lead. I will keep you safe my little one.
Crying... I would like it if you picked me up and carried me Jesus. That will be better.
I can do that my little one if you are willing.
Yes. Ok. Crying... Hold me tight Jesus... Crying... Hold me very tight…
Yes my little one I am holding you very tight. I will not let you go.
Crying...
You are safe in my arms of love my little one. There is nothing to fear. Nothing that the enemy will do that I am not in control of, nothing that he can bring against you that I am not greater than. Hold on to me my little one. I am all that you need.
Crying...
My dearest one I will not ever leave you. All that you are is safe in my arms of love. Each part of you is held safe and secure my little one. I will not ever let you go.
Is this part of bringing me back together?
Yes my little one it is.
I don't like it.
I know my little one.
I am not liking very much of this journey Jesus.
My little one you travel with me. Keep your eyes fixed upon me and upon who I am. I will hold you safe and bring you through this time. There is light and life waiting for you my little one.
I hope so Jesus. I didn't see this coming.
I know my little one, but I am with you. Your hope is in me my little one. I will not fail you.

Aj was doing ok on the outside most of the time but I suppose it was all getting mixed up with all of the dollies. Most of the time we coped with outside life because we had already let go of so much of it. Most of our days were spent at home doing chores and other things that I thought were really dull and boring, but it was enough for us I suppose. When we got stressed, we didn't always cope very well.

There was a problem with the smoke alarm the other night and it was beeping and beeping and I couldn't make it stop and I didn't know what to do. It is connected to the mains but even turning the electric off didn't help. I took it apart and tried to pull out the wire bits even though I think that was dangerous. I was upset and crying, and I didn't care if I died. Somehow, I wanted to die so I did dangerous things. There was a lot of angry thoughts and swearing stuff going on in my head and that upset me too. I don't know if it was me or someone else or the enemy. I don't know Mr. Mike but it took me a lot to control it and not let it out. Richard was trying to help but he didn't know what to do and I couldn't be all angry and upset. So I don't know what was happening but it upset me that I reacted like that, wanting to die and hurt myself and all of the swearing stuff. Is that me, I don't know. Anyway, I did a lot of praying and maybe Jesus fixed it because it stopped and has been fine since. So I am ok until something like that happens and then I feel all alone and don't know what to do and it is bad. Apart from that things are ok. I am still waiting to hear about the money I applied for. I should have heard by now, so I am a bit worried about that. I haven't paid the rent. So that isn't good, but I expect it will work out. I have been reminding myself that I have a daddy who loves me and that I am in this pickle because Jesus wants me on the outside and he made it happen, so he is going to look after me isn't he. I hope he is because I need looking after Mr. Mike.

Jesus helped me to understand what was happening which helped a lot. He talked to me a lot about the healing that he was doing and what he was asking of me. I knew he wanted me to accept dolly 4's memories as mine and I knew that the memories that were being stirred up were ones that came from her. He showed us the locket a lot of times to help us understand what was happening.

In the worship time I was in Jesus arms and we were dancing. I like that very much Mr. Mike. I love to be with him. I saw something I thought was strange. I saw the locket round his neck and the top and middle layer were still merging like I saw last time, that is dolly 2 and dolly 3 (me) but the bottom layer, dolly4, looked more separate than it was before, I could see a gap between that layer and the middle one. I thought that was strange, so I asked Jesus and he told me he was repositioning her? Maybe her I don't know but kind of like he had separated us so he could put her into a better position ready for putting us back together. I still thought that was strange but that's what I thought he said.

He asked me to allow him to take my suffering so I said I would. I knew this was about dolly 4. Then he took the locket between his finger and thumb and pressed the bottom layer into place with a clicking noise so that the bottom layer and the middle one doesn't have a gap between them anymore. They aren't merging yet though. That must mean something important happened mustn't it Mr. Mike, like dolly 4 is in position ready to be merged with me? That is a bit scary, but I know Jesus is in control, so I don't feel too afraid.

My thoughts and feelings were getting mixed up with dolly 4's too which made it a bit more confusing for me. It made me feel even younger than I already did. I didn't mind that so much, but it made me a bit confused again about who I was. Dolly 4 felt a lot of shame and like she was bad and dirty, so I felt those things too.

Lamby is so cute I can't look at her without smiling. And you were kind Mr. Mike. I am sorry I cried when you had to go. I had to be very brave and hold on to Jesus. I didn't like that you had to go. I talked with Jesus and daddy this morning and I cried a bit Mr. Mike. I think most I cried because I feel like I am so horrible, but they still love me anyway. Daddy said I was clean and white like snow and I know that is true for them but for me I feel like the middle of a rubbish dump. But it is so good that I am loved even when I feel like that and I think I do know that I am loved Mr. Mike.

Jesus said I needed to help dolly 4 tell her story by letting her write and draw so I did even though it was hard because I didn't want to see or know the things she remembered. Some of them I knew about, some of them were new to me but they were all horrible. I needed all Jesus help to trust him to hold me so I could be strong enough to let dolly 4 share her memories with me. Jesus wanted me to help dolly 4 trust him and get to know him like I did so that he could help her and heal her and protect her from the enemy.

Jesus says dolly 4 knows who he is and that he is there, but she doesn't trust him or know his love like I do because of all the stuff she is holding that gets in the way... like all the fear and stuff. I asked if when I take back all that stuff, I would lose my trust in him, but he said I wouldn't lose the ground I've gained. He said I am strong enough. I felt like I was getting lost in all that pain and fear, but Jesus was holding on to me. What scares me most is knowing that it is mine Mr. Mike. Those things happened to me and all those feelings are my feelings. Jesus says all I have to do is one day at a time and keep following but it does feel a bit like I might disappear down a black hole. Would you help me if I did? I still don't know. If I get scared of you again, please don't be angry I will try very hard to keep on trusting you like Jesus says. I keep crying all the time Mr. Mike. He said that I am already connected to dolly 4. I got the feeling it is kind of like I am connected in a lot of places ... and Jesus said once I can accept that these things are mine and take them back then the walls between us will dissolve and we will become one again. He said it had to be the right memories and things to do this the best way but that he is in control and knows how to do it best. He said that everything wouldn't be healed but that there was healing in the process. So then I asked him how I would be when I had all dolly 4's stuff, when it is mine again, and wouldn't it mean that I would be very vulnerable… something like that and that I would maybe have flashbacks and things and be triggered a lot more. He said yes it did mean that, but I would be much stronger when the dollies were back together, and I am blended with Jennifer so it's not like I would become like dolly 4 is now. And he is my strength he said, and he would help me, and it doesn't really matter if I think I can't do things because it is just the same as now. I have to rely on him. I asked him why it had to be now, and he

said it couldn't be before because I had to be strong enough and I had to trust him enough and you too Mr. Mike. He said that the dolly blending had to happen before the blending with Jennifer is finished so that she can blend with one whole me. That is maybe why it has seemed long Mr. Mike, because it has to be done in that order. So, I am understanding better I think, and I am a bit relieved that I don't have to go through all the memories, not now anyway, just enough for the blending to happen. Maybe it won't take so long Mr. Mike.

Up until now I hadn't really met dolly 4. I had seen her memories and felt how she felt, and she had done some writing through me, but I didn't see her up until now. Mostly I felt scared because of the memories and the things the enemy was doing. But when I did see her it helped a lot.

I saw that she is like me. She is a little girl who is hurting, and she needs help. And I am the one who has to help her Mr. Mike. I am the one who can help her get the hurt out of her heart. That is what I saw. It made me cry to see that, but it helps because now I am doing it for her as well as for me. When Jesus said it was time to do some drawing later, I was helping her by asking little questions and not running away, letting her tell. It hurt so much, and I had to hold on to Jesus, but I did better. It was the picture of me laid out on the ground with my hands and feet tied to wood stuck in the ground and the goat. This is what I wrote Mr. Mike. It is hard to tell.

They put a goat on us. They made it lick they held its thingy and put it in us. They squeezed its parts and it did go in us. They took a knife and cut its throat, so it was dead. They put its blood in a cup and they drank it.

We are by the lake. It is for drowning. It is the white people with the big man. He hurts us a lot. They poured the blood down our belly and in our legs. Then they do it with us. All of them. They take off their robes and wash in the lake. They leave me there. I don't know what they do. Grandad washes me in the lake.

There was a lot of crying Mr. Mike and a lot of gaps where I was holding on to Jesus. I asked questions to help her talk but it was very bad. I saw it Mr. Mike, this time I saw it. And I hurt inside like cramps, it lasted for a while. I don't know what else to say Mr. Mike. Jesus says I am washed pure and clean, but I think I would have been better dead.

After writing to Mike for a little while dolly 4 came out to talk with him in our chat time. It was a big fight for her to get to the outside and I had to ask Jesus to help. Dolly 4 had a much better idea of what was going on than I did.

Hello Mr. Mike and Lamby, it is dolly 4. It is strange to be writing to you and I don't know what I am going to say. Hello. I liked talking to you yesterday. You were kind and said nice things. Did you mean them Mr. Mike? Maybe you did because I don't think you tell lies like some people, but I am not knowing how you can love me or think nice things about me when I am so bad. Nobody ever loved me Mr. Mike. When I was coming out and the bad ones were trying to stop me, I thought of asking Jesus to help me, but I didn't know if I could but dolly 3 asked him for me so now I know that is what to do. Um. I am supposed to tell you about bad things I remember. I remembered a bad thing. It was when we were very small. I am going to say we were three. That might be right. I didn't know where it was, I didn't see proper, but it was the vicar man. His name was father T and he was very bad, I think. Why was he bad Mr. Mike if, he was working for Jesus? I don't understand. Why does Jesus let bad people work for him? Or maybe he wasn't bad, and it was me and I was the bad one. I don't know but I didn't like it what he did. He did a lot of things, but this one I remembered was when we were very little.

We had no clothes on Mr. Mike. I like having my clothes on and I don't ever want to take them off. Clothes are good and bare is bad. He stood us on the bed I think and got us to take off his belt. It was a very thin leather one round his middle and you had to pull hard to make it open. He had this long black thing on with buttons all the way down and he made us undo all of them. That is hard Mr. Mike when you are so little, but he made us do it. He liked it. So, then we had to help him take it off. I don't think we did very well because he was so big, and we were so little. um... This is the bad bit. He had on his vest and pants and he put our hands down his pants. We didn't like that. And then he got us off the bed and stood us on the floor and he knelt down in front of us. So, then we had to put our hands on his thing and move them up and down until it was sick. It is a bad thing to do Mr. Mike. I think so but he said it was to get the bad out of him and we were helping, and we were a good girl to do it. Then he said he had to get the bad out of us. So, he laid us down and touched us Mr. Mike till we did that thing. He said we was a good girl. I don't understand. Barbara said we was a bad dirty girl, but he said we was good for doing those things. I don't want to be good if you have to do that Mr. Mike. Anyway, so now I am going to draw. Dolly 3 will send it to you I expect. I would like to leave some little kisses for your Lamby. Here they are xxxxxxx bye bye Mr. Mike. From dolly 4

She was learning about who Jesus was through all the things that were happening, and she had found her own voice for the first time. Even though it was very hard at times it was easy to see that Jesus was doing exactly what he said. Aj was looking after us both of course because she was still the one on the outside most of the time. She bought some coloring books and children's DVD's mostly for dolly 4 I think but I liked them too. I felt much closer to dolly 4 than I did to dolly 2. We seemed kind of the same even though she was much younger than me. Aj seemed a lot more grown up than me and didn't seem to hurt or get scared like I did. We would talk to each other about things like how Jesus was healing us together. But I was getting scared and I think the enemy was telling me lies too and that was all getting mixed up with dolly 4's stuff too.

I am not doing very good today. I am having trouble with things that I don't understand and feeling confused and scared. I am scared that now dolly 4 is here I will have to away and you won't talk to me again. I have been crying and crying because I think it will be like dolly

2. She doesn't talk to you or write to you anymore Mr. Mike and I don't know why. I don't understand and I didn't think about it before because I didn't see that we were different, but we are so why did she stop and go away and not write or talk any more. I don't want to go away. I don't know who Aj is or even if she is any of us. I am confused and I know it maybe doesn't matter but somehow it does. I am crying and crying, and I feel like I lost myself all over again and that you will not be my friend anymore and I will have to go away. I don't understand who I am Mr. Mike. I have been talking with Jesus, but I am not really trusting what I hear because I feel like I get everything wrong. And I feel like I am bad and selfish because it is supposed to be about dolly 4 and not me and I should go away, but I don't want to. I don't want to go away and you forget about me. I don't understand why that happened with dolly 2. And now it is my turn. I can't talk no more.

Dolly 4 thought she was bad because of how scared I was, and she wanted to make it better for me. We were both trying to help each other as best we could.

Hello Mr. Mike, it is dolly 4. It has been bad here and dolly 3 has been crying and crying. It is my fault Mr. Mike because I came out. I don't want dolly 3 to go away. She loves you Mr. Mike I don't want her to go away. I am coming out because Jesus says I need to get the hurting out of my heart and I can do that by writing and talking to you. He says that is good for dolly 3 too and he doesn't want her to go away so I hope you can fit us both in Mr. Mike because I don't want dolly 3 to be sad because of me. I am a bad girl Mr. Mike because of what I did but I don't want to be bad any more or make anyone sad. Do you know what I did Mr. Mike.? I have hurt people. They gave me a knife and made me hurt them. I didn't want to Mr. Mike. I am a very bad girl. I don't want to tell you how bad I am. I don't remember anything today, but I know that I am bad because of what I did. I am not telling until I remember because I don't want to. I would like stop being bad. Maybe when I give all the bad things to Jesus, he will take them, and I won't be bad anymore. Maybe it is me that should be going away Mr. Mike. Dolly 3 is a good girl, I think. She didn't do anything bad it was all me. I am the bad one. When they put me in the hole with the worms and I cried and cried they made me eat one Mr. Mike. I had to eat it and it made me sick and then they hurt me Mr. Mike. Being sick is bad and crying is bad and doing the thing with men is bad and the things with women is bad and hurting people is bad and I did it all and I am bad bad bad. I don't think you will want to be my friend when you know all these bad things but I am telling you now so I will go away if you want me to. I will go away and hide and not be seen no more not never. Dolly 4 is the bad one not dolly 3. You keep dolly 3 and I will go away. I don't want to go away. I don't want to be bad. Can you make me not bad Mr. Mike? Maybe Lamby cuddles will help me not be bad. I never had no cuddles. I think they might be good. Maybe I am too bad for cuddles and that is why.

The enemy kept up their attacks. Sometimes it was hard to know which one of us they were attacking but maybe it was both. The closer we got I suppose the easier it was to attack us both at the same time.

Hello Mr. Mike. I wish you was here. There is nobody here and we are all alone. We are always alone Mr. Mike and it makes us sad. There aren't any friends for me and dolly 3. We are not good girls to have friends maybe. We just had a bad thing happen Mr. Mike it was the bad ones, I think. I could see them hurting dolly 3 but I couldn't move or speak and then I was in the lake and they were holding me under Mr. Mike, and I couldn't breathe. I couldn't breathe and they made me stay under the water and when I came up they pushed me down again over and over until I didn't want to breathe no more Mr. Mike I just wanted to die and then when I wanted to die they made me live all over again.

It isn't fair Mr. Mike. Why can't we die and be in heaven and not have to keep on being drowned. I don't know what it is that is happening. When it stopped, I didn't see dolly 3 no more I just saw Jesus. He was there Mr. Mike and he held me tight so I could breathe again. I think maybe he is the one who made me live when they were drowning me. I think he was because I remembered that I was being helped then just like I was now. It is the same Mr. Mike and I remembered it. I think he was the one who did it and I don't know why Mr. Mike. He says he loves me like you say it Mr. Mike but I don't understand what it means. What does it mean Mr. Mike? Does it mean that I have to keep on being alive even when I want to be dead? I don't know. Maybe it means holdings and cuddles and no hurting. Does it mean that Mr. Mike? That would be better, I think. I don't want to be drowned any more.

So then I -dolly 3- heard Jesus telling me to help her because she stopped talking for a long time. He said to tell her about love and I said I didn't really know about it.
Dolly4
Yes
Jesus says I should tell you a little bit about his love.
Ok. Do you know?
A little bit maybe dolly 4, but it is hard for me too... I think Jesus love is kindness and comfort. I think he cares for us and protects us. He is the shepherd and we are his lambs, did you know about that?
I don't know. Am I a lamby?
Yes. We are both lamby's that Jesus cares for. Like today when the bad ones made you remember. Jesus came and held you and made them go away. That is his love looking after you.
Oh. Did he know?
He knows everything about everything dolly 4. He knows everything that has happened and everything that will happen.
But does he think I am his lamby?
He made you his lamby. He chose you and said I want dolly 4 to be my lamby and his daddy who is the big daddy of everything said it was a good choice and gave you to Jesus to be his lamby.
And did the daddy think I was a good lamby for Jesus?
Yes. He did.
I think the daddy doesn't know nothing.
The daddy knows everything just like Jesus does. He knows everything about you dolly 4.
Oh. But I am a bad lamby.
But Jesus makes us good dolly 4. The love he gives us takes away the bad in our hearts and makes us good like him. We need to get full of his love and the fuller we are the more we get to be like him, and he is good good good.
So…when he loves me I get gooder?
I think you need to say to him that you want his love but yes it makes you gooder. I think so.
I want to be good not bad. I don't want to be bad anymore.
You need Jesus love then dolly 4 just like I do.
Yes please. Can I have some?
You ask him dolly 4. He has got lots and lots of love to give to you.
He does? What about you? Will he run out?
No he won't run out. He has enough love for the whole world. You ask him.
Ok I will. I want to be good.

Dolly 4 told us how it had been before we had started to get to know her, before I knew she was there. Jesus had been showing her the way even before then.

Hello Mr. Mike

I am writing to you again. It is a bit strange to be talking and sometimes I don't know what to say. I have been hiding Mr. Mike. All of the time I was hiding in a dark place but I don't know where it was and then there was a light and it hurt my eyes, but it stayed and I got used to it and there was a nice voice and it said kind things and I was scared, but nothing bad happened. And then the light got a bit more and more until I could see me, and I was not a nice thing Mr. Mike. I was all dirty. But then the light said it could make me clean. I didn't know it was Jesus in the light that was talking to me. I didn't know that for a long time. The voice said that I wasn't a dirty bad girl, I was a lovely girl who had got dirt on her but that he could wash it off for me.

I was scared Mr. Mike and I thought I would rather stay dirty than see underneath, because I thought the dirt might go right through me. But then I started to hear other things Mr. Mike and I think that was dolly 3 maybe. And she was talking to the light too. She cries a lot Mr. Mike. More than me. I don't cry a lot. But dolly 3 cried because she is sad, and Jesus is kind and looks after her. I heard it all Mr. Mike and so I thought maybe I might like to get clean even though I was scared about it. And then I started to see the outside things that I didn't see before and I found out about the life that the others are having. And I watched Mr. Mike and I listened. And sometimes I got scared, but mostly I just thought it was interesting. And the light stayed Mr. Mike it never went away. And sometimes it spoke to me and was kind. I have been talking back to the light Mr. Mike, I know it is Jesus I have been

talking to. I have told him I want to be clean and good and do you know what happened Mr. Mike? All my muck has been gone and I don't know where it went, and I got a clean white dress with little pink flowers and it is the most beautiful thing I ever saw and now I am not dirty anymore because Jesus did clean me, but I don't know if I am bad still maybe the bad and the dirt went together I am not sure. So I have been in the light now Mr. Mike and it is good there. Now I am clean I can go and when I am there it is all gold and I am all gold and shiny and Jesus is there, and he hugs me, and it is nice.

He told me all about his love like dolly 3 said and I thought it sounded very good and nice, so I said yes please Jesus, so he gave me some love and it was the pink flowers on my dress. They are to remind me about the love he gave me. They look like teeny weeny hearts and I love them. And Jesus said I am his now and not dirty no more and not bad no more and he will keep on giving me his love to make me more and more gooder like dolly 3 said. I am better now Mr. Mike and all the bad is gone that's what he is saying to me. I don't know where it went Mr. Mike maybe it went down the plug when I got washed. I don't know now what I am doing with all the bad things. I don't know if they are grown or not. Maybe they are not I don't know, I will ask Jesus because I forgot because of the light and the pink flowers he gave me. I have had a good time Mr. Mike. I am better but dolly3 is still so sad. I don't know why she get so sad if she has Jesus love, but I think maybe she is crying for other reasons I don't know. I hope you will hold her and hug her Mr. Mike. If you can because you are far away. I will come and talk with you if I can. I liked to talk with you. I will find out about the bad things. Bye from dolly 4.

She wrote some of her chats with Jesus down too as she was learning about him and who he was. He was helping her to understand about the blending and what it would mean for her too.

Hello Mr. Jesus, I am come to talk with you like dolly 3 does.
Hello my little one.
Jesus what is the only way to get to daddy?
I am the only way to daddy little one. Only I can take you to him.
What is daddy like? Dolly 3 says he is the big daddy over everything... ohh I sneezded.
Bless you my dearest one. Daddy is just like me. He is kind and loves you very much.
Oh. Why?
Because he is the one who thought of you little one. He is the one who thought of every good thing that there ever was.
What about you Mr. Jesus did you think of anything?
My thoughts and daddy's thoughts are the same little one. We thought of you together.
But I am not a good thing to think of Mr. Jesus. I am just a little thing.
You are very precious little one even if you are small and you were a very good thing for us to think of.
I liked those stories they were funny Jesus when I am better can I come out and play?
You can come out and play now little one as it is safe for you to do so.
How will I know if it is or not?
You must ask me little one. I will always tell you the truth about everything.
No more lies Mr. Jesus.
I did not ever lie to you my little one.
I don't know Mr. Jesus sometimes I think maybe you did when you said that I was yours and I was good. I don't know if that can be true.
It is true my little one. Me and daddy thought of you together. You were our idea little one and it was a very good idea. You belong to us and now you have said that want to be ours we can make you as good as good can be. That is because our love fills you up and makes you like us and we are very very good.
So I am good?
Yes little one you are.
Oh. No more lies Mr. Jesus I don't like them.
I don't like them either little one. They hurt people and I never like it when people are hurt.
Because you love them.
Yes little one because I love them.
Can I talk to daddy?
Yes little one you can.
What would I say?
Anything that you want. What would you like to say to him little one?
I don't know. I don't know about daddys and what to say to them. I only know about the bad men who said they were daddies, but they were lying wasn't they Mr. Jesus.
Yes little one they were. My daddy and your daddy are not like those men. He will never hurt you little one. He is kind and gentle and loves you very much.
Will he hold me?
Yes little one he will.
I don't know bout that Mr. Jesus... I got a new dress and everything. I like it. Did you make it Jesus?
Yes little one I did.
Thankyou. I like it very much. And did you make the flowers on it Mr. Jesus?
Yes little one they were made especially for you.
I don't know but I think they are growing Mr. Jesus but how can they be?
The flowers are my love for you my little one. They grow as you accept more of my love.
Oh so when I am full I will be covered in flowers?

Yes little one you will.
But Jesus if I am going to be made a big blob with dolly 3 I won't have a dress anymore.
Little one when you are a little bit better than you are now and you are able to be a part of who dolly 3 is you will be a little girl just as you are now and you will have a pretty dress with pink flowers little one.
But... won't I have to share dolly 3s dress?
Yes little one but it will also be your dress. You will share it together because you will be one little girl again.
And will it have pink flowers on?
Yes little one it will.
But dolly 3 doesn't have pink flowers Mr. Jesus. I seed her dress and it has white flowers with yellow middles.
But when you are one again and you share a dress it will have both kinds of flowers on it little one.
That will be a pretty dress Mr. Jesus. I will like that.
Yes my little one I know that you will.
Mr. Jesus when I am in the dolly 3 dress will I be yours?
Yes little one just as you are now.
And will you love me more?
No little one I cannot love you any more than I do now.
Why Jesus because I think dolly 3 is nicer than me so if I am in with her won't you like me better?
No little one I love you both just the same amount. I love you both with all the love that I am. I cannot give you any more than that little one.
Is it a lot Jesus?
Yes little one it is a very lot.
Oh. That is good. When I am in the dress with dolly three how many legs will I have?
Just two little one.
One each.
You will share in one body little one you will have two legs just as you do now.
And two arms.
Yes little one just the same.
Oh. And will it be good?
Yes little one it will be very good.
What about all of the bad things in my heart and in my brain, Jesus are you making them go?
I am taking them from you little one. As you remember and tell your story I take them from you, and they aren't there any more to hurt you.
Like bubbles coming up and you take the bubbles.
Yes little one like that.
What do you do with them Mr. Jesus?
I take all the pain and all the tears my little one and I use it for great good. I take all the bad and the evil and I destroy it so it can never be seen again.
Oh. Jesus... Mr. Jesus.
Jesus is enough my little one.
But we call Mr. Mike a Mr.?
But you do not need to little one.
Oh. What can we call him?
Why don't you ask him little one? Ask him what he would like you to call him.
Ok. When I am in the dress with dolly 3 will I be having a name properly with her Jesus.
Yes little one you will have your own name.
But we share it.
Yes little one you will be one little girl with one name.

Ok Jesus. Will I be liking the name? Is it like a present?
Yes little one your name will be a gift to you and to many. You will like it very much.
It is sounding good Jesus. When can I go and get in the dress?
When you are a little better than you are now.
I am getting better Jesus.
Yes little one you are.
You are making me betterer so I can be in the dress with dolly3 so then we can have a name and it will be good.
Yes little one I am.
I think dolly 3 is very sad Jesus.
Yes little one she is but I will help her just as I am helping you.
Does she need to get better as well Jesus. Is she a poorly girl?
She is not poorly little one, but she carries a lot of grief and hurt which cause her to lose hope even when she sees my promises to her which are good.
What did you promise her Jesus?
I promised her a good life little one where she can be the person, I made her to be.
And will she be happy?
Yes little one for the most part she will be very happy.
And I will be happy too because I will be part of her? Is that right Jesus?
Yes little one it is.
But why is she so sad Jesus. I got lots of bad things, but I don't feel so sad like she does.
Little one the things that happened to you were very bad and they happened to you and to dolly 3 just the same. She does not remember them as you do but she carries the pain of them little one.
So I got the pictures and she got the hurt.
Something like that little one though you were also hurt by the things that happened.
But I didn't get so sad.
No little one you didn't.
So... Her sad need to get better and my pictures need to go bye bye?
Yes little one.
And then we can be in the dress and have the name and be happy.
Yes little one you can.
That will be better Jesus. I would like that very much. Can we do it now?
We are doing it now little one. It cannot happen all at once for that would hurt both of you too much, but I am helping you and I will take all of the pain and sadness and the bad pictures from your brain and then you will be ready.
Will you take it all Jesus?
Yes little one I will. You will still be aware of the things that happened little one, but it will not be as it is now and dolly three will be sad from time to time but she will not carry the pain and despair that she does now.
Ok Jesus. I am a bit tired now and that was a big talk. I want to have drink please and maybe something to eat if dolly 2 will let us.
Dolly 2 is trying to help all of you in the best way she knows little one.
I think she does it good Jesus. We are doing ok and you are helping us too.
Yes little one I am.
When I talk to Mr. Mike will you help me say the bad things to him Jesus.
Yes little one I will help you tell your story to him.
Ok Jesus. I am going to say bye, now but I like your light Jesus and it doesn't go.
No little one I don't ever leave you.
I think maybe I love you Jesus and you are my bestest friend and then it is dolly three and then it is Mr. Mike and his Lamby. I have friends Jesus.
Yes little one you do.
Ok. Bye.

Little one I will still be here.
Ok but I am stopping writing now.

As dolly 4 got stronger Jesus started healing us together. We would both sit on his lap and hold hands with each other, and I would see the things that she was remembering. Jesus would hold us both tight and comfort us. We were getting closer each time we did this, I think.

Hello Mr. Mike
I haven't really been out much since I talked with you. Dolly2 talked with Ester. She told her about me and dolly 4 and that was ok, but I didn't want to go out and talk with anyone. I am feeling too sad and I don't want to find out my friends are not my friends anymore. It is better to stay on the inside. Yesterday I was hurting so much Mr. Mike. I did spend some time with Jesus, and he did something I think. I was sat on his knee on one side and dolly 4 was sat one the other side. He had his arms round us. Me and dolly 4 held hands and I was remembering something very bad. It wasn't anything with people or places in it except for grandad. He was touching me and doing it to me and that is what it was. I was crying and crying and saying he is hurting me over and over. Jesus held me tight Mr. Mike. It hurt a lot. I saw dolly4 in her dress. She is very cute with curly blonde hair just like in her picture. When I think about her it is like I think we are twins and I feel like we are very the same Mr. Mike. Not like with dolly2... she seems a lot more like Jennifer and not very much like us because she is older. It is nice to have someone like me but then I get sad and I think when we are blended, she will be gone again, like Jennifer. I keep losing people Mr. Mike. That is how it feels to me. So I just get sad about it all and even though I see that Jesus is doing things and healing us it is making me feel so sad because of losing things over and over. Dolly two stayed with Cheryl last night and spent the day with her. She didn't say anything about dolly 4 or me. I am very tired, and I don't want to think about it anymore. Night night Mr. Mike. Love from dolly 3.

I was very sad a lot of the time. Losing things over and over was hard and it made me lose hope. Jesus was doing good things, but I felt sad about my life even so. I did like dolly 4 very much though. She made me smile and it was nice not to feel so alone.

Hellooooo Mr. Mike
Do you know what Jesus has been telling me about? He has been telling me about his big throne in the sky and how he is in charge of everything and how his daddy has made him boss of all the world Mr. Mike did you know that. That is a lot to be bossing. I don't want to be bossing anything except maybe my rabbits. I think they don't mind though. I have my dress Mr. Mike and that is very good, and I have flowers in my hair too now. They are like the ones on dolly3s dress. They are pretty. I would like to show you sometime Mr. Mike but I don't think you can see them from America. Do you have flowers there? I think it is a big place to be with lots of things I never seen before. When I am in dolly3s dress I will come and see all the things and it will be good. Jesus, he told me that I am a big girl cos I am five. Did you know Mr. Mike? That means that I can be a big girl and do things for Jesus when he asks me to like now, he said he wants me write to you about all the things in my heart, so I do it Mr. Mike. Sometimes I don't know all the things in my heart till I write to you and then they come out and I see them. Mr. Mike some things in my heart are bad but Jesus takes them away when I find them. He says I don't need them anymore and then he puts good things in to fill up the holes because it is bad to have holes in your heart Mr. Mike. I am saying goodbye to the bad things and I am saying hello to the good things and it feels weird but not too bad. I am thinking about when I come and be in dolly3s dress and Jesus will be with us too. I hope I can bring my rabbits. Will you have room for them Mr. Mike they are very little, and I can hold them in my hands if you like. They are very good rabbits cos I look after them good. Will you look after me good Mr. Mike and keep me safe and be kind

to me. I think maybe Jesus is giving me to you so you can be kind and so I can help with the work. I can do some things Mr. Mike see I can write and talk and show my rabbits to people and maybe I can cuddle them too... the people I mean if they would like that. I don't know cos I only ever cuddled with Jesus, but he says he will make my cuddles special and full of him so when I cuddle people it is like being cuddled by Jesus and that is good Mr. Mike. I am going to draw you a picture now. Bye bye from dolly4.

Dolly 4 was getting stronger and we were getting closer. Jesus healing was drawing all the dollies back together again so that we could be one dolly. We didn't know how long that would take. It had been a long time now since the blending with Jennifer had started and that wasn't finished yet so we thought it might be a long time before there was only one dolly, me.

My little one you are my child and you belong to me. Everything that you are and will be is in my hands. I am making you into a servant for the kingdom my little one so that the darkness can be driven back by the light in the lives of many. Being a servant for the kingdom is a special thing my little one and there are not many who choose this path. Many are content simply to be my child and to wait for heaven to come to them but you my dearest one you will bring heaven to those who need it most for you carry it within you and I will enable you to give it away. My dearest one kingdom rule is my desire for the earth and its people, but it comes only as my children bring it. That is who you are and who I am making you to be my little one, a carrier of the kingdom, bringing heaven to the places that I send you. I know you do not fully understand this my little one but all that I am giving to you is to enable you to do this so that many will be drawn to me and be saved and healed and will come to know the kingdom for themselves.

Chapter 29

Together Again

    We were going to visit Ruth for a few days. She had moved a long way away, so we hadn't seen her since she left. She didn't know about the dollies or the blendings and thought it was Jennifer who was going to visit but it wasn't of course it was Aj. We didn't like it. It felt like a really bad thing to do to pretend with one of Jennifer's best friends but Jesus said it wasn't time to tell her about the blendings yet so we had to go and hope it would be ok. It was ok. It was scary for us, but Jesus helped us, and Ruth and her husband didn't seem to notice. I thought that was kind of sad. That Jennifer was gone and one of her closest friends didn't even notice but I was glad of it anyway. We knew now that Jennifer was gone now and that her blending with Aj was all the way finished.

    I think... the new dolly 2 is doing good Jesus.
Yes my little one she is. I have been healing her my little one just as I have been healing you. She is well able to do this my little one.
She does seem able Jesus.
Yes my little one so do not be afraid. The outside life is not so fearsome as you believe I am making all of you able my little one.
I think Jennifer is blended with dolly 2 now Jesus is that right?
Yes my little one it is.
And Jennifer on her own doesn't exist anymore..
Not as you would understand it my little one.
And she won't be on the outside anymore.
No my little one she won't for she is not needed any more.
And she is ok.
Yes my little one she is. Everything is good my little one.
I think... it is better Jesus.
Yes my little one it is much better.
Will it be better when we are all together Jesus?
Yes my little one it will be much better.
But...why me Jesus? I don't see how it can be me if I am going to stay eleven because... I need to be grown up if I am doing the outside life.
My little one you will be able to do everything that I will ask of you. There is not anything my little one that you will not be able to do with my help and with the help of those I am giving you to.
What do you mean Jesus?
My little one right now you are able because of all that dolly 2 is and what she is becoming because of the healing and the blending. I am making her able my little one. And when you are the one on the outside and all the other dollies are in you then you will be able my little one for, I will make you so. My dearest one there are many ways in which I can enable you. I can heal you and make you stronger. I can give you the courage and the skills and abilities you need, and I can also bless you with people who will enable and help you for you will not be able to do everything for yourself my little one. Right now, you live independently for the most part and you are able to do this because I am enabling dolly 2 but it will not always be necessary or desirable for you to live independently as you do now my little one. You will not need to do and be all that you believe you will. My dearest one my plans for you are many and they are good, but they do not include you living an independent adult life in the way that you do now. That is not my desire for you my little one. I will help you my little one when the time comes and give you all that you need so that you can live as the person, I have made you to be my little one. It will not be necessary for you to

do everything that you do now.
You mean us.
Yes my little one, the things that you can do together.
But if we get stronger and more with the blending... why will I be able to do less Jesus?
Not less my little one but different. The skills and abilities of the other alters will be given to you my little one but you will express them in different ways. My dearest one a child can have many strengths and abilities, many great giftings in different areas but they still remain a child my little one with the needs of a child.
I suppose Jesus but how...I still have, we still have to be grown up and not needing other people like that.
Yes my little one for now you do my dearest one my timing is perfect and as you are healed and blended I will give to you the life that you are able to live, where there are people to help you and care for you in the ways that you need.
Mostly I don't think that can happen Jesus.
I know my little one but remember all that I have promised you. It will come my little one.

It was hard for me to see that it could be me on the outside and it be ok, so I kept on asking Jesus about it. Sometimes I hoped it was a mistake and sometimes I hoped it meant that I would be going to America very soon because how could I live Jennifer's life? But then how could I leave. It was hard to find any answers that I liked.

While we were visiting with Ruth we went to a meeting. I suppose I knew that Jesus was going to do something, but I was still were surprised by what happened.

When we got to the meeting place in the evening, we started to feel the Holy Spirit straight away even before it started. When we were worshipping, I was on Jesus knee with dolly 4 and I knew what was going to happen. I cried Mr. Mike because it seemed sad to me, but Jesus held me and told it me was a good thing. Me and dolly 4 kind of hugged and it was like she melted into me and then it was just me on Jesus knee. He told me over and over that it was a good thing. I saw my dress Mr. Mike and it was like Jesus said. It is daisies and little pink rosebuds and it is very pretty, and I got blonde bits in my hair too. I know it is good, but it is kind of sad and I got surprised that it happened so fast and then I got worried I was making it up because how could it happen so fast. But even though I asked a lot Jesus always said it was true.

Who will I be Jesus?
You will be my child just as you are now. My dearest one none of these changes who you are. You were always the person that you are becoming for that is how you were created in the beginning my little one. I am restoring you and making you whole, but I am not changing who you are.
But you are changing who I know I am Jesus and the things I can do and be.
Yes my little one I am and because this is difficult at times you must hold on to me just as you have been doing. I will give you the strength and the security that you need. You will not get lost in this my little one. I am holding you tightly to me and I will not let you go.
Tell me about dolly 4 Jesus.
She Is now a part of who you are my little one. The healing was complete enough for this to happen and both of you were willing, that is all that was needed my little one.
It seemed very quick Jesus.
My dearest one I have been working in many ways that you have not seen. This was the completion of a work that was started long ago.
I suppose... you know Jesus.
Yes my little one I do.

Will I notice Jesus. Will I see her in me?

Yes my little one you will. All that she is has been given back to you. She is a part of who you are now my little one and that is good.

It seems sad Jesus. She was cute.

Yes my little one but she is not gone. All that she is, is now found in you. She is not lost my little one. Nothing is lost.

I kind of see it with Jennifer and dolly 2. I think I kind of understand Jesus, but I'm still worried I will be a grownup and because it's hard to see how I wouldn't be... they seem…bigger than me and like when we are blended I will be overwhelmed by them and disappear.

But that is not what I have said my little one. They are a part of who you are. You will not be overwhelmed or disappear my little one you will be strengthened and more able to be the person you were created to be. That does not mean that you will be older my little one.

I know… it is up to you who I am Jesus and I shouldn't worry about it because it will be better than I think.

Yes my little one it will be much better than you think. My dearest one everything that I am doing is to bring you life and hope and joy. There is nothing that is bad my little one. You will not be disappointed in who I have made you to be. I am not disappointed my little one.

It... seems wrong to…have me as the one who is left though Jesus.

But it is not my little one it is my will and desire that it should be so and that is never wrong my little one.

Jesus... I am always going to be weird.

You will always be special my little one but that is a good thing and not one to be feared. My dearest one acceptance from others will come but do not look for it my little one. Be who you are without fear and trust in me. I have made you who I want you to be my little one and to be anyone else would be wrong. That would be a sad thing my little one.

I think being who I am without fear is the hardest thing ever Jesus.

Yes my little one but I will help you and as you learn and grow and become more secure in who you truly are it will not be so hard as you believe. My dearest one who you are is found in me. You are safe and you are loved and there is nothing to fear from anything. My dearest one no-one can take you from me. You are safe in my arms of love and will always be so.

Help me remember that Jesus because I forget...I forget a lot of things.

Yes my little one but I will help you remember all that is needed.

Now the blending is done… does that mean memory healing is done?

For the moment my little one. There is yet more to be done my little one but that is sufficient for now.

So now Jennifer and Aj were blended and me and dolly 4 were blended. There was still dolly 5 but I hadn't met her yet. It didn't seem to be time. Jesus said I was blending with Aj still like I had seen in the locket and that was what was happening for now. I was still very worried about how I was going to be able to live Jennifer's life all by myself. I didn't think I could do it. I didn't want to do it. Things were changing though, and I was spending more and more time on the outside.

I am noticing that I am spending more time on the outside now. Sometimes I am out with Cheryl and she doesn't know, and I am out more with Ester and tonight I was out at home when I was watching the telly. Sometimes it is hard to know it is me, but I like to cuddle things like with my rabbits, so I know it is me when I need to be holding something like that. It seems ok but I don't really know how it can work with me on the outside all the time. I suppose it will be different when I am blended with dolly 2 like she is different now she is blended with Jennifer. I don't want to be grown up Mr. Mike but I have to trust that Jesus knows who I am, and it will be ok when it is done. I am doing good I think Mr. Mike and it seems different somehow, but I am not very sure why. It seems easier and better, like... skating instead of walking, or like when you have been carrying a heavy bag and then you put it down and you feel light. Something like that.

I suppose Jesus had been waiting until I was ready but then it at last it was time.

Today I was feeling bad, like I wanted to die. I didn't really know why because I have been doing so good and nothing bad has happened. I went into town with Cheryl, but I didn't have fun... well it was dolly 2 but anyway we didn't enjoy it. I love Cheryl very much, but she isn't very happy and sometimes when I am not ok it doesn't help too much to be around her. I/we knew she was wanting to come and spend the evening at our house because she was complaining about her flatmate and saying how awful it was going to be... but we just couldn't Mr. Mike. And then I felt like I am bad. I suppose when I don't do what people want me to I think that means I am bad. Maybe it does I don't know but we were not feeling good and we knew we couldn't, so we didn't. We came home and had a bath and I was feeling like I wanted to die, and I was kind of wondering and asking why because I didn't know. And it came to me that it was dolly 5 and not me at all. I didn't like that thought much Mr. Mike. So, I talked with Jesus, but I started to cry and cry. There was so much pain Mr. Mike. It was very bad.

Jesus
My little one I am here. I am here with you my little one and I will not ever leave you.
Crying... I don't know what the matter is with me today Jesus.... Crying... I cried and cried and all I could think was I don't want to be me.
My little one it is time to begin healing dolly 5.
Crying... But you made it sound like that was a long way off. Why do you do that Jesus? Things, bad things are always closer.

There was so much pain Mr. Mike I couldn't stop crying

Help me... Crying... Help me.... Crying...
My little one my arms are around you. You are safe and you are loved. My little one dolly 5 needs your help. I know my dearest one that this is hard for you but my little one when dolly 5 is healed and made one with you things will be much better for you. She needs my healing my little one will you help her?
Crying... I don't know how... Crying...
Hold on to me my little one. My dearest one do you see her?
Crying...

I did see her Mr. Mike. She is a very little girl with short blonde hair. I thought she looked about two. She was sitting on the floor in dirt. She was eating dirt and she looked so unhappy. Her face was wet with tears. I never saw anyone who looked so unhappy.

Crying... Yes... Crying...
My little one the pain you are feeling belongs to her. Hold on to me. I will give you my strength. Do you see her my little one?
Crying... Yes.
Speak to her my little one. Let her know that you are there.

I put the laptop down because I was crying too much and I crouched down in front of dolly 5 and I said hello to her. She looked at me and I took her in my arms and hugged her tight. There was so much pain Mr. Mike, even worse than before and it made me cry out and curl up in a little ball, but I didn't let go, I just kept on holding her. And Jesus was holding me and telling me it was ok, that he was my strength and I just needed to hold on to him. I was holding dolly 5 and Jesus was holding me. After a while the pain got less, and Jesus took dolly 5 from me and cradled her in his arms. She lay there sucking her thumb and looking up at him with big blue eyes. She looked better, she just looked into his eyes and she was quiet. He hugged me too and I cried a bit and it took me a while to recover but then we had a little chat.

Jesus
My little one the healing of dolly 5 will continue but it is begun my little one and it is good.
I wasn't expecting it Jesus.
I know my little one but my dearest one I will give you everything that you need. This is a good thing for you my little one and will help you in many ways.
I know Jesus.
My little one dolly 5 is in need of much love and much comfort. Most of all she needs to be held my little one, but she is safe in my arms. When it is time my little one, I will ask you to help her release some of the pain she holds but it is not yet time for that my little one.
Why do you need my help with that Jesus?
Because my little one it is your pain that she is holding. As she releases it you will experience it my little one, but I will be holding you my little one and I will take the pain from you even as you receive it.
Is it a bit like dolly 4's memories?
Yes my little one it is like that. Just as you had to accept dolly 4's memories as your own so you must accept dolly 5's pain.
Crying... Crying... Crying...
My little one I am your strength and I will help you through this. My dearest one.
Crying...
it is my great desire to bring healing to you. Do not be afraid to follow wherever I lead.
Crying...
My little one my plans for you are good. This is part of my great plan for you my little one not only to bring hope and healing to you but through you to many. I know my dearest one that the path seems strange to you, but I am holding you my little one and no matter where I lead you, you are safe and you are loved. I am always with you.
I thought we were doing something else Jesus. I thought it was about... serving you, doing things.
And so it is my little one but your healing is part of that. My dearest little one my will for you depends upon you being healed and whole in me. You cannot do all that I am calling you to do when you are still so broken my little one. I am healing your broken heart piece by piece and restoring it to you. I will do this many times as we travel together my little one and each time I do it will enable you to take another step forward in serving me. My dearest one my healing comes out of my great love for you and even were you to say no to my plans for you I would still desire to heal you my little one but my plans for you spring out of the healing that I am doing. They cannot be separated my little one.
Yes. Tell me about dolly 5 then Jesus. She looks about two to me.
She is a little younger than that my little one. She is able to speak only a very little and she has not yet found her voice. I will comfort and heal her my little one.
Maybe you can tell me more another time Jesus. When I feel better than I do now.
Yes my little one for it will help you to know a little more of who she is.
Does she have memories?
Yes my little one she does but mostly these are expressed in the way she feels for

she is too young to understand the things that she remembers. It is the pain that is most real to her my little one.

Ok. Is there anything else Jesus? I am tired.

Yes my little one you need to rest. That is enough for today. Dolly 5 is safe in my arms as are you. Rest now my little one and do not be afraid. I will always be sufficient for you.

I love you Jesus.

Yes my little one I know that you do. Rest now.

Jesus said that dolly 5 held the earliest trauma and that she needed to be held most of all. So dolly 5 stayed in Jesus arms until it was time for more healing.

This morning I was hurting a lot and I knew that there was going to be more healing. I worshipped for a bit but then I knew it was time. I was sitting on Jesus lap and so was dolly 5. He had one arm round me and one arm around her. He asked me to hold her hands, so I did. As soon as I did, I could feel so much pain Mr. Mike and I curled up and cried. And then dolly 5 was in my arms and Jesus wrapped us both up in his arms. It hurt so much Mr. Mike but I don't get scared because I know I am safe. It was the same feelings again, loneliness and being unloved and unwanted but there was something else too. I looked at her Mr. Mike with her little arms and legs and her blonde curls and I felt so very sad that she would feel that way and that she wasn't loved when she should have been and knowing that really it was me... it was all mixed up Mr. Mike and I cried and cried because it is so wrong. After a while Jesus said it was enough and he took dolly 5 from me and he held us both again like before. When I felt a bit better, he said he wanted to talk.

My little one I am with you. My arms of love are around you and I am holding you close. My dearest one this healing will continue until it is complete, but it will not be long my dearest one. Keep holding on. Dolly 5 is growing stronger my little one and soon she will be ready for the healing that must come.

What is this Jesus?

I am reconnecting you my little one. The pain that you are feeling is held by dolly 5 and as you connect you are also experiencing it. My dearest one as she releases these feelings to you, she grows stronger and more able to receive the love and healing that I have for her. My little one the things of the past are hard to bear but I will give you my strength and enable you in every way that you need.

Crying... Crying... Crying...

My little one the grief that you are feeling will pass for my love makes all things new. Hold on to me my little one.

I understand the feelings she has Jesus, but they aren't trauma... you said trauma.

Yes my little one I did. My dearest one the feelings that you are connecting to are only a part. There are deeper feelings yet to come my little one from the things that she experienced.

Bad things.

Yes my little one bad things.

How could they Jesus… Crying.... How could they? Crying...

My little one evil does not discriminate in its victims. The young and the innocent are easy targets my little one. It has always been so. My dearest one those who should have protected and cared for you failed to do so and instead they hurt you but my little one I am the great healer and everything that they have done will be made right again. Hold on to me my little one. I am your strength and your courage. Do not be afraid but be willing to follow wherever I lead.

Jesus told me I needed to take back her pain and her fear like I had taken dolly 4's memories and that it would be difficult for both of us. He needed to wait until dolly 5 was strong enough.

Today Jesus did the healing he has been talking about with dolly 5. I don't understand everything that happened, but I will tell you about it. I knew Jesus was wanting to do something, so I was listening to some worship music and waiting and wondering. I knew something was happening and I felt like I was just supposed to cuddle up on my bed, so I did, me and my rabbits. I thought I saw that there were angels around me and then I was sitting with Jesus and dolly 5 again. He put her hands in mine and he said that the connection between us was complete. Then he stood up and carried us both across some grass to a river. I don't know what this was Mr. Mike but I will just tell you what I saw he took us in the river, and we all went under the water. Jesus was still holding me and dolly 5 and we weren't scared or anything. Then he carried us out and we sat down with him. He kind of joined my hands to dolly 5's hands with golden threads. I don't know what that was Mr. Mike but then I started to see and feel. I think they were dolly 5's memories. I saw granddads face like he was coming for me and I felt afraid and kept saying over and over make him go away make him go away. Dolly 5 was crying, and I was crying but Jesus was holding us close and he told me I was safe, and he kissed us both. Then I saw the Goatman's face and there were flames. Lots and lots of flames. It was pictures and not a happening... but it was frightening. And I started saying over and over mamma, mamma, mamma... I suppose maybe that was dolly 5 calling out. And we were both crying. And then there was something else, like we couldn't breathe, and I think that was someone putting something over our face and stopping the crying maybe... and then it was over, and Jesus was comforting us both. And then he undid the golden threads round our wrists, and he put dolly 5 on my lap and she kind of melted into me just like dolly 4 did and then it was just me and Jesus and I cried because I get sad when they go.

My little one I am here with you holding you close. My little one as you are healed you grow stronger. I am making you all that you can be. Dolly 5 is not lost my little one but is now part of who you are once again. My dearest one the healing that I am doing is good and is bringing you life. Continue to hold on to me my little one. I will strengthen you and give you my hope. All that you need is found in me my little one. There is nothing to fear... My little one now that you are stronger you can begin to do all that I am asking of you. I know my little one that there is as yet much you do not understand but I am with you my little one and will help you with everything. My dearest one everything that you need will be given to you. There is nothing that will be withheld from you as you walk with me. My little one the way ahead is clear, and I will enable you to keep on walking forward with me. There is nothing that can stand in your way my little one. I will hold you and love you and when you are ready, I will ask you to take the next step that I have for you my little one. For now, rest and then continue with your day. I will be with you my little one. I will help you and though you do not yet see it there is a new thing that I have for you. Hold on to me my little one. All that I have spoken of is coming.
Jesus
Yes my little one.
I feel sad.
I know my little one but there is nothing to fear. Dolly 5 is not lost to you my little one. She is a part of who you are just as it should have been my little one. Healing will continue as you are ready but that is sufficient for now my little one.

So now dolly 5 is gone and it is just me and dolly 2 and I get sad when I think that she will go too. Somehow it seems sad to me and like I will be left alone but I know it is good what is happening, and Jesus isn't going to go is he.

It was very strange to think that now it was just me and dolly 2. I didn't want her to go and leave me alone, but I knew that was Jesus plan.

In the worship I saw something... you know like I see stuff that Jesus shows me... I saw the locket he wears. Usually the part that is dolly 2 is on the top but now I saw that my part is on the top and her part that is a lot thinner is on the underneath. That means that we have swapped places and now I am the one on the outside. I think that's what it means. I didn't have time to think about it much then but later I got scared about it because I am just a girl Mr. Mike and it is a very scary thing to be all alone being grown up and a mummy and looking after a house and having friends and all of those things.

Crying...
My little one I am here with you. I will not ever leave you.
Crying....
My little one you are able to do this. I would not ask it of you otherwise.
Crying... So I get stronger.
Yes my little one strong enough to do everything that I will ask of you. My dearest one you are safe in my arms of love. There is nothing that can harm you.
Crying... I don't want to be here all alone.... Crying....
You are not alone my little one you are never alone.
Crying....
My dearest one I am with you in every moment and will give you all the help that you will need. My dearest one this life is given to you because it is yours my little one. Do not be afraid to take hold of all that I am giving to you my little one. This life is part of that, even though it is not the life I am leading you into this is still for you my little one. It is my gift to you to make you strong in me so that everything I have spoken of will be possible for you. My dearest one there is nothing to fear. You walk with day by day in my strength and in my courage. I will not ever leave you my little one.
Crying... I know what you are saying is true Jesus.... Crying....
My little one I would not ask it of you if it were not necessary for all that is to come. My dearest one I have great purpose in this. Hold on to me and do not be afraid. I am enough for you my little one.
Help me Jesus... Crying...
My little one you are safe in my arms.
Yes I am.... Crying....
There is nothing to fear.
No there isn't... Crying....
My little one let me show you the truth of where you are and who you are.
Crying... What do you mean Jesus?
You are safe in my arms my little one. That is where you are. You are surrounded by my angels my little one who are ministering to you constantly. My little one you are not alone. You are safe and you are loved, and you have everything that you need.
Ok... show me Jesus so I can know it.
So I saw that there were four angels. One at each corner of my bed. And that I am I Jesus arms.
They are watching over you my little one. They are sent to protect you and guide you. My dearest one you are so very precious to me. I will not ever leave you alone.
Crying....
I will never abandon you my little one. Not ever.

But I did feel like I was getting lost in all the changes that were happening and having to pretend to be Jennifer and do all the grownup stuff I didn't want to do.

It is hard because I keep on crying. Yesterday was very bad. I don't know I think it is a mix of things. Knowing that it will just be me makes me feel like I am being left all alone and that is making me very sad. I don't feel like I can do it. I have to be Jennifer and Jenny and Aj and there is no place for me. There is nobody who wants me. When I was crying in the night, I decided I should be put in the bin and just be whoever people want me to be. I can't be me. I put my rabbits away because I can't be me. I know you didn't mean to Mr. Mike but when you didn't come it felt like you left me. And you called me Aj again and so I think you don't even know who I am, and you don't want me, and I should go in the bin where I belong. I cried all day Mr. Mike and even more after you didn't come, and it was bonfire night and even though you didn't think it was anything I think it was. When it got dark and I could hear the fireworks I had memories of drownings in a dark lake. I held on to Jesus Mr. Mike. I held on so tight, but I wanted to not be. I still want to not be. I don't really understand why he is asking me to be other people and not letting me be me when he keeps saying he wants me to be me. I am so confused about who I am and getting lost in all these other people. It is better if I am in the bin and nobody would care. But I can't because how do you get in there I don't know. I can't get rid of me it would only be pretend. Everything is pretend Mr. Mike and it is hard to know what is real. I didn't know what I would write to you because it hurts so bad and maybe you don't want me to come and talk with you. I am not sure anymore. I am not sure if you are my friend or maybe you just put up with me.

I was still being called dolly 3. It didn't help not having a real name. It made me feel like I wasn't real or important enough to have my own name. I said that to Mike in our chat time and he said I should ask Jesus if he had a name for me, right there and then. I was scared and didn't want to do it, but I did. I asked Jesus and he said that my name was Blossum because that is what I was doing. I was blossoming and becoming. He said it was only my name for now and that one day I would be given a new name. I thought it was a bit of a strange name, but I quite liked it and I told Mike. So from then on I had my own name and that was better. It made me feel like more of a real person. That was good that I had a name because now it was time. It happened unexpectedly like it had with dolly 4. I had gone to visit Sophie on the train, and it was me on the outside the whole time. That was scary but I did ok.

Anyway, so I went, and we had a very nice time. I kept asking Jesus if it was me and he kept saying it was. As far as I know I have been on the outside now for a few days without dolly 2 even though I have been feeling so very bad most of the time. We went for a nice meal and had some drinks and chatted and laughed. I just had a nice time and I did ok with everything. She said something that tells me she thinks of me as her friend. I think that is nice Mr. Mike. Jesus said a long time ago that maybe I couldn't be a mummy, but I could be a friend and love her and Richard. So that made me feel good. On the way home on the train I was thinking about how it had been, and I knew then that I didn't have to be afraid about it being just me. That it would be ok. And that is when it happened. I was stood facing dolly 2 and Jesus was behind her. And we kind of stepped towards each other, so dolly 2 and me kind of merged, then I was in Jesus arms. I felt sad and cried Mr. Mike and I thought it was a strange place for it to happen but maybe it was because I was ready.

So now it was just me. It was scary to be just me, and I was still trying to understand who I was because it seemed like I kept on changing. But I knew that Jesus knows who I am and none of the changes were confusing to him. It felt like a new start for me, but I didn't know who I was, and I felt very alone.

Hello Jesus
Hello my little one.
Thankyou that I had a good day yesterday and that you looked after me.
My little one I will always help you in every way that you need. My dearest one as you learn how to be the person I have created to be you will discover not only that you are so much more than you have believed yourself to be but also that I am able to be

more than you imagine through you.
I don't think I understand.
My little one in me you are able to do all things. Everything that I ask of you, you can do in my strength my little one. The things that I will ask of you will flow out of the person that I have made you to be. I will enable you in everything my little one but all of it will flow through the person that you are. My little one I have made you special in so many ways so that I can be and do things through you that I cannot do through anyone else in the way that I can do through you. As you learn to be that person my little one you will discover many things about the person, I have made you to be but also about who I can be through you.
Do you mean... You can be... things... through me because of who I am?
Yes my little one I do. My dearest one I have made you special and unique and with purpose. My purpose in you will be fulfilled as you become the person that you were created to be. You cannot be that person without me my little one for it is as I live and breathe in and through you that you become that person. As you become that person I can do and be through you what I cannot do and be through anyone else my little one for your spirit and my spirit join together in a unique way to accomplish things that could not be accomplished through any other person.
That sounds mysterious and difficult Jesus, but I think I sort of understand.
My little one do not ever regret that you are you. My little one you were made on purpose, not by accident. You were made in love and for love my little one and everything that you are is precious to me.
I am feeling confused about who I am Jesus because it keeps changing.
I am not changing who you are my little one, but I am helping you to become all that you are. That will change many things about you my little one. It will change the things that you can do and be, but it does not change who you are.
I suppose... who I am is kind of fixed in the spirit place where I am eternal or whatever it is but I am still not being that here... so even though I am that person I have to keep on changing and growing to become that.
Yes my little one that is so and you are changing my little one and you are growing and that is very good. My dearest one all that you are belongs to me and I will help you to change and to grow and to become but my dearest one I will not ever change you into someone that you are not. I will help you to learn who you are my little one for as you learn and accept who you are you are able to become that person my little one.
Yes. I see that sort of Jesus because you... my ideas about me are kind of changing but sometimes I get scared about that and it gets hard. But I get scared too because I don't know who I am, and I don't know. I keep looking different to me and being different and I think is that me or someone else because I don't know, and I can't tell and that's why I kept asking is this me.
Yes my little one I understand that it is hard for you to know what is truly you, because of all the changes that have happened and are happening. My little one as you have blended with others you have grown and become and the person that you see has changed my little one. That is a good thing but now it is time for you to grow into the person that you have become and not to be afraid of being that person my little one.
I want to know...did it happen?
Yes my little one it did. You are now one my little one and though there are many others in the inside world for now you are one on the outside. It is you my little one that you are seeing. It is you that is speaking and acting and thinking. There are no others there with you my little one.
But dolly2... Crying...
Is part of who you are now my little one.

They are all gone... Crying...
No my little one they are not gone. They are all a part of who you are. My dearest one this is a good thing and you are now strong enough to walk forward with me on the path that I have for you. My little one I will help you to grow into the person that you are and to learn about the person that I am making you to be. Do not be afraid my little one. There is nothing to fear.
Crying... It feels like you took them all away.
But I did not my little one I gave them all back to you and you are now one and whole again. I know my little one that there are so many more and much more healing to be done but I have made you able my little one to walk forward with me on the path that I have for you. More healing will come my little one but for now I will help you to grow into the person that you are.

So now it was time for me to be the one on the outside, just me with no one else for the first time in my life. But I wasn't alone. I couldn't do it if I was alone. It was very strange it being just me. It felt very lonely and kind of empty. Sometimes it scared me because it had never been like that for me before, not ever.

Yesterday I was feeling sad and very alone. I miss the conversations that went on in my head... it was a bit like my own thoughts really and sometimes that's what I thought they were but really, they were everyone's thoughts and there would be conversations going on. I suppose that can happen even now if I talk to myself which I do because I am used to getting an answer :(but it's not the same and I does feel very strange and lonely. I would be very scared if I didn't have Jesus, but I do... but sometimes I still feel scared.

Most people didn't notice the difference of course because I had to keep on pretending to be Jennifer. But I had to tell Cheryl and I had to tell Esther and her alters. I was scared because I thought they wouldn't want me, that they would want me to go away. I had to do it though. Cheryl seemed to accept it and not be worried about it. She asked about Jennifer and when I said she was blended now she seemed to accept that too. When I told Esther, she seemed ok but kind of puzzled like she didn't know what to make of it. I suppose that might have been because I am only eleven and who would expect me to be the one Jesus chose for the outside life? It doesn't make sense. I am not very sure what they were thinking or feeling but to me the things they said and did in the next few weeks told me I had been right to be worried.

Monday wasn't very good at all and I did a lot of crying. I have been getting upset about being me and wondering why and I am confused about what Cheryl said when I told her about me and Aj blending and that it was me now. She said it didn't matter to her who I was. I don't understand that Mr. Mike. How can you say you love someone if it doesn't matter who they are? It matters to me who you are Mr. Mike. I love you because of who you are to me. So I have been confused about that and I am feeling confused about Esther too. Since I have been me something is different. I think she still talks to me on skype and on chat of course but when I get emails, they are always from Penny Milly and Kitty. Esther's name is never on now. It always was before. That makes me sad and a bit confused. I wanted to talk to you about it on Tuesday, but I was scared to. I don't know why. Maybe it feels like I am saying something bad about her I don't know. Tuesday, I did talk with Jesus in the morning.

My little one my arms are around you. I will not ever let you go.
Crying...
My little one everything that you are is precious to me. It matters to me who you are for I am the one who created you in love my little one. I am the one who dreamed of you and made you mine.

Crying...
My little one it matters to me so much that I gave everything I am for you.
Crying...
My little one you are not alone in this world no matter how it feels to you.
Crying... Crying...
My dearest little one all that you are is held by me and nothing is forgotten. There is nothing that is not precious to me. My dearest one this is not the life I have for you.
Crying... Don't tell me that. Stop it.... Crying
My little one I have prepared something wonderful for you and I am making you ready to receive it. My little one everything that you have given to me will be used for great good including this time.
Crying....
My dearest little one I know you so much better than you know yourself. I know everything that you need my little one. I know everything that you are and everything that you can be. My little one as you walk forward with me you will find I will ask many things of you that you do not want to do. It is a life of sacrifice my little one a life of sacrifice of love to me just as my life was a sacrifice of love. My little one I will give you all that you need to live this way just as all that I needed was given to me. My dearest one I know the cost for I bear it with you. I understand the pain and the loneliness my little one, but I am with you.
Crying....
I am always with you and will not ever leave you.
Crying......
My little one I am holding you close to my heart and I am loving you back to life. I know it does not feel that way to you my little one for the pain that you bear runs so very deep, but I will make you able to continue with me. Every step that you take is in my hands of love. My little one the journey I am taking you on is not for nothing. I have great purpose in it my little one I know that is hard for you to see.
Crying...
My little one all of my promises to you are true and will be fulfilled as you follow me. Do not lose hope my little one. Do not lose hope of seeing the life I have promised you.
Crying...
It is only just ahead of you.
Crying...
My little one my love for you is unending. It will not ever end my little one and you will spend eternity in my arms of love. This life that is given to you is only for a brief time my little one, but I will accomplish a great deal through it if you surrender it to me. My dearest one your life will be used for my eternal purposes which far outweigh the suffering that you endure. My little one that does not mean that your suffering is unimportant to me or that I do not care only that I walk through it with you because I understand all that will come from it. It is a sacrifice of love my little one offered up to me with many tears. I know my little one that you wish it were not so. I know that you do not understand but cling to me my little one. Keep coming to me with all that you are. I am doing something so special my little one. Every tear that falls is precious to me none of it is wasted.
Crying...
My little one I am teaching you to rely on my strength and mine alone. I will not fail you my little one. I will give you everything that you need.
Crying... I don't want to be here. I can't do it. Crying... I have reached the end.
I know my little one I know that you have but where you end that is where I begin. My dearest little one you have not yet seen all that I can do. You have only glimpsed my strength and my power in you. My little one as you learn to trust and rely on me

alone, I can do so much more than you imagine.
Crying... What are you going to do? Crying...
I am going to capture your heart in a new way and enable you to follow me where few dare to go. I am going to show you who I am in a new way my little one so that you will know that you are loved and that you belong to me.
Crying
My little one all of this is to reveal my love to you and through you to others. I understand the cost my little one, but it is a cost worth bearing because of all that I will do.
I don't think I can do it. I am not... I can't... Crying
Yes my little one you can. You can do all that I say you can and be everything that I have made you to be. All you must do is continue to choose me.
Crying...
My little one the way I have for you is hard and it is costly, but it is good. It is so very good. I will help you my little one. You are not alone.
Crying... You picked the wrong person.... Crying...
No my little one I did not for I see you completely, I did not make a mistake my little one.
Crying... Crying...
My little one will you stay here just a little bit longer so that I can complete my work in you. So that I can make you ready for all I am longing to give to you. Will you do it for my sake my little one and for the sake of those you will reach for me?
But... Crying... I can't.... Crying
My little one will you trust me to help you. Will you trust me to give you the strength and the courage that you need. Will you trust me to lead and guide you and fulfil all of my promises to you?
Can I do it? Crying...
Yes my little one you can.
Crying... Crying
You can be everything that I say and do everything that I have told you if only you do not give up my little one. Hold on to me and do not let go. I am the one who will carry you through this time and enable you in everything.
Crying... Crying
My dearest little one your heart belongs to me and I am making it new. I know the pain that you bear my little one and the deep loneliness that you feel. It cannot be overcome in a moment my little one but only as you walk with me and receive my love for you. My dearest one I know that you fear that it will never be overcome, that it will always be this way for you but my dearest one I am able, and I am willing, and I will do all that I have said. Come to me my little one and rest in my arms and I will strengthen you for the journey that is ahead of you. Your hope lies in me my little one and not in anything that you see.

We had learned that we could do Jennifer's life with Jesus helping us when it had been Aj on the outside and it didn't seem very much different now. But I got worried and upset a lot because I am just a child and even more than Aj did I didn't really believe I could live an adult's life and I didn't want to either. But to Jesus whether I was a child or not he said I could do everything he asked me to. One morning in church Jesus spoke to me through a bible passage.

> **Jeremiah 1:4-9:**
> **The word of the Lord came to me saying 'before I formed you in the womb I knew you, before you were born I set you apart, I appointed you as a prophet to the nations'. Ah sovereign Lord I said, I do not know how to speak, I am only a child. But the Lord said to me 'do not say I am only a child. You must go to**

everyone I send you to and say whatever I command you. Do not be afraid of them for I am with you and will rescue you' declares the Lord. Then the Lord reached out his hand and touched my mouth and said to me 'now I have put my words in your mouth'.

I knew the Holy Spirit was talking to me. Not about being a prophet to the nations lol but the bit about do not say you are a child and about going and saying what he tells me... that part. I knew that was for me Mr. Mike and it went right into my heart. He proved it to me too. When the service finished Kate wanted to talk to Annette and I had to be there too, I don't know why... anyhow so really it was Kate telling Annette off again like on Wednesday and it wasn't going well because Annette wasn't saying what Kate wanted her to. There was some music playing and I prayed for what was happening and went to Jesus... I was just sitting there being quiet on the outside... He started to dance with me and seemed to be having fun. I wasn't sure that was right to do that and said to him about what was going on with Kate but he said to me that he could meet all of our needs at the same time and I didn't need to be part of what was happening there. So, I was dancing with Jesus and snuggling in his arms while this argument was going on. Eventually Annette left, but not in a good way and it was just me. Jesus gave me a big hug. And I said to him something like ok you said you put your words in my mouth... now would be a good time. And he did Mr. Mike. It was not me. And I was fearless, even though I was speaking truth that Kate did not want to hear I was not afraid at all... That is not me! She seemed to listen, and I prayed for her... I was very... firm (!) ...with her. Lol. So, he made those verses come true for me straight away. Oh dear Mr. Mike. I am not sure who Jesus thinks I am, but it isn't the same as, I think… It is hard for me to understand Mr. Mike when I am wanting to be a little girl and be looked after, that Jesus is doing these things, but I am learning that he really can do things through me that I can't do. I am learning that because it is all very silly. I am even supporting and encouraging Annette because she is not happy with all of this.

So Jesus showed me a lot of times that being me didn't mean that I couldn't do everything he was asking. But I didn't really know who me was. Now that everyone else was 'gone' I could see me much more clearly. There wasn't anyone else to get confused with. Everything that was done and said was done and said by me. That was very strange and sometimes I didn't like what I saw.

My little one you are my beloved child. You are growing stronger and more able my little one. You are following me faithfully and you are learning and growing into all that I have made you to be. My dearest one whether you are what people think you should be or not does not matter all that matters is that you are following me and being yourself my little one. Which is my desire for you.
I still find that hard to understand Jesus but suppose I'm not a very nice person.
My little one I am making you like me. That means that you will become more and more filled with all that I am my dearest one. You may not yet be all that I want you to be, but you are on the way to becoming so my little one. That is all that I will ask of you. My little one if you make a mistake, if you do or say something that is not kind or loving all you must do is admit your mistake and make amends as you are able. I know my dearest one that you find this hard for many reasons but part of learning how to be in relationship is knowing and being able to put things right when you make a mistake.
Yes... but suppose it's not that I made a mistake, but it is… part of who I am that... I don't like and that others don't like.
My little one you are not bad and all that you are is in my hands. Everything that needs to be redeemed will be redeemed. My dearest one all that you need do is surrender yourself into my hands. I know my dearest one that you fear you might not like the person that you are but my dearest one there are so many wonderful things about yourself that you have not yet seen. There is nothing to fear from discovering

who you are my little one.

But... I want you to help me not say things I shouldn't Jesus.

Yes my little one I know that you do but remember my dearest one that part of who you are is to be my messenger of truth. My dearest one people do not always want the truth nor are they always willing to accept it. Sometimes they will reject and blame the one who brings it but my dearest one that is part of who I am making you to be. A bringer of truth my little one. What you lack is the wisdom of when to speak and when to hold back and this I will teach you my little one but speaking the truth does not make you bad. It is part of who you are my little one.

I know you want me to tell people the truth about you Jesus but...

My little one I will help you with the things that you say. I know my dearest one that you desire only to bring life to those you are with and that your intent is for good but my dearest one sometimes those you are with do not understand the things that you are saying to them. They do not see you as I do my little one. I know your heart, but others may not. That is what is troubling you my little one.

I say things Jesus and they might be true... but maybe I shouldn't say them and maybe I could say them different. I don't want to hurt people with the things I say.

I know my little one. My dearest one even though sometimes the things that you say may come across in a way that you don't mean them to that does not mean that what you said was wrong or bad. It is about learning how to speak the truth my little one, how to express yourself. For you are only just beginning to learn what is in your heart and your mind and you are only just beginning to learn how to express these things. You will grow in this as in everything my little one.

I get surprised by the things I say Jesus.

Yes my little one for you are still discovering who you are. My dearest one as you spend time with people and become more who you are you will be able to see yourself more clearly my little one. The mistakes you make are part of discovering the person that you are my little one for your mistakes will help you to become all that you can be if you learn from them.

Maybe I am thinking... You made me so I will speak my mind... because you want to me to tell people the truth but... I need to do it better and that is about learning and growing.

Yes my little one it is. My dearest one you are only just beginning in everything. The things that you see in yourself are as yet only signs towards what can be. My little one I will help you bring the truth to others in kindness and in love but being honest and straightforward in your relationships is a good thing my little one. It is not hiding away as you would once have done.

I suppose it is letting people see me. That is strange too. Even me seeing me is strange. It is a lot to get used to.

Yes my little one it is but whatever you see do not be afraid. I am always here to help you my little one in every way that you need.

You never make me feel bad Jesus.

My little one my love for you will help you to grow and become. I know what you need my little one and it will be given to you.

I talked to Jesus a lot asking the question who I am. It was very hard to know. It kept on changing it seemed to me and I was having to be two people at the same time. A grown-up woman with children and a dependent child who was healing and growing and becoming. I didn't have much time or space to find out about me, so I had to ask the only person who knew.

Hello Jesus
Hello my little one.
I am feeling sad Jesus. Who am I?
You are my beloved child my little one and my servant also. My little one all that you

are will be revealed slowly. You are in the process of becoming my little one and cannot yet be seen fully for the person that you are.

Yes... I know that I don't know much about me or what I can do or what I'm like... I know. Why is it bothering me so much?

My little one you have been through a great many changes. All that you are is in my hands my little one. I am shaping and molding you to become the person that you were created to be. Your final shape cannot yet be seen my little one. All that you can see is hints and beginnings of what will be. My dearest one I am making you so very special. I know my dearest one that you long to be the child that you never were, to be loved and cared for and to have the freedom to laugh and play and feel safe in who you are. They are deeply unmet needs my little one and you are longing for a life where those things will be fulfilled. That life will be given to you my little one and those needs will be met but they will be met in the way that you need them to be my little one for you are not like an ordinary child. You are extraordinary in every way my little one. Do not be afraid that your deepest needs and longings will not be met. They will all be met my little one in just the right way and at just the right time.

Is that why I get scared… because I think I won't be able to have the things I want most.

Yes my little one it is but that is not what I have said my little one. I will give you everything that you need my little one. I know who you are and everything that you need. My dearest one you are a child and will be able to express that childlike nature but you are also more than that my little one for you know what it is to be an adult and are capable of many of the same things that an adult is. My dearest one you will learn what this means for you but do not be afraid that I will not give to you everything you need my little one. It will all be given to you and more my little one.

I'm sorry. I know you've promised me a lot of lovely things Jesus. I forget that you know what's right for me to have and I get scared I can't have what I want because I still think I shouldn't have it.

Yes my little one but that is not so. My little one rest in me and in my provision for you. Be who you are my little one and do not try to be anything that you are not. You do not need to be anyone except the person that you are my little one.

That is so confusing to me Jesus when I am always being someone that I'm not.

Are you my little one? All that I see is my beautiful child living life in my strength and my power showing the people around her different parts of who she is according to what it is needed. I do not see anything other than you my little one.

Maybe. I am still confused, I think.

Yes my little one but you will soon begin to see and understand that the person that is seen is you no matter what name is given to you. My dearest one I know that you have still to fully understand these things, but you are always you my little one. You are not being someone else.

It is hard for me to say because I don't know who I am.

No my little one you don't. Don't be afraid my little one but continue to live your life out of my strength which is given to you. I will continue to reveal to you all that you are. You are so many things my little one and that is good it is very good for it means that you can accomplish many things and reach many people for me.

I… want to be what you want me to be. Help me not be scared of what that is Jesus.

Yes my little one. I will help you to see understand who you are. You are so much more than you believe or even desire to be but my dearest one I am making you so many wonderful things not only for your sake but for mine.

But being a grown up almost all the time made me feel like I had lost Blossum just when I was starting to find her. It was different now. When I had been on the outside to begin with it had only been with Jesus or Mike and I could be me. Now most of my outside time was spent being Jennifer and I felt like Blossum had got lost, like that person was gone. It scared me because I felt like I was turning into

Jennifer and I didn't want to be her I wanted to be me. It helped that Jesus said he only saw me, but it was very frightening sometimes and I knew that all I could do was to hold on to Jesus and trust that he was holding the true me and that I wouldn't get lost or forgotten again. That was always my biggest fear that somehow, I would disappear again into a nothing place and be forgotten.

It wasn't just the here and now person I was trying to get to know though there was this future person, the Blossom of the future that Jesus kept talking to me about and kept showing me. She didn't seem very much like the Blossom I could see now, when I could see her at all. I wanted to know who I was and to me it felt like I couldn't get hold of that at all. I know now that Jesus was wanting me to learn the truth about who I am in him and for that to be the person that I see and know as me but it was very difficult for me to even want to do that when I was looking for something to help me feel safe in who I was. Of course, that is what Jesus wanted too just not the way I thought he should.

I have been crying again today. I am very confused and scared about who I am. I don't know who it is Mr. Mike and when I kind of begin to see the person Jesus says I am and will be that is even more scary. I can't even put that person in words. I can't tell you what I see but... I think the person Jesus has in mind and the person I think that maybe I am, they are very different. And when I see the Jesus me, I get scared. Like looking in a mirror and seeing something... you don't recognize. I don't know how to explain it but anyway that is falling on me a lot too.

My little one all that you are is held in my hands of love. I know who you are my little one and who you are is wonderful and nothing to fear. My dearest one your ideas of who you are are formed from the past and from the present but who you are is found in me my little one. Who you are is formed in my hands of love. The past may have told you many things my little one, but it did not tell you the truth about who you are. Only I can do that. My dearest one the truth of who you are will set you free to become everything that you were created to be. There is nothing my dearest one that I cannot do in and through you. You are my beloved child, created in love to be loved and to give that love away to others. There is nothing to fear from this my little one. Do not try to hold on to your ideas of who you are. Hold on to me my little one. I am making you new. My dearest one many of the things that you see now as being part of who you are will fall away and many new things will be discovered. That does not change who you are my little one but only how you see yourself and who you can be in this world. I know my dearest one that you are afraid to be anything or anyone that stands out from the crowd but my dearest one you are already special. You are already unique. All I am doing is revealing what is already there, the wonderful person that you already are my little one. Do not be afraid but allow me to work in your heart and in your mind to accomplish all that I desire. Do not fear who I am making you to be my little one. You are safe in my arms of love. There is nothing that can harm you.

End part one – 'Out of the Darkness'

www.ingramcontent.com/pod-product-compliance
Lightning Source LLC
Chambersburg PA
CBHW061139230426

43662CB00026B/2469